PASSION for COLLECTING...

When it comes to passion for collecting, dedication to the hobby, and amassing high-grade, award winning runs... few measure up to Pedigree Comics' CEO and President, Doug Schmell, who sold his personal collection of Silver Age Marvels in 2012 for over 3.94 Million Dollars (a record price for a comic book collection).

So, who is best qualified to help you build your collection and find you the books and upgrades you need?

Over the past 20 plus years, I have amassed over fifteen thousand Marvel comic books, most of which are in very high grade condition. When CGC was in the process of forming in March, 1999, I was one of a handful of collectors asked to attend their start-up meeting and provide input to the creation of this third party grading service. When the CGC commenced operations later that year and began encapsulating and grading comic books for the public, I began submitting my runs of Marvel titles. Now, known as "Captain Tripps" on the CGC Registry and chat boards, I have come to be recognized as one of the leading collectors of Marvel Silver and Bronze Age comics, with many of my books being the highest graded copies in existence. In fact, I received the coveted Achievement in Comics Collecting 2006, awarded by the CGC Comics Registry, in honor of the outstanding runs of Marvel comics I had registered since November, 2003, including the highest graded set of virtually every Marvel Silver Age and Bronze Age title.

Although I sold the majority of my Bronze Age titles when I moved to Florida in 2004, I kept and continued to add to my Silver Age sets, looking for upgrades on any individual issue whenever possible. The formation of this collection, which has been painstakingly pared down to around 700 books, took an incredible amount of effort, time, expense, and patience. The stories I could tell of meeting at diners, post offices in Northern New Jersey, law offices, street corners in New York City, dealers' tables, and comic stores around the country in order to obtain that missing issue or coveted upgrade, would blow your mind. My decision to sell the collection was based on my feeling that I had reached a sort of collector's Nirvana, that I had finally obtained every sought after pedigreed issue or top of the CGC census book I could possibly find. The long journey has taken me to this point in time and I couldn't be any happier.

**Let me help you find the same fulfillment I have!
Email me at dougschmell@pedigreecomics.com
or call me today at 1-561-422-1120.**

PedigreeComics.com

SOLD $12,197

SOLD $13,244

SOLD $94,875

SOLD $64,936

SOLD $6,109

SOLD $95,200

FULL SET
SOLD $22,278

SOLD $37,041

SOLD $22,412

SOLD $7,100

THE CONSIGNOR'S BEST CHOICE OVER 1 MILLION ITEMS SOLD

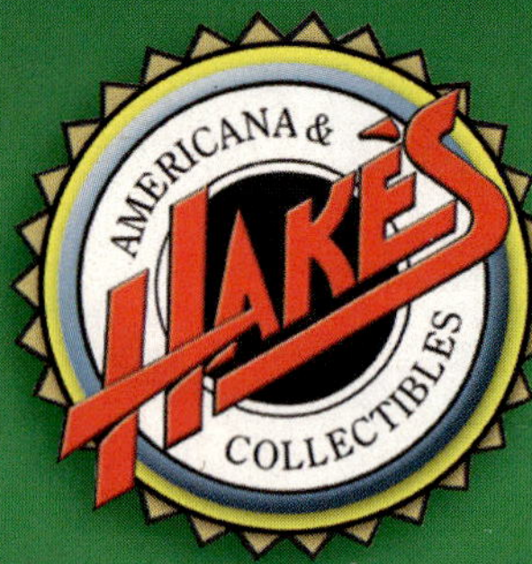

Since 1967 Hake's has been the premier source for Pop Culture Collectibles. We are America's first and most diversified collectibles auction house.

SOLD $151,534

★ OVER 200 CATALOGED AUCTIONS CONDUCTED SINCE 1967 ★

★ WORLD RECORD PRICES SET IN EVERY AUCTION ★

★ OUR EXPERTS USE THEIR COMBINED 250 YEARS OF KNOWLEDGE IN THE FIELD TO SHOWCASE YOUR ITEMS ★

★ 20 AUTHORITATIVE COLLECTIBLE PRICE GUIDES PUBLISHED ★

SOLD $75,000

SOLD $31,625

SOLD $12,776

SOLD $41,264

SOLD $8,114

SOLD $33,674

CONSIGN NOW
WWW.HAKES.COM

P.O. Box 12001
York, PA 17402
(866) 404-9800

A DIVISION OF

THE OVERSTREET®
GUIDE
TO COLLECTING
COMICS

BY ROBERT M. OVERSTREET

WRITTEN BY J.C. VAUGHN

ADDITIONAL MATERIAL WRITTEN BY WELDON ADAMS,
JON BERK, ARNOLD T. BLUMBERG, BRADY BONNEY,
SCOTT BRADEN, PAT CALHOUN, GARY M. CARTER,
JOHN CLARK, ART CLOOS, WILLIAM M. COLE,
CHUCK DIXON, STEVE GEPPI, TOM GORDON III,
TED HAKE, BRUCE HERSHENSON, MARK HUESMAN,
ROB HUGHES, COURTNEY JENKINS, CAITLIN MCGURK,
WILL MURRAY, MICHAEL NAIMAN, CHARLIE NOVINSKIE,
ROBERT M. OVERSTREET, JIM SHOOTER, BILLY TUCCI,
MIKE WILBUR, AND MARK ZAID

DESIGN & LAYOUT BY MARK HUESMAN

COMIC ART SEQUENCES BY GENE GONZALES

ADDITIONAL ART BY ANTHONY CASTRILLO,
COLORS BY THOMAS MASON (ATLAS),
AND LEE GARBETT AND TREVOR SCOTT, COLORS BY
PETE PANTAZIS, LETTERS BY TRAVIS LANHAM
("CHRISTMAS WITH THE BEETLES"),
RENATO GUEDES AND MARC CAMPOS, COLORS BY
ALEX SINCLAIR AND MIKE CALLARO, LETTERS BY
ROB LEIGH ("HOW COMICS ARE MADE")

PHOTOS BY MICHAEL A. SOLOF

SPIDER-MAN COVER BY JOE JUSKO
VALIANT COVER BY SEAN CHEN, LEE GARBETT,
AND BOB HALL, COLORS BY DAVID BARON

EDITED BY J.C. VAUGHN AND MARK HUESMAN

ADDITIONAL EDITING AND PROOFING BY
ROSINA ALLY, COURTNEY JENKINS,
CHARLIE NOVINSKIE, AND MARK SQUIREK

GEMSTONE
PUBLISHING

Stephen A. Geppi
President &
Chief Executive Officer

Robert M. Overstreet
Publisher

J.C. Vaughn
Vice-President
of Publishing

Mark Huesman
Creative Director

Michael Solof
Advertising Sales
Coordinator

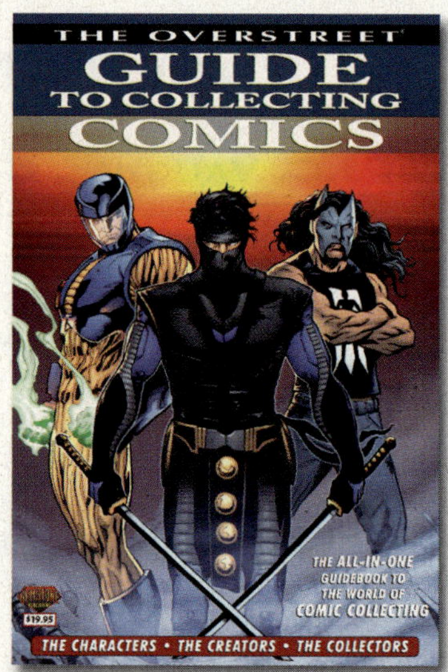

Spider-Man by Joe Jusko. Spider-Man ©2013 Marvel Characters, Inc. Used by permission. All rights reserved.

Valiant by Sean Chen, Lee Garbett, and Bob Hall. Colored by David Baron. X-O Manowar, Ninjak, and Shadowman ©2013 Valiant Entertainment. Used by permission. All rights reserved.

Overstreet® is a Registered Trademark of Gemstone Publishing, Inc.

Spider-Man Edition ISBN: 978-1-60360-142-9
Valiant Edition ISBN: 978-1-60360-154-2

Printed in Canada

10 9 8 7 6 5 4 3 2

Second Printing: November 2013

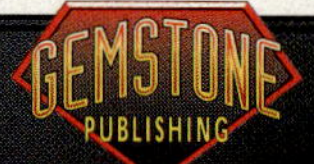

www.gemstonepub.com

AMAZING INVENTORY OF GOLD SILVER AND BRONZE
WANT-LIST MATCHING SERVICE
THE ADVENTURES OF
SUPERWORLD
COMICS.COM
WE ENCOURAGE OFFERS. MOST BOOKS BIDDABLE
GIANT HALF-PRICE SECTION. NEW BOOKS ADDED WEEKLY
SEE US AT MAJOR SHOWS AROUND THE COUNTRY!
SUPERWORLD
FRIENDLY, KNOWLEDGEABLE STAFF!
EXPERT GRADING AND ADVICE!
SUPERB PACKING AND SHIPPING!
508-829-2259
508-UB-WACKY
TED@SUPERWORLDCOMICS.COM
SUPERWORLDCOMICS.COM
456 MAIN ST. SUITE F
HOLDEN, MA 01520
FOLLOW US ON FACEBOOK AND YOUTUBE

TOP PRICES PAID!
WE BUY COMICS

COLLECTIBLES, GRAPHIC NOVELS, ORIGINAL ART, AND VINTAGE TOYS!

WE BUY AT OUR STORES AND AT OUR WAREHOUSE IN QUEENS, NY! CONTACT ALEX FOR AN APPOINTMENT:

✉ WEBUY@MIDTOWNCOMICS.COM ☎ 646.452.8173

NEW WEBUY/SELL PROGRAM - COMING SOON!

MIDTOWNCOMICS.COM

MIDTOWN COMICS ®
NYC

NEW YORK CITY'S LARGEST COMIC SHOPS!

800.411.3341 ☎ 212.302.8192

TIMES SQUARE
200 W. 40TH ST.

GRAND CENTRAL
459 LEXINGTON AVE.

DOWNTOWN
64 FULTON ST.

FAO SCHWARTZ
MINI-BOUTIQUE (767 5TH AVE.)

Collecting Is Cool!

SORRY. JUST HAD TO GET THAT OUT OF THE WAY.
WELCOME TO THE OVERSTREET GUIDE TO COLLECTING COMICS, OUR NEW BOOK ALL ABOUT WHAT MAKES COMIC BOOK COLLECTING GREAT!

THIS BOOK IS WRITTEN AND DESIGNED FOR THOSE WHO MIGHT BE NEW TO COMIC BOOK COLLECTING, WHETHER BEGINNERS OR SERIOUS INVESTORS!
AND IT'S ALSO FOR SEASONED COLLECTORS WHO MIGHT BE LOOKING FOR NEW INSIGHTS TO REFOCUS OR REVITALIZE THEIR COLLECTING EXPERIENCE!
IN OTHER WORDS, IT'S FOR EVERYONE!
OR AT LEAST ANYONE WHO WANTS TO GIVE SERIOUS THOUGHT AS TO HOW, WHAT AND WHY THEY COLLECT!

OF COURSE, IT'S JUST ABOUT ALWAYS A GOOD TIME TO DISCOVER OR RE-DISCOVER THE MAGIC OF COMICS!
THERE ARE MANY DIFFERENT WAYS TO COLLECT, AND WE'LL GET INTO A BUNCH OF THEM.

THERE'S A LOT TO TALK ABOUT, SO LET'S GET STARTED!

WITH MOVIES LIKE THE IRON MAN SERIES, THE SPIDER-MAN SERIES, THE X-MEN SERIES, THE BATMAN SERIES, 300, ROAD TO PERDITION, GHOST WORLD, WATCHMEN AND SO MANY OTHERS...
MORE PEOPLE THAN EVER ARE GETTING TO KNOW COMIC CHARACTERS.

IN FACT, THE DARK KNIGHT MADE MORE THAN $1 BILLION AT THE BOX OFFICE ALONE.
AND OF COURSE THERE ARE TV SHOWS, VIDEO GAMES, MOTION COMICS AND MORE...

ALL OF THE GREAT STUFF IN OTHER MEDIA LEADS US BACK TO THE PLACE IN WHICH THESE GREAT STORIES WERE CREATED...
COMICS!

THROW ME THE ACTION COMICS #1 AND I'LL THROW YOU THE WHIP!

WHETHER YOU'RE JUST STARTING OUT OR YOU'VE BEEN COLLECTING FOR A LONG TIME, THERE'S ALWAYS A LOT TO LEARN ABOUT COMICS.
Action Comics
JUNE, 1938
No. 1
10¢

ONE OF THE COOL THINGS ABOUT COMIC BOOKS IS THAT THERE ARE LOTS OF NEW ONES TO DISCOVER...

AND THERE ARE LITERALLY HUNDREDS OF THOUSANDS OF DIFFERENT BACK ISSUES, TOO!

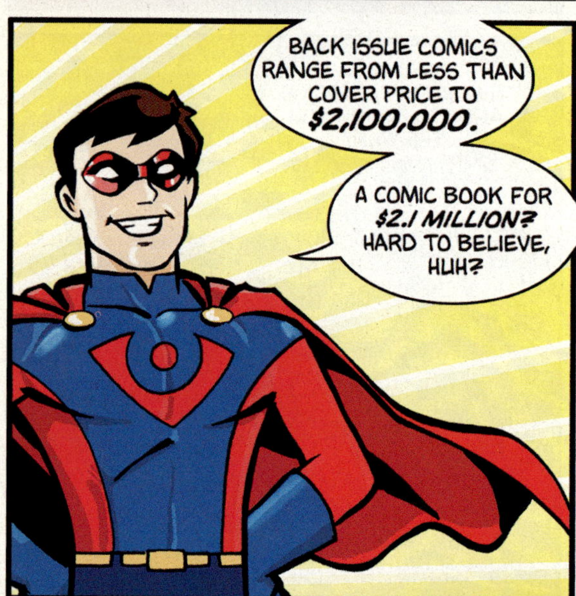

BACK ISSUE COMICS RANGE FROM LESS THAN COVER PRICE TO $2,100,000.
A COMIC BOOK FOR $2.1 MILLION? HARD TO BELIEVE, HUH?

THE FIRST COMIC TO HIT $1 MILLION WAS ACTION COMICS #1, THE FIRST APPEARANCE OF SUPERMAN.
THE SECOND, JUST A FEW DAYS LATER, WAS DETECTIVE COMICS #27, THE FIRST APPEARANCE OF BATMAN.
ANOTHER ACTION #1 SOLD FOR $1.5 MILLION JUST A SHORT WHILE AFTER THAT.

MANY OTHERS HAVE SOLD FOR RECORD PRICES IN THE LAST YEAR OR SO, EVEN WITH THE TOUGH ECONOMY NATIONALLY.

THE GRADE AND SCARCITY OF THE ISSUES HAVE A LOT TO DO WITH THAT. WE'LL GET INTO THAT IN JUST A BIT...

THE BEST PART IS THERE ARE MANY DIFFERENT WAYS TO COLLECT.

YOU CAN CHOOSE TO FOLLOW INDIVIDUAL PUBLISHERS, WRITERS, ARTISTS, CHARACTERS...

YOU CAN COLLECT SUPERHEROES, WAR COMICS, WESTERNS, ROMANCE OR WHATEVER YOU LIKE...

YOU CAN CHOOSE #1 ISSUES, FIRST APPEARANCES, CROSSOVERS, OR MANY OTHER VARIATIONS.

THE BEST THING TO COLLECT IS WHAT YOU LIKE, NOT WHAT SOMEONE ELSE LIKES.

WHETHER IT'S SPIDER-MAN OR EVERY COMIC THAT CAME OUT THE MONTH YOU WERE BORN, IT'S BEST TO DO IT WITH A PLAN.

CAPTAIN ACTION ©2012 CAPTAIN ACTION ENTERPRISES. ALL RIGHTS RESERVED.

DOCTOR EVIL ©2012 CAPTAIN ACTION ENTERPRISES. ALL RIGHTS RESERVED.

SHI ©2012 WILLIAM TUCCI. ALL RIGHTS RESERVED.

SHERLOCK DOME ©2012 J.C. VAUGHN & GENE GONZALES. ALL RIGHTS RESERVED.

BILLY BOB DRIWAHL ©2012 J.C. VAUGHN & VINCENT SPENCER. ALL RIGHTS RESERVED.

A SENSE OF...
WONDER

• GOLDEN-AGE COMICS
• SILVER-AGE COMICS
• BRONZE-AGE COMICS
• ORIGINAL COMIC ARTWORK

40 YEARS OF BUYING AND
SELLING THE VERY BEST IN
FINE VINTAGE COLLECTIBLES

SENIOR
ADVISOR
OVERSTREET
PRICE
GUIDE

© DC

ARCHANGELS
4629 CASS STREET
SUITE #9
PACIFIC BEACH, CA
92109 • USA

ROB HUGHES
310-480-8105
rHUGHES@ARCHANGELS.COM
ARCHANGELS.COM

CGC
Comics Guaranty, LLC
CHARTER
MEMBER DEALER

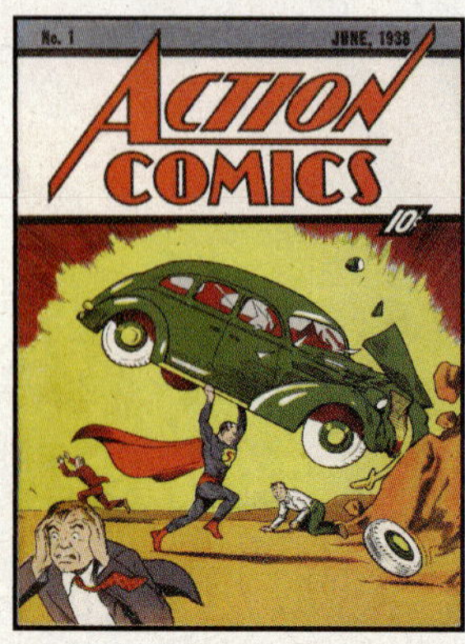

Action Comics #1

First appearance of Superman
1970 Mint Price: $300
2013 NM– Price: $1,900,000

All-American Comics #16

First appearance of Green Lantern
1970 Mint Price: $50
2013 NM– Price: $550,000

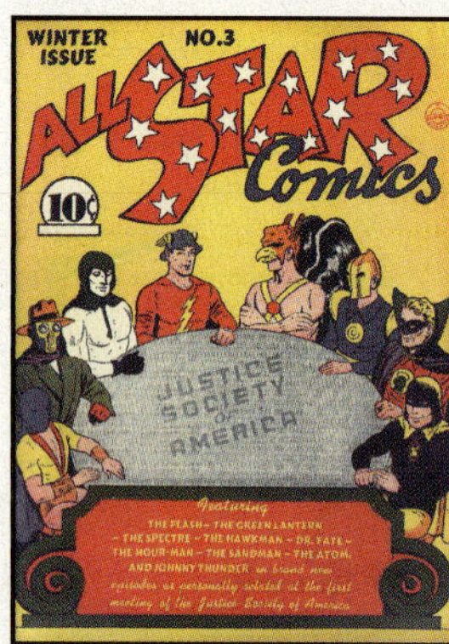

All Star Comics #3

First Justice Society of America
1970 Mint Price: $135
2013 NM– Price: $100,000

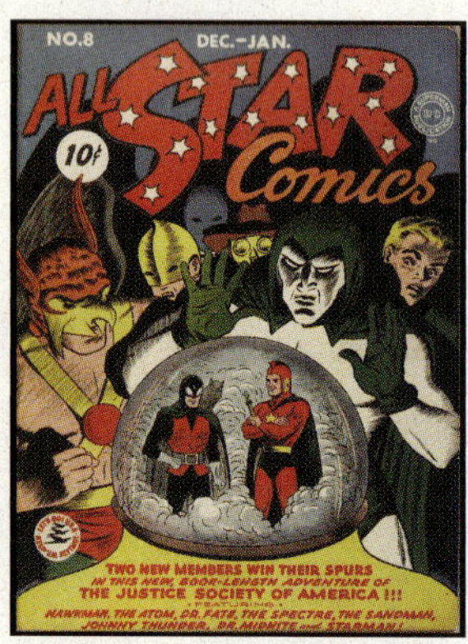

All Star Comics #8

First appearance of Womder Woman
1970 Mint Price: $45
2013 NM– Price: $90,000

Archie Comics #1

First Teen-Age comic
1970 Mint Price: $10
2013 NM– Price: $110,000

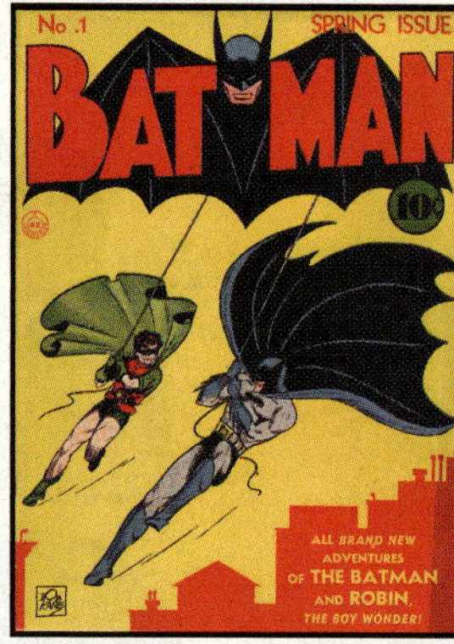

Batman #1

Debut of the Joker and Catwoman
1970 Mint Price: $175
2013 NM– Price: $420,000

Captain America Comics #1

First appearance of Captain America
1970 Mint Price: $150
2013 NM– Price: $300,000

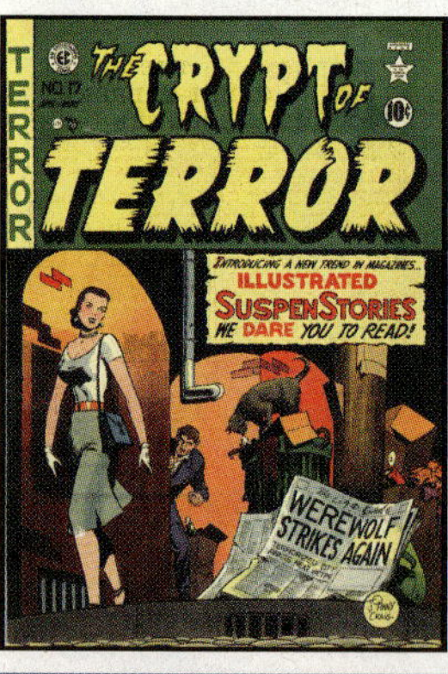

Crypt of Terror #17

First of the EC New Trend issues
1970 Mint Price: $30
2013 NM– Price: $5,300

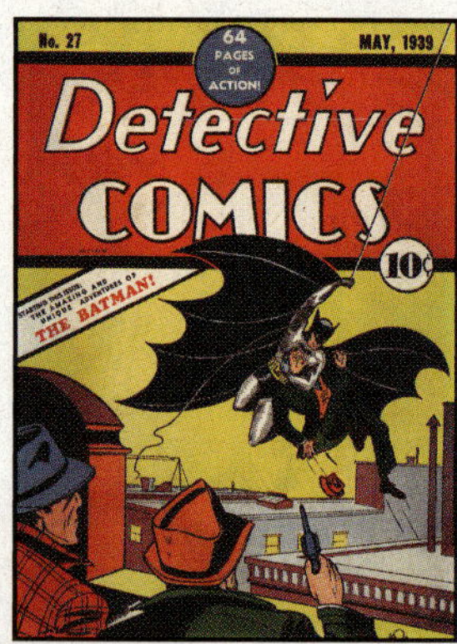

Detective Comics #27

First appearance of Batman
1970 Mint Price: $275
2013 NM– Price: $1,500,000

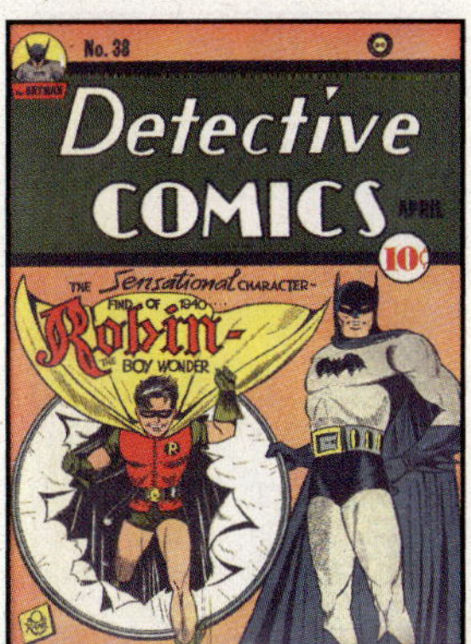

Detective Comics #38
First appearance of Robin
1970 Mint Price: $60
2013 NM– Price: $92,000

Flash Comics #1
Debut of the Flash and Hawkman
1970 Mint Price: $125
2013 NM– Price: $170,000

Marvel Comics #1
First Sub-Mariner and Human Torch
1970 Mint Price: $250
2013 NM– Price: $485,000

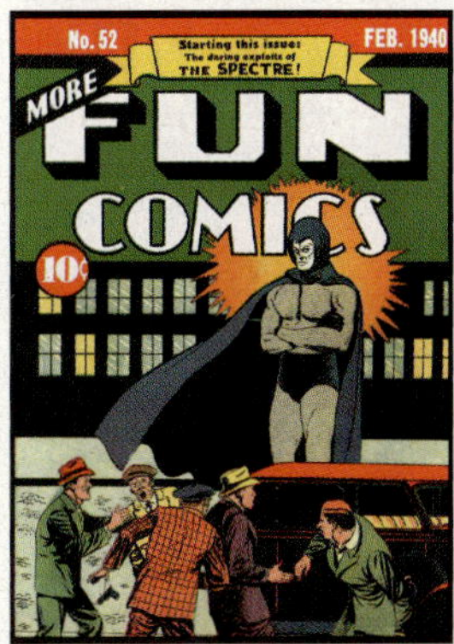

More Fun Comics #52
First appearance of The Spectre
1970 Mint Price: $100
2013 NM– Price: $155,000

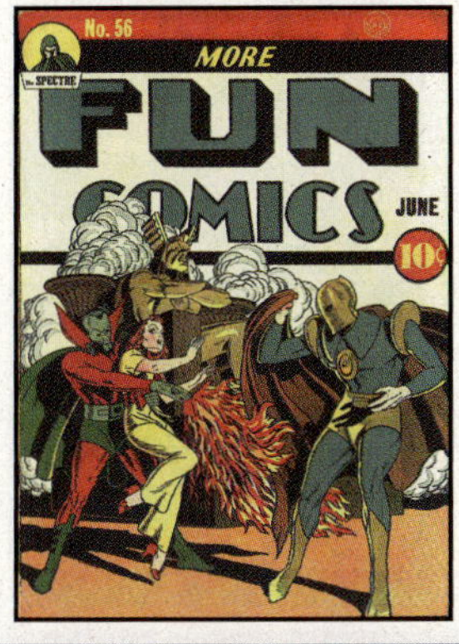

More Fun Comics #56
First cover appearance of Dr. Fate
1970 Mint Price: $40
2013 NM– Price: $16,500

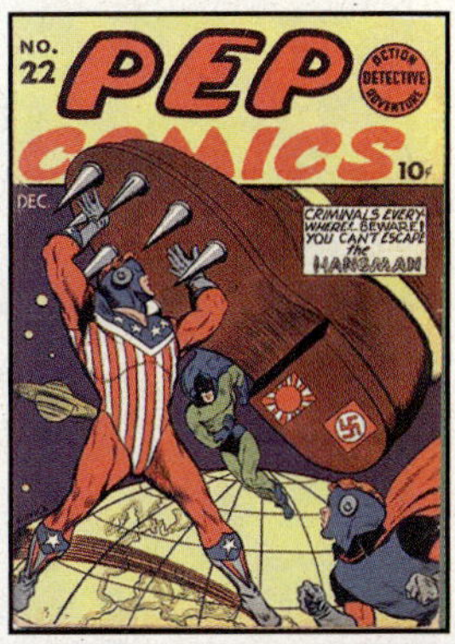

Pep Comics #22
First appearance of Archie
1970 Mint Price: $10
2013 NM– Price: $140,000

Superman #1
Superman's origin
1970 Mint Price: $250
2013 NM– Price: $720,000

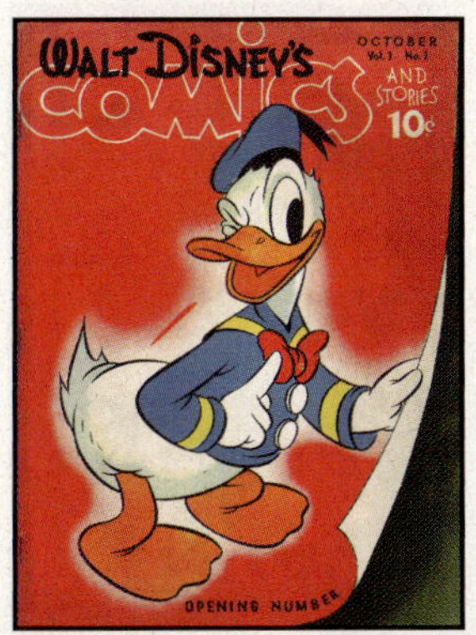

Walt Disney's Comics & Stories #1
Donald Duck, Mickey Mouse reprints
1970 Mint Price: $115
2013 NM– Price: $45,000

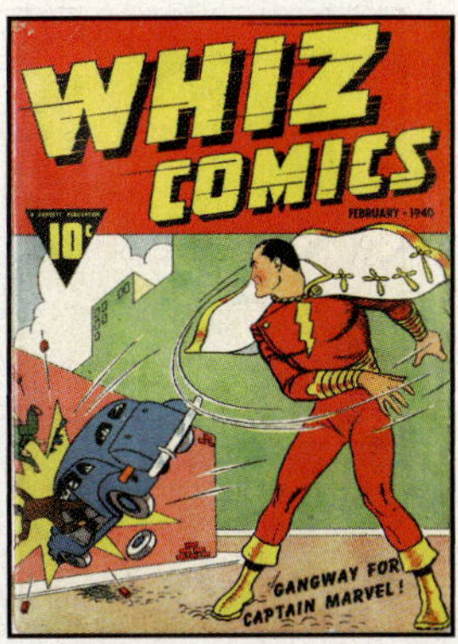

Whiz Comics #2 (#1)
First appearance of Captain Marvel
1970 Mint Price: $235
2013 NM– Price: $130,000

Amazing Fantasy #15
First appearance of Spider-Man
1970 Mint Price: $16
2013 NM– Price: $175,000

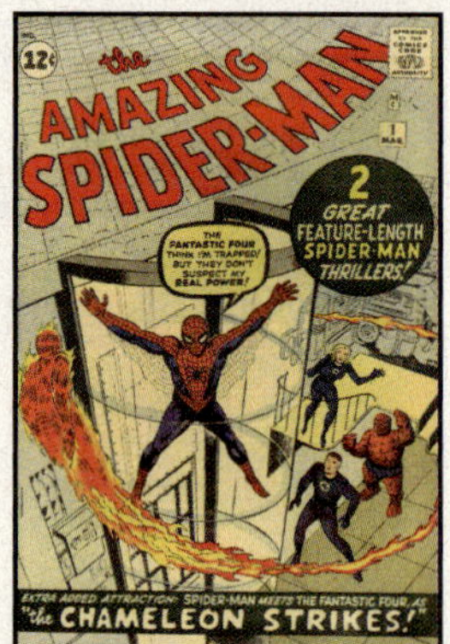

Amazing Spider-Man #1
Spider-Man's 2nd appearance
1970 Mint Price: $16
2013 NM– Price: $58,000

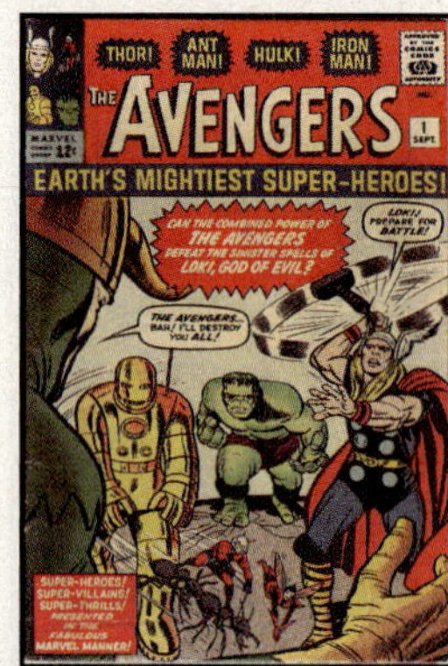

The Avengers #1
First appearance of the Avengers
1970 Mint Price: $6
2013 NM– Price: $28,000

Brave and the Bold #28
First Justice League of America
1970 Mint Price: $5
2013 NM– Price: $26,000

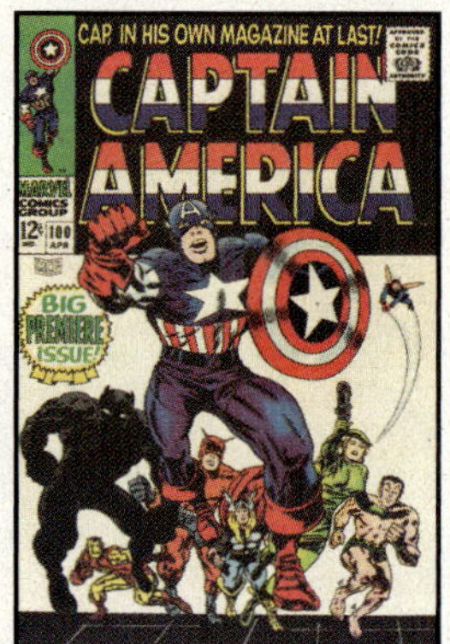

Captain America #100
1st Silver Age Cap in his own title
1970 Mint Price: $1
2013 NM– Price: $700

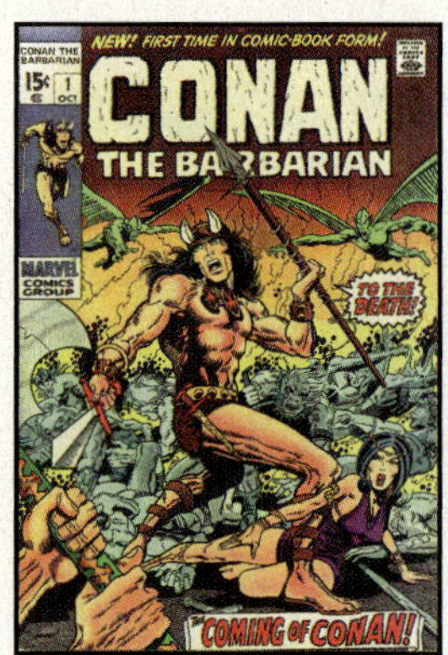

Conan the Barbarian #1
Comic book debut of Conan
1970 Mint Price: 15¢
2013 NM– Price: $500

Fantastic Four #1
First appearance of the Fantastic Four
1970 Mint Price: $12
2013 NM– Price: $105,000

Fantastic Four #48
Debuts of Silver Surfer & Galactus
1970 Mint Price: $1
2013 NM– Price: $1,600

Green Lantern #76
O'Neil/Adams issues begin
1970 Mint Price: 65¢
2013 NM– Price: $2,700

Incredible Hulk #1
First appearance of the Hulk
1970 Mint Price: $14
2013 NM– Price: $105,000

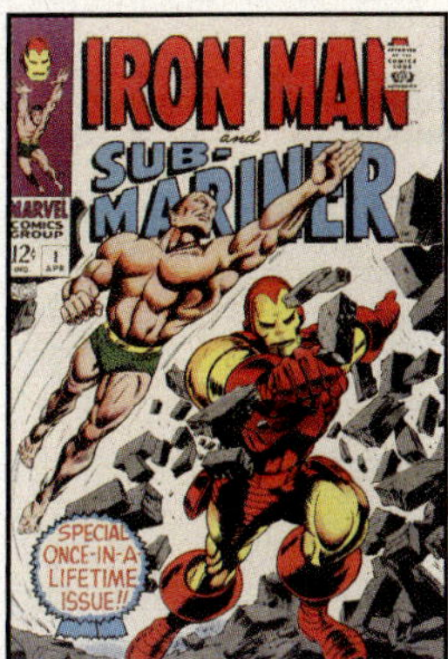

Iron Man & Sub-Mariner #1
Prelude to new #1 issues
1970 Mint Price: $1.15
2013 NM– Price: $340

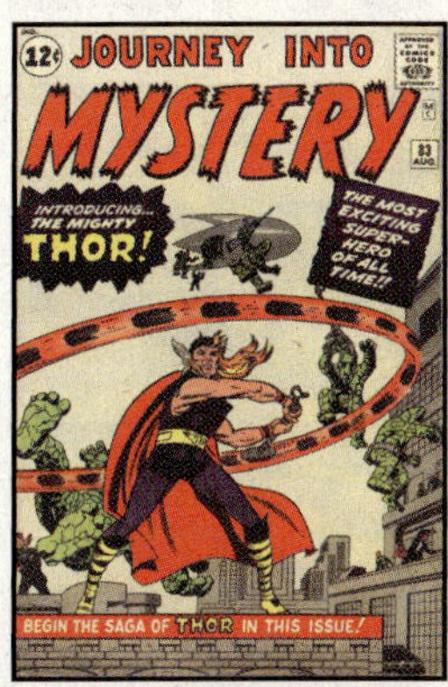

Journey Into Mystery #83
First appearance of Thor
1970 Mint Price: $10
2013 NM– Price: $50,000

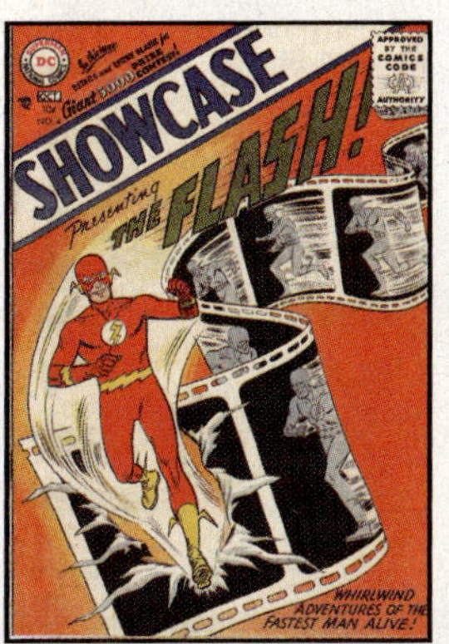

Showcase #4
First appearance of Silver Age Flash
1970 Mint Price: $12
2013 NM– Price: $65,000

Showcase #22
First Silver Age Green Lantern
1970 Mint Price: $6
2013 NM– Price: $30,000

Strange Tales #110
First appearance of Dr. Strange
1970 Mint Price: $3
2013 NM– Price: $6,500

Tales of Suspense #39
First appearance of Iron Man
1970 Mint Price: $6
2013 NM– Price: $36,000

Tales to Astonish #27
First appearance of Ant-Man
1970 Mint Price: $12
2013 NM– Price: $25,000

X-Men #1
First appearance of the X-Men
1970 Mint Price: $6
2013 NM– Price: $40,000

FIRST APPEARANCES
SPIDER-MAN AND HIS FRIENDS AND FOES

SPIDER-MAN
AMAZING FANTASY #15
AUG. -SEPT. 1962

GWEN STACY
AMAZING SPIDER-MAN #31
DECEMBER 1965

MARY JANE WATSON
(1ST TIME FACE SHOWN)
AMAZING SPIDER-MAN #42
NOVEMBER 1966

HARRY OSBORN
AMAZING SPIDER-MAN #31
DECEMBER 1965

J. JONAH JAMESON
AMAZING SPIDER-MAN #1
MARCH 1963

HUMAN TORCH
FANTASTIC FOUR #1
NOVEMBER 1961

GREEN GOBLIN
AMAZING SPIDER-MAN #14
JULY 1964

DOCTOR OCTOPUS
AMAZING SPIDER-MAN #3
JULY 1963

THE KINGPIN
AMAZING SPIDER-MAN #50
JULY 1967

THE VULTURE
AMAZING SPIDER-MAN #2
MAY 1963

VENOM
AMAZING SPIDER-MAN #300
MAY 1988

BATMAN
DETECTIVE COMICS #27
MAY 1939

ROBIN
DETECTIVE COMICS #38
APRIL 1940

BATGIRL
DETECTIVE COMICS #359
JANUARY 1967

ALFRED
BATMAN #16
APRIL-MAY 1943

CATWOMAN
BATMAN #1
SPRING 1940

THE JOKER
BATMAN #1
SPRING 1940

HARLEY QUINN
BATMAN ADVENTURES #12
SEPTEMBER 1993

COMMISSIONER GORDON
DETECTIVE COMICS #27
MAY 1939

THE RIDDLER
DETECTIVE COMICS #140
OCTOBER 1948

POISON IVY
BATMAN #181
JUNE 1966

THE PENGUIN
DETECTIVE COMICS #58
DECEMBER 1941

BANE
BATMAN: VENGEANCE OF BANE #1
JANUARY 1993

FIRST APPEARANCES
THE JUSTICE LEAGUE

SUPERMAN
ACTION COMICS #1
JUNE 1938

WONDER WOMAN
ALL STAR COMICS #8
DECEMBER 1941

THE FLASH
SHOWCASE #4
SEPT.-OCT. 1956

GREEN LANTERN
SHOWCASE #22
SEPT.-OCT. 1956

MARTIAN MANHUNTER
DETECTIVE COMICS #225
NOVEMBER 1955

AQUAMAN
MORE FUN COMICS #73
NOVEMBER 1941

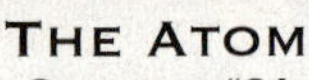
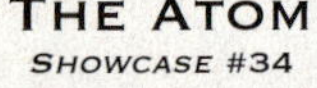

THE ATOM
SHOWCASE #34
SEPT.-OCT. 1961

HAWKMAN
BRAVE AND THE BOLD #34
FEBRUARY-MARCH 1961

GREEN ARROW
MORE FUN COMICS #73
NOVEMBER 1941

RED TORNADO
JUSTICE LEAGUE OF AMERICA #64
AUGUST 1968

FIRESTORM
FIRESTORM, THE NUCLEAR MAN #1
MARCH 1978

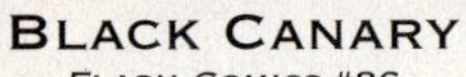

BLACK CANARY
FLASH COMICS #86
AUGUST 1947

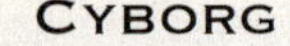

CYBORG
DC COMICS PRESENTS #26
OCTOBER 1980

ZATANNA
HAWKMAN #4
OCT.-NOV. 1964

FIRST APPEARANCES
THE AVENGERS/X-MEN

THOR
Journey Into Mystery #83
August 1962

IRON MAN
Tales of Suspense #39
March 1963

CAPTAIN AMERICA
Captain America Comics #1
March 1941

ANT-MAN
Tales to Astonish #27
January 1962

BLACK PANTHER
Fantastic Four #52
July 1966

WASP
Tales to Astonish #44
June 1963

THE VISION
The Avengers #57
October 1968

HAWKEYE
Tales of Suspense #57
September 1964

SCARLET WITCH
X-Men #4
June 1964

BLACK WIDOW
Tales of Suspense #52
April 1964

THE X-MEN
X-Men #1
September 1963

WOLVERINE
Incredible Hulk #181
November 1974

COLOSSUS
Giant-Size X-Men #1
Summer 1975

STORM
Giant-Size X-Men #1
Summer 1975

NIGHTCRAWLER
Giant-Size X-Men #1
Summer 1975

FIRST APPEARANCES
THE GOLDEN AGE

CAPTAIN MARVEL
WHIZ COMICS #2 (#1)
FEBRUARY 1940

ARCHIE
PEP COMICS #22
DECEMBER 1941

DAREDEVIL
SILVER STREAK COMICS #6
SEPTEMBER 1940

PLASTIC MAN
POLICE COMICS #1
AUGUST 1941

HUMAN TORCH
MARVEL COMICS #1
OCTOBER-NOVEMBER 1939

THE SPECTRE
MORE FUN COMICS #52
FEBRUARY 1940

SUB-MARINER
MOTION PICTURES FUNNIES WEEKLY #1
1939

BUGS BUNNY
LOONEY TUNES & MERRIE MELODIES #1 1941

UNCLE SCROOGE
FOUR COLOR COMICS #178
DECEMBER 1947

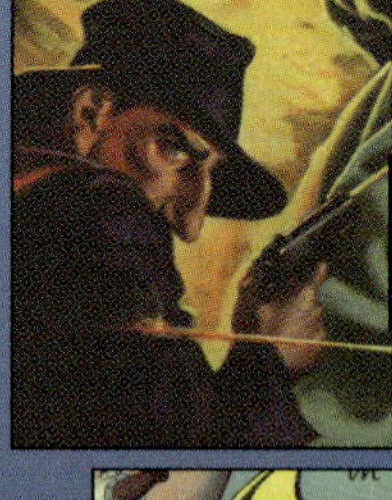

THE SHADOW
SHADOW COMICS #1
MARCH 1940

THE SPIRIT
THE SPIRIT (NO NUMBER)
JUNE 1940

BUCK ROGERS
FAMOUS FUNNIES #3
SEPTEMBER 1934

PHANTOM LADY
POLICE COMICS #1
AUGUST 1941

THE CRYPT KEEPER
CRYPT OF TERROR #17
APRIL-MAY 1950

DEADPOOL
New Mutants #98
February 1991

RICK GRIMES
The Walking Dead #1
October 2003

MICHONNE
The Walking Dead #19
June 2005

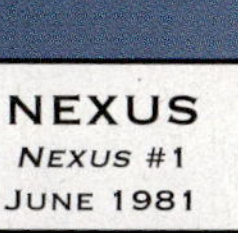

JOHN CONSTANTINE
Saga of the Swamp Thing #37
June 1985

NEXUS
Nexus #1
June 1981

GEN 13
Deathmate Black
September 1993

KATCHOO & FRANCINE
Strangers in Paradise #1
November 1993

TEENAGE MUTANT NINJA TURTLES
Gobbledygook #1 (Back cover)
1984

MARV (SIN CITY)
Dark Horse Presents
Fifth Anniversary Special
April 1991

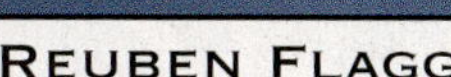

THE ROCKETEER
Starslayer #1
February 1982

REUBEN FLAGG
American Flagg! #1
October 1983

WITCHBLADE
Cyblade/Shi #1
1995

HELLBOY
San Diego Comic Con Comics #2
1993

THE GOON
The Goon #1 (Avatar)
March 1999

Batman and Wonder Woman Collectors

WE BUY PRE-1975 BATMAN COMICS
AND MEMORABILIA
AND WONDER WOMAN COMICS
AND MEMORABILIA FROM ALL ERAS.

P.O. Box 604925
Flushing, NY 11360-4925

email: batt90@aol.com
wwali@aol.com

THE OVERSTREET COMIC BOOK PRICE GUIDE
43RD EDITION
2013-2014
ROBERT M. OVERSTREET
WHILE I REALLY LIKE *READING* THE COMIC BOOKS IN MY COLLECTION, THERE'S A LOT OF FUN IN ACTUALLY PUTTING A COLLECTION TOGETHER!

"WHILE WE ALL MIGHT NOT HAVE THE MONEY TO PICK-UP CGC-CERTIFIED 8.0 COPIES OF *ACTION COMICS #1* OR *DETECTIVE COMICS #27*, IT'S A GREAT IDEA TO KEEP TRACK OF WHAT'S GOING ON IN THE MARKET."

"WHEN YOU KEEP UP WITH *RECORD PRICES*, WHAT'S *SELLING*, WHAT'S *NOT* SELLING, AND WHAT'S SUDDENLY *IN DEMAND*, IT HELPS YOU KNOW WHAT YOU SHOULD BE WILLING TO PAY OR WHEN TO SELL."

BUYING AND *SELLING BACK ISSUES* CAN BE ONE OF THE MOST INTIMIDATING PARTS OF COLLECTING COMIC BOOKS, BUT IF YOU'RE PREPARED IT'S NOT REALLY SCARY AT ALL.

ON THE NEXT PAGE, WE'LL TAKE A LOOK AT SOME OF THE BASICS. BUT REMEMBER, THERE'S *NO SUBSTITUTE FOR EXPERIENCE!*

With record prices paid for *Action Comics* #1, *Detective Comics* #27, *Amazing Fantasy* #15, *Incredible Hulk* #1, and many other comics, it's a very interesting time to sell your comics. "Interesting," though, doesn't automatically mean "great."

It seems pretty basic, but you should only patronize dealers who treat you well. Whether you're purchasing a single new issue or setting a record price for a "Holy Grail" back issue, any customer deserves to be treated with respect, as do the dealers with whom you do business.

When it comes to spending serious amounts of money on a comic, you should never deal with a dealer without fully checking their references. The more serious the money, the more patient you should be in getting additional verification, such as checking with The Better Business Bureau. While it is not in and of itself any kind of guaranty, advertisers and advisors in *The Overstreet Comic Book Price Guide* are more likely to have an established reputation.

If you are looking to sell, potential buyers who are dealers will be most concerned with the retail value of your entire collection. Based on demand at that time, which in turn depends on the dealer's customer base, some issues may sell for prices above *Guide*, while others retail below *Guide* prices. More recent issues may only be worth a percentage of cover price. Take into account how the collection breaks down into fast-, moderate-, and slow-moving issues. To expect someone to pay full retail for comics that usually sell at considerably lower prices is unrealistic.

Regardless, you should learn as much as you can about the market so that you can formulate an informed opinion as to what percentage of *Guide* price is acceptable to you. It's also simply good business to get competing offers.

Some buyers may want to purchase only certain key or high grade issues from your collection. While you may be paid a high percentage of retail for their selections, you will find that "cherry-picked" collections are much more difficult to sell, since all of the most desired books will be sold by the time the second or third potential buyer examines your collection.

Auction houses offer another outlet for your comics. For the rarest, high-grade, vintage comics, some auction companies will even offer you cash advances against the expected sales of your comics. Most of the established auction houses will gladly discuss their track records and how they perceive current market conditions.

Another venue, of course, is eBay, which bypasses the auction house structure. It is not exclusively the domain of bargain hunters, but many eBay shoppers expect a discount on the price they would pay dealers or fellow collectors in person.

If you are listing your comics for a prospective buyer, an auction house, an eBay listing or even your insurance company, don't forget how important it is to understand the condition of your comics. Learning how to grade with the top graders in the business can take years, but getting a good understanding of the process doesn't take that long at all.

You should think along the same lines when you are going to purchase collectible comics. Learn what the give and take in the market is about, and develop your understanding of how important grades are to pricing.

Most of us can't afford to go out and buy a 9.6 copy of *Amazing Fantasy* #15 on a whim, but low grade copies are still easily within reach of many collectors.

Whether buying or selling, the key is to get informed.

MARKET BOBSERVATIONS

by Robert M. Overstreet

As I was preparing my market observations for this new book, I reflected on what I had written in *The Overstreet Comic Book Price Guide* #40. Not only was it our 40th annual edition, it came after two of the roughest years our economy had seen since the 1930s.

"The Financial crisis of 2008-2009 changed forever the banking structure of this country. Lehman Brothers went out of business, Merrill Lynch and Bear Stearns were sold at liquidation prices and Fannie Mae and Freddy Mac were placed into conservatorship by the U.S. government in September 2008. Also the insurance giant AIG, who insured many of the failed banks toxic loans, defaulted and was taken over by the federal government that same month.

"Furthermore, with the steep decline in the economy during this time and millions of workers being laid off, the car industry imploded with the U.S. government becoming shareholders of General Motors, and forcing the sale of Chrysler to Fiat at a salvage price. Hundreds of car dealerships across the country went out of business.

"This 2008-2009 faltering of the U.S. economy spread all over the world and has been dubbed by the President "the worst crash since 1929." The unemployment rate reached double-digits (higher than 17% when we count the people who have simply stopped looking for work) while the U.S. government kept spending and dumping cash into the economic system in an attempt to soften or slow down its decline.

"With all the bad economic news permeating the media outlets month after month, one might think the comics market would have suffered a dramatic decline as well, but this is not the case," I wrote in 2010.

Well, as I write this several years later, things have not improved dramatically, if at all, and yet we have not seen any drop in the number of record prices reported for rare, vintage, high grade comic books. There are certainly some keys to this, and most of them fall in the phrases "rare," "vintage," and "high grade." This does not mean that those comics that aren't rare or vintage or high grade do not have a market, just that those are fairly accurate predictors of success. There are of course many others. By the way, while we like to refrain from blanket statements, the same factors seem to have played out in many other collecting niches beyond comics as well.

The million dollar prices paid for copies of *Action Comics* #1 (the first appearance of Superman), *Detective Comics* #27 (first Batman) and *Amazing Fantasy* #15 (first Spider-Man) all have all three factors working in their favor, with the "rare" factor increasing almost exponentially the higher up the 10.0 grading scale they go. If you do your research, you'll see that there are many other issues to which these categories apply as well.

Here's an example we have used before: In the case of *Action Comics* #1, most industry experts

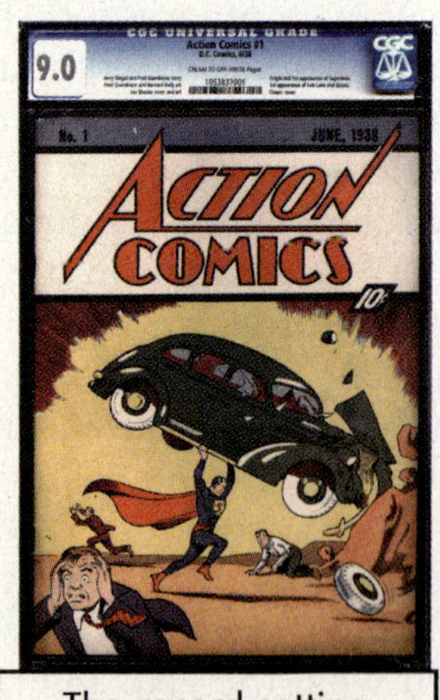

The record setting $2,161 million copy of *Action Comics* #1.

agree that there are about 100 copies of this issue. If we're wrong and there turn out to be 200 copies, this would still be an amazing purchase. We live in a nation of more than 300 million people and Superman is the most recognized character in the world. *Action Comics* #1 will always be in high demand, particularly the better the grade.

Likewise, the first appearance of Batman in *Detective Comics* #27 is an appealing purchase as well. With the strong box office performance of *Batman Begins* (2005) and phenomenal success of *The Dark Knight* (2008), and another powerful outing with *The Dark Knight Rises* (2012), it seems safe to suggest that more people than ever are at least aware of Batman, and that if even a small percentage of those people are interested in acquiring the character's first appearance this will also turn out to be a smart investment.

In the case of *Amazing Fantasy* #15, which is two decades younger than the other two million dollar comics, grade becomes even more important because there are more copies, though not that many more in high grade.

The Golden Age and Silver Age issues that dominate the high profile sales are likely to continue doing so because they have a proven track record. This would include Golden Age mainstays like *Batman* #1, *Captain America Comics* #1, *Daredevil Battles Hitler* #1, *Marvel Comics* #1, *Red Raven* #1, *Richie Rich* #1, *Sub-Mariner* #1, *Superman* #1, *Walt Disney Comics & Stories* #1, and *Whiz Comics* #2 (#1), and Silver Age highlights such as *Avengers* #1, *Avengers* #4, *Brave & the Bold* #28, *Daredevil* #1, *Fantastic Four* #1, *Flash* #105, *Incredible Hulk* #1, *Iron Man* #1, *Journey Into Mystery* #83, *Justice League* #1, *Showcase* #4, *Showcase* #22, and *Tales of Suspense* #39 among many, many others.

To get a really good dose of long term perspective, you can see many of these on Pages 20-23 and compare their prices from 1970, the first year of *The Overstreet Comic Book Price Guide*, to their values in 2013 (and they are updated every year in the *Guide* as well).

The Walking Dead #19 doesn't need to be "vintage" to command high prices.

It's very important to note that not all three of those descriptors apply each time, particularly when demand for an issue increases significantly in a short period. For instance, *The Walking Dead* #1 and *The Walking Dead* #19 could hardly qualify as "vintage," but they have seen their high grade prices skyrocket in just a few years as awareness of the series has spiked upward since the debut the popular television series it inspired. Simply put, demand went up, supply remained static, so the prices went up accordingly.

There are also many, many comics that don't fit into the vintage, rare, high grade mold. That does not mean they're not desirable – in the end, only *you* can decide what *you* want – but the price you pay should reflect all of these factors and the demand for them. In some cases, if you're the one selling them, you may actually work harder for the same return or even less of a return than a few years ago. That may not always be the case, but it seems to be as I write this.

We would never say comic prices only go up. That's just not true. We can, however, say that looking at the track record over more than four decades of researching, writing, assembling and publishing *The Overstreet Comic Book Price Guide*, that comics have performed admirably, consistently and in a fashion that appears to be readily discernable to the trained observer. The same, of course, can't be said for every investment we make.

If you are just getting into comic collecting, my personal encouragement to you is to study the market. Acquire knowledge as readily as you do the comics themselves. Establish relationships with dealers and other collectors you trust, and don't do business with those you don't. If you can do those things, then it probably only comes down to one more step: enjoy what you collect, collect what you enjoy, and the rest will likely take care of itself.

Liquidity

In the Comic Book Market

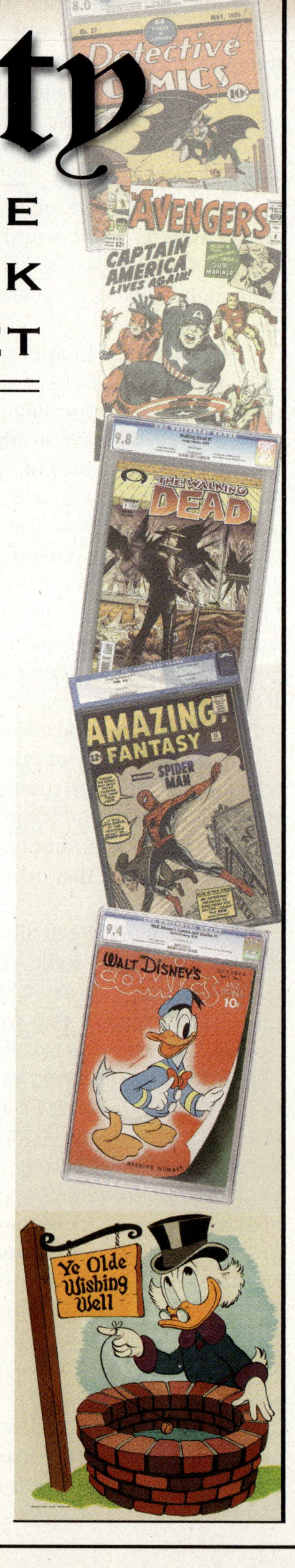

As Bob Overstreet indicated in his overview of the market-place, vintage comic books offer many different factors that can appeal to collectors and investors. One of the key factors is liquidity.

"Liquidity is the ability to sell an item in a fast and easy process without causing a significant negative movement in price," said Vincent Zurzolo, Chief Operating Officer of Metropolis Collectibles and ComicConnect.com.

Under normal conditions, he said, increased liquidity should promote trade and increase prices because easier transactions allow more people to make those transactions in a confident manner. That increased consumer confidence is at the heart of it: if you are convinced that any investment in any field is safer, if all things are equal then you are more likely to make that investment.

"In a consistent fashion every month I am getting calls from brand new buyers who have never collected or invested in comic books looking to get into the market. They are motivated by finding a place to invest in Batman, Superman and Spider-Man. Long time collectors and investors are motivated financially but they are also motivated by their passion for the comic books, their love of the characters and trying to recapture the joy they felt in their youth when they read comics," he said.

But why is liquidity important in the first place? It is probably – and understandably – more of an issue for an investor, but given the substantial prices paid by collectors for vintage, rare, high grade comics these days there is no denying that it's part of the equation for them as well. The higher the prices investors and collectors have to pay for a given comic book, the more they want to know what their short-term downside is in case they have to sell sooner than they planned.

"A bidder doesn't want to feel foolish by going too far beyond what anyone has paid before. Or to put it another way, if you overpay you want to be doing so consciously because you just want the item that much," said Barry Sandoval, Director of Operations, Comics for Heritage Auctions.

Sandoval said that each high result from an auction provides other bidders a certain comfort level, particularly if the price is the result of an unreserved auction (meaning there was no bottom price for which the issue could have sold) because it takes a minimum of two people to get to a certain price.

With high-dollar private treaty sales that were rumored or announced over the years, you never quite knew for sure if a partial trade or other considerations were involved.

"The presence of investors in the market alongside collectors, though, does not by itself increase liquidity in the marketplace," said Josh Nathanson, President of ComicLink.com.

"Bringing investors into the market helps increase prices realized for certain segments of comic books at certain periods of time, but I don't think it increases liquidity. It just affects the demand side of the equation. If the supply side does not increase as quickly as the demand side, or the supply on the market diminishes, prices go up," Nathanson said.

"Accurate grading and pricing by sellers and third party grading services help to promote liquidity," he said.

Most experts agree that reliable, independent, third-party grading has played an enormous role in shaping the comic book market's past decade, including the robust growth in five-, six-, and now seven-figure sales.

"The advent of Comics Guaranty, LLC (CGC) has been an enormous factor. I believe the days are gone where a non-CGC-certified book of value gets bought or sold. Most dealers and sellers realize you will receive a lot more money for a certified comic book compared to a non-certified one (primarily for comics worth hundreds of dollars and higher) and most collectors and buyers will not pay a premium for a book of value unless it is certified," said Doug Schmell, President and CEO of Pedigree Comics.

"It is the confidence and trust factor of the CGC product that drives this market, knowing that at least three expert graders have reviewed any given comic for its condition, knowing whether it has been restored or not, and having an impartial and accurate grade assigned to it," he said.

No single factor, not even independent third-party grading, can make a market, though. There are many significant changes that we can enumerate, but the presence of the internet has changed the comics market – and so many others – in ways that we cannot entirely comprehend at this point.

In addition to the relative ease of finding the material compared to even just 10 years ago, there has also been a change in the social acceptance. The "Bam! Pow! Bop!" lead sentences in news articles about record prices have given way – not quickly enough for our tastes, but still – to more articulate descriptions of our marketplace.

The financial success of comic characters or properties in other media has also helped. Blazing box office successes for *The Dark Knight* trilogy, the *Avengers* films, the *Spider-Man* movies, and *The X-Men* series, and along with television series such as *The Walking Dead* have helped raise the profile of comics as well.

In the end, however, there are no assurances that comic values will always go up. Anyone who peddles such a notion probably would have said the same thing about housing values prior to 2007. So, what is an appropriate way for a collector or investor to moderate his or her expectations?

"Collect and invest with a plan in mind. Come up with a strategy that fits your budget and talk to people like me once you have put your plan and goals together," said Zurzolo.

Experienced, reputable dealers or seasoned collectors can help you to refine your plan and let you know if your goals are realistic ones. If you as the purchaser are willing to spend a substantial amount of money with them, they should be able to provide you with references that will increase your confidence.

COMIC BOOK AGES

by J.C. Vaughn & Gene Gonzales

THE YELLOW KID IN MCFADDEN'S FLATS COLLECTED R.F. OUTCAULT'S SUCCESSFUL CHARACTER IN BOOK FORM.
LIKE MANY OTHERS IN THAT TIME, IT WAS A HUGE SUCCESS.
BUT NO ONE WOULD CALL THIS COLLECTION A COMIC BOOK, WOULD THEY?
50 Cents
THE YELLOW KID IN MCFADDEN'S FLATS
BY E.W. TOWNSEND AUTHOR OF "CHIMMIE FADDEN"
DIS BOOK IS DE STORY OF ME. SWEET YOUNG LIFE
AND R.F. OUTCAULT CREATOR OF THE "YELLOW KID"
G.W. DILLINGHAM CO. PUBLISHERS NEW YORK
THIRTIETH THOUSAND.

THE MOST POPULAR COMIC BOOKS EVER PUBLISHED.

THE MOST POPULAR COMIC BOOKS EVER PUBLISHED.
ARTEMUS WARD.
HIS COMPLETE COMIC WRITINGS, WITH BIOGRAPHY AND ONE HUNDRED ILLUSTRATIONS. THE BIOGRAPHICAL SKETCH BY "ELI PERKINS." CLOTH BOUND, PRICE $1.50.
JOSH BILLINGS.
HIS WORKS COMPLETE (FOUR VOLUMES IN ONE), WITH ONE HUNDRED ILLUSTRATIONS, BY THOMAS NAST, AND OTHERS. CLOTH BOUND, PRICE $2.00.
VERDANT GREEN.
A RACY ENGLISH COLLEGE STORY, BY CUTHBERT BEDE. PROFUSELY ILLUSTRATED, AND CLOTH BOUND. PRICE $1.50.
SOLD EVERYWHERE, AND SENT BY MAIL, POSTAGE FREE, ON RECEIPT OF PRICE, BY G.W. DILLINGHAM CO., PUBLISHERS, 33 WEST 23D STREET, NEW YORK.

SO, LET'S GET THIS STRAIGHT . . .
IN 1897 THESE GUYS KNEW IT WAS A COMIC BOOK, BUT THERE ARE STILL PEOPLE OUT THERE NOW WHO DON'T?
G.W. DILLINGHAM CO. PUBLISHERS NEW YORK

WHO ELSE MIGHT HAVE BEEN DOING COMICS?
I CREATED LITTLE NEMO IN 1905 AND SOON IT WAS BEING COLLECTED INTO COMIC BOOK REPRINTS.
LADIES AND GENTLEMEN, WINSOR McCAY.
LATER, COMIC MONTHLY, WHICH DEBUTED IN 1922, WAS THE FIRST MONTHLY NEWSSTAND COMIC BOOK.
DREAM OF THE RAREBIT FIEND
LITTLE NEMO IN SLUMBERLAND
BANG!
Comic Monthly
PRICE 10¢
POLLY & HER PALS
BY CLIFF STERRETT.
Published By

BY GEORGE, THE REPRINTS OF MY STRIP, BRINGING UP FATHER, SOLD MORE THAN 4 MILLION COPIES EACH . . .
. . . IN A NATION OF ONLY 100 MILLION PEOPLE!
BRINGING UP FATHER
by GEO McMANUS

FUNNIES ON PARADE, WHICH IS LITTLE MORE THAN AN INTERESTING FOOTNOTE IN COMICS HISTORY, WAS PUBLISHED IN 1933 . . .
IT WAS, OF COURSE, A COLLECTION OF REPRINTS . . .

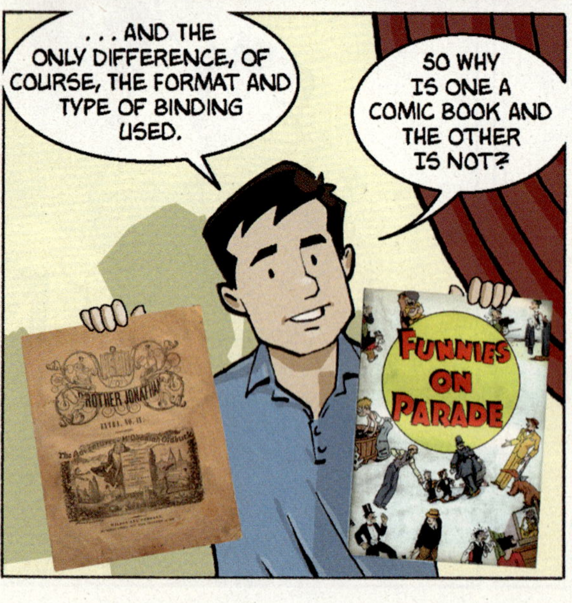

. . . AND THE ONLY DIFFERENCE, OF COURSE, THE FORMAT AND TYPE OF BINDING USED.
SO WHY IS ONE A COMIC BOOK AND THE OTHER IS NOT?
BROTHER JONATHAN
FUNNIES ON PARADE

COMICS, OF COURSE, STARTED EARLIER.
THEY WENT THROUGH A LONG DEVELOPMENTAL STAGE IN THE PIONEER AGE AND VICTORIAN AGE

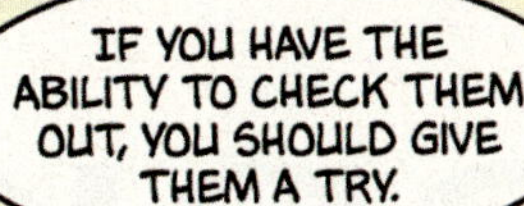

STILL, IT'S HARD TO IGNORE WHAT FOLLOWED.

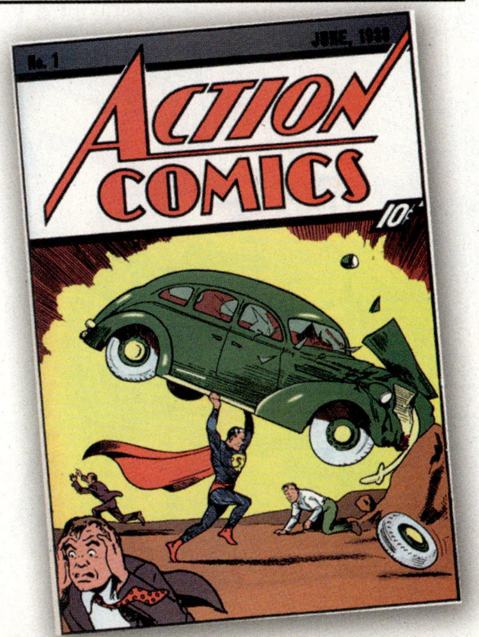

THE DEFINITIONS OF COMIC BOOK AGES CAME WITH A LOT OF GIVE AND TAKE OVER THE YEARS.

WHILE WORKING ON THE SECOND EDITION OF *THE OVERSTREET COMIC BOOK GRADING GUIDE*, A CONSENSUS WAS REACHED.

THE ARTICLE THAT FOLLOWS DESCRIBES THE PROCESS.

AS THE INDUSTRY SEEKS OUT DIVERSITY TODAY, THE IMPACT OF THOSE CHANGES IS STILL BEING FELT.

COMIC BOOK
DEFINING

By Dr. Arnold T. Blumberg & J.C. Vaughn
(with additional material and
timeline graphics by Douglas Gillock)

AGES: ERAS

In **The Official Overstreet Comic Book Price Guide** *#33, we offered the beginnings of a discussion on Comic Book Ages. This article features the results of that discussion.*

The search for agreement on comic book ages has proven to be one of those topics, the kind for which no one is without an opinion or two (or twelve). It has produced scores of animated e-mails, letters and even academic papers, all of them from collectors, dealers and historians who care deeply about where comics have been and where they're going.

As we worked to arrive at a consensus, we've heard from many different fans of the four-color medium in a wide variety of capacities. While there are still some elements to be decided, a great deal of agreement was found in some areas of understanding.

COMICS DIDN'T START IN 1933

More than 90 years before *New Fun* hit the stands, *The Adventures of Obadiah Oldbuck* presented a story in sequential comic form. Someone made the decision to publish it and influenced the next generation of cartoonists. More than 50 years before *New Fun*, Palmer Cox collected his Brownies cartoons into one publication, influencing 60 years of comics publishing during which a tremendous variety of packaging and presentations were tried out.

If you still think it's the comics themselves and not the creative and business people behind them that the Ages denote, consider these questions: If Vin Sullivan and his contemporaries hadn't been looking to try something different, would *Action Comics #1* ever have happened? If Julie Schwartz hadn't been interested in reviving the superheroes, would *Showcase #4* have witnessed the reinterpretation of the Flash? If Stan Lee hadn't stepped away from the day-to-day operations at Marvel, would Gwen Stacy have died? If the

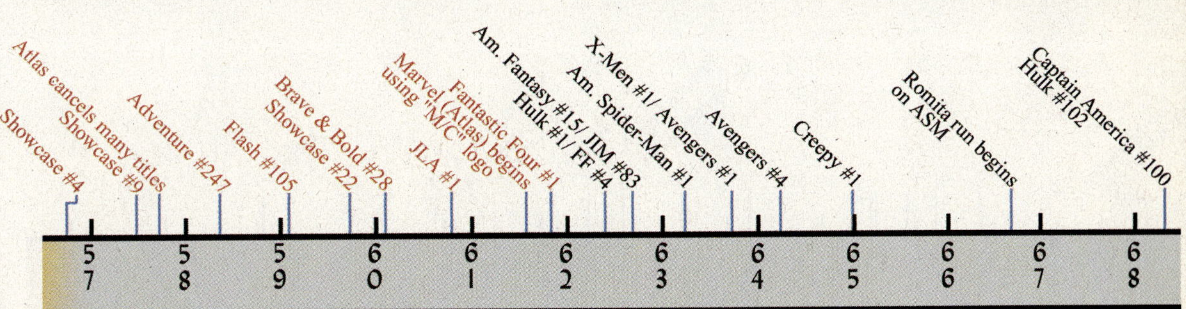

limited series format hadn't proved successful, how would *Crisis on Infinite Earths* have been handled?

It's simple: the comics we have come to recognize as indicators of significant changes, like those noted in the previous paragraph, are the manifestations of *editorial or publishing decisions* that were made several months before. It is actually these decisions we are marking when we note the importance of the publication of *The Adventures of Obadiah Oldbuck*, the collection of Palmer Cox's Brownies into their first book, or the introduction of the Barry Allen Flash. Bill Gaines, Harvey Kurtzman and Al Feldstein wouldn't have done anything that hadn't already been done. Denny O'Neil and Neal Adams wouldn't have told their classic Green Lantern/Green Arrow tales. Gwen Stacy never would have died, the Punisher never would have appeared, and Conan would never have been a licensed comic book title.

A SEARCH FOR THE AGES

We must first acknowledge that comic book Ages really exist only to facilitate the ease of conveying information to other parties. In other words, they help create a verbal shorthand to make it easier to explain the creative, editorial or publishing work involved in a specific comic or set of comics (or the present day value we attach to a specific comic or set of comics) in comparison to other comics.

The act of splitting comics up into groups creates the illusion that these are not part of a much bigger picture, but believing that illusion would be a mistake. Comics are just one part of the much larger world of comic character collectibles, and that world itself is just a piece of the even larger entire history of popular culture.

Comic book Ages are important and they're fun, but they're truly nothing more than an intellectual exercise. If it were more serious, we'd have to take a look at why the comic book Ages run backwards (Golden, Silver, Bronze instead of Bronze, Silver, Golden as does the rest of human history). Picking the landmarks by which we navigate comics history isn't easy though, as we have often discovered.

CODIFYING THE AGES

Does one incident or single comic book issue define an Age? Surely *Action Comics #1* begins the Golden Age just as *The Brownies* begin the Platinum Age, but some have observed that the Comics Code might be the deciding factor in dividing the various eras. That idea did in fact help to suggest an even more innovative way of looking at the whole Age issue that finally breaks away from the narrow-minded reliance on the superhero genre as the end-all be-all of Comic Book Age definition. In the final analysis, we determined that it was not the superheroes *alone* that dictated when these Ages began or ended. They were merely the superficial result of a much deeper motivating force that ultimately serves as the primary shaper of every Comic Book Age; namely, the editorial and publishing decisions that drive the industry and influence the content of the comics themselves. Seen from this perspective, the entire Age issue takes on even greater resonance and even the already established Ages fall neatly into place.

As we will see, the Comics Code can serve to illuminate this theory. Though the original incarnation of the Comics Code Authority and its system of strict self-regulation only existed for 16 years (Oct. 1954 to Jan. 1971), its influ-

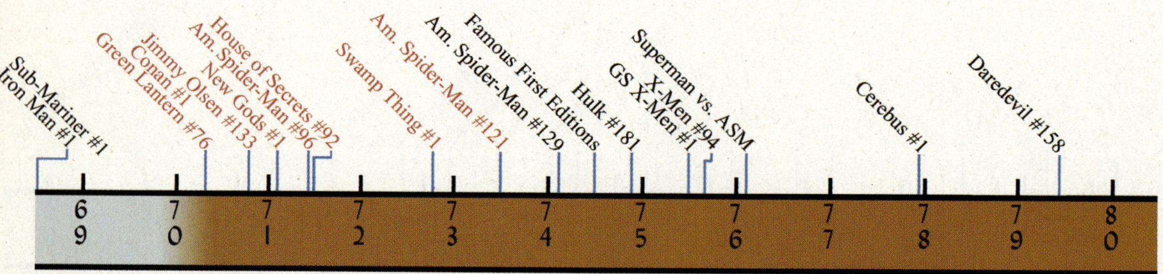

ence on comic book history has been enormous. Primarily, the implementation of the CCA suggested – and perhaps necessitated – the resurrection of a stagnating superhero genre and heralded the beginnings of the Silver Age. But as this genre was given new life with the inclusion of a fresh, realism-based perspective and a growing social consciousness, creators quickly found themselves restricted by walls of content regulation that had been used in the '50s to protect an industry under public siege. It was this desire for greater content flexibility on the part of Silver Age creators that was the first sign of things to come.

Social issues had been creeping into the pages of comics for a few years, but by the end of 1970 there seems to have been a general consensus within the business that the CCA needed revision. In 1971, the Comics Magazine Association of America ratified a general overhaul of the Code, the first since its inception in 1954. Not only did this revision allow for the inclusion of content that for more than a decade had been absent from the pages of comic books, but it denoted a fundamental shift in thinking by the industry as a whole. From this point on, it was clear that the industry itself was in control of the specifics of the CCA. If they saw fit, they could change the Code to keep it current with their perception of public standards.

And change it they did. A mere three months after the original revision of the CCA, the members of the Association found themselves meeting once again to amend the specifics of the system of self-regulation. The topic at hand was the portrayal of drugs, and on April 15, 1971, an agreement was reached to allow stories depicting graphic drug use with the understanding that "narcotics addiction shall not be portrayed except as a vicious habit." This unexpected amendment was directly inspired by Stan Lee's decision at Marvel to distribute three issues of *Amazing Spider-Man* that failed to meet Code approval because of the portrayal of drug abuse. With the inconsistencies in the Code rectified, Carmine Infantino – then editor at DC – followed suit and released a Code-approved story in *Green Lantern* dealing with heroin addiction.

Just as the implementation of the Code can be seen as a defining aspect of the dawn of the Silver Age, the growing social consciousness of certain comic creators and the resulting decision to amend the CCA stands as a herald of the shift into the Bronze Age. With a revised Code, genres and topics that had been forbidden for years suddenly re-emerged in the pages of mainstream comics. The major publishers began launching a multitude of new titles and re-invigorating others that had floundered under the original content restrictions. Without a conscious decision by the industry to expand the range of allowable material, many of the characters, titles, and stories that are now considered foundational to the Bronze Age never could have been published.

In looking beyond the Bronze Age to define the Copper Age, we can see another important reconsideration of the CCA playing a role. Just as publishers had realized in the early '70s that they themselves were in control of the particulars of the Code, in the mid-'80s they decided that for certain kinds of comics the restrictions were not necessary at all. These comics were targeted at an older audience, many of whom had grown up with the socially relevant comics of the '70s. This audience realized the potential the medium

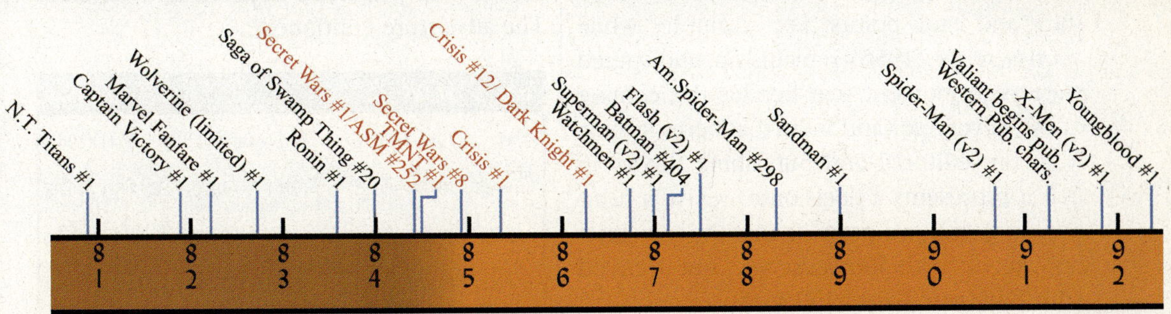

had for a broader type of storytelling and they demanded more "mature" content. Comics like Frank Miller's *Dark Knight Returns* and Alan Moore's *Watchmen* played a major role in defining this new Copper Age and pointed the way to yet another revision of the Code in 1989.

But just as we are suggesting that no single issue can be used to wholly define an era of comic book history, it is important to point out that the CCA was not the only factor in the evolution of the industry. Many creative, social, economic, and technological factors combined to make comics what they are today. But the Code does stand out as a profound, industry-wide influence that can be very helpful in charting the progression of the medium since the mid-'50s. Only now, almost fifty years after the CCA was first imposed, are the publishers of comic books moving away from a single system of content regulation. This "deregulation" of the industry will surely be a determining factor in Ages yet to be defined.

THE SHIFTING SANDS OF TIME

Another aspect of the debate was also clarified for us during this process. For years, we have struggled to define Comic Book Ages based on a single turning point – an individual issue of one comic book from one genre and one company that straddles the line between the end of one era and the start of the next. But since these Ages are arbitrary, applied to real-world developments that never truly reach an end, the flow of history often obscures any specific turning point and instead suggests that one era might subtly segue into another over a period of time. Therefore, we establish here that the later eras on the Comic Book Age scale can be defined through gradual transitions that have start and end points. For example, while *Showcase* #4 (1956) remains an undisputed watershed moment that heralds the coming of the Silver Age (and indeed adheres strongly to our editorial and publishing theory in that it represents a decision to revive a nearly-dead genre), we propose that the transition only *began* with *Showcase* #4…but it ended with *Fantastic Four* #1 (1961).

This same thinking can be applied to the later Ages as well. Perhaps one of the reasons the Bronze Age has been so difficult to nail down at either its beginning or conclusion is that it represents a volatile shift in editorial and publishing philosophy on both ends. Here we propose that the Bronze Age began arriving with *Green Lantern* #76 (1970), the first of a series of books in 1970 and 1971 to break boundaries, explore new editorial and publishing opportunities in storytelling and theme, and start a march toward maturity in the medium. But where did this transformation reach its *climax*, signaling the death of innocence embodied by the Silver Age and opening the door to a more adult era of heightened violence and heightened consequences? *Amazing Spider-Man* #121 (1973).

Finally, we introduce a new Age: the Copper Age, spanning the years from the end of the Bronze Age in 1985 to the debut of Image Comics in 1992. As before, we propose that the transition begins with Marvel's editorial and publishing decision to embark on a twelve-issue maxi-series that ties in their entire superhero universe while introducing changes to their primary characters that would echo forward for years to come. That series was *Marvel Super-Heroes: Secret Wars* (1984-85). The Copper Age then fully arrives when DC takes the notion one step further, utilizing the same editorial and publishing concept to completely remake their fictional universe and wash away the last vestiges of the Silver and Bronze Ages with *Crisis on Infinite Earths* (1985-86).

Now, with what is hopefully a much clearer understanding of this approach to the organization of comic book history, we look forward to the future, and countless other Ages to be explored, enjoyed and defined. The adventure continues…

AGE	YEARS	CATALYSTS
Silver	1956-1970	*Showcase* #4 (1956), *FF* #1 (1961)
Bronze	1970-1984	*GL* #76 (1970), *AMZ* #121 (1973)
Copper	1984-1992	*Secret Wars* (1984-85), *Crisis* (1985-86)
Modern	1992-Present	Image Comics debut

GRADING
ONE OF THE MOST IMPORTANT FACTORS IN DETERMINING A COMIC'S VALUE IS THE GRADE IT RECEIVES.
JUST FOR INSTANCE, A 9.8 COPY OF GREEN LANTERN #76 SOLD FOR $37,343.75 LAST YEAR. A 2.0 COPY OF THAT SAME ISSUE MIGHT NOT EVEN BE $100.
SO, HEY, I'M NOT TRYING TO TELL YOU WHAT TO DO, BUT YOU MIGHT WANT TO LEARN A BIT ABOUT GRADING?
PAINKILLER JANE © 2012 QUESADA & PALMIOTTI ALL RIGHTS RESERVED.

THE DEFINITIVE GUIDE TO GRADING COMIC BOOKS!
OFFICIAL
OVERSTREET COMIC BOOK GRADING GUIDE
THIRD EDITION
10 POINT GRADING SYSTEM
ROBERT M. OVERSTREET AND DR. ARNOLD T. BLUMBERG
It's a good practice to develop relationships with dealers and other collectors who prove themselves trustworthy.
MANY PEOPLE HAVE STARTED USING INDEPENDENT, THIRD-PARTY GRADING SERVICES, SUCH AS CGC.
HEY, SOMEONE TOOK A BITE OUT OF THIS COMIC!

OKAY, THE BASICS OF GRADING ARE PRETTY STRAIGHTFORWARD. THE TOP OF THE SCALE IS 10.0 AND THE BOTTOM IS 0.5.
IF YOU'RE NEW AT THIS, DON'T EXPECT TO BE AS GOOD AS A VETERAN COLLECTOR OR DEALER RIGHT AWAY. YOU'LL GET BETTER AT IT QUICKLY, AND IT'S SOMETHING EVERY COLLECTOR SHOULD LEARN.
WHEN YOU'RE READY, TURN THE PAGE AND YOU'LL FIND THE DEFINITIONS OF EACH GRADE.

10.0 **GEM MINT (GM):** This is an exceptional example of a given book - the best ever seen. The slightest bindery defects and/or printing flaws may be seen only upon very close inspection. The overall look is "as if it has never been handled or released for purchase." Only the slightest bindery or printing defects are allowed, and these would be imperceptible on first viewing. No bindery tears. Cover is flat with no surface wear. Inks are bright with high reflectivity. Well centered and firmly secured to interior pages. Corners are cut square and sharp. No creases. No dates or stamped markings allowed. No soiling, staining or other discoloration. Spine is tight and flat. No spine roll or split allowed. Staples must be original, centered and clean with no rust. No staple tears or stress lines. Paper is white, supple and fresh. No hint of acidity in the odor of the newsprint. No interior autographs or owner signatures. Centerfold is firmly secure. No interior tears.

9.9 **MINT (MT):** Near perfect in every way. Only subtle bindery or printing defects are allowed. No bindery tears. Cover is flat with no surface wear. Inks are bright with high reflectivity. Generally well centered and firmly secured to interior pages. Corners are cut square and sharp. No creases. Small, inconspicuous, lightly penciled, stamped or inked arrival dates are acceptable as long as they are in an unobtrusive location. No soiling, staining or other discoloration. Spine is tight and flat. No spine roll or split allowed. Staples must be original, generally centered and clean with no rust. No staple tears or stress lines. Paper is white, supple and fresh. No hint of acidity in the odor of the newsprint. Centerfold is firmly secure. No interior tears.

9.8 **NEAR MINT/MINT (NM/MT):** Nearly perfect in every way with only minor imperfections that keep it from the next higher grade. Only subtle bindery or printing defects are allowed. No bindery tears. Cover is flat with no surface wear. Inks are bright with high reflectivity. Generally well centered and firmly secured to interior pages. Corners are cut square and sharp. No creases. Small, inconspicuous, lightly penciled, stamped or inked arrival dates are acceptable as long as they are in an unobtrusive location. No soiling, staining or other discoloration. Spine is tight and flat. No spine roll or split allowed. Staples must be original, generally centered and clean with no rust. No staple tears or stress lines. Paper is off-white to white, supple and fresh. No hint of acidity in the odor of the newsprint. Centerfold is firmly secure. Only the slightest interior tears are allowed.

9.6 **NEAR MINT+ (NM+):** Nearly perfect with a minor additional virtue or virtues that raise it from Near Mint. The overall look is "as if it was just purchased and read once or twice." Only subtle bindery or printing defects are allowed. No bindery tears are allowed, although on Golden Age books bindery tears of up to 1/8" have been noted. Cover is flat with no surface wear. Inks are bright with high reflectivity. Well centered and firmly secured to interior pages. One corner may be almost imperceptibly blunted, but still almost sharp and cut square. Almost imperceptible indentations are permissible, but no creases, bends, or color break. Small, inconspicuous, lightly penciled, stamped or inked arrival dates are acceptable as long as they are in an unobtrusive location. No soiling, staining or other discoloration. Spine is tight and flat. No spine roll or split allowed. Staples must be original, generally centered, with only the slightest discoloration. No staple tears, stress lines, or rust migration. Paper is off-white, supple and fresh. No hint of acidity in the odor of the newsprint. Centerfold is firmly secure. Only the slightest interior tears are allowed.

9.4 **NEAR MINT (NM):** Nearly perfect with only minor imperfections that keep it from the next higher grade. The overall look is "as if it was just purchased and read once or twice." Subtle bindery defects are allowed. Bindery tears must be less than 1/16" on Silver Age and later books, although on Golden Age books bindery tears of up to 1/4" have been noted. Cover is flat with no surface wear. Inks are bright with high reflectivity. Generally well centered and secured to interior pages. Corners are cut square and sharp with ever-so-slight blunting permitted. A 1/16" bend is permitted with no color break. No creases. Small, inconspicuous, lightly penciled, stamped or inked arrival dates are acceptable as long as they are in an unobtrusive location. No soiling, staining or other discoloration apart from slight foxing. Spine is tight and flat. No spine roll or split allowed. Staples are generally centered; may have slight discoloration. No staple tears are allowed; almost no stress lines. No rust migration. In rare cases, a comic was not stapled at the bindery and therefore has a missing staple; this is not considered a defect. Any staple can be replaced on books up to Fine, but only vintage staples can be used on books from Very Fine to Near Mint. Mint books must have original staples. Paper is cream to off-white, supple and fresh. No hint of acidity in the odor of the newsprint. Centerfold is secure. Slight interior tears are allowed.

9.2 **NEAR MINT− (NM−):** Nearly perfect with only a minor additional defect or defects that keep it from Near Mint. A limited number of minor bindery defects are allowed. Cover is flat with no surface wear. Inks are bright with only the slightest dimming of reflectivity. Generally well centered and secured to interior pages. Corners are cut square and sharp with ever-so-slight blunting permitted. A 1/16"-1/8" bend is permitted with no color break. No creases. Small, inconspicuous, lightly penciled, stamped or inked arrival dates are acceptable as long as they are in an unobtrusive location. No soiling, staining or other discoloration apart from slight foxing. Spine is tight and flat. No spine roll or split allowed. Staples may show some discoloration. No staple tears are allowed; almost no stress lines. No rust migration. In rare cases, a comic was not stapled at the bindery and therefore has a missing staple; this is not considered a defect. Any staple can be replaced on books up to Fine, but only vintage staples can be used on books from Very Fine to Near Mint. Mint books must have original staples. Paper is cream to off-white, supple and fresh. No hint of acidity in the odor of the newsprint. Centerfold is secure. Slight interior tears are allowed.

9.0 **VERY FINE/NEAR MINT (VF/NM):** Nearly perfect with outstanding eye appeal. A limited number of bindery defects are allowed. Almost flat cover with almost imperceptible wear. Inks are bright with slightly diminished reflectivity. An 1/8" bend is allowed if color is not broken. Corners are cut square and sharp with ever-so-slight blunting permitted but no creases. Several lightly penciled, stamped or inked arrival dates are acceptable. No obvious soiling, staining or other discoloration, except for very minor foxing. Spine is tight and flat. No spine roll or split allowed. Staples may show some discoloration. Only the slightest staple tears are allowed. A very minor accumulation of stress lines may be present if they are nearly imperceptible. No rust migration. In rare cases, a comic was not stapled at the bindery and therefore has a missing staple; this is not considered a defect. Any staple can be replaced on books up to Fine, but only vintage staples can be used on books from Very Fine to Near Mint. Mint books must have original staples. Paper is cream to off-white and supple. No hint of acidity in the odor of the newsprint. Centerfold is secure. Very minor interior tears may be present.

8.5 **VERY FINE+ (VF+):** Fits the criteria for Very Fine but with an additional virtue or small accumulation of virtues that improves the book's appearance by a perceptible amount.

8.0 **VERY FINE (VF):** An excellent copy with outstanding eye appeal. Sharp, bright and clean with supple pages. A comic book in this grade has the appearance of having been carefully handled. A limited accumulation of minor bindery defects is allowed. Cover is relatively flat with minimal surface wear beginning to show, possibly including some minute wear at corners. Inks are generally bright with moderate to high reflectivity. A 1/4" crease is acceptable if color is not broken. Stamped or inked arrival dates may be present. No obvious soiling, staining or other discoloration, except for minor foxing. Spine is almost flat with no roll. Possible minor color break allowed. Staples may show some discoloration. Very slight staple tears and a few almost very minor to minor stress lines may be present. No rust migration. In rare cases, a comic was not stapled at the bindery and therefore has a missing staple; this is not considered a defect. Any staple can be replaced on books up to Fine, but only vintage staples can be used on books from Very Fine to Near Mint. Mint books must have original staples. Paper is tan to cream and supple. No hint of acidity in the odor of the newsprint. Centerfold is mostly secure. Minor interior tears at the margin may be present.

7.5 **VERY FINE– (VF–):** Fits the criteria for Very Fine but with an additional defect or small accumulation of defects that detracts from the book's appearance by a perceptible amount.

7.0 **FINE/VERY FINE (FN/VF):** An above-average copy that shows minor wear but is still relatively flat and clean with outstanding eye appeal. A small accumulation of minor bindery defects is allowed. Minor cover wear beginning to show with interior yellowing or tanning allowed, possibly including minor creases. Corners may be blunted or abraded. Inks are generally bright with a moderate reduction in reflectivity. Stamped or inked arrival dates may be present. No obvious soiling, staining or other discoloration, except for minor foxing. The slightest spine roll may be present, as well as a possible moderate color break. Staples may show some discoloration. Slight staple tears and a slight accumulation of light stress lines may be present. Slight rust migration. In rare cases, a comic was not stapled at the bindery and therefore has a missing staple; this is not considered a defect. Any staple can be replaced on books up to Fine, but only vintage staples can be used on books from Very Fine to Near Mint. Mint books must have original staples. Paper is tan to cream, but not brown. No hint of acidity in the odor of the newsprint. Centerfold is mostly secure. Minor interior tears at the margin may be present.

6.5 **FINE+ (FN+):** Fits the criteria for Fine but with an additional virtue or small accumulation of virtues that improves the book's appearance by a perceptible amount.

6.0 **FINE (FN):** An above-average copy that shows minor wear but is still relatively flat and clean with no significant creasing or other serious defects. Eye appeal is somewhat reduced because of slight surface wear and the accumulation of small defects, especially on the spine and edges. A FINE condition comic book appears to have been read a few times and has been handled with moderate care. Some accumulation of minor bindery defects is allowed. Minor cover wear apparent, with minor to moderate creases. Inks show a major reduction in reflectivity. Blunted or abraded corners are more common, as is minor staining, soiling, discoloration, and/or foxing. Stamped or inked arrival dates may be present. A minor spine roll is allowed. There can also be a 1/4" spine split or severe color break. Staples show minor discoloration. Minor staple tears and an accumulation of stress lines may be present, as well as minor rust migration. In rare cases, a comic was not stapled at the bindery and therefore has a missing staple; this is not considered a defect. Any staple can be replaced on books up to Fine, but only vintage staples can be used on books from Very Fine to Near Mint. Mint books must have original staples. Paper is brown to tan and fairly supple with no signs of brittleness. No hint of acidity in the odor of the newsprint. Minor interior tears at the margin may be present. Centerfold may be loose but not detached.

5.5 **FINE– (FN–):** Fits the criteria for Fine but with an additional defect or small accumulation of defects that detracts from the book's appearance by a perceptible amount.

5.0 **VERY GOOD/FINE (VG/FN):** An above-average but well-used comic book. A comic in this grade shows some moderate wear; eye appeal is somewhat reduced because of the accumulation of defects. Still a desirable copy that has been handled with some care. An accumulation of bindery defects is allowed. Minor to moderate cover wear apparent, with minor to moderate creases and/or dimples. Inks have major to extreme reduction in reflectivity. Blunted or abraded corners are increasingly common, as is minor to moderate staining, discoloration, and/or foxing. Stamped or inked arrival dates may be present. A minor to moderate spine roll is allowed. A spine split of up to 1/2" may be present. Staples show minor discoloration. A slight accumulation of minor staple tears and an accumulation of minor stress lines may also be present, as well as minor rust migration. In rare cases, a comic was not stapled at the bindery and therefore has a missing staple; this is not considered a defect. Any staple can be replaced on books up to Fine, but only vintage staples can be used on books from Very Fine to Near Mint. Mint books must have original staples. Paper is brown to tan with no signs of brittleness. May have the faintest trace of an acidic odor. Centerfold may be loose but not detached. Minor tears may also be present.

4.5 **VERY GOOD+ (VG+):** Fits the criteria for Very Good but with an additional virtue or small accumulation of virtues that improves the book's appearance by a perceptible amount.

4.0 **VERY GOOD (VG):** The average used comic book. A comic in this grade shows some significant moderate wear, but still has not accumulated enough total defects to reduce eye appeal to the point that it is not a desirable copy. Cover shows moderate to significant wear, and may be loose but not completely detached. Moderate to extreme reduction in reflectivity. Can have an accumulation of creases or dimples. Corners may be blunted or abraded. Store stamps, name stamps, arrival dates, initials, etc. have no effect on this grade. Some discoloration, fading, foxing, and even minor soiling is allowed. As much as a 1/4" triangle can be missing out of the corner or edge; a missing 1/8" square is also acceptable. Only minor unobtrusive tape and other amateur repair allowed on otherwise high grade copies. Moderate spine roll may be present and/or a 1" spine split. Staples discolored. Minor to moderate staple tears and stress lines may be present, as well as some rust migration. Paper is brown but not brittle. A minor acidic odor can be detectable. Minor to moderate tears may be present. Centerfold may be loose or detached at one staple.

3.5 **VERY GOOD– (VG–):** Fits the criteria for Very Good but with an additional defect or small accumulation of defects that detracts from the book's appearance by a perceptible amount.

3.0 **GOOD/VERY GOOD (GD/VG):** A used comic book showing some substantial wear. Cover shows significant wear, and may be loose or even detached at one staple. Cover reflectivity is very low. Can have a book-length crease and/or dimples. Corners may be blunted or even rounded. Discoloration, fading, foxing, and even minor to moderate soiling is allowed. A triangle from 1/4" to 1/2" can be missing out of the corner or edge; a missing 1/8" to 1/4" square is also acceptable. Tape and other amateur repair may be present. Moderate spine roll likely. May have a spine split of anywhere from 1" to 1-1/2". Staples may be rusted or replaced. Minor to moderate staple tears and moderate stress lines may be present, as well as some rust migration. Paper is brown but not brittle. Centerfold may be loose or detached at one staple. Minor to moderate interior tears may be present.

2.5 GOOD+ (GD+): Fits the criteria for Good but with an additional virtue or small accumulation of virtues that improves the book's appearance by a perceptible amount.

2.0 GOOD (GD): Shows substantial wear; often considered a "reading copy." Cover shows significant wear and may even be detached. Cover reflectivity is low and in some cases completely absent. Book-length creases and dimples may be present. Rounded corners are more common. Moderate soiling, staining, discoloration and foxing may be present. The largest piece allowed missing from the front or back cover is usually a 1/2" triangle or a 1/4" square, although some Silver Age books such as 1960s Marvels have had the price corner box clipped from the top left front cover and may be considered Good if they would otherwise have graded higher. Tape and other forms of amateur repair are common in Silver Age and older books. Spine roll is likely. May have up to a 2" spine split. Staples may be degraded, replaced or missing. Moderate staple tears and stress lines may be present, as well as rust migration. Paper is brown but not brittle. Centerfold may be loose or detached. Moderate interior tears may be present.

1.8 GOOD– (GD–): Fits the criteria for Good but with an additional defect or small accumulation of defects that detracts from the book's appearance by a perceptible amount.

1.5 FAIR/GOOD (FR/GD): A comic showing substantial to heavy wear. A copy in this grade still has all pages and covers, although there may be pieces missing. Books in this grade are commonly creased, scuffed, abraded, soiled, and possibly unattractive, but still generally readable. Cover shows considerable wear and may be detached. Nearly no reflectivity to no reflectivity remaining. Store stamp, name stamp, arrival date and initials are permitted. Book-length creases, tears and folds may be present. Rounded corners are increasingly common. Soiling, staining, discoloration and foxing is generally present. Up to 1/10 of the back cover may be missing. Tape and other forms of amateur repair are increasingly common in Silver Age and older books. Spine roll is common. May have a spine split between 2" and 2/3 the length of the book. Staples may be degraded, replaced or missing. Staple tears and stress lines are common, as well as rust migration. Paper is brown and may show brittleness around the edges. Acidic odor may be present. Centerfold may be loose or detached. Interior tears are common.

1.0 FAIR (FR): A copy in this grade shows heavy wear. Some collectors consider this the lowest collectible grade because comic books in lesser condition are usually incomplete and/or brittle. Comics in this grade are usually soiled, faded, ragged and possibly unattractive. This is the last grade in which a comic remains generally readable. Cover may be detached, and inks have lost all reflectivity. Creases, tears and/or folds are prevalent. Corners are commonly rounded or absent. Soiling and staining is present. Books in this condition generally have all pages and most of the covers, although there may be up to 1/4 of the front cover missing or no back cover, but not both. Tape and other forms of amateur repair are more common. Spine roll is more common; spine split can extend up to 2/3 the length of the book. Staples may be missing or show rust and discoloration. An accumulation of staple tears and stress lines may be present, as well as rust migration. Paper is brown and may show brittleness around the edges but not in the central portion of the pages. Acidic odor may be present. Accumulation of interior tears. Chunks may be missing. The centerfold may be missing if readability is generally preserved (although there may be difficulty). Coupons may be cut.

0.5 POOR (PR): Most comic books in this grade have been sufficiently degraded to the point where there is little or no collector value; they are easily identified by a complete absence of eye appeal. Comics in this grade are brittle almost to the point of turning to dust with a touch, and are usually incomplete. Extreme cover fading may render the cover almost indiscernible. May have extremely severe stains, mildew or heavy cover abrasion to the point that some cover inks are indistinct/absent. Covers may be detached with large chunks missing. Can have extremely ragged edges and extensive creasing. Corners are rounded or virtually absent. Covers may have been defaced with paints, varnishes, glues, oil, indelible markers or dyes, and may have suffered heavy water damage. Can also have extensive amateur repairs such as laminated covers. Extreme spine roll present; can have extremely ragged spines or a complete, book-length split. Staples can be missing or show extreme rust and discoloration. Extensive staple tears and stress lines may be present, as well as extreme rust migration. Paper exhibits moderate to severe brittleness (where the comic book literally falls apart when examined). Extreme acidic odor may be present. Extensive interior tears. Multiple pages, including the centerfold, may be missing that affect readability. Coupons may be cut.

It can be difficult to visualize the degradation that takes place as you move from the best example of a given comic to the worst copy. To demonstrate this progression, we've taken one specific comic book - DC Comics' **The Atom #25** - and presented it here in conditions ranging from 9.6 to 1.0, to further illustrate how a comic might degrade as it moves down the major steps of the 10 Point Scale. Who better than the Atom to aid us with this quick visual guide to the amazing shrinking scale?

9.6 Near Mint+ NM+

The overall look is "as if it was just purchased and read once or twice."

Color fleck

Almost imperceptibly blunted corner

All copies © DC Comics

Slight staple stress lines

Slight staple stress lines

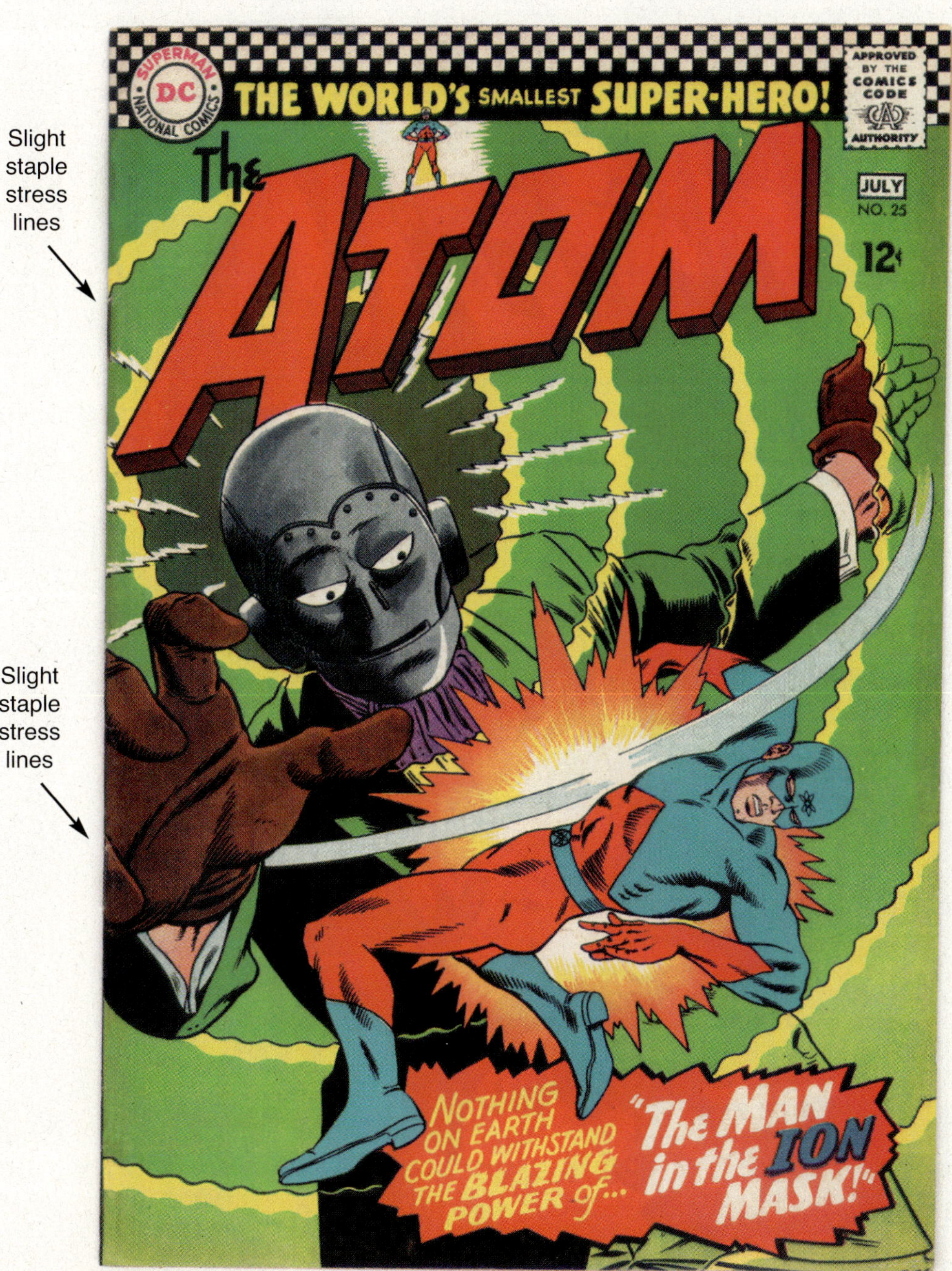

High cover reflectivity

Slight edge wear

8.0 Very Fine VF

A comic book in this grade has the appearance of having been carefully handled.

Minor spine wear

Slight staple stress lines

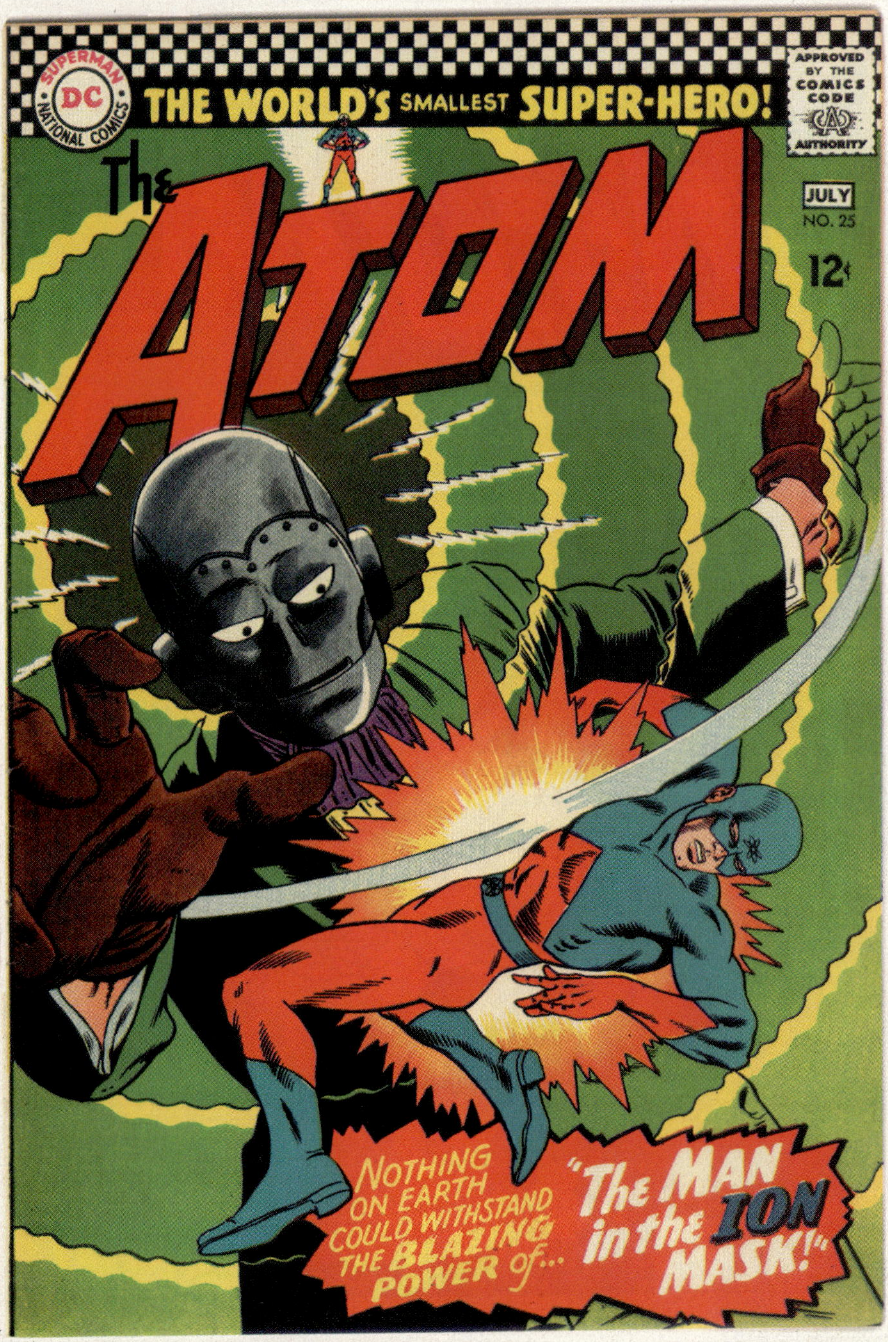

Slight staple stress lines

Minor spine wear

Corner wear

1/8" light crease

Light spine wear

Staple stress lines

Light spine wear along spine

1/8" light crease

6.0 Fine FN

An above-average copy that shows minor wear but is still relatively flat and clean with no significant creasing or other serious defects.

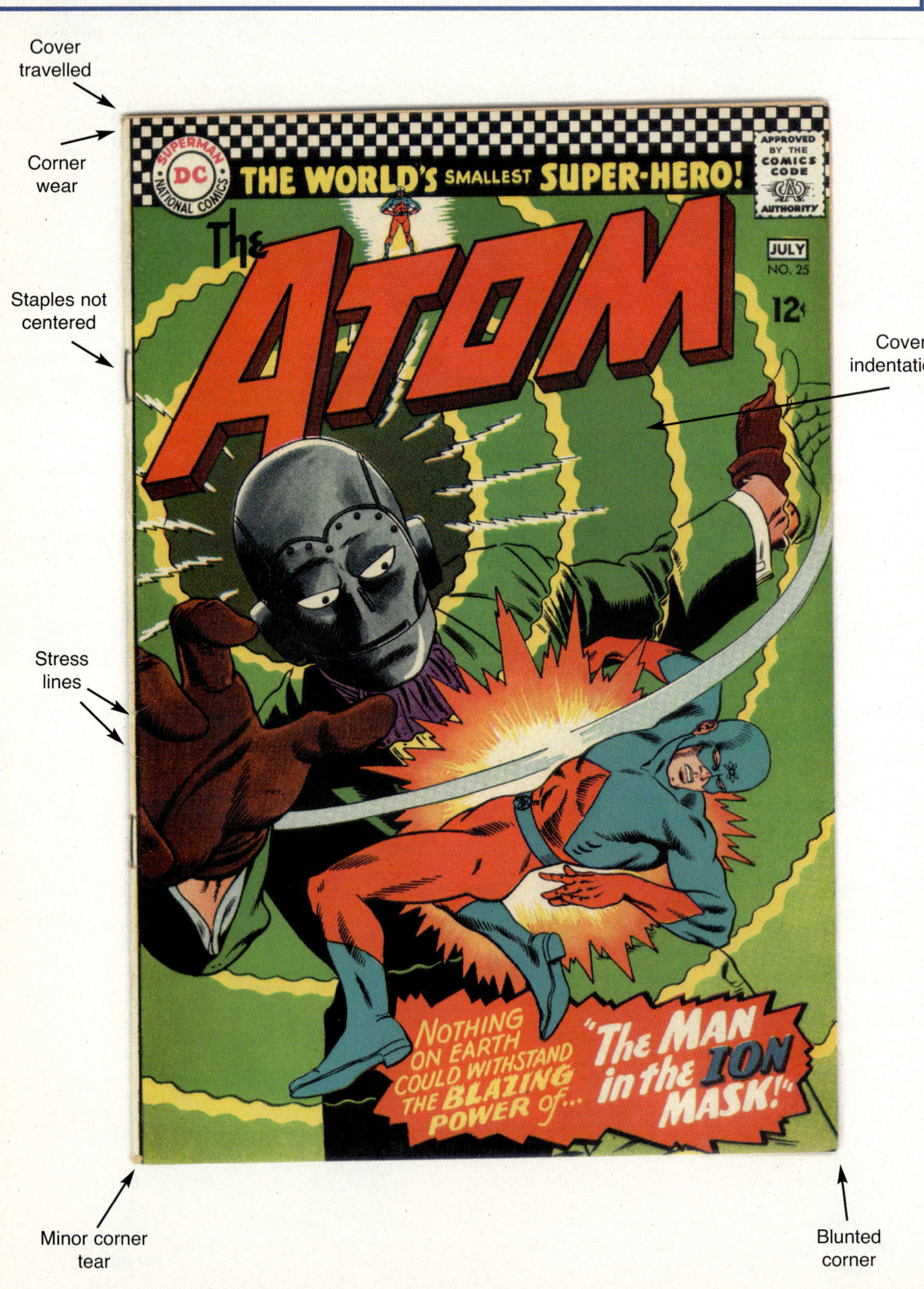

1/8" minor corner crease

Minor edge wear

Cover indentations

Staple stress lines

Spine stress

Staple stress

Spine stress

Moderate wear

Cover indentations

4.0 Very Good VG

Significant moderate wear, not accumulated enough total defects to reduce eye appeal to the point that it is not a desirable copy.

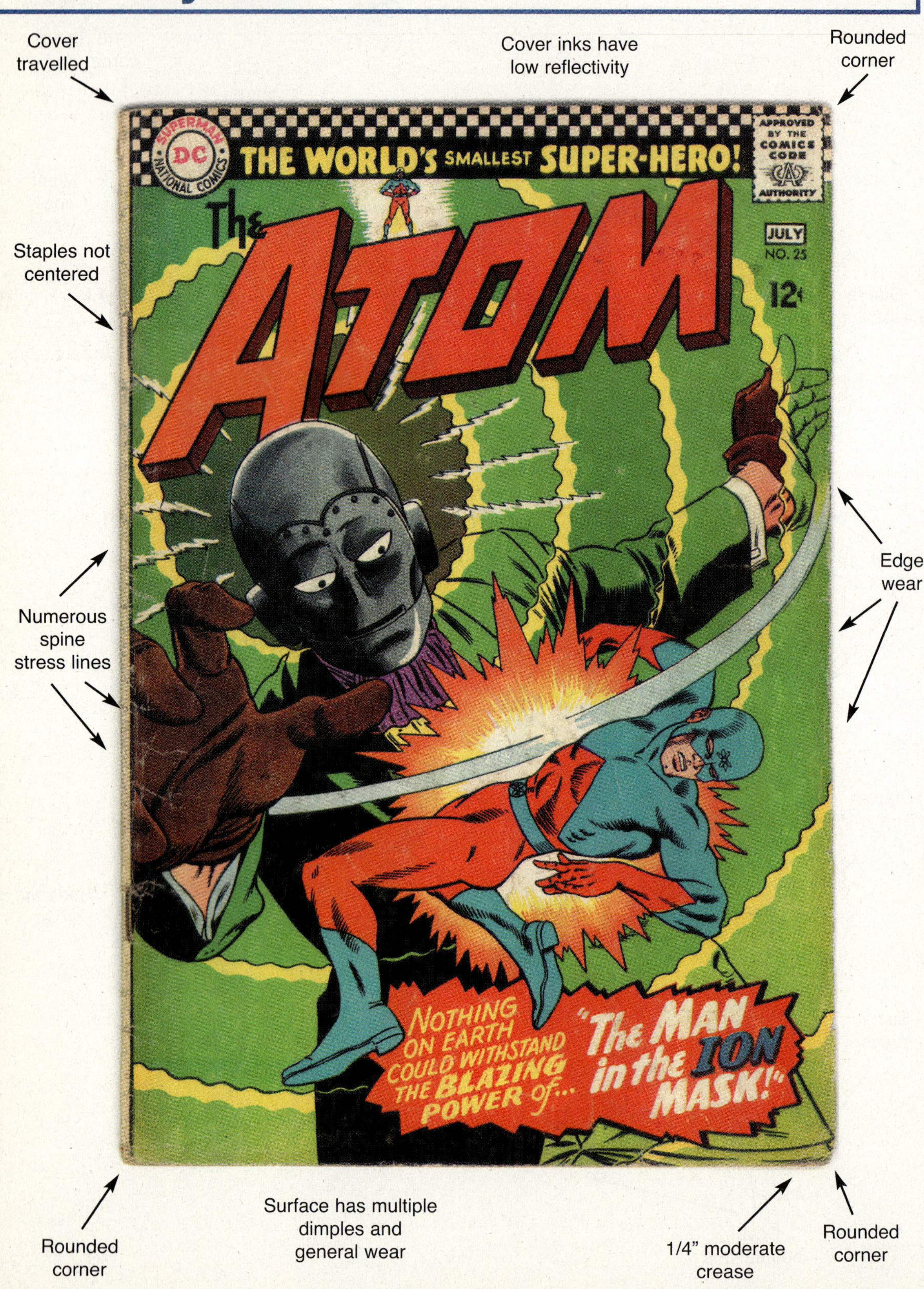

Cover travelled

Cover inks have low reflectivity

Rounded corner

Staples not centered

Edge wear

Numerous spine stress lines

Rounded corner

Surface has multiple dimples and general wear

1/4" moderate crease

Rounded corner

Cover shows
substantial wear

Rusted
staple

Spine
stress
and
tears

Edge
wear

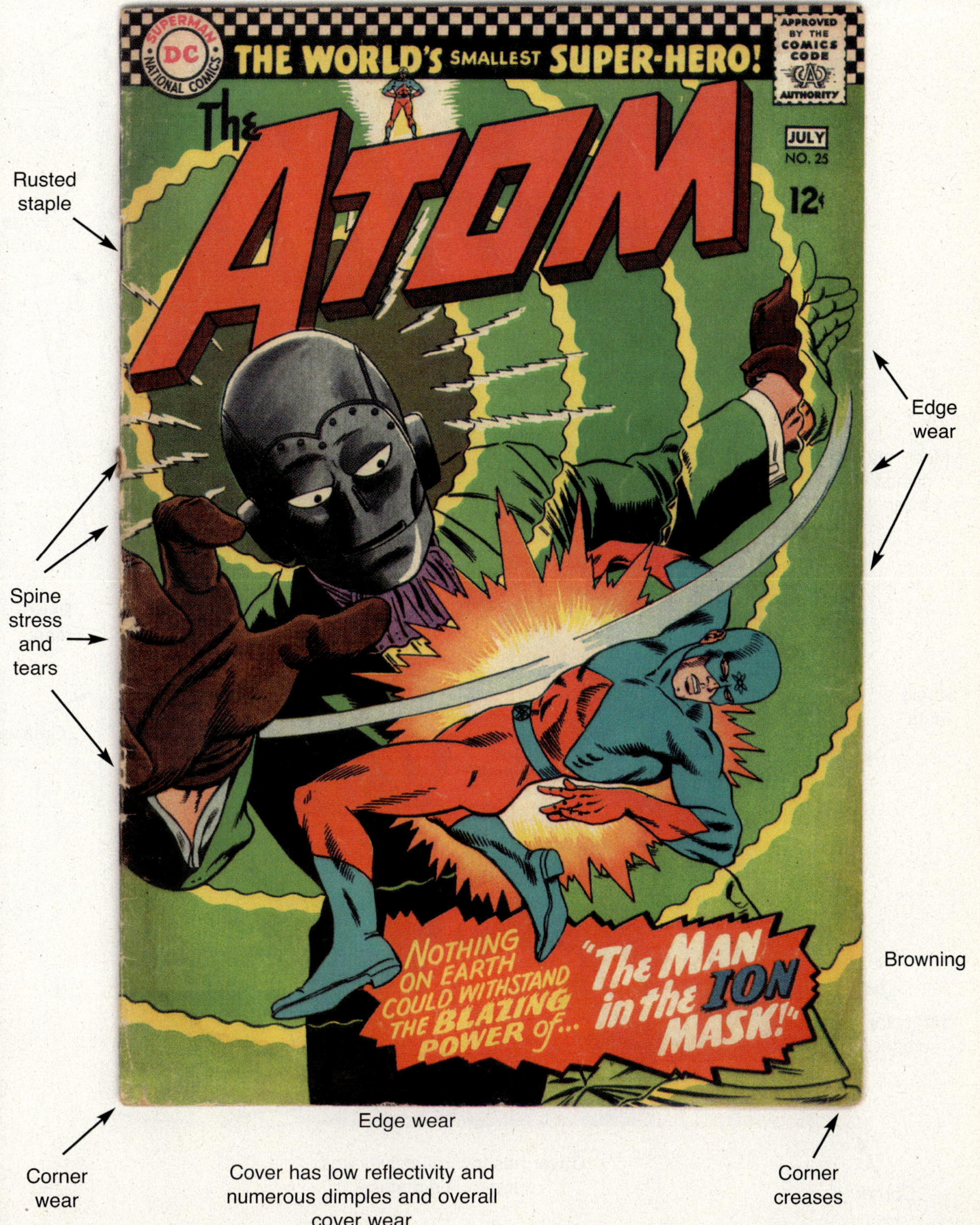

Browning

Corner
wear

Edge wear

Cover has low reflectivity and
numerous dimples and overall
cover wear

Corner
creases

2.0 Good GD

Shows substantial wear;
often considered a "reading copy."

Corner
wear

Significant wear
on cover

Rounded
corner

Color
fleck

Moderate
spine
wear

Edge
wear

Pencil
marks

Creases

Staple
tears

1/8" color
scrape

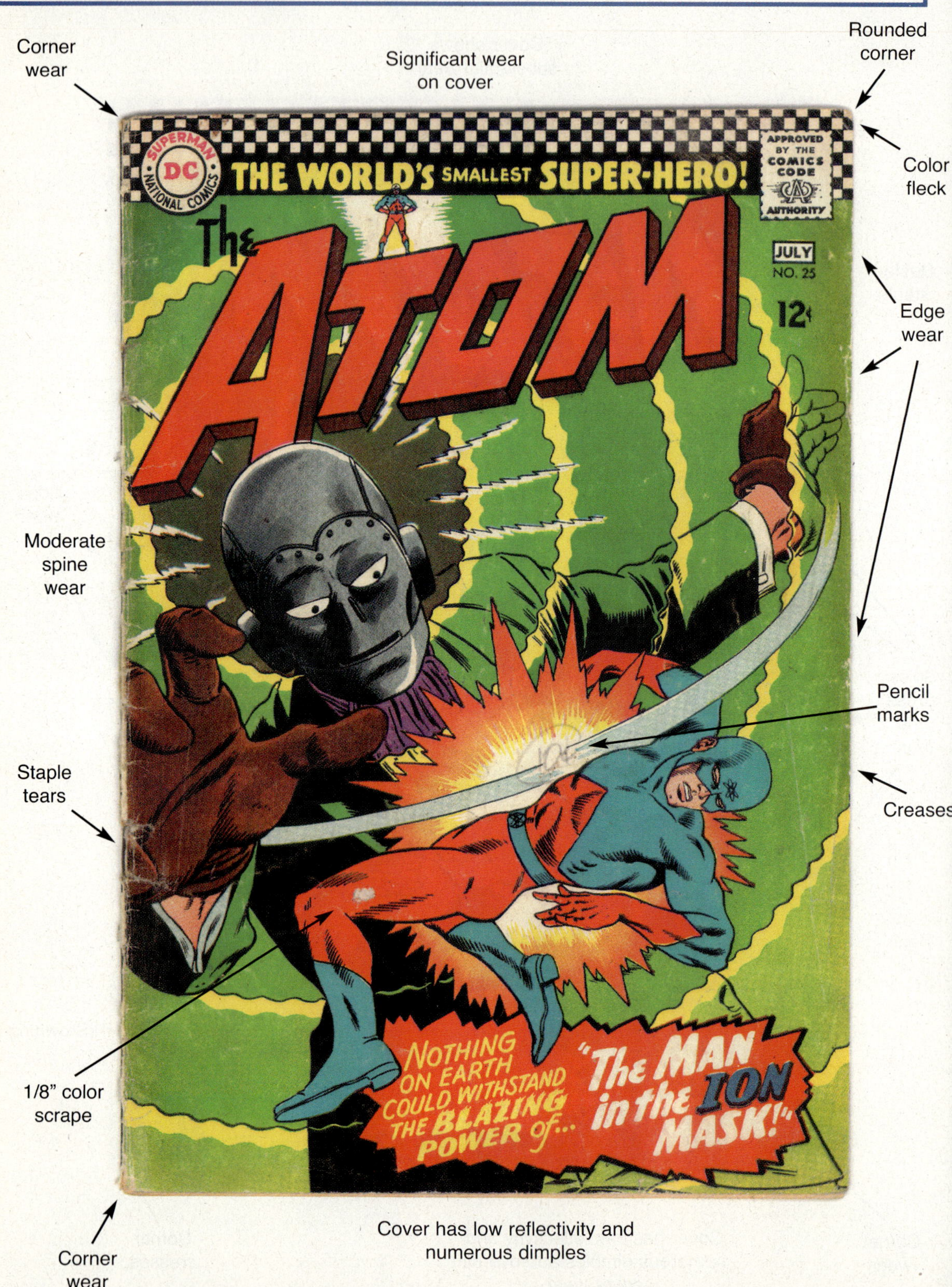

Corner
wear

Cover has low reflectivity and
numerous dimples

1.0 Fair FR

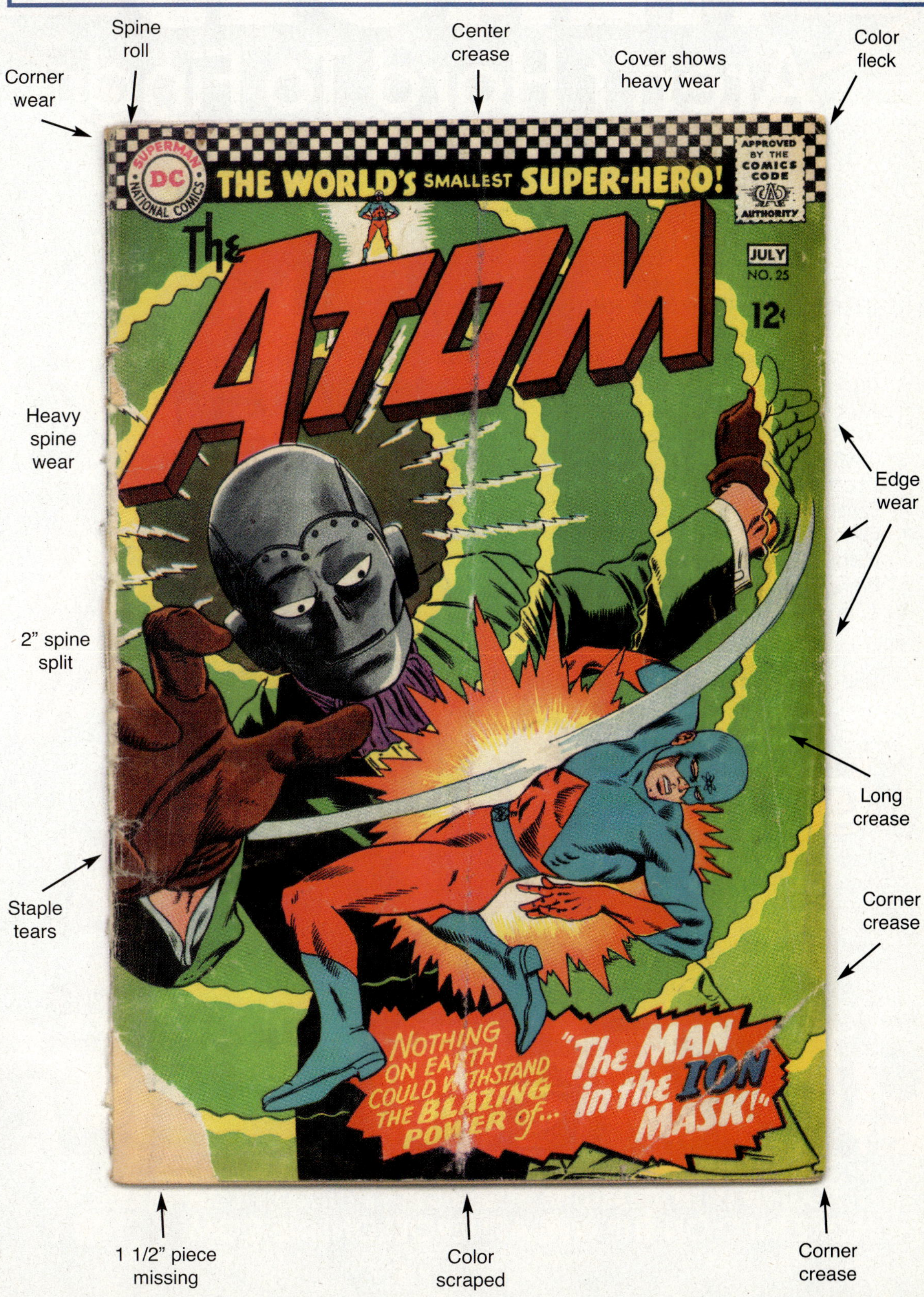

Corner wear

Spine roll

Center crease

Cover shows heavy wear

Color fleck

Heavy spine wear

2" spine split

Staple tears

Edge wear

Long crease

Corner crease

1 1/2" piece missing

Color scraped

Corner crease

HEROES
Aren't Hard To Find
AMERICA'S COMIC SOURCE

HEROES AREN'T HARD TO FIND is one of the largest and most well-known comics retailers in the country. We carry a complete line of new comics, graphic novels, and manga; as well as back issues, Silver and Golden Age comics, statues, specialty items, and our own line of comics collecting supplies.

Located in the heart of the historic Elizabeth neighborhood near Uptown Charlotte, we work hard to foster a family-friendly atmosphere, while carrying an incredibly diverse line of comics from every genre. Heroes is always buying comic collections, give us a call.

We are also the proud organizers of

America's Favorite Comic Convention every summer since 1982, featuring the best creators and dealers in the business! You don't want to miss our **Annual Art Auction** where guests of the show create one-of-a-kind artwork while you watch!

1957 EAST 7th STREET, CHARLOTTE, NC 28204 10-9 MON-SAT, 1-6 SUN, 704.375.7462
MORE INFO ON THE WEB AT HEROESONLINE.COM

Captain America created by Joe Simon & Jack Kirby © & ™ 2012 Marvel Comics Art by Travis Charest

There are a number of powerful foes waiting to strike at collectors, not least of which are the comic books themselves, or rather the effects of time on them.

Comics, after all, were not manufactured for the long haul. They were built to last just a short time, made with acidic newsprint paper, thin covers, and inconsistent inks. They weren't originally made with bags and boards, long boxes, Mylar snugs or CGC slabs. They were created, as painful as this is for a true collector to think about, to be disposable.

Is there any way to combat the ravages of time on your comics? Yes! We might not be able to keep comics in Gem Mint condition forever, but we can slow the damage with good methods of preservation and storage.

Some of the best advice for preserving a comic is simply to handle it carefully. Most dealers would prefer to remove the comic from its bag and show it to the customer themselves. In this way, if the book is damaged, it would be the dealer's responsibility and not the customer's.

When handling high-grade comics, always wash and dry your hands first, eliminating harmful oils from the skin. Lay the comic on a flat surface or in the palm of your hand and slowly turn the pages. This will minimize the stress to the staples and spine.

Careful storage is also a key element in the preservation of a cherished comic book. They must be protected from the elements, including the dangers of light, heat, and humidity. In addition to thinking about where you store your comics, you should also consider what you store them in. For years there have been arguments about what materials are acceptable.

For many years, it has been the policy of *The Overstreet Comic Book Price Guide* that in the *short term*, under good conditions, most plastic bags and boards are acceptable. It is vital to remember that it is up to you as a collector to find out what materials are used to make your collector supplies and to understand that when combined with negative conditions, particularly heat and humidity, the safe lifespan of bags that might otherwise be fine in the short term is quickly decreased.

For long term preservation, only archivally sound materials should be used. Generally speaking, this means Mylar snugs and acid-free backing boards, but there are numerous variations on these subjects. The time you spend learning about these materials, though, will be time you don't have to spend later wondering what happened to your collection.

Even when it comes to boxes, care must be taken. Some contain chemicals that will actually help to destroy your collection rather than save it. Always be aware whether you are purchasing materials designed for long-term storage or not.

You can read more about these subjects in *The Official Overstreet Grading Guide*, available at local comic shops.

PRESERVATION AND STORAGE OF COMIC BOOKS

By William M. Cole, P. E.

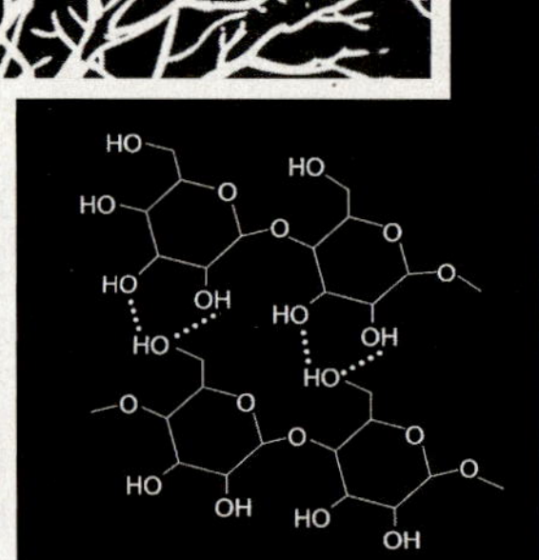

Comic Book collecting today is for both fun and profit. Yet, the comic book you thought was going to increase in value year after year has suddenly turned yellow after only three months and is now worthless. What happened? What could have been done to prevent the yellowing? This article will discuss how paper is made and what materials are best suited for long term storage and the guidelines for proper preservation.

How Paper Is Made

Paper generally has plant fibers that have been reduced to a pulp, suspended in water and then matted into sheets. The fibers in turn consist largely of cellulose, a strong, lightweight and somewhat durable material; cotton is an example of almost pure cellulose fiber. Although cotton and other kinds of fiber have been used in paper making over the years, most paper products today are made from wood pulp.

Wood pulps come in two basic varieties: groundwood and chemical wood. In the first process, whole logs are shredded and mechanically beaten. In the second, the fibers are prepared by digesting wood chips in chemical cookers. Because groundwood is the cheaper of the two, it is the primary component in such inexpensive papers as newsprint, which is used in many newspapers, comic books and paper backs. Chemically purified pulps are used in more expensive applications, such as stationery and some magazines and hardcover books.

Since groundwood pulp is made from whole wood fiber, the resulting paper does not consist of pure cellulose. As much as one third of its content may consist of non cellulose materials such as lignin, a complex woody acid. In chemical pulps, however, the lignin and other impurities are removed during the cooking process.

Deterioration Of Paper

The primary causes of paper deterioration are oxidation and acid hydrolysis. Oxidation attacks cellulose molecules with oxygen from the air, causing darkening and increased acidity. In addition, the lignin in groundwood paper breaks down quickly under the influence of oxygen and ultraviolet light. Light induced oxidation of lignin is what turns newspapers yellow after a few days' exposure to sunlight (Light can also cause some printing inks to fade.).

In acid hydrolysis, the cellulose fibers are cut by a reaction involving heat and acids, resulting in paper that turns brown and brittle. The sources of acidity include lignin itself, air pollution, and reaction by products from the oxidation of paper. Another major source is alum, which is often used with rosin to prepare the paper surface for accepting printing inks. Alum eventually releases sulfuric acid in paper.

Acidity and alkalinity are measured in units of pH, with 0 the most acidic and 14 the most alkaline. (Neutral pH is 7.0) Because the scale is based on powers of 10, a pH of 4.5 is actually 200 times more acidic than a pH of 6.5. Fresh newsprint typically carries a pH of 4.5 or less, while older more deteriorated paper on the verge of crumbling, may run as low as pH 3.0. Although some modern papers are made acid free, most paper collectibles are acidic and need special treatment to lengthen their lives. Other factors which contribute to the destruction of paper include extremes of temperature and humidity, insects, rodents, mold and improper handling and storage.

Guidelines For Preservation

First and foremost, keep your paper collectibles cool, dark and dry. Store books and other items in an unheated room, if possible, and regularly monitor the humidity. Excess heat and humidity should be controlled with an air conditioner and a dehumidifier. Storage materials such as envelopes, sleeves and boxes, should be of *archival quality* only to prevent contamination of their contents.

According to the U.S. Library of Congress, the preferred material for preserving valuable documents is Polyethylene Terephthalate polyester film, such as Mylar type D or equivalent material. The film must be clear containing no plasticizers, surface coatings, UV inhibitors, or absorbents. The material must be guaranteed to be dimensionally stable, and resistant to most chemicals, moisture and abrasion.

Mylar is an exceptionally strong transparent film that does resist moisture, pollutants, oils and acids. With a life expectancy of hundreds of years, Mylar will outlast most other plastics. In addition, the brilliance and clarity of Mylar enhances the appearance of any paper collectible. (Mylar is a Registered Trademark of DuPont Teijin films.) Their brands of archival quality polyester films were and are Mylar type D and Melinex 516 of which they are exclusive manufacturers.)

Note: Mylar type D is no longer being manufactured by the Dupont Company. The use of the name Mylar is now being used generically for all material that meets the above specifications for the archival storage of paper documents.

Polyethylene And Polypropylene

For years collectors have stored their movie posters, comic books, baseball cards and other collectibles in polyethylene bags, PVC sheets and plastic wraps. Although such products may be useful in keeping away dirt, grease and vermin, many plastic sleeves contain plasticizers and other additives which can migrate into paper and cause premature aging. Both polyethylene and polypropylene contain solvents and additives in their manufacture to assure clarity and increase the flexibility in the plastic. Polyethylene when uncoated without any solvents is a good moisture barrier but has a high gas transmission rate, and eventually shrinks and loses its shape under warmer conditions.

In recent years polypropylene bags have been sold under the guise of being archivally sound. This is far from the truth. Only uncoated and untreated material is suitable for archival protection. Currently, the only way to seal polypropylene is to add a substance called PVDC (Polyvinyl Dichloride which is a relative of PVC) to allow the material to be heat sealed. Therefore, once you add the harmful additive, the sleeve now becomes non-archival and should not be used for long term storage.

Acid Free Boards And Boxes

Because ordinary cardboard is itself acidic, storage in cardboard boxes may be hazardous to your collection, and is a leading cause of premature deterioration of comic collections. For proper storage, only acid free boards that meet the US Government's *minimum* requirements are acceptable. These requirements have been defined as boards having a 3% calcium carbonate buffer throughout and a minimum pH of 8.5. Anything less will hasten your collection's destruction. While many advertisers claim that their boards are "acid free at time of manufacture," they are in reality only spray coated with an alkaline substance making them acid free for only a very short time. Boards termed "acid free at time of manufacture" do not offer sufficient protection or storage for anything other than short term. True acid free boards have been impregnated with a calcium buffer resulting in an acid free, alkaline pH content of 8.5 throughout.

Deacidification

Another way to extend the longevity of your collectibles is to deacidify them before storage. Deacidifying sprays and solutions are now available for home use. By impregnating the paper with an alkaline reserve, you can neutralize existing acids and inhibit oxidation, future acidity and staining due to certain fungi. However it is best left to the professionals to deacidify your comic books. Deacidification with proper storage conditions will add centuries to the lifetime of paper.

In summary, we recommend the following guidelines for the maximum protection of your collectibles: Deacidify the paper; store in Mylar sleeves with acid free boards and cartons; and keep the collection cool, dry and dark. Periodic inspections and pH and humidity tests are also recommended. By following these simple guidelines you can be assured of a comic book collection that not only will increase in value, but will also last for many years to come.

Bill Cole has been manufacturing collectors supplies for almost 40 years and is the owner and CEO of Bill Cole Enterprises, Inc. in Randoph, Massachusetts. Mr. Cole is a retired Army Officer and also the author of numerous articles on preservation. Questions or comments may be directed to him at sales@bcemylar.com. Their website is www.bcemylar.com.

PRESERVING COMICS LONGER THAN ANYONE ELSE!

YOUR COMICS, MAGAZINES, AND POSTERS ARE...

SLOWLY DYING!

AIR, UV LIGHT, WARMTH, HUMIDITY, DIRT, FUNGI, VERMIN, INSECTS, ACIDS, CHEMICALS, & MORE ARE CAUSING THIS TO HAPPEN!

You can prevent this from happening by using heat-sealed Mylar® sleeves and acid-free boards! Want to know more? Go to **www.bcemylar.com!**

Check out our all-new ebay store & auctions!

Want to sell your old comics?
See our website for full details!

PO Box 60· Dept. ECBD ● Randolph, MA 02368-0060 ● P: 1-781-986-2653 ● F: 1-781-986-2656 ● E: sales@bcemylar.com

Comic Book Maintenance and Preservation for Archives and Special Collections

by Caitlin McGurk

From Richard Outcault's first *Yellow Kid* newspaper strip, capturing life in the tenement ghettos of New York City in the 1890s, to Peter Bagge's *Hate* series that so accurately and sarcastically depicts the Seattle grunge scene in the 1990s, it's clear that comics are doing more than telling stories - they're unwittingly documenting our cultural heritage. By combining descriptive powers similar to those of photography and novels — be it a historical event or a personal tragedy captured in a minicomic — what comics can represent about ourselves and our society is boundless. And with the wild insurgence of comic-adapted films, indie-conventions popping up in more cities than ever, and sequential art being taught in colleges worldwide, there's no arguing that now more than ever comics have become serious business. With that in mind, as librarians, educa-tors, and devoted lovers of the form, it's crucial that dedicated time and attention is paid toward the preserva-tion and maintenance of comics and graphic novels in our collections to aid in resounding their enduring sig-nificance.

Before we discuss preventative methods, it's important that we under-stand a little bit about the deeper make-up of our materials. We're all familiar with that thin, yellowy look that pre-modern age comics wear so well, and be it aesthetically pleasing in an esoteric kind of way - that little novelty hue is the harbinger of sick-ness in our collection. Up until the mid-1980s when EPA regulations changed the acidity content in paper, comics, like all other "pulp" material, were printed on cheap wood pulp paper, brimming with highly photo-synthetic lignin and cellulose. Just like a flower soaking up sunlight to grow, these plant compounds are by nature hungry for the elements, oxidizing with their exposure to air and light, making them a ticking time-bomb from the moment of their creation without any help from us. However, this internal war is waged mostly within the pages of Golden and Silver Age comics, as most comics produced in the past 20 years are printed on high quality glossy paper which has been chemically de-pulped, and coated with an alkaline buffer to better protect against environmental pollutants that cause acid hydrolysis. Regardless, all paper degrades over time, and the external key factors of deterioration remain the same: light and air pollutants, handling, storage, and upkeep.

Now that we're aware of the internal menace lurking in the very fibers of our books, our only means for gaining control is preventative action! It may seem like a no-brainer that comics should not be stored within the reach of sunlight, but what not all collectors realize is that paper is affected by all kinds of light. Be it natural light, fluorescent bulbs, or even incandescent - all of these contribute some degree of UV or infrared light, quickening the process of decay. Luckily, there are a number of vendors out there offering UV protective tube guards for fluorescent lights at a fairly inexpensive cost, averaging about $7.00 per cover, and typically guaranteed to last up to 10 years.

However, if light fixture renovations aren't in your budget, simply using the right storage materials for your collection will do the trick. Sites

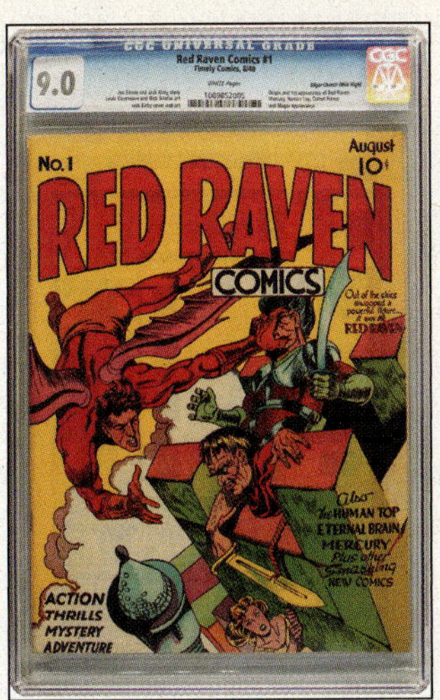

like www.comicsupply.com, as well as Gaylord Brothers (www.Gaylordmart.com) offer acid-free storage boxes in a variety of sizes. Pay close attention while shopping around for these materials that the products you choose are in fact archival quality and acid free - those coated with a calcium carbonate buffer will maintain a steady pH content, avoiding contamination from the wood pulp in ordinary cardboard boxes. Be sure to double-check your dimensions as well, as shoving Silver Age books into boxes specified for Modern age sizes will not only damage the material, but any obstruction of the lid is easy exposure to pollutants, let alone vermin or bugs! Boxes should be watertight, and stored vertically in cool, dry, dark environments. Silica gel packs can work long lasting wonders as well, and Gaylordmart also specializes in tiny Desiccant Canisters with color-changing indicator gel, which can be placed inside each storage box and are reusable for life by baking them in the oven once they've been saturated.

An item of frequent debate and confusion is the proper sleeves to store comics in, as polyethylene and polypropylene bags are typically the cheapest and easiest to find. In terms of longevity and superior quality though, uncoated archival quality polyester film, more commonly known as Mylar® bags, are by far the best option. These bags will outlast other plastics by hundreds of years, as polyethylene and polypropylene products are manufactured with solvents and additives that break down over time, causing premature aging in the paper. Stiff, acid free backing boards made of cotton rag or wood and cellular fiber should be inserted in each bag behind the comic as well to prevent bending and cracking. These will also have a calcium carbonate buffer, and can be purchased in bulk from any comic book supplies store. I would recommend Thin-X-Tender brand, as an inexpensive and high-quality option. You will also want to invest in tape with which to seal the flap of each sleeve, settling for nothing other than acid-free products as the off-gassing of old tape can cause serious damage to your books over time.

Now that you've gathered all of your proper storage weapons of prevention, one item worth looking into is MicroChamber interleaving paper. This product is your one sure bet for combating against the unavoidable internal-aging process occurring within the pages of your comics. MicroChamber technology uses lignin-free and sulfur-free material that actually absorbs air-borne pollutants and acidic by-products of degradation. Upon interlacing one sheet inside of the back and front covers of your comic, these sheets immediately begin working to actively soak up the hazardous toxins being released from the book, as well as preventing the ink from transferring from one page to another. MicroChamber paper only needs to be replaced every 7 years, and has been used by the CGC for every comic they grade.

Now, if the comics or graphic novels you're maintaining are receiving high circulation and handling, and these technical details are beyond

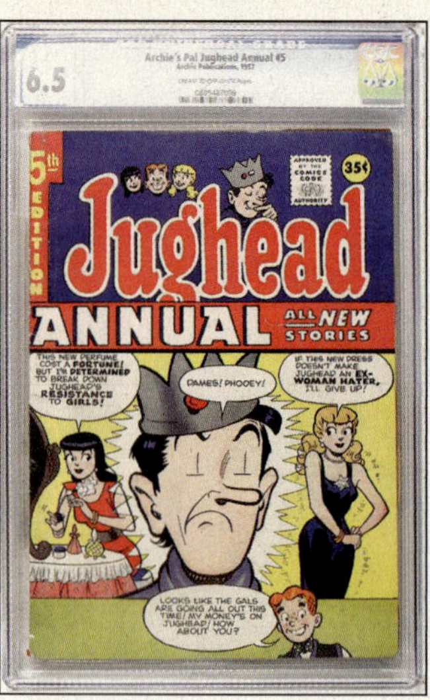

consideration, the same basic principles for care of any book apply. The low-grade paper that older comics were printed on is highly susceptible to grease and oils, so always handle with clean hands and an eye for brittle pages. I've found that loosely packed rotating racks are the best for displaying comics, although they can become quickly unorganized. Another quick and easy option for storage is three-ring binders with sealable sleeves, which can also be found in age-specific sizes made from archival materials.

Whichever route you take for maintaining your comics collection, do it economically and sensibly. If you're using MicroChamber paper, be sure to not counteract it with acidic storage boxes. There are more options on the market for these products than ever before, so shop around, be sure you're getting the best for your buck, and always acid free! Be it for business or pleasure, consider yourself a guardian of comic book history, and remember: with great power comes great responsibility!

This article was originally published by Diamond Comic Distributors on their Bookshelf website.

Caitlin McGurk self publishes the zine and mini-comics series Good Morning You, *and is currently finishing her MLIS degree at the Palmer School in New York City. She has worked to build and maintain the collections for Marvel Comics, The Schulz Library at The Center for Cartoon Studies, and the Bulliet Comics Collection of Columbia University. She aspires to promote the advancement of comics research by broadening their accessibility in the collections of universities and libraries worldwide.*

THE INDUSTRY'S LEADING "TOP OF THE LINE" BAG!

Preserve and protect your comic book collection with the most respected bags and boards in the business. E. Gerber Products, LLC.'s Mylites2 mylar bags coupled with their absolutely acid-free backing boards are exactly what you need to keep your collection safe from the elements!

Full-Back Pricing:

Item Code	Size	Description	Price Per 50	Price Per 200	Price Per 1000
675FB	6 ¾ x 10 ½	Current Comics - fits 700	$9.50	$31.00	$135.00
700FB	7 x 10 ½	Standard Comics - fits 725	$10.00	$32.00	$140.00
750FB	7 ½ x 10 ½	Silver/Golden Comics - fits 775	$10.50	$35.00	$150.00
		Shipping & Handling	$5.00	$16.00	$60.00

Half-Back Pricing:

Item Code	Size	Description	Price Per 100	Price Per 500	Price Per 2000
675HB	6 ¾ x 10 ½	Current Comics - fits 700	$8.00	$35.00	$120.00
700HB	7 x 10 ½	Standard Comics - fits 725	$8.50	$36.00	$125.00
750HB	7 ½ x 10 ½	Silver/Golden Comics - fits 775	$9.00	$39.00	$135.00
		Shipping & Handling	$5.00	$16.00	$60.00

Mylites 2 Pricing:

Item Code	Size	Description	Price Per 50	Price Per 200	Price Per 1000
700M2	7 x 10 ½	Current Comics: 1990's & up	$10.75	$36.00	$155.00
725M2	7 ¼ x 10 ½	Standard Comics: 1970's-1990's	$11.00	$37.00	$160.00
775M2	7 ¾ x 10 ½	Silver/Gold Comics: 1950's-1970's	$11.50	$38.00	$165.00
		Shipping & Handling	$2.00	$6.00	$15.00

Minimum Ship Charge: $10.00

Call E. Gerber today at 1-800-79-MYLAR to place your order today!

CGC

How the Company Has Grown and How It Works

By the CGC Grading Team

The world of comic book collecting has grown and matured since the 2000 introduction of CGC (Certified Guaranty Company). Before the founding of CGC comic book transactions were mainly face to face deals with buyers and sellers reviewing the books and negotiating the sales price. The advent of the internet changed all that. The world of the internet opened up new opportunities in that comic books from across the country were as easy to buy as those across the street. But with this new market came risk. Risk of not knowing the seller and risk of buying a book virtually sight unseen except for an online image.

CGC was created to put an end to the risk and the chaos that accompanied it, and to help bring order and stability to comic book sales. CGC is the first independent, impartial, third-party comic book grading service. A proven and respected commitment to integrity, accuracy, consistency and impartiality has made CGC the leader in its field, becoming a tool to help people with their buying and selling decisions. The universally accepted grading scale ensures consistency and gives both dealers and collectors a sense of dependability when making purchasing decisions. With CGC certification, a collector knows what he or she is getting based on an accurate and comprehensive description that can be found on the CGC certification label.

Here's a look at how CGC came together and how a book is certified.

The Formation of the Company

In January of 2000 CGC was launched under the umbrella of the Certified Collectibles Group, which includes Numismatic Guaranty Corporation (NGC), the largest third-party coin grading company in the world, Numismatic Conservation Services (NCS), the leading authority in numismatic conservation and Paper Money Guaranty (PMG), the world's leading currency certification company. The Collectibles Group sought out talented and ethical individuals to grade comic books. Experts needed a history of nec-

essary skills to verify a comic book's authenticity and to detect restoration that can affect its value. To identify these individuals, many of the most respected individuals in the hobby were consulted, and, based on their recommendations a core grading team was selected.

The members of the CGC grading team come from diverse backgrounds, and many were comic book dealers at some time in their careers. Experience in the commercial sector can be an essential ingredient in becoming familiar with market standards. Upon joining CGC, all graders immediately cease all commercial trading. All CGC employees are prohibited from commercially buying and selling comic books to ensure they remain completely impartial, having no vested interest other than a dedication to serving clients through accurate and consistent grading.

When it was time to develop a uniform grading standard, the hobby's leaders were once again called upon. Everyone agreed that the *Overstreet Comic Book Price Guide* was the foundation of this standard, but there were a number of subjective interpretations of its published definitions. It was critical to understand how these guidelines were being applied to the everyday buying and selling of comics. To accomplish this, approximately 50 of the hobby's top experts took part in an extensive grading test. Their grades were averaged and an accurate grading standard reflecting the collective experience of the hobby's most prominent figures was thus developed. CGC now had the best standard and the best team to apply it.

With the graders in place and the grading scale established, the next step was to develop a tamper-evident holder for the long-term storage and display of certified comics. This proved to be a technical challenge. Exhaustive material tests were conducted to determine that the holders were archival safe. To create a true first line of defense, it was determined that the comic book should be sealed in a soft inner well, then sealed again inside a tamper evident hard plastic case with interlocking ridges to enable compact storage. The CGC certified grade appears on a label sealed inside the holder for an additional level of security.

Submitting your Books

Comic books may be submitted for certification in two ways - they can be submitted by authorized dealers or by Collectors Society members. The Collectors Society is an online community with direct access to certification service from CGC, and submissions can be prepared online. Both dealers and Collectors Society members typically send their comics to CGC's offices by registered mail or through an insured express company. Submissions are also accepted at many of the Comic Cons that occur around the country throughout the year.

The Comic Books are Received

Every day, CGC's Receiving Department opens newly arrived packages and immediately verifies that the number of books in each package matches the number shown on the submitted invoice. Once this is done, a more detailed comparison is made to ensure that their invoice descriptions correspond to the actual comics. This information is entered into a computer, and from this time forth, the comics will be traceable at all stages of the grading process by their invoice number and their line number within that invoice. Each book is checked to see that it is properly prepared for grading in an appropriately sized comic bag with backing board and then is labeled with a numbered barcode containing the pertinent data of invoice number and line item information for quick reading by the computer.

Before any grading is performed, the book is examined by a CGC Restoration Detection Specialist. If any form of restoration work is detected, this information is entered into the computer, making it available to the grading team.

Each comic book receives a restoration check and the results appear on the label.

The Grading Begins

After being examined by a Restoration Detection Specialist, the book is then passed on to the graders. At this stage the comics have been properly sleeved and barcoded for grading and have been separated from their original invoice. This step is taken to ensure that graders do not know whose books they are grading, as a further guarantee of impartiality. The grading process begins by having the book's pages counted and entering into the computer any peculiarities or flaws that may affect a book's grade. Some examples of this would be "a tear on third page," "a corner crease – does not break color," "a 1/4" inch spine split," and so forth. This information is entered into the "Graders Notes" field and a grade is assigned.

When other graders examine the comic, they are not able to see any previous assigned grades, so as to not influence their evaluation. Graders are only able to view previous Graders Notes after determining their own grade. The Grader may then add to the existing commentary if he believes more remarks are in order. The Grading Finalizer is the last person to examine the book. He makes a final restoration check before determining his own grade, at which time he reviews the grades and notes entered by the previous graders. If all grades are in agreement or are very close, he will assign the book's final grade. The book is then forwarded to the Encapsulation Department for sealing. If there is disagreement among the graders, a discussion will ensue until a final determination is made and the book forwarded.

Encapsulating the Comics

After each comic has been graded and the necessary numbers and text entered into their respective data fields, all the comics on a particular invoice are taken from the Grading Department into the Encapsulation Department. Here, appropriately color-coded labels are printed bearing the proper descriptive text, including each book's grade and identification number. This is critical, as it serves to make each certified comic unique and is also a significant deterrent to counterfeiting CGC's valued product. All of the above information is duplicated in a barcode, which appears underneath the written text on the comic's label.

The newly-printed labels are stacked in the same sequence as the comics to be encapsulated with them, ensuring that each book and its label match one another. The comic is now ready to be fitted inside an archival-quality interior well, which is then sealed within a transparent capsule, along with the book's color-coded label. This is accomplished through a combination of compression and ultrasonic vibration.

The Comics are Shipped

After encapsulation, all comics are returned briefly to the Grading Department for a quality control inspection. Here, they are examined to make certain that their labels are correct for both the grade and its accompanying descriptive information. Quality control also inspects each book for any flaws in its holder, such as scuffs or nicks. While these are quite rare, CGC is careful to make certain that the comics it certifies are not only accurately graded, but attractively presented as well. When all the comics have been inspected, they're delivered to our Shipping Department for packaging. The comics are counted and their labels checked against the original invoice to make certain that no mistakes have occurred. A Shipping Department employee then verifies the method of transport as selected by the submitter on the invoice and prepares the comics for delivery or they are held in CGC's vault for in-person pick-up by the submitter.

No matter whether the US Postal Service or some private carrier is used, the method of packaging is essentially the same. The encapsulated comics are placed vertically inside sturdy cardboard boxes. In 2005, CGC developed a custom shipping box to enable the highest level of stability during shipping. A copy of the submitter's invoice is included before the box is sealed and heavy tape is used to prevent accidental or unauthorized opening of the box while it's in transit.

The barcode of every comic book is scanned before it is placed into its shipping box. The status of the book is changed to "shipped" in our tracking system, and we retain a record of what books were shipped in which box. This is the final crucial step of our detailed internal tracking system.

The CGC Label

Comic books certified by CGC bear color-coded labels that have different meanings. Whenever purchasing a CGC-certified comic, be certain to note not only the book's grade but also its label category. A Universal label is denoted by the color blue and indicates that a book was not found to have any qualifying defects or signs of restoration. There is one exception to this policy: At CGC's discretion, comics having a very minor amount of glue and/or color touch-up may still qualify for a Universal label provided that they were produced approximately 1950 or earlier and that such restoration is noted underneath the assigned grade.

As its name implies, the Restored label, identified by its purple color, is used for books found to have restoration work performed on them. The grade assigned is based on the book's appearance, with the restoration noted. A distinction is made between Amateur and Professional restoration, this judgment being based on the materials used. Since the degree of work performed is also significant with restored books, there are a total of seven possible descriptions under the Restored label. Each description is prefaced

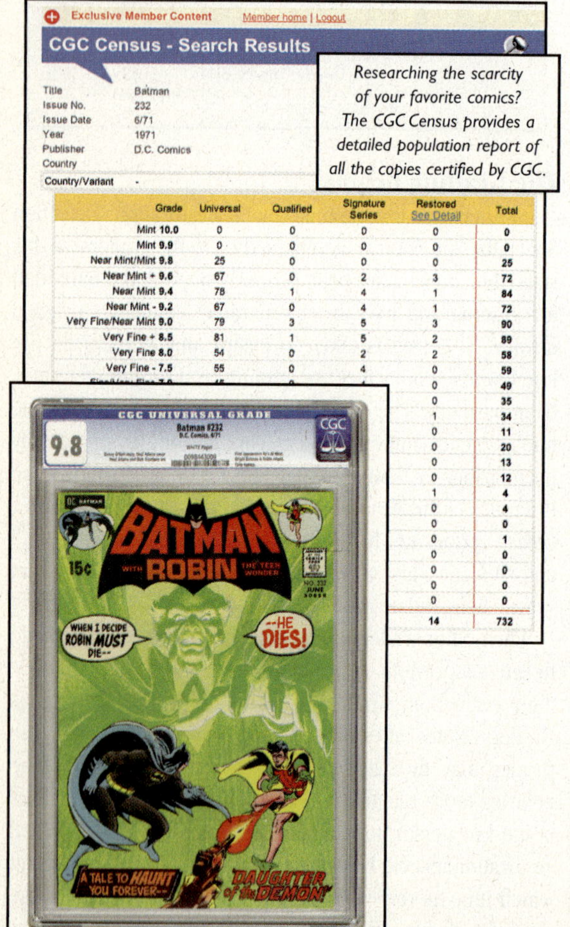

CGC Census - Search Results

Title	Batman
Issue No.	232
Issue Date	6/71
Year	1971
Publisher	D.C. Comics
Country	
Country/Variant	-

Grade	Universal	Qualified	Signature Series	Restored See Detail	Total
Mint 10.0	0	0	0	0	0
Mint 9.9	0	0	0	0	0
Near Mint/Mint 9.8	25	0	0	0	25
Near Mint + 9.6	67	0	2	3	72
Near Mint 9.4	78	1	4	1	84
Near Mint - 9.2	67	0	4	1	72
Very Fine/Near Mint 9.0	79	3	5	3	90
Very Fine + 8.5	81	1	5	2	89
Very Fine 8.0	54	0	2	2	58
Very Fine - 7.5	55	0	4	0	59

Researching the scarcity of your favorite comics? The CGC Census provides a detailed population report of all the copies certified by CGC.

with the word Apparent, followed by Slight, Moderate or Extensive in combination with the final descriptors Amateur or Professional. Examples of Restored labels might read Apparent Moderate Professional or Apparent Slight Amateur, both descriptions then being followed by the book's grade. Finally, comics which have had no restoration other than a trimming of their covers or edges are labeled as simply Apparent, followed by their grade.

The Qualified label is green, and this indicates that one qualifying defect is present on a book. An example of such a qualifying feature would be a missing Marvel Value Stamp that does not affect the story. While such a book technically may grade 1.5, it may appear to grade 9.6. In such instances, assigning a grade of just 1.5 does not fully represent the value of the comic to a collector. Through use of the green Qualified label, a comic buyer is able to make an informed decision as to what he is purchasing in terms of its overall desirability. Because of the complexity involved, green labels are assigned quite seldom and then only when considered absolutely necessary. In addition, comic books that have an unwitnessed signature, and therefore are not eligible for the Signature Series label (see below), get the Qualified label. This is the most common use for the Qualified label. This shows what the grade of the book would have been if the signature was not present.

CGC's Signature Series label is yellow, and this is used when a comic book has been signed or been sketched on

A Signature Series encapsulation provides an assurance of authenticity for the signature (and in some cases a sketch as well.) **The Walking Dead** team of Robert Kirkman and Tony Moore signed this copy.

by a creator in the presence of a CGC representative, assuring the signature's or sketch's authenticity. Only books that meet CGC's strict criteria for authenticity are eligible for the Signature Series label. In addition to the certified grade, the yellow label includes who signed it and when it was signed. If appropriate, a Signature Series label may state where a book was signed. In 2007, CGC introduced a Signature Series Restored label. Similar to the CGC Signature Series label in color, it is differentiated by a purple bar across the top. Restoration is noted in the same fashion as on the purple CGC Restored label, and, as with the regular Signature Series label, restored books must be signed in the presence of CGC representatives in order to be eligible for signature authentication.

In October of 2003, CGC began to certify comic book related magazines. The certification process and label system for magazines is exactly the same as for comic books. Some examples of comic book related magazines CGC certifies are *MAD Magazine*, *Vampirella*, *Creepy*, *Eerie* and *Famous Monsters of Filmland*.

More recently CGC introduced grading and encapsulation for *Sports Illustrated* and *Playboy* magazines, Movie Lobby Cards and Photographs making us the first independent, impartial, expert third-party grading service for all types of collectibles.

For more information on comic book certification and CGC's many services, please visit our website at www.CGCcomics.com

What are comic book pedigrees? Why are they important?

According to the forthcoming book *The Guide To Comic Book Pedigrees*, "A pedigreed collection must have been accumulated by one individual during the time the comics were released on the newsstand. This is a critical factor because a pedigree's appeal comes from their homogenous quality and singular genesis. The books have aged together in the same environment, creating a uniform 'feel' that does not exist for comics in a collection with diverse origins."

As the book's website points out, there are three other commonly accepted stipulations for what makes a collection a pedigree collection:

- A pedigreed collection must primarily consist of high quality comic books.
- A pedigreed collection must contain a substantial number of key or rare issues, or represent a significant portion of a particular genre, company, period, or classic title/character.
- Comics Guaranty, LLC (CGC) and the collecting community must continue to recognize the pedigree name of a collection past the point of initial sale.

The first widely recognized comic book pedigree was (and is) the Edgar Church collection, which is also known as the Mile High collection, which was unveiled in the 1970s. Since it first gained notoriety, others have surfaced including the following:

Allentown	Davis Crippen	Lost Valley	River City
Aurora	("D")	Massachusetts	Rockford
Bethlehem	Denver	Mohawk Valley	Salida
Big Apple	Don & Maggie	Northford	Spokane
Boston	Thompson	Northland	Tom Reilly
Bowling Green	Edgar Church	Nova Scotia	(San Francisco)
Carson City	(Mile High)	Ohio	Twilight
Chicago	Gaines File	Okajima	Vancouver
Circle 8	Green River	Pacific Coast	Western Penn
Cosmic Aeroplane	Hawkeye	Palo Alto	White Mountain
Crowley	Kansas City	Pennsylvania	Windy City
Curator	Lamont Larson	Recil Macon	Winnipeg

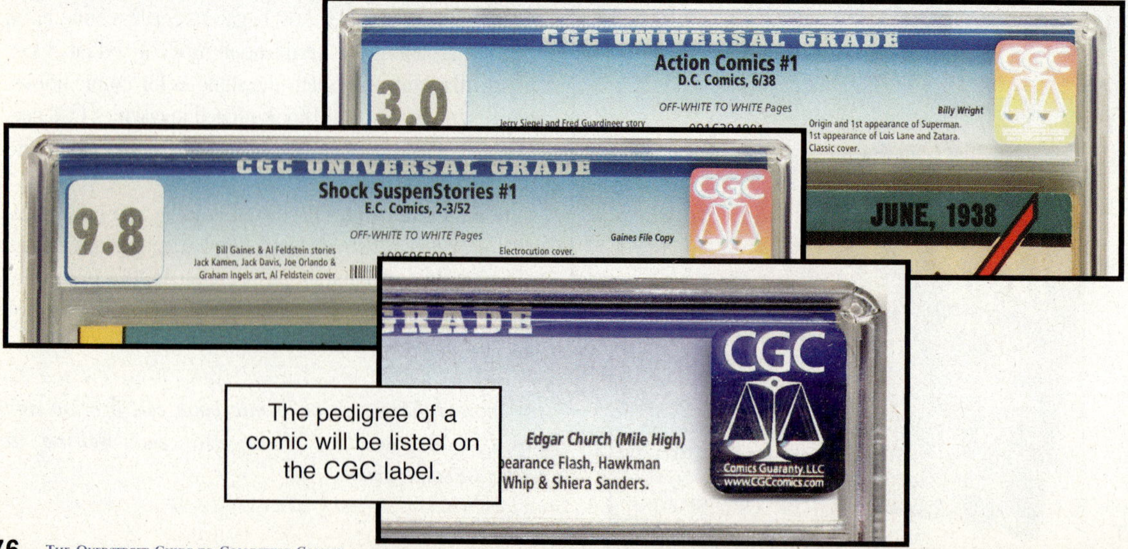

The pedigree of a comic will be listed on the CGC label.

THE LAMONT LARSON COLLECTION

BY JON BERK

In the summer of 2005, unbeknownst to the majority of the attendees at Comic-Con International: San Diego a special collector was on the floor and later attended a dinner in his honor. Lamont Larson, whose comic collection is considered in the top tier of the Golden Age pedigrees by pedigree collectors, had been invited to attend. Those who had the chance to meet him knew that it was truly a once in a lifetime opportunity.

Longtime collector and Overstreet Advisor Jon Berk details the history of the Lamont Larson Collection and the man behind hit.

I was going to start off and proclaim that "I had found Lamont Larson!". However, from the perspective of Lamont Larson, he had never been "lost". And, frankly, from my point of view, although I had often wondered about Lamont Larson, I never actively made this a crusade. I mean did I really think I could locate the man, who had amassed, as a boy, over 50 years ago, a collection of Golden Age comics which forms one of the most collectible and recognizable "pedigree" set of comic books in today's marketplace? Well, with some perseverance and a whole lot of luck I "located" Lamont Larson and have had the opportunity to speak with him as to his recollections of reading comics in the late 1930s and early 1940s.

But first, a little background. For reasons which I cannot fully articulate, I have been intrigued by collecting Golden Age comicbooks known as "Larson" books. The collection, uncovered by Joe Tricarichi in the early 1970s, comprises about 1000 comic books. Although there are a couple of books from 1935, the bulk of the collection runs from 1936 to September 1941; the heart of the pre-Golden Age and Golden Age. (Please note, except for the "lost Larsons" described below, there are *not* any Larson copies covered dated after September 1941.) Although the Larson collection contains many of the early Golden Age keys, notable among the missing key issues is *Detective Comics* #27, *All Star Comics* #3 and *Flash Comics* #1. Notwithstanding these omissions, the collection contains major keys and significant runs of hard core and esoteric Golden Age. Unique to the Larson collection is that it contains several "pre-hero" comic books missing from the Church collection. The collection also contains many Big Little Books, pulps and mystery novels.

As pedigree collections go, the Larson collection contains some of the earliest books of any pedigree collection. The earliest issues for some pre-Golden Age titles are: *Famous Funnies* #10 (May 1935), *Tip Top* #2 (June 1936), *Funny Pages* #3 (July 1936), *More Fun* #15 (November 1936), *New Comics* #11 (November 1936), *Funny Picture Stories* #1 (November 1936), *Detective Picture Stories* #1 (December 1936), *King Comics* #9 (December 1936), *Detective Comics* #3 (May 1937), *New*

Adventure #17 (July 1937), *Feature Funnies* #9 (June 1938). Due to my interest in books from this early time period and Centaur comics, I kept on "bumping" into "Larson" books as the only specimens I could find. Eventually, as my awareness of the Larson collection grew, I took pleasure knowing that these books could be traced back to a single owner. I would search out books from this remarkable collection.

Although the condition of the books is variable (a few have been chewed by mice (see *Red Raven* #1), or have water damage or have had coupons clipped out (including *Jungle Comics* #1, *Planet Comics* #1 and *Target Comics* #1 - the coupon of these books unfortunately being on the inside of the front cover), many books are in the VF/NM range or better. Whatever the grade, most books have outstanding page quality with light to moderate "foxing" due to apparent exposure to water. Books from this collection sell for *Guide* to a premium over *Guide* for simply being a "Larson copy".

Many "Larsons" are easily identifiable by the name "Larson" prominently written in pencil on the cover. Besides the "flowing cursive" Larson signature (see *Funny Pages* 4/1 and *Whirlwind Comics* #2), many books have a "different" Larson signature (see *Red Raven Comics* #1 and *Zip Comics* #16) or "Lamont" in a different handwriting (see *Thrilling Comics* #8 and *Top-Notch Comics* #18). In many instances, the initial buyers of these books would try to erase the name from the cover, a perceived "defect." Today that "defect" is sought out by the more avid Larson collectors. Some books just have a "number" on the cover, many books have "on" on the cover with the Larson "signature" (see *Popular Comics* #57), or without the Larson "signature"(see *Crackajack Funnies* #13); others have no markings at all. Late issues of the poorly distributed Fox Comics had an "ad" on the cover.

Some collectors have been told that books with just an "L" are Larson copies. This simply is not the case. The "signature" present or erased is always in the upper left hand quadrant of the book.

The oldest books from 1936 have "P.N." with a number (see *Detective Picture Stories* #2 and *Funny Pages* #6). Almost all the books have some degree of the distinctive foxing.

Unfortunately, due to an early lack of information about these books, unless a particular book has a distinctive identifying mark, many "Larsons" have been assimilated anonymously into the comic book marketplace. (Although not absolutely definitive, the Larson list compiled by Joe Tricarichi is quite helpful. Grading of the books on the list is generally under the more liberal grading standards of the 1970s. However, Joe notes some specific defects on books, which is critical to identifying books as Larson copies if the lineage of the book is unknown.)

What draws me to "Larson" copies (beside their generally nice condition) is the knowledge that the books are part of a single identifiable collection. Although not generally of the superior virginal (i.e. "not read") quality of the Church collection, these books were <u>read</u> and accumulated by one person. My interest with Larson books prompted many questions. What is the meaning of the markings on the covers? Why the variation of the "signatures"? Was this the result of a father-son collaboration? What got him going on comics? How old was he? I thought these questions would never be answered. Wrong!

I had been offered a book which was a "Larson". Inquiring how the book was identified as a "Larson", I was told that it was from the coupon filled out inside the book (of *All-Star Comics* #1). Did it give an address? "Wausa, Nebraska". I called telephone information but, alas, no listing for "Lamont Larson". They did have three other listings for "Larson". What the heck, I called the first on the list, and although not a relative, she put me on the path to locate Lamont Larson in Clay Center, Nebraska. Lamont Larson was then 74 years old and a retired English teacher.

In my initial telephone conversation I spent much time convincing Mr. Larson that I had both feet planted firmly on the ground and that I was genuinely interested in events that had taken place over 50 years ago. He is totally disassociated from the world of comics and had no idea of the prominence of his comic books. After convincing him that I was not crazy, I said, "Ah, you don't know me, but I am interested in comics and, well, you collected them 50 years ago…" He interrupted me at that point and said, "I did not collect them, I read them." This was a refreshing start.

Larson was surprised at my call. He had not given any thought to these books for many years. They were something that formed a part of his childhood, a part that he had let go as his interests turned to mystery novels and model airplanes. Understandably, Larson's recollection of the events of reading comic books as a boy is vague at best. It came as "a very big surprise" for him to learn that his books had such notoriety for comic collectors. He admitted that his initial reaction to this information was that this was all "very strange". As we talked, he warmed and found it "pleasant" as to the place his books hold in collecting circles.

Lamont Larson grew up in Wausa, Nebraska, a small farming town in northeast Nebraska about 150 miles from Omaha (Actually "Lamont" is his middle name. Growing up in the late 1930s he was not fond of the phonetic sameness of his first name "Rudolph" with a certain German leader of that time.). The town population was about 700. His family ran the local movie theater. As a boy Larson described himself as an "avid reader". He read comics from about the age of nine through the age of 15. As he told me, "I always liked comics in the daily and particularly in the Sunday paper. As they came up with comic books, I began to prize and enjoy them". (Remember the "modern" comic book only hit the newsstands in 1934, with original material beginning in 1935/1936.) He did not buy to "collect" comics, but rather, as Larson stated, "to read and enjoy them". He stated that he always enjoyed the comics in the newspaper. Comic books represented "a step beyond that. I was developing a desire to read and I liked the high adventure that you got in some of those comics."

Larson would purchase the comics at Cruetz' Drugstore. Because Larson missed some issues as they came out, the owner of the drugstore, Fred Cruetz, suggested that he put aside all comics that came in and have Larson pick them up periodically. As Larson recalls Fred Cruetz said, "Well, I tell you what. We'll put them away and put your name on them…and when you want to come in and get them, they'll be here." Larson accepted this arrangement. Tryg Hagen and Cecil Coop, employees at different times at the drugstore, were primarily responsible for placing Larson's name on the books which were put aside for him. It is <u>their</u> handwriting, not Larson's, that appears on the books. (This information explains the variation in the handwriting for "Larson" or "Lamont" appearing on the books, and puts to an end one of the small mysteries about the books.) This arrangement probably started some time in 1939 - Larson would have been 12 - as I am not aware of any "signed" Larsons before this date. (In fact, based on review of my "Larson" books it appears this arrangement started with books cover dated July 1939. Interestingly, his name did not appear on all titles on a consistent basis until those cover dated January 1940. This may also explain some of the gaps in the early runs. Additionally, as indicated below, it appears that certain gaps are explained by the fact that he gave some of his books away.) All comics were purchased new; no second-hand comics were purchased to fill gaps.

The "Larson" name on his copy of *Marvel Mystery Comics #3* from 1940.

Mr. Larson had no explanation for the numbers written on the books, or the "P.N." or the "on" written on the books, except to state that many of the magazines sold at the drugstore, whether comics or not, would have the notation "on". To answer these questions, Larson put me in contact with Norman and Bob Cruetz, the sons of the drugstore owner. (Cruetz' Drugstore has been in continuous operation and run by the same family since 1895.) They stated that the initials identified the distributor of the books in order to make returns. "P.N." stood for "Publishers News" and "on" stood for "Omaha News". They also were able to identify <u>who</u> wrote Larson's name on the books. The flowing cursive "Larson" and "Lamont" as appears on *Funny Pages #4/1* and *Whirlwind Comics*, respectively, was written by Tryg Hagen while the handwriting for "Larson" as it appears on *Red Raven Comics* and *Zip #16* was written by Cecil Coop (who helped out at the drugstore after Hagen died in 1940).

As to the numbers on some of the covers, the answer is less clear. Norman Cruetz believes it is a "call back" number by which the distributor identified books that were then ready to be returned. The retail outlet would then tear off the covers and return these books for credit. Cruetz believes this was the procedure for Publishers News. (Apparently after 1937 only Omaha News would be specifically indicated by a symbol on the cover.) In support of this theory it is noted that numbers do not appear on any book that has the "on" (Omaha News) symbol. This supposition of Kruetz appears to be correct in that the number for the Larson titles that do have numbers are all the same.

Larson's parents would pay for the comics. They had no problem with him reading them. Larson stated that his parents viewed it as a cheap way "to keep me out of trouble". He started reading them at the end of the Depression. As he reflected, "They were only a dime so it really wasn't a big thing, although, sometimes, that dime was kinda hard to come by." Although many of the books in the Larson collection were "reprint" books, Larson confided that he did not like these "funny books," preferring "high adventure," "far out," and "fantastic" stories. His favorite characters read like a who's who of the Golden Age: Captain America, Captain Marvel, Superman, and, his favorite, Batman (Interestingly, his "handle" for CB was "The Shadow" due to the shared name "Lamont"). He also had a tremendous interest in Dick Tracy both in comic books and Big Little Books which he adored.

Larson stated he was always careful about things he owned. Generally, he would put the comics away after he read them, although he acknowledged that some might have been thrown away. (This further explains the gaps that appear in many of the collected series). Initially, the books were in a box in a storeroom, but when his family moved in 1940 they were stored in a barn. This outdoor storage explains the mice chews on some books and the exposure to moisture - resulting in foxing - present on many copies. (This "storage method" of subjecting books to the extremes of the Nebraskan weather while sitting of the floor of a barn in a cardboard box and yet maintaining white pages is remarkable considering the elaborate procedures advocated by "experts" on how to properly preserve one's collection.) Larson has no specific recollection of why he stopped reading comics, except to note that he had become interested in other things, such as mystery novels and anything to do with aviation. In fact, latter in life he started to collect hardback and paperback mystery novels.

Larson obtained a job as a teacher and moved away from Wausa leaving the comics in the barn. In the late 1970s, a local antique dealer, Dwaine Nelson, asked Larson's mother (for whom he did odd jobs) about the books and an arrangement was made. Larson was surprised that they had been saved. Mrs. Larson who was anxious to remove the material in the barn sold Nelson the comics and many magazines such as *The Saturday Evening Post* and *Colliers*. Nelson had the books for about 18 months before he resold them. Nelson (with whom I spoke) recollected that he sold the comics and magazines for about $50 to $100. They eventually found their way into the hands of Joe Tricarichi.

As one looks back, it was the thousands and thousands of kids who, like Lamont Larson, latching on to this new form of entertainment, catapulted the nascent comic book business into the thriving business it would be. And out of those thousands and thousands of books only a few survived through the years to be snapped up by anxious collectors today. Who would have thought that one of the most prominent collections of comic books would survive to this date, due to the idea of an owner of a drugstore in a small Nebraskan town and a boy who took good care of what he owned?

Epilogue

After my article came out in late 1994, Larson's hometown newspaper in Nebraska asked if they could reprint it. I naturally gave my permission. About two weeks after the newspaper articles appeared, I received a letter from a boyhood friend of Larson's (Larson had even been his best man.). He had read with much interest my articles. It prompted an old memory. Recently, he had cleaned out his mother's house and discovered a box of his old comics. He remembered as a boy that Larson had given him comics after he was done with them. Sure enough he found six books with "Lamont" or "Larson" on them. He "wondered" if I "might" be interested in them. MIGHT BE!

As described none of the books sounded like they were in particularly good condition. However, driven by curiosity and this incredible quirk of luck that these books even existed, I dickered over a price and purchased the books. These books are, for the record, *Smash Comics* #8 (March 1940), *Feature Comics* #34 (July 1940), *Minute Man Comics* #2 (September 5- December 5, 1941), *Super Mystery* #2/4 (October 1941), *Victory Comics* #3 (November 1941) and *Star Spangled Comics* #2 (November 1941). As testament to the uniqueness of the storage condition of the original collection, the "lost Larsons" are of variable condition with none grading better than VG+ and none displaying the page whiteness of the original collection.

These "lost Larsons" prompt several thoughts and observations. There are, obviously, "Larsons" that were purchased after the September 1941 cover date. However, it is clear that at this point Larson lost interest. Of the six "lost Larsons" four are from the very end of his comic reading career. The fact that he gave away the books is evidence of that. He may have been more willing to part with his comic books at this point. However, since two of the books are from 1940, the "gaps" in the Larson collection may be attributed as much to the common boyhood trait of sharing books as to the possible distribution quirks of the comic books themselves. The more intriguing question is if Larson gave away any *other* books. Are there more "lost Larsons" out there waiting to be found?

A version of this article originally appeared in Overstreet's Gold and Silver Quarterly #6 (Oct.-Dec. 1994). *Following that, additional information was discovered concerning this collection, most notably author Berk's acquisition of Joe Tricarichi's "Larson List." Additionally, previously unknown "Larson" copies were discovered prior to its revised publication in* Comic Book Marketplace.

AND WHEN THE VAULT WAS

It was an oddly cold day in August 1989. The mist settled in among the Manhattan skyscrapers creating a spooky EC setting as Russ Cochran and I walked over to Bill Gaines' apartment from our hotel. It still seems like only yesterday when Russ called me with the news that Bill Gaines has decided to sell his EC collection. Russ would be handling the sale and I was needed to verify the collection and to arrange the copies of each issue by grade. We both knew that he had put away twelve copies of every EC 35-40 years earlier and sealed them away in boxes. Now the time had come to open those packages.

Thoughts were rushing through our heads about the significance of the day. We had many questions to be answered. We wondered what the condition would be like, how white the pages would be, if any issues would be missing, and if something new would be discovered.

We finally arrived at the Gaines' apartment at 10:15 AM. After clearing security, we arrived at his doorstep. Bill and his wife Anne cheerfully invited us in. Their apartment was like a curio shop, filled with mementos, souvenirs, and Statues of Liberty which they had collected for many years. Over to the right were bookshelves filled with bound ECs and *MAD*s. But what really caught our eyes was a genuine shrunken head sitting on the shelf (see the *Haunt of Fear* #8 cover). After gasping and choking for a second, we settled down around a large dining room table where the work would be performed.

In the closet were six large cardboard boxes which contained the ECs. The comics were wrapped in brown paper by issue number and sealed in the boxes. Before the comic books were handled, Russ and I put on white cotton film editor's gloves.

The first box was opened and the first package of comics was set on the table. We began with *Vault of Horror* #40 and worked backwards to *War Against Crime* #10. Russ cut open each package, counted the issues and handed them to me for arrangement by grade. Anne placed the ID labels on Mylar bags while Bill supervised.

Legendary EC Publisher Bill Gaines during the evaluation of the Gaines File collection.

OPENED...

by Robert M. Overstreet
with Gary M. Carter

After each stack was graded, Russ placed them in Mylar sleeves. At this point the copies were divided into two groups, one to be sold and one to be retained by Bill. Depending on shortages, Bill wanted to keep up to four copies for his personal use.

It soon became apparent, after going through just a few packages, that we were seeing something out of the ordinary. The books were dazzling. They were essentially in brand new condition with full cover gloss and extra white pages. The cover colors were brilliant, with only a few exceptions. All of the noticeable defects either occurred during printing or trimming or the way they were wrapped. Some corners were bumped, and some issues were wrinkled.

We were disappointed to find no annuals or Pre-Trend comics, except for *War Against Crime* #10 and 11, and *Crime Patrol* #15 and 16. But we were surprised to find most all of the different versions of M.C. Gaines' books: *Picture Stories from the Bible, Science, American History* and *World History*. Some carried the All-American seal, some the DC seal, and others had the familiar EC seal.

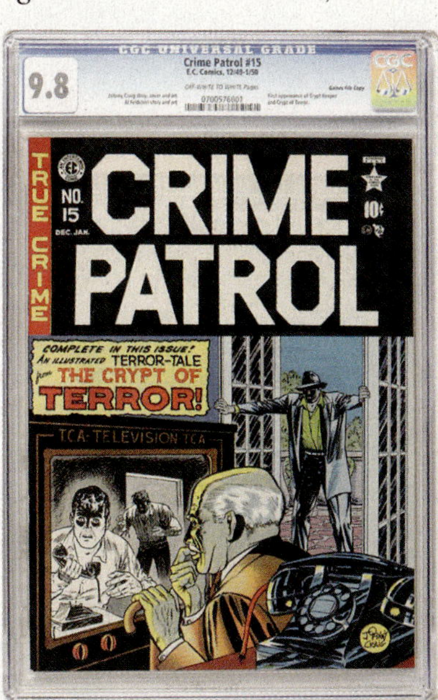

The Gaines File Pedigree is one of the most sought-after collections of comic books, with its high-grade copies selling for record prices. This **Crime Patrol** #15 CGC-graded 9.8 copy sold for $9560 in 2008.

Haunt of Fear #17 (#3)
CGC-certified 9.6 copy
sold for $7475 in 2005.

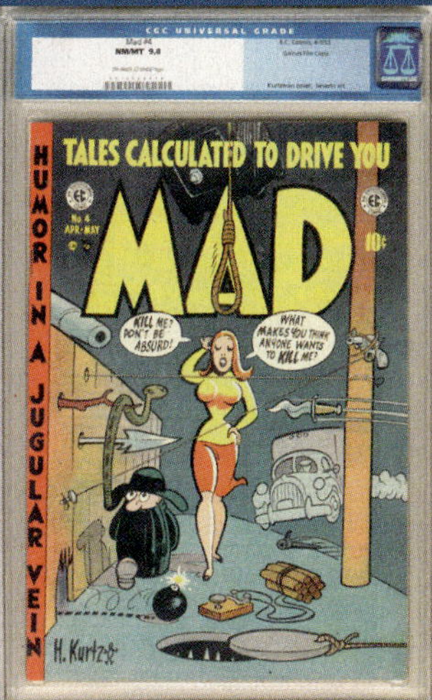

Mad #4
CGC-certified 9.8 copy
sold for $5750 in 2001.

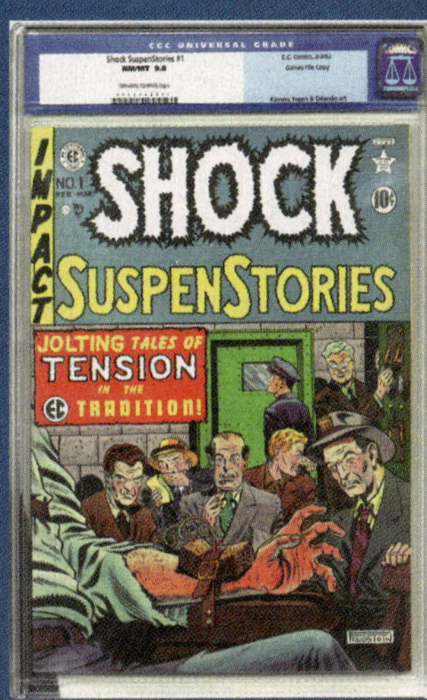

Shock SuspenStories #1
CGC-certified 9.8 copy
sold for $5750 in 2004.

Shock SuspenStories #6
CGC-certified 9.8 copy
sold for $7170 in 2006.

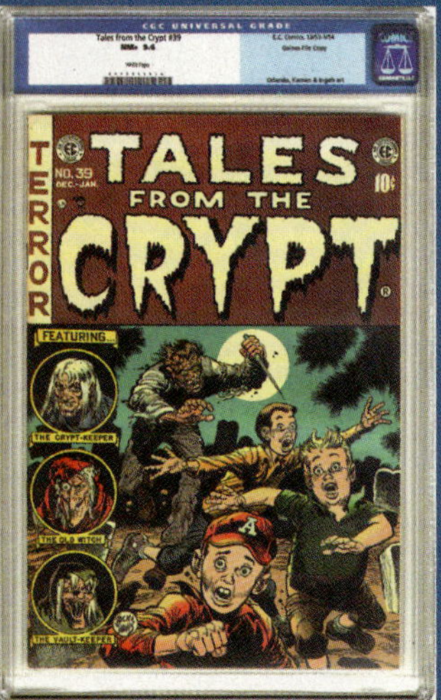

Tales From the Crypt #39
CGC-certified 9.6 copy
sold for $2990 in 2002.

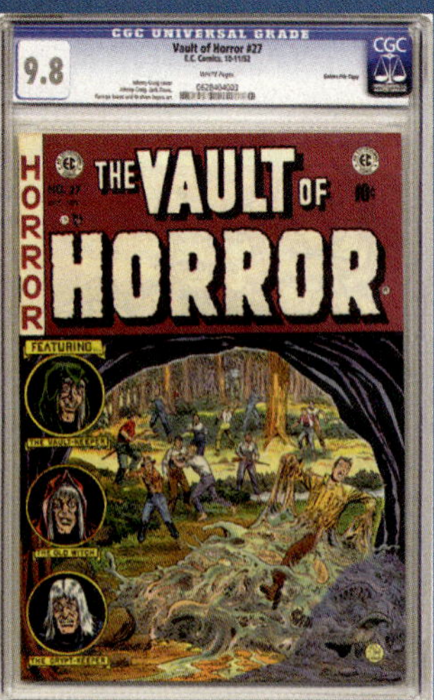

Vault of Horror #27
CGC-certified 9.8 copy
sold for $4887 in 2005.

Robert M. Overstreet evaluates a then-freshly opened issue of *Frontline Combat* #4, documenting the now legendary Gaines File collection.

After opening a few of the packages and seeing the pristine condition of the books, we just had to check out their smell. The white pages and inks were still so fresh, that opening the books and smelling the insides swept us back to 1950. It was a smell we all remembered. Those of us who can recognize an Edgar Church Collection (Mile High) comic by its smell would have trouble distinguishing between it and the Gaines smell. It soon became obvious that we were looking at probably the best surviving sets of EC comics.

As a comparison, many of the Harvey file copies had brown edges due to the way they were stored. Some of the Dell file copies also had minor browning on the edges. Since the Gaines collection was

Longtime EC enthusiast, historian and publisher Russ Cochran with **Frontline Combat** copies from the Gaines File collection.

never read, and was wrapped air-tight, the only comparable collection would be the Church collection. In the Dell and Harvey file copies there were issues missing from the runs, and in some cases there were probably as many as 100 copies of each issue.

Bill had remembered that there were twelve copies in each package, but we found that many had been opened, probably before Gaines moved to that apartment in 1961. We found that most issues did have twelve copies, but there were many packages that contained nine, ten, or eleven copies, and a few with only seven copies, and one issue with only one copy (*Vault of Horror* #12).

The work was tedious, the days were long, but they were filled with memories that we shall never forget. As we looked at these books, we traded stories about our memories of seeing each cover for the first time, and stories of how we tracked down that particular issue for our collections. Each day we played Christmas music and sang Christmas carols as we continued processing the mountain of unopened packages. At each day's end we returned to our hotel immersed in EC dust, Christmas Spirit, and childhood memories.

After spending a few days going through these books, Russ and I agreed that it was an experience that any EC fan would have enjoyed — the historic unveiling of the Gaines File collection. It was like opening 300 little time capsules that hadn't seen the light of day for 35-40 years. Being small-town collectors we both felt privileged and honored to be present at such a historic occasion. We hope that these notes will in some way make it possible for all other collectors and fans to have been there also.

On Friday, August 11, we processed *Vault of Horror*, *Tales from the Crypt*, *Haunt of Fear*, *Crime SuspenStories* and *Shock SuspenStories*. On Saturday, August 12, we did *Weird Science*, *Weird Fantasy*, *Weird Science-Fantasy*, *Incredible Science-Fiction*, all of the New Direction titles (such as *Valor* and *Impact*), *MAD* and *Panic*. On Sunday we were joined by Russ's daughter, Sylvia, and Angie Meyer, and we did *Two-Fisted Tales*, *Frontline Combat*, the 3-D comics, and the various *Picture Stories* series. The actual sets of books were put together Sunday afternoon, which finished the project.

As an interesting footnote, we learned that *Impact* #1 was originally printed by Charlton Press. The printing quality was poor, so Gaines had the entire run destroyed, saving only one copy. It was then printed again and distributed to the stands.

Years later, of course, the Gaines File collection has become one of the most sought-after pedigreed collections of comic books. As has been documented in our Market Reports over the past few editions of the *Guide* and from the incredible success of Gemstone's *EC Archives* project, the interest in these classics shows no signs of waning now.

This article appeared in different form in Overstreet's Golden Age & Silver Age Quarterly *and* The Overstreet Comic Book Price Guide #38.

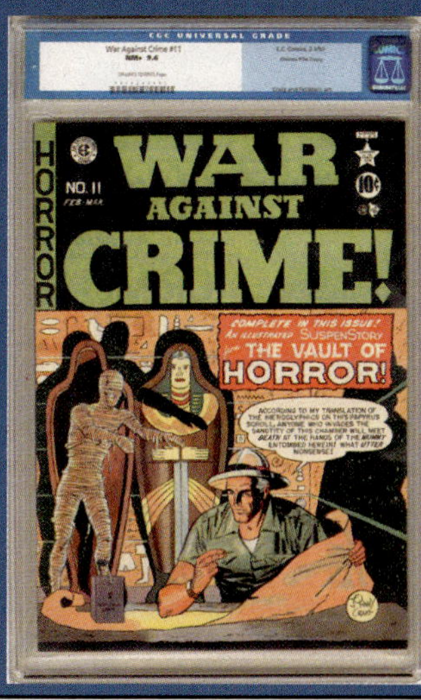

War Against Crime #11
CGC-certified 9.6 copy sold for $4600 in 2001.

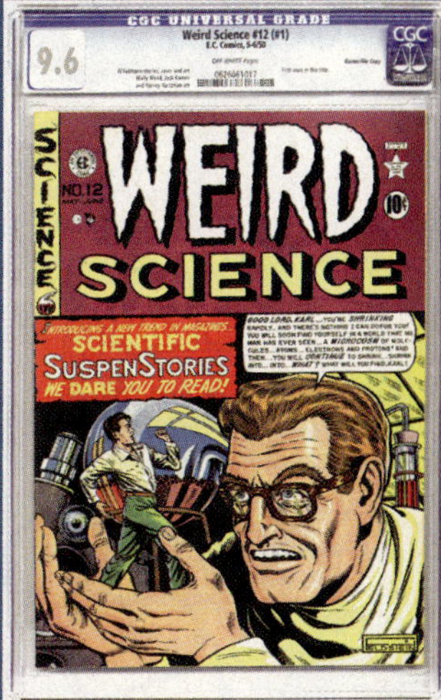

Weird Science #12 (#1)
CGC-certified 9.6 copy sold for $8799 in 2006.

Weird Science-Fantasy #29
CGC-certified 9.6 copy sold for $13,255 in 2002.

Follow us on Twitter and find us on Facebook.
LOOKING FOR A COMIC SHOP NEAR YOU?
COMIC SHOP LOCATOR SERVICE
COMICS
comicshoplocator.com
888-COMIC-BOOK

Actress Ming-Na (*Joy Luck Club*, *ER*, voice of Mulan) at her first Comic-Con in San Diego.

Even Halo soldiers need snacks. Presuming they can find their wallets and open their faceplates.

Cosplay has become an increasing presence at many larger shows and even some smaller ones.

CONVENTIONS!

Comic book conventions are a great way to meet fellow fans, creators, publishers, dealers and others who share your passion for your favorite titles, characters and events. Conventions range from small, one-day events on the local level all the way up to Comic-Con International: San Diego and the New York Comic Con, the two biggest comic book events in North America.

Beyond buying, selling and trading comic books with dealers and fellow fans, there are many different activities at conventions including meeting creators and getting their autographs, attending and participating in panel discussions, costuming or cosplay, TV, movie and anime presentations, debuts of convention-exclusive editions of comics, and more. At larger shows, there are frequently activities to participate in after the normal dealer room hours have ended. There's also a huge social component to some conventions after hours as well. Some shows bring in celebrities for special signings. At other conventions you might find celebrities in attendance because many of them are fans, too.

On the pages that follow are just some of the shows on the convention circuit. Check with the promoters for the dates of the next installments of these shows and keep your eyes open for new ones in your area.

One of the main aisles at Comic-Con International: San Diego (yes, it's during a slow time).

Sgt. Rock writer-artist Billy Tucci with Pvt. David Katagiri, F Co., 2nd Battalion 442nd RCT.

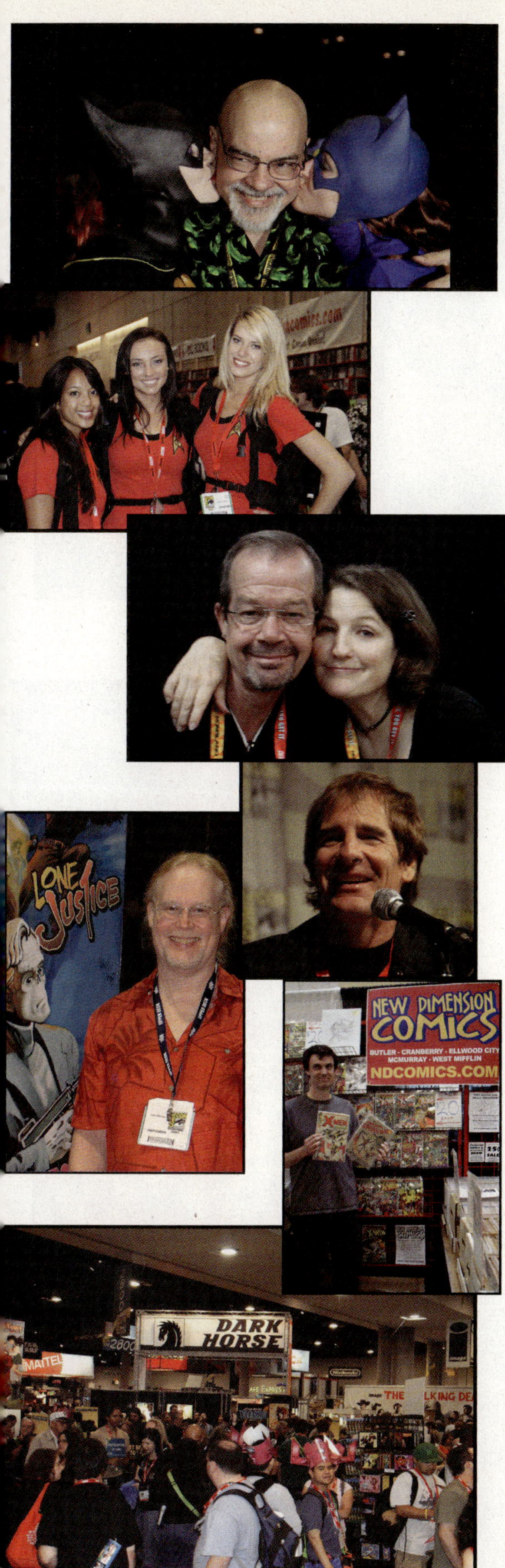

East Hanover Comic Book Expo
Ramada Conference Center
130 Route 10
East Hanover, NJ 07936
www.njcomicbookshows.com

HeroesCon
Charlotte Convention Center
501 S. College Street
Charlotte, NC 28202
www.heroesonline.com

Long Beach Comic Con
Long Beach Convention Center
300 East Ocean Boulevard
Long Beach, CA 90802
www.LongBeachComicCon.com

Meadowlands Secaucus Comic Book Expo
Holiday Inn Secaucus (2nd floor)
300 Plaza Drive
Secaucus, NJ 07094.
www.njcomicbookshows.com

MegaCon
Orange County Convention Center,
Center Hall D,
9800 International Drive,
Orlando, FL 32819
www.megaconvention.com

New York Comic Con
Jacob K. Javits Center
11th Avenue (between 34th and 39th St.)
New York, NY 10001
www.NewYorkComicCon.com

Pittsburgh Comicon
Monroeville Convention Center
209 Mall Boulevard
Monroeville, PA 15146
www.Pittsburghcomicon.com

Small Press Expo (SPX)
Bethesda North Marriott Hotel
& Conference Center
5701 Marinelli Road,
N. Bethesda, MD 20852
www.spxpo.com

Virginia Comicon
Ramada Plaza West
6624 West Broad Street
Richmond, VA 23230
www.vacomicon.com

West Virginia Popular Culture Convention (WVPOP)
Mylan Park Expo Center
500 Mylan Park Lane
Morgantown, WV 26501
http://wvpop.com/

Wizard World Austin
Austin Convention Center
500 East Cesar Chavez Street
Austin, TX 78701-4121
www.wizardworld.com/austin.html

Wizard World Chicago
Donald E. Stephens Convention Center
(Rosemont)
5555 N. River Road
Rosemont, IL 60018
www.wizardworld.com/chicago.html

Wizard World New Orleans
New Orleans Ernest N. Morial
Convention Center
900 Convention Center Boulevard
New Orleans, LA 70130
www.wizardworld.com/neworleans.html

Wizard World Ohio
Greater Columbus Convention Center
450 North High Street
Columbus, OH 43215
www.wizardworld.com/home-ohio.html

Wizard World Philadelphia
Pennsylvania Convention Center
1101 Arch Street
Philadelphia, PA 19107
www.wizardworld.com/philadelphia.html

Wizard World Portland
Oregon Convention Center
777 NE Martin Luther King Jr. Boulevard
Portland, OR 97232
www.wizardworld.com/portland.html

Wizard World Toronto
Metro Toronto Convention Centre
255 Front Street West
Toronto, ON, M5V 2X7 CANADA
www.wizardworld.com/home-toronto.html

WonderCon
Moscone Center South,
747 Howard Street
San Francisco, CA 94103
www.comic-con.org/wc

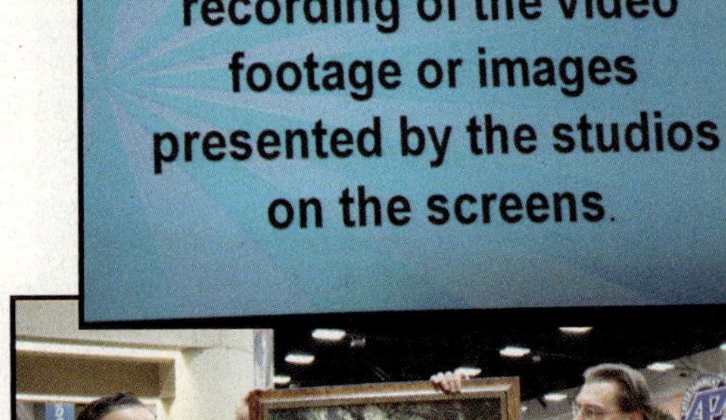

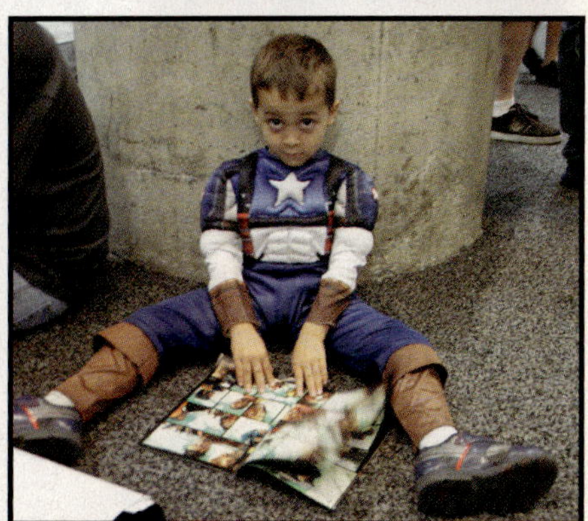

FREE COMIC BOOK DAY ™

FREE COMIC BOOK DAY ™
BEHIND THE SCENES

Each year, the first Saturday in May is Free Comic Book Day. Since 2002, the entire industry has seen Free Comic Book Day reach the point where dozens of publishers large and small take part in an effort to expand the reach of comics by helping participating retailers give away free samples – often comics specifically created for the event – to new and returning readers.

Comic book retailer Joe Field, proprietor of Flying Colors Comics, has been a driving force behind many things in the industry, perhaps none of them bigger than Free Comic Book Day.

"I used to write a monthly column for the comic industry's trade magazine. In one of my columns I proposed doing something similar to Baskin Robbins 'Free Scoop Night' (these days, it's now 'Dollar Scoop Night'). I had the foresight to ask for comments from Diamond Comic Distributors since I was essentially asking them to serve as coordinators for the event. Their response was very positive, so things took off from there," he said.

In addition to kicking off Free Comic Book Day, Field is a recipient of the Will Eisner Spirit of Comics Award for Comics Specialty Retailing Excellence, president of the comics retailer trade association ComicsPRO and a founder of WonderCon. We talked with him about Free Comic Book Day, its history and its future.

As you talked to people in the industry about starting a Free Comic Book Day, what were the different reactions you got?
Joe Field (JF): Most of the reactions seemed to be along the lines of the forehead-slapping "Why didn't we think of doing this sooner?" The minority reaction was from some retailers feeling they could just give away unsold older comics and get the same result. I believe that has since been proven faulty.

What were the first steps you took in the effort to get organized?
JF: After discussing it with Roger Fletcher, Diamond's VP of Marketing, it was agreed that we should get some of the major players together to find a way to do it. Diamond had one of their Retailer Summits in Las Vegas in October '01 and that's where I sat down with Diamond's management team and the publishers of DC, Marvel, Image, Dark Horse and Maggie Thompson from Comics Buyers' Guide. All of them were enthusiastic and thought it was worth pursuing.

Who were some of the early key contributors to making it a success?
JF: Definitely the whole Diamond team. The art department at DC came up with the FCBD logo. And when it came time to actually have the first FCBD, retailers came through in remarkable ways!

Whether it's been conventions or other promotions, you've always been a forward-thinking kind of guy. Did you think it would grow to the size it has or maybe just hope it would?
JF: The way I look at FCBD is the way cereal marketers advertise Corn Flakes — they are a part of healthy diet for breakfast, but there are other things needed to complete the balance. I know FCBD has been a healthy part of the comics biz, and it came along at a time when we weren't as steeped in comics culture as we are now. I strongly believe that the outpouring of media that pays attention to FCBD more than ten years into it is a very positive thing that leads to sales.

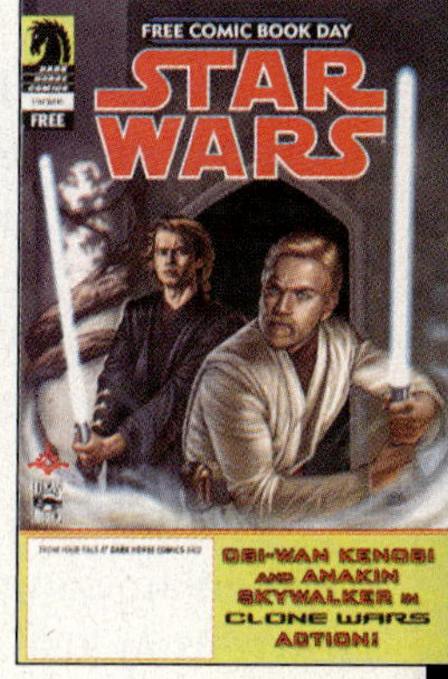

Originally the date moved around a bit. How was the first one decided upon?
JF: In that meeting in Vegas, it was then-Image publisher Jim Valentino who suggested we time the event with the release of the first *Spider-Man* movie. After that, the date moved to the July 4th weekend for one year, but has settled as the First Saturday in May since 2005.

On a personal level, what are some of the things you've done at your store to promote FCBD over the years?

JF: At Flying Colors, FCBD is our biggest party of the year. Besides the thousands of comics we give away, we add to the party atmosphere with creator signings, refreshments, costumed characters, some special deals, and occasional exclusive items. In 2012, for instance, we had a video crew here to shoot a mini-documentary about the origins of Free Comic Book Day. That can be seen at *FreeComicBookDay.com* and on YouTube.

On a national level, what are some of the best promotions you've seen or heard about?

JF: Some retailers have really turned FCBD into major community events. I'm blown away that more than a thousand folks show up here, but there are FCBD events that draw in excess of two thousand or more! Some of my retailer colleagues make FCBD a full-on community event, with charity fund-raisers and a carnival atmosphere. There are so many different ways to approach FCBD—and it shows the creativity and hard work of the best retailers to take FCBD to the next level every year.

How would you like to see Free Comic Book Day grow from here?

JF: I take these one at a time and I'll continue to advocate for retailers and publishers doing all they can to promote the event outside our core base of die-hard consumers.

As FCBD has developed since 2002, it's been amazing to watch how it has grown from just a few publishers to more than three dozen, from a few countries to start to nearly 50 now and having more than one million people visit comic shops on FCBD.

Free Comic Book Day is the largest single comics-related event in the world, and is now the focal point for promotion of comics and specialty retailers that sell comics. FCBD is part of a healthy comics

Joe Field and his wife Libby model the finest in FCBD fashions.

market and I'm always gratified and humbled to see how much effort everyone puts into it.

Have you seen its success affecting the comic industry as a whole in terms of the mainstream culture?

JF: FCBD puts comics and comic shops into the public spotlight in huge ways. Besides the tie-in to movies, there's a huge out-pouring of support from the education community. Many libraries participate in conjunction with local comic shops and many teachers at all levels from elementary school through college give students extra credit for attending FCBD events and then reporting on the comics and the scene. Also, given that FCBD happens in nearly 50 countries around the world, in a sense, FCBD is exporting American popular culture.

There are always people who work behind the scenes to make big things happen. Over the decade since Free Comic Book Day got started, who are some of the unsung heroes?

JF: The marketing team at Diamond really do a great job, so Roger Fletcher and Dan Manser deserve more than this name-drop. Previous FCBD marketing coordinators Barry Lyga [now a successful novelist] and especially Elissa Lynch (now Tierney) really did special things for FCBD. That Hugh Jackman video promoting FCBD? That was all Elissa's doing. Leslie Bowser continues the great tradition that Barry and Elissa established. On the operations' side at Diamond, Cindy Fournier and her team do a phenomenal job of making sure that 3+ million comics are moved through the system with precision and pride. Every picker and packer in each of the Diamond warehouses deserves a lot of credit.

There are some retailers who don't participate. What's the funniest or strangest reason you've heard for a retailer not taking part in it?
JF: A couple of years ago, I called and talked with a number of retailers that had not signed up to participate. One told me he didn't need to buy the FCBD comics because he still had an unopened case of *Badrock* #1 he could give away! Wow! Talk about missing an opportunity. I had another retailer bristle at the suggestion that, by asking him to be an official FCBD retailer, I was telling him how to run his business!

Look, the beautiful thing and the maddening thing about comic book specialty retailers is that we are a fiercely independent lot. It's beautiful because we

Lavish cakes are only one part of the festive carnival atmosphere of FCBD celebrations.

can each carve our own niche and create unique store environments that fit our personalities and communities. It's maddening because some retailers just don't get it and don't want to do a little work for a good return.

On the more serious side, how would you encourage those not participating to reevaluate things?
JF: I'd kindly ask them to consider that there are no other international promotions that draw over one million people to comic shops on a single day and yet cost as low as $50 to participate.

Anything else you'd like to add?
JF: Among the primary goals of Free Comic Book Day is to get people to visit their local comic shops. I hope everyone reading this will do what they can to promote and support FCBD and their local comic shop. Comic book retailers used to have competition that was primarily other small specialty collectibles' shops. These days, the primary competition for comic shops are behemoths like Amazon, eBay, Barnes & Noble and Wal-Mart! So please support your local retailers!

An ever more healthy comic book business is as great for readers and fans as it is for those of us who work in the business! Everyone reading this has my personal invitation to score free comics at your local comic shop every First Saturday in May on Free Comic Book Day!

You can visit the website for Free Comic Book Day at **www.freecomicbookday.com**.

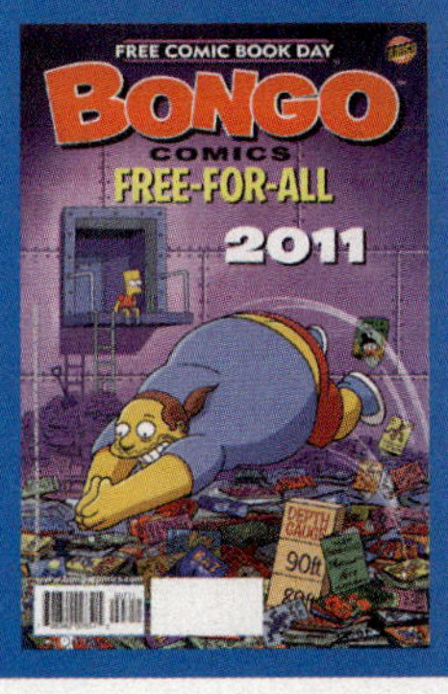

HOW COMICS ARE MADE

SUPERMAN Script

"CLOSE CALL"
Script: Chuck Dixon
Pencils: Renato Guedes
Inks: Marc Campos
Colors: Alex Sinclair & Mike Cavallaro
Lettering: Rob Leigh

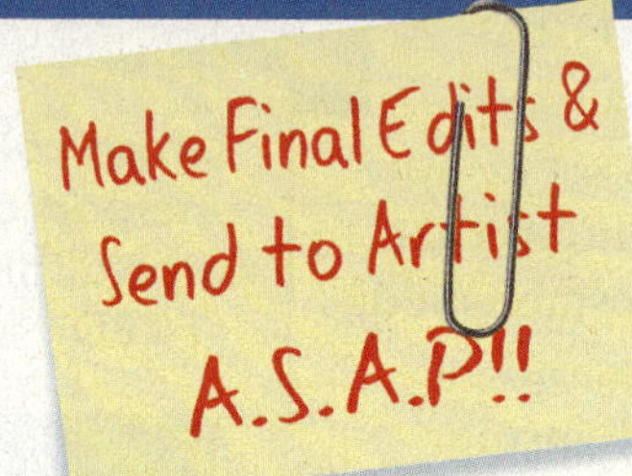

PANEL ONE
LOIS LANE is speeding along a multi-lane bridge speaking on her cell phone as she tools along. She's in a convertible and we're looking down at her as she drives. On the front seat, we see an open laptop, notes and other reporter paraphernalia from the Daily Planet.

    CAPTION: METROPOLIS.

    LOIS: I'M TELLING YOU…I THINK I'VE UNCOVERED WHO'S BEHIND THESE RECENT ATTACKS!

    PHONE: (ELECTRONIC, SMALL) SHOULDN'T YOU GO TO THE AUTHORITIES, LOIS?

     **LOIS:** AND MISS BREAKING THE BIGGEST STORY OF THE YEAR? NOT ON YOUR--

PANEL TWO
Closer shot - LOIS looks alarmed and grabs the wheel with both hands, dropping the cell phone.

[handwritten margin note: stet: keep cell phone in hand]

    LOIS: (SMALL) ---LIFE?

    PHONE: (ELECTRONIC, SMALL) LOIS?

    LOIS: SOMETHING'S **WRONG** WITH THE BRAKES!

PANEL THREE
LOIS' convertible crashes through a guard rail and off the bridge. It sustains damage from going through the guard rail.

    LOIS: NO!!!

PANEL FOUR
Our Big Money shot and the largest panel on the page. We're looking down at a dramatic angle as SUPERMAN catches the falling convertible. He's stopped the car from plunging into the river below. LOIS stares at him in stunned surprise. SUPERMAN is smiling. Below him we can see the long drop to the river. Add some river traffic for scale. Maybe have a tug pushing a barge.

[handwritten margin note: Try Drawing from a few different angles]

    LOIS: SUPERMAN!

    SUPERMAN: YOU REALLY SHOULD **THINK** ABOUT A HANDS-FREE CELL PHONE, LOIS.

    CAPTION: (SMALL) CONTINUED IN ACTION COMICS! *[handwritten note: Use comic logo]*

STAGE TWO: THE PENCIL ARTIST, IN THIS CASE THE VERY TALENTED RENATO GUEDES (24: MIDNIGHT SUN), ROUGHS OUT THE PAGES. SOMETIMES THIS IS DONE IN BLUE PENCIL, WHICH WILL NOT NORMALLY REPRODUCE.

GREAT SCOTT!
P1 11

STAGE FIVE: NEXT COMES THE COLOR, IN THIS CASE BY ALEX SINCLAIR AND MIKE CAVALLARO. IN THE MODERN WORLD OF COMPUTER COLORING, THEY CAN USE A FULLER AND MORE VIBRANT RANGE THAN WAS POSSIBLE IN THE PAST.

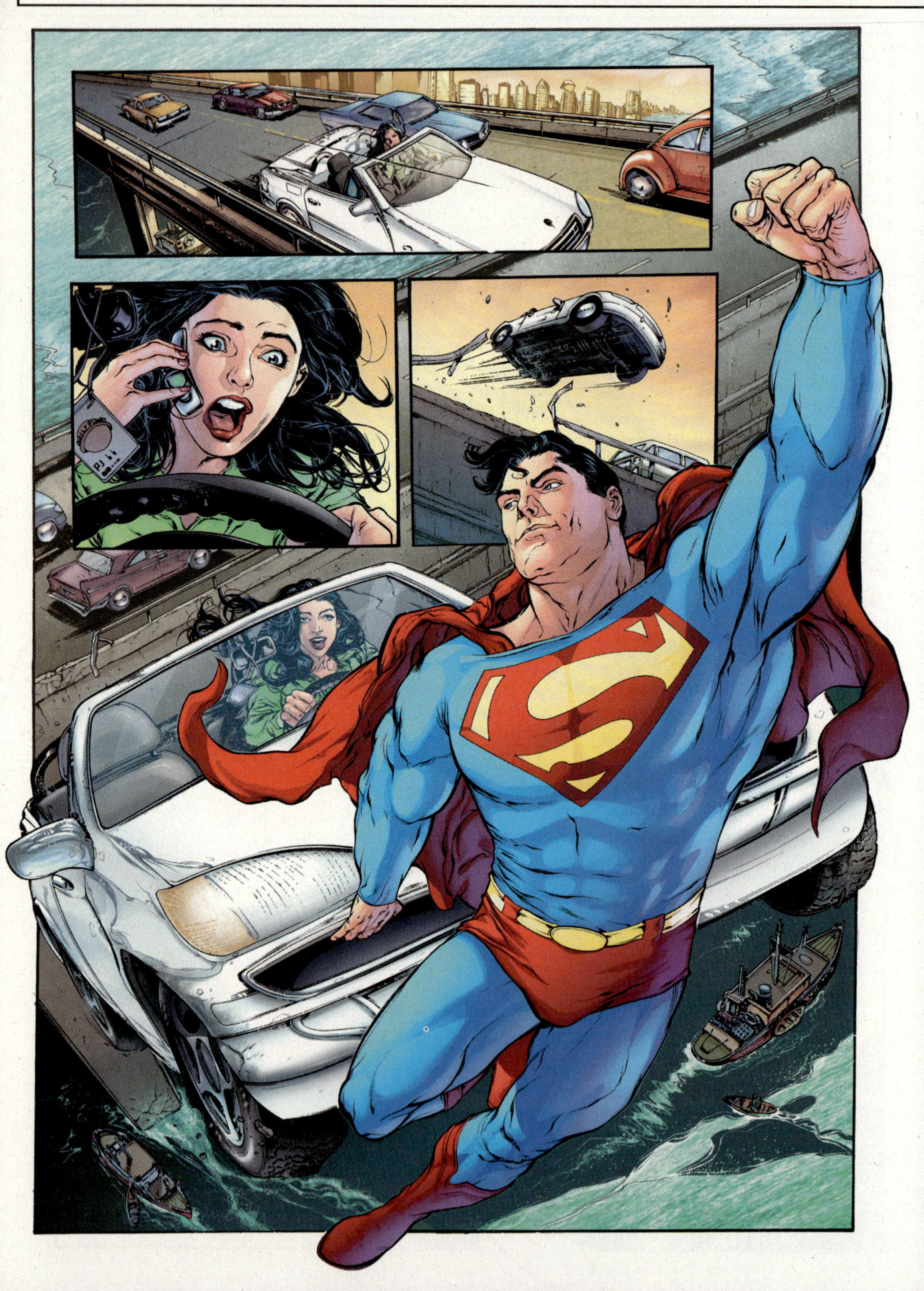

STAGE SIX: FINALLY THE LETTERER (FOR THIS STORY, ROB LEIGH) APPLIES THE WORD BALLOONS, CAPTION BOXES, LOGOS AND TEXT. THE PAGE IS THEN ASSEMBLED WITH THE OTHERS THAT COMPRISE THE REST OF THE STORY!

METROPOLIS.
I'M TELLING YOU... I'VE UNCOVERED WHO'S BEHIND THESE RECENT ATTACKS!
AND MISS BREAKING THE BIGGEST STORY OF THE YEAR? NOT ON YOUR--
SHOULDN'T YOU GO TO THE AUTHORITIES, LOIS?
--LIFE?
LOIS?
SOMETHING'S WRONG WITH THE BRAKES!
NO!!
SUPERMAN!
YOU SHOULD REALLY THINK ABOUT A HANDS-FREE CELL PHONE, LOIS.
Continued in ACTION COMICS

Jerry Siegel's Scripts

ComicConnect.com offered the Man of Steel's co-creator Jerry Siegel's Superman scripts from *Action Comics* #27, *Action Comics* #29, *Action Comics* #30, and *Action Comics* #31 as well as the radio script entitled "Frozen Death" from the *Adventures of Superman* in their August 2012 Event Auction.

While we don't have each stage of their development available as we do with more modern interpretations, it's still interesting to compare these treasured, typed script pages to the finished product, in this case *Action Comics* #29 from October 1940 with art by Jack Burnley.

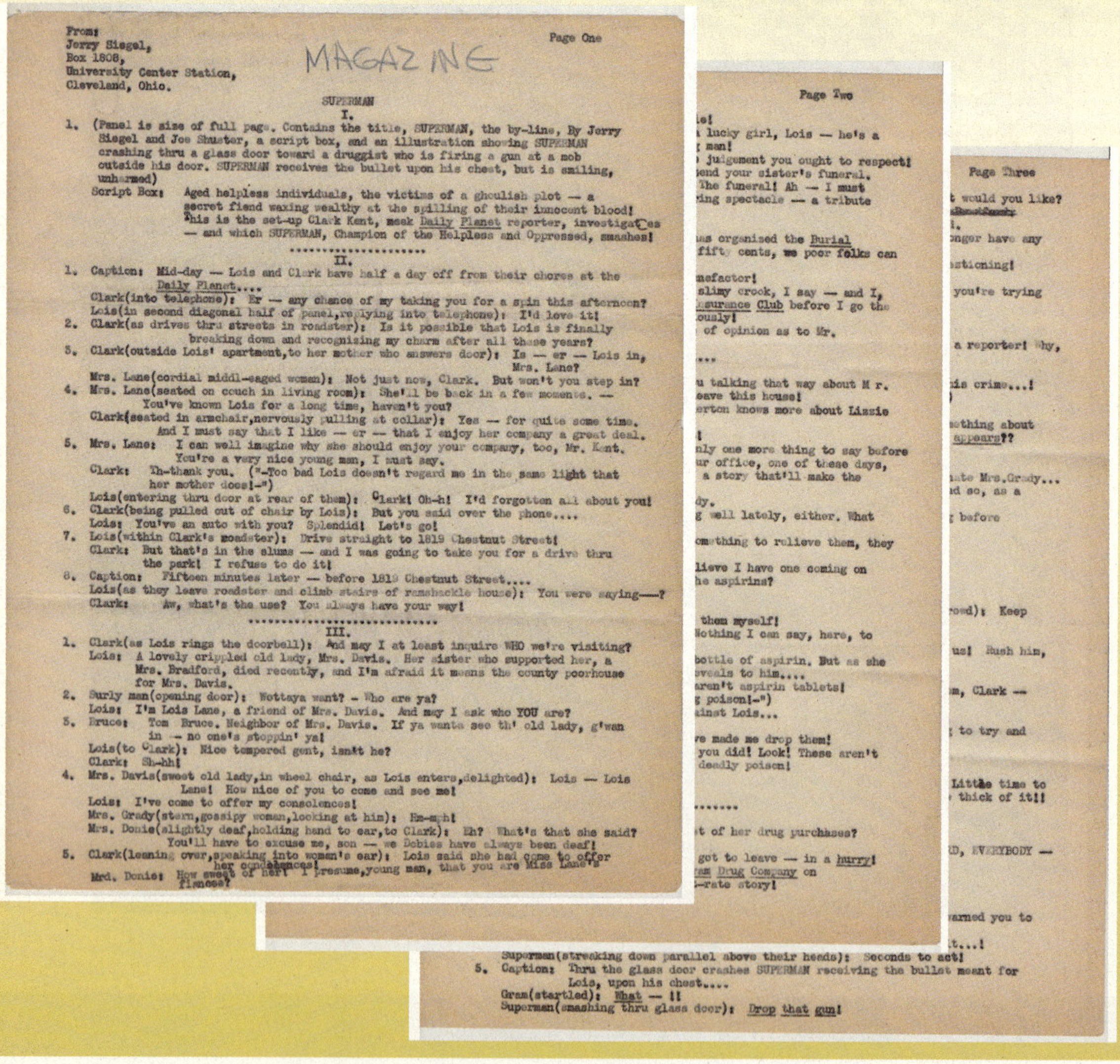

From:
Jerry Siegel,
Box 1808,
University Center Station,
Cleveland, Ohio.

MAGAZINE

Page One

SUPERMAN

I.

1. (Panel is size of full page. Contains the title, SUPERMAN, the by-line, By Jerry Siegel and Joe Shuster, a script box, and an illustration showing SUPERMAN crashing thru a glass door toward a druggist who is firing a gun at a mob outside his door. SUPERMAN receives the bullet upon his chest, but is smiling, unharmed)

Script Box: Aged helpless individuals, the victims of a ghoulish plot — a secret fiend waxing wealthy at the spilling of their innocent blood! This is the set-up Clark Kent, meek Daily Planet reporter, investigates — and which SUPERMAN, Champion of the Helpless and Oppressed, smashes!

II.

1. Caption: Mid-day — Lois and Clark have half a day off from their chores at the Daily Planet....
Clark(into telephone): Er — any chance of my taking you for a spin this afternoon?
Lois(in second diagonal half of panel, replying into telephone): I'd love it!
2. Clark(as drives thru streets in roadster): Is it possible that Lois is finally breaking down and recognizing my charm after all these years?
3. Clark(outside Lois' apartment, to her mother who answers door): Is — er — Lois in, Mrs. Lane?
Mrs. Lane(cordial middl-eaged woman): Not just now, Clark. But won't you step in?
4. Mrs. Lane(seated on couch in living room): She'll be back in a few moments. — You've known Lois for a long time, haven't you?
Clark(seated in armchair, nervously pulling at collar): Yes — for quite some time. And I must say that I like — er — that I enjoy her company a great deal.
5. Mrs. Lane: I can well imagine why she should enjoy your company, too, Mr. Kent. You're a very nice young man, I must say.
Clark: Th-thank you. ("-Too bad Lois doesn't regard me in the same light that her mother does!-")
Lois(entering thru door at rear of them): Clark! Oh-h! I'd forgotten all about you!
6. Clark(being pulled out of chair by Lois): But you said over the phone....
Lois: You've an auto with you? Splendid! Let's go!
7. Lois(within Clark's roadster): Drive straight to 1819 Chestnut Street!
Clark: But that's in the slums — and I was going to take you for a drive thru the park! I refuse to do it!
8. Caption: Fifteen minutes later — before 1819 Chestnut Street....
Lois(as they leave roadster and climb stairs of ramshackle house): You were saying——?
Clark: Aw, what's the use? You always have your way!

III.

1. Clark(as Lois rings the doorbell): And may I at least inquire WHO we're visiting?
Lois: A lovely crippled old lady, Mrs. Davis. Her sister who supported her, a Mrs. Bradford, died recently, and I'm afraid it means the county poorhouse for Mrs. Davis.
2. Surly man(opening door): Wottaya want? - Who are ya?
Lois: I'm Lois Lane, a friend of Mrs. Davis. And may I ask who YOU are?
3. Bruce: Tom Bruce. Neighbor of Mrs. Davis. If ya wanta see th' old lady, g'wan in — no one's stoppin' ya!
Lois(to Clark): Nice tempered gent, isn't he?
Clark: Sh-hh!
4. Mrs. Davis(sweet old lady, in wheel chair, as Lois enters, delighted): Lois — Lois Lane! How nice of you to come and see me!
Lois: I've come to offer my consolences!
Mrs. Grady(stern, gossipy woman, looking at him): Em-mph!
Mrs. Donie(slightly deaf, holding hand to ear, to Clark): Eh? What's that she said? You'll have to excuse me, son — we Dobies have always been deaf!
5. Clark(leaning over, speaking into woman's ear): Lois said she had come to offer her condolences!
Mrs. Donie: How sweet of her! I presume, young man, that you are Miss Lane's fiancee?

Page Two

...! lucky girl, Lois — he's a ... man!
... judgement you ought to respect! ... end your sister's funeral. ... The funeral! Ah — I must ... ing spectacle — a tribute

... as organised the Burial ... fifty cents, we poor folks can

... nefactor! ... slimy crook, I say — and I, ... Insurance Club before I go the ... ously! ... of opinion as to Mr.

... u talking that way about M r. ... leave this house! ... erton knows more about Lizzie

... nly one more thing to say before ... ur office, one of these days, ... a story that'll make the

... dy.

... g well lately, either. What

... omething to relieve them, they

... lieve I have one coming on ... he aspirins?

... them myself! ... Nothing I can say, here, to

... bottle of aspirin. But as she ... reveals to him.... ... aren't aspirin tablets! ... g poison!-") ... ainst Lois...

... ve made me drop them! ... you did! Look! These aren't ... deadly poison!

... t of her drug purchases?

... got to leave — in a hurry! ... Drug Company on ... -rate story!

Page Three

... t would you like?

... nger have any

... stioning!

... you're trying

... a reporter! Why,

... is crime...!

... thing about ... appears??

... ate Mrs. Grady... ... d so, as a

... g before

... road): Keep

... us! Rush him,

... m, Clark —

... to try and

... Little time to ... e thick of it!!

... D, EVERYBODY —

... rned you to

... t...!

Superman(streaking down parallel above their heads): Seconds to act!
5. Caption: Thru the glass door crashes SUPERMAN receiving the bullet meant for Lois, upon his chest....
Gram(startled): What — !!
Superman(smashing thru glass door): Drop that gun!

XIII.

1. Superman(smashing in thru wall): Let me in on this!
   Martin(turning,startled): Who ─── ?
   Bruce(terrified,loosing hold on LOIELMAN): SUPERMAN!
   Lois(to Superman): Am I glad to see YOU!
2. Caption: As the tree criminals flee SUPERMAN heaves a huge desk before them,
            blocking their exit...
   Superman: Stick around!
3. Bruce(crouching in croner in terror,as SUPERMAN advances): No! No!
   Martin(hands up in fear): Don't touch us!!
   Superman(grimly): Don't worry! This won't hurt ─── much!
4. Caption: With lightning-speed, SUPERMAN touches the mobsters upon certain nerves
            so that they drop unconscious....
   Superman(dropping last men): The last man!
   Lois(into telephone): Get me the police!
5. Lois(as Superman rips open great safe with bare hands): Why are you doing that?
   Superman(as performs feat): There'll be enough evidence in here to hang all
                             three of them!
6. Sergeant Casey(entering with other police): What's happening here?
   Superman(leaping away thru window,pointing to Lois): She'll tell you!
   Lois: Martin and those two thugs were behind the Insurance Racket Deaths!
7. Caption: Later...ath the Daily Planet....
   Lois(to Clark): And the best news of all is that the rightful legal heirs will
                   probably get the insurance money, now! That means Mrs. Davis
                   won't go to the poorhouse!
   Clark: What I'd like to know is how you ever managed to get such a swell scoop!
8. Lois(half view of her and Clark): All credit should go to SUPERMAN, for the
                                    assistance he gave me!
   Clark: ─── I wish SUPERMAN would give ME assistance like that, sometime!
   Small script box in lower right hand bottom corner of panel: The End.

• •

From:
Jerry Siegel,
Box 1808,
University Center Station,
Cleveland, Ohio.

Special thanks to Rob Reynolds, Director of Consignments for ComicConnect.com, for the quality scans of the script pages.

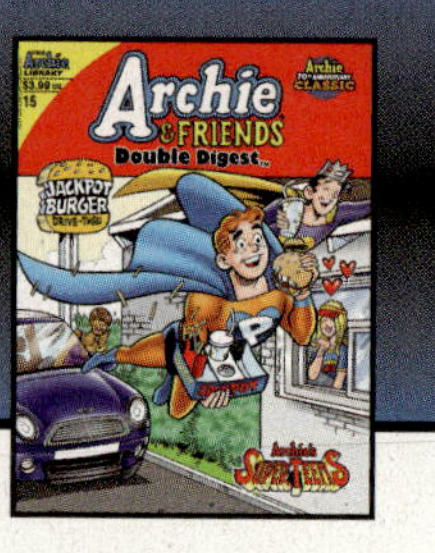

By J.C. Vaughn

Think about your favorite comic book character. You don't have to follow the crowd. You can pick anyone from the most obscure to the most popular. After all, it's *your* favorite that we're talking about.

Batman. Spider-Man. Superman. Captain America. Green Lantern. Iron Man. Green Arrow. Harbinger. Wolverine. Catwoman. Thor. Static. Cerebus. The Flash. The Incredible Hulk. G.I. Joe. The Teen Titans. Uncle Scrooge.

Painkiller Jane. The Spirit. The Avengers. Nexus. Richie Rich. The Justice League of America. Cerebus. The Rocketeer. Zorro. Bone. Shi. The Punisher. CyberForce. X-O Manowar. Sam & Max, Freelance Police. Fighting American.

Shadowman. Hardcase. Badrock. The Fish Police. Superboy. Rom, Space Knight. Supergirl. The Defenders. Young Justice. The Champions. The Badger. Firearm. Magnus Robot Fighter. The Micronauts. Starslayer. Daredevil. Somerset Holmes. The Human Fly. Shogun Warriors. Godzilla. Mickey Mouse.

These characters and so many others populate both the successful comic book universes and those less fortunate. What they have in common is that just about every character or group of characters is *someone's* favorite, and that collecting by character presents some great opportunities and potentially some massive challenges.

How are you going to define exactly what your collecting goal is? The best part about this, though, is that *you* make the rules and *you* set the goals.

So, you can collect a moderately popular character that has had very few appearances such as The Rocketeer or the Fighting American. You can collect a character who has (with few exceptions) been a team member and rarely a solo character, such as The Vision at Marvel or Cyborg at DC.

Aside from *Sgt. Fury and His Howling Commandos*, Nick Fury's various series at Marvel have never run very long. The char-

acter, however, has been integral to many Marvel adventures over the years and might make a tantalizing focus for a back-issue hunt. Or you could collect Krypto and the other super-pets at DC or the superhero versions of Archie and the gang from Riverdale.

The keys are first and foremost to enjoy yourself and to be flexible. Publishers are switching things up more and more frequently these days. Whereas *The Cat* became *Tigra* not too far into her career and that sort of stood out for years, in more recent times we've had Kyle Rayner as Green Lantern, Hal Jordan as the villain Parallax, Bucky Barnes as Captain America, Wally West as the Flash, Dick Grayson as Batman, and so on.

As characters change identities or reboots wipe out whole parcels or even all of a character's back story – like Power Girl or the Huntress after *Crisis on Infinite Earths* – you can take those changes as the opportunity to wrap up that distinct, character-based set, or those same events can be the reason to expand or redefine your goals.

If, for instance, you were a big *New Teen Titans* fan back in the day and have dozens of original convention sketches of Robin kissing Starfire, well, then you probably don't even want to explain to younger readers that it's not *that* Robin and yes, they were an item. Since several different characters have been Robin, perhaps you would only want to collect the Dick Grayson Robin and then spin that into a pursuit of Nightwing.

Collecting by character is, of course, just one more way to define how you collect. It also brings up other questions as well. For instance, if you say you collect Superman, does that mean that you collect the Superman toys as well? Or are you just collecting the Man of Steel's comics?

There is no single answer to that, but it can be fun getting to your own personal conclusion.

THE KID WHO COLLECTS
SPIDER-MAN

BY
CHARLIE
NOVINSKIE

It started simply enough: a tattered, brown grocery bag with 20 comic books inside. Not so much a collection, but rather a nudge in the right direction. Now, forty-four years later, that simple gesture of being given a bag full of comics has grown into a collection of well over 20,000 comics.

A sampling of issues from *Amazing Spider-Man* #38-51: quite a way to start a comic collection.

It always starts with something little, insignificant at the time if you think about it. But from the time that that first seed is planted—if properly cared for—can grow into a utopia. That's how it pretty much happened to me. The year was 1968 and I was a typical fifth grader enjoying typical fifth-grade pleasures.

Collecting comic books was one of those pleasures. Plenty of kids grew up reading comics, but very few had that spark to turn it into a lifetime passion. That bag of comics was indeed the spark that sent me down the path of comic collecting—and why not, the mystery bag, which I had traded for, contained a beautiful run of then current comics, *Amazing Spider-Man* to be specific. Imagine being 10 years old and being handed *Amazing Spider-Man* #31-50! Wild horses couldn't drag me from my bedroom that weekend as I devoured the comics like a contestant in a hot dog eating contest!

It wasn't just the adventures of Spider-Man, but the villains—the Green Goblin, the Molten Man, Kingpin, Kraven the Hunter—and wow, the first Mary Jane story; I was introduced to the Marvel universe and that's where I wanted to stay. After all, the talents of Stan Lee, Steve Ditko and John Romita, Sr. made the adventures leap off the pages! I was hooked on Marvel Comics, Spider-Man in particular!

The bonus for me was that Peter Parker was like a real teenager, he experienced life's ups and downs and did it in such a way that you really cared about what was going to happen to him next. In many ways, Peter Parker was the precursor to what my life was going to be like in a few short years. (True, I was never bitten by a radioactive spider and give the proportionate strength of a spider, but I did experience the bullying in school, the cruelness of your peers, and even the adventures of dating). The fact that Peter Parker was also Spider-Man was like the icing on the cake.

Early-day comic collecting was also an adventure: no eBay, no online subscription services, comic specialty shops, nope, none of that, comic collecting in the 1960s entailed an intricate race against time to visit every newsstand and mom and pop shop in a five mile radius to hunt down all of your favorite comics. Oh, there was the option to buy your comics directly from Marvel by subscribing, but who wanted to get a comic in the mail that had a crease down the middle because of how they folded them when shipping them?

It was Richard Howell that coined the phrase, "Marvel Zombie," although I think he might have meant it to be a bit derogatory towards people that blindly purchased all Marvel comics regardless of quality or content. As for me, I wore the badge of Marvel Zombie proudly, after all, I know what I enjoyed and it was definitely Marvel Comics. Not only were those books in the sixties classics in the making, but they had Stan Lee as head huckster—a guy that could make *Team America* sound like a great book!

Through it all, I still had Spider-Man as my top tier book. If I could only buy one book a month (and thankfully I could always buy more), Spider-Man would always be the first choice. The flagship title will always be *Amazing*, but when books like *Marvel Team-Up*, *Peter Parker,*

The Spectacular Spider-Man, the adjective-less *Spider-Man* and a plethora of others sprang up, I had to add them to my collection. Collect 'em, read 'em, enjoy 'em, that's the motto of a true collector! By Marvel's own count, taking all of the books featuring Spider-Man—one-shots, mini-series, Point One issues and so on, there are 1,757 comics featuring the adventures of Peter Parker as I write this (more already by the time you read it), and I have most of them. That's what a collector does, he collects!

I find that there are two types of true collectors in the world. First, those that find something at an early age who receive so much pleasure and enjoyment in something that they stick with it clear into adulthood. The second type of collector is much older, someone that has a fondness for something from their childhood that they now miss but want to collect to relive those days of innocence when they were growing up.

I'm thankful for being part of the first group of collectors—those that, at an early age, developed a love for something and was able to hang on for a lifetime. Unlike collectors that purchase things from their childhood for the fond memories, I'm able to live that deja vu quality of what it was

When more Spider-titles sprang up, it meant there was more to collect.

like to experience reading that comic the day it was put on sale—re-reading it instantly transports me to that time of my youth allowing me to re-experience that exuberance that we sort of lose in adulthood.

The bottom line is that the purest collector hangs on to things that bring them great pleasure with no thought of what value their collection might bring in today's marketplace. For me, comics of the '60s and '70s are the best ever produced, because I grew up in that era. After all, we all have fond attachments for things in our childhood.

It doesn't matter how you collect or what you collect—some people collect comic books, or, like myself, certain comic characters, like Spider-Man. Others collect original artwork, or follow the work of a particular writer or artist. The main focus is that no one can tell you what to collect, no one can decide for you. It truly is a personal decision based on personal preference. If collecting it makes you happy, then that's what you should collect.

Amazing Spider-Man has just surpassed the 700-issue mark, and I can look back over the decades at the nearly 700-issue run in my collection and fondly remember all of the enjoyment that I've received from reading and re-reading these comics. The most important factor in collecting is that it is fun, and that it should remain fun.

With warmest regards to Roger Stern, Ron Frenz, and Terry Austin for *Amazing Spider-Man* #248.

One of the many ways to collect is following a specific character or group of characters. Collecting high profile creations such as Spider-Man, Batman, Superman, The X-Men or many others will keep a reader busy since they have multiple new titles and many older ones as well. While other characters might have a slightly lower profile, the task can still remain a worthy challenge, particularly when one is dedicated to getting everything associated with the character and not just the comic books themselves.

With a name like Magnus, it might seem automatic for collector Magnus Ramström to be interested in Magnus, Robot Fighter. It didn't start out that way, though. Like many Europeans, he first started with a healthy love of the Disney Ducks. In fact, he didn't even become familiar with Russ Manning's creation until he was on this side of the pond.

That late start, however, didn't stop him from becoming in the opinion of many other collectors the top collector of the character in the world.

"Here in Sweden it was kind of obvious, almost taken for granted, that kids read Donald Duck and/or the Swedish comic *Bamse, the World's Strongest Bear*. My parents got me a subscription to Donald earlier than I can remember, and I still enjoy the duck stories. When I started school, me and my friends turned to superhero comics. At that time four DC comics were reprinted in Swedish. I read them all and later some Marvels. The books with teams were my early favorites (Legion of Super-Heroes and Justice League of America); later Spider-Man became more popular," Ramström said.

Then, in 1994 after moving the States, he happened to see a comic shop.

"I could not resist it and found lots of comics reminding me of my youth. I also found back issues of VALIANT's Magnus. That was a huge discovery for me and it was just the beginning. I still had Gold Key's Magnus to discover as well as the rest of the VALIANT universe (and basically all about how comics had developed in the decade I had missed). Especially [Jim] Shooter's writing impressed me so much that I wanted to learn more," he said.

After acquiring the VALIANT run of the character, he expanded and sought out the original Gold Key series. Since neither is a particularly long run, once that mission was completed, he turned to other VALIANT titles, then DEFIANT and other Gold Key series, international editions and more.

"Most important is that my habits have grown to represent how comics are created and the community of creators and fans," he said. He also expanded into Magnus-related original comic book art.

"Pencils, inks, colors, panel pages, splashes, covers, card art, published, unpublished, commissions and so on, preferably representing every aspect of the creation process that I have learned to admire so much," he said.

His collection includes some original Gold Key covers, covers and interiors from key VALIANT issues, concept pieces, private commissions and more, enough to make another fan green with envy. That said, neither these pieces nor the comics are what he thinks is best about collecting. What is?

"The community! To get in contact with people having the same tastes as me and to be part of discussions on forums and over email. Sometimes of course discussions can get rough, as even creators have experienced, but often, so much more often, one experiences how people help and care for each other," Ramström said. And the creators. I have had such good times talking, emailing and even meeting with creators. That's just so cool beyond words."

Collector Magnus Ramström with Frank Bolle's unpublished cover for Gold Key's *Magnus Robot Fighter #47*.

ELRIC
of Melniboné

While characters like Superman or Spider-Man reside with their original publishers, many characters from the Golden Age and many others from the creator-owned era have been produced under numerous imprints. This can make collecting all the appearances of a specific character a worthy challenge.

Few characters have had as diverse a comic book publishing history as Michael Moorcock's sword-and-sorcery fantasy anti-hero Elric. Like Conan, in whose title his first comic book appearance came, Elric was first introduced in the world of prose fiction (writer Roy Thomas, who has long been associated with both characters, was the driving force in getting both into the four color world).

Elric was a manifestation of Moorcock's "Eternal Champion," who at other times would be embodied by his characters Hawkmoon, Corum, Jerry Cornelius and numerous others, walking between the forces of order and chaos.

Notable runs for the character have come at Pacific Comics, First Comics, Topps Comics, Dark Horse Comics, and DC Comics. Elric was most recently published by BOOM! Studios.

Conan The Barbarian #14-15
Marvel Comics; 1972

Elric #1
Windy City Publications; 1973

The Jewel in the Skull
Big O Publishing; 1978
(UK graphic novel, first Hawkmoon)

Marvel Graphic Novel #2: Elric: The Dreaming City
Marvel Comics; 1982

Elric of Melnibone #1-6
Pacific Comics; April 1983 – April 1984

Elric: The Sailor on the Seas of Fate #1-7
First Comics; June 1985 – June 1986

First Comics Graphic Novel #6 - Elric of Melnibone
First Comics; May 1986
Signed & Numbered HC by Graphitti Designs

Elric: Weird of the White Wolf #1-5
First Comics; October 1986 – June 1987

**First Comics Graphic Novel #11:
Elric: The Sailor on the Seas of Fate**
First Comics; August 1987
Signed & Numbered HC by Graphitti Designs

Elric: The Vanishing Tower #1-6
First Comics; August 1987 – June 1988

Elric: The Bane of the Black Sword #1-6
First Comics; August 1988 – June 1989

First Comics Graphic Novel #21: Elric: Weird of the White Wolf
First Comics; September 1990
Signed & Numbered HC by Graphitti Designs

Elric #0
Topps Comics; 1996

Elric: Stormbringer #1-7
Dark Horse Comics/Topps Comics; 1997

Michael Moorcock's Multiverse #1-12
DC Comics/Helix; November 1997 – October 1998

Michael Moorcock's Multiverse
DC Comics/Vertigo; 1999

Michael Moorcock's Elric: The Making of a Sorcerer
#1-4
DC Comics; 2004 – 2006
TPB *2007*

Hawkmoon and Corum were also featured in mini-series from First Comics.

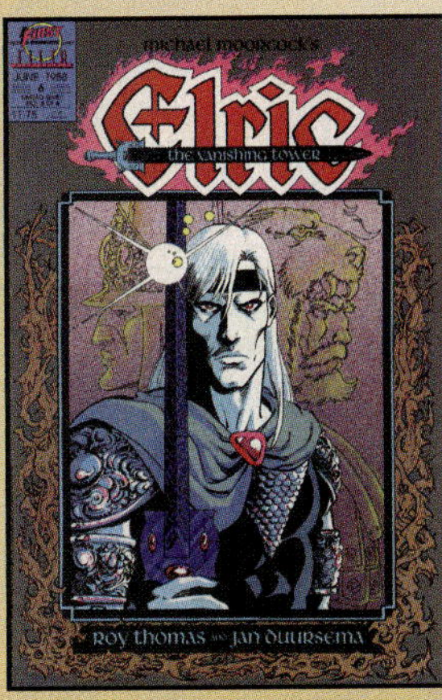

REBOOTS

By Scott Braden
& J.C. Vaughn

The success of rebooting characters and bringing them into a new comic book universe didn't start in 2011 with DC Comics' "New 52." In fact, this successful phenomenon is only the latest attempt to take established heroes, polish them up, and use them again in a whole new way.

The New 52 – with its young Superman and godly Wonder Woman – garnered major success, set the start of this incarnation of the DC universe just five years ago, and was ostensibly aimed at making the DC heroes more accessible to readers.

But truth be told, this is no different in concept than when Stan Lee and his "House of Ideas" created the "Marvel Age of Comics," or when DC editor Julie Schwartz heralded the Silver Age by rebooting the Golden Age incarnations of DC's top superheroes.

The excitement of DC's then-new Flash and Green Lantern in the dawn of the Silver Age led to a wholesale revival of the company's superhero line. Even the company's premiere super-team, the Justice League of America, was a modernization of the first superhero team, the Justice Society of America.

Marvel, for its part, sometimes used only the names of the characters, seeing the Golden Age android Human Torch replaced by the young Johnny Storm Human Torch in the pages of *Fantastic Four* #1. Not too many years after that, the names Vision and Black Widow resurfaced at Marvel with little relation to the originals.

When the character Captain America was revived in *Avengers* #4 and when the Sub-Mariner appeared in *Fantastic Four* #4, they were not new versions of the characters but instead were the originals. The story of Captain America's disappearance and his sidekick Bucky's demise at the end of World War II, though, did in fact create the need for a substantial retro-continuity change since in the real world Cap's adventures had continued through the end of the war and even experienced a strange, brief revival in the 1950s. It took many twists and turns over

DC's New 52, accessible to a new generation of readers.

more than a decade of real time to fill in the continuity gaps and explain what had happened. The Sub-Mariner's youth and vitality decades later was an easier explanation. As a human-Atlantean hybrid, a mutant, he had a longer lifespan as well as incredible power.

Over a period of decades, DC has acquired entire catalogs of other comic book publishers and introduced them into their universe with varying levels of success. There were the Quality and Fawcett comics heroes, including Captain Marvel, Spy Smasher, Bulletman, Blackhawk, Uncle Sam, Black Condor, and Doll Man, among others.

Although no such time of heroes existed at Quality, Len Wein and Dick Dillin assembled the former Quality characters into *The Freedom Fighters*, who initially resided on Earth X (probably not the Marvel *Earth X*, but you can see how this might get confusing) and then were

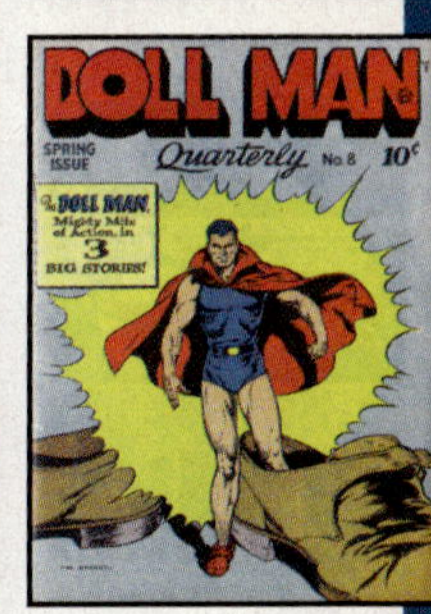

The Quality characters found new life as the Freedom Fighters from Earth X.

cast adrift for a period when *Crisis on Infinite Earths* came along and wiped out the multiple realities in favor of a unified world. Later they were simply integrated into DC's war-era heroes. They were also revived more recently as well.

For the 1980s (and in terms of lasting effect), reboots don't get much bigger than *Crisis on Infinite Earths*. It brought the characters onto a more manageable stage and gave them generational counterparts. For instance, you had the retired or semi-retired Golden Age Flash and Green Lantern occasionally popping up alongside their present day replacements.

While streamlining their continuity, *Crisis* also was used to introduce another library of characters DC had acquired, the Charlton superheroes such as Captain Atom, Blue Beetle, The Question, Peacemaker, Judomaster, and Nightshade. Blue Beetle himself is a case study in reboots. The original Blue Beetle was Dan Garrett, whose adventures were published by Fox. When Fox quit publishing, they sold the character to Charlton. Eventually they launched a new Blue Beetle, Ted Kord, who was said to be one of Garrett's students.

It was the Ted Kord Blue Beetle who first

Too many incarnations of the same character can necessitate some cleanup.

appeared at DC, but years later, he would be replaced by young Jaime Reyes, who has survived long enough (just a few years really) to be reconfigured as part of the New 52. *[**Editor's note:** If you want to see the three Blue Beetles in action, check out the story following this article.]*

And don't think that it's only DC doing it. Marvel's "Ultimate" universe gave us the first African-American Nick Fury and new versions of Spider-Man, the Fantastic Four, The X-Men, the Avengers (called "The Ultimates") and so on. Then they killed the Ultimate version of Peter Parker and replaced him with another character as Spider-Man. As we've been wrapping up this book, Marvel has been announcing their big changes with their "Marvel Now" initiative.

Magnus Robot Fighter, *Doctor Solar, Man of the Atom*, and *Turok, Son of Stone*, had their original incarnations at Gold Key, second versions during Valiant's original incarnation, third versions during Valiant's Acclaim Comics era, and most recently were brought back by Dark Horse (joined there by the Mighty Samson, who was not part of the Valiant revival).

Valiant itself, of course, has been the subject of a revival, having launched initially the early '90s. They rebooted in the mid-1990s after being acquired by videogame maker Acclaim Entertainment. They attempted

Some of Marvel's Ultimate line of characters.

a reboot again in 2000 (with a great premise for how to do these sorts of things). The Valiant name and characters were acquired out of Acclaim's bankruptcy, and the new Valiant has launched a number of their familiar characters in new titles. *[Editor's note: You will find information about them in both our "Collecting By Company" and "Fan To Pro" sections].*

Dynamite has created universes out of many (at least theoretically) public domain Golden Age characters and Jack Kirby's creator-owned characters (Topps had a Kirbyverse previously). DC has licensed T.H.U.N.D.E.R. Agents. Archie has licensed their Red Circle superhero characters to DC in two separate instances and have now relaunched them themselves.

All of these instances of ret-con (retro continuity) or reboots provide natural jumping on or jumping off points for fans. Some of the fun may come in trying to figure out when a title has been changed just to get the spike in sales thought to accompany a new first issue, and when it's really starting over. Marvel's Captain America might be a great case study in this.

The "Marvel Now" series *Captain America* will be the tenth on-going title to feature the Star Spangled Avenger. While some of them have been short-lived, others have spanned decades. They include *Captain America Comics* (1941-1950, 1954), *Captain America* (1968-1996), *Captain America* (1996-1997, "Heroes Reborn"), *Captain America* (1998-2002, "Heroes Return"), Captain *America: Sentinel of Liberty* (1998-1999), *Captain America* (2002-2004, "Marvel Knights"), Captain *America and The Falcon* (2004-2005), and *Captain America* (2005 - 2011).

Following *Captain America* #50, the 2005 series took the cumulative issues

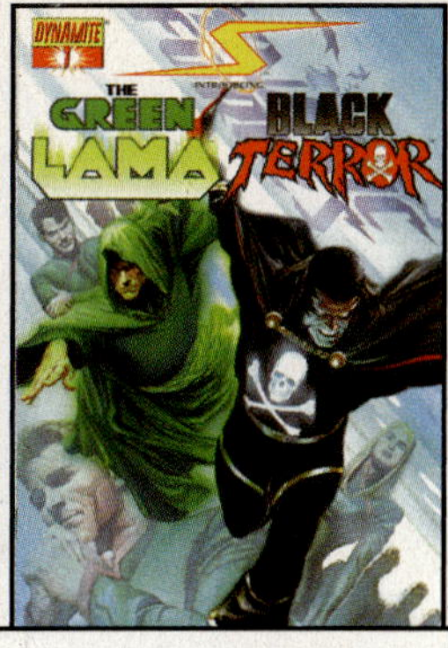

Golden Age characters in the public domain, like The Black Terror, were ripe for revival by Dynamite Entertainment.

and adopted the number of the 1968 series, making the following issue *Captain America* #600 in keeping with the character's raised profile, Marvel's 70th corporate anniversary, and the then-upcoming Marvel Studios *Captain America* film.

Following *Captain America* #619, Marvel decided to introduce a new Captain America series with *Captain America* #1 (the ninth series), so *Captain America* (eighth series) changed its title to *Captain America & Bucky* with #620, followed by *Captain America & Hawkeye* (one story arc), *Captain America & Iron Man* (one story arc), *Captain America & Namor* (one issue), and *Captain America & Black Widow* (one story arc).

Of these, *Captain America Comics* and the Silver Age *Captain America* represent two different takes on the same character, with the anomalies of the 1950s revival explained away with new story elements later. After that, the only distinctly different Cap prior to "Marvel Now" was the "Heroes Reborn" version, although the Marvel Knights version didn't entirely square with other stories.

Regardless, there's fun to be had in collecting any or all of them. Even if you can't quite figure them all out.

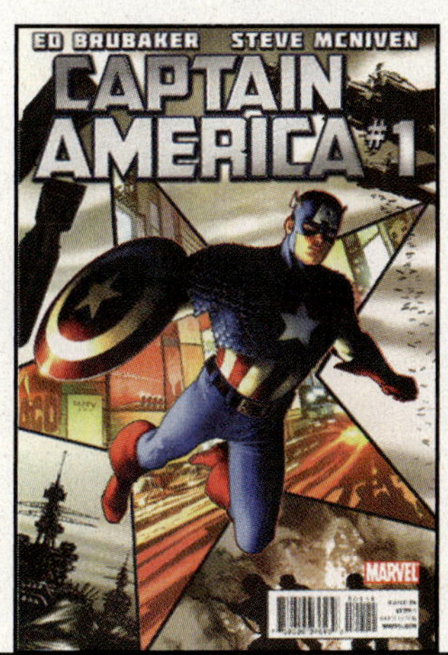

One of the recent reboots, *Captain America* #1 from 2011.

CHRISTMAS WITH THE BEETLES

writer: J.C. VAUGHN   pencils: LEE GARBETT
inks: TREVOR SCOTT   color: PETE PANTAZIS   letterer: TRAVIS LANHAM

TODAY. SANCHEZ STATE JAIL, EL PASO, TEXAS.

A 1,001-BED FACILITY FOR MEN INCARCERATED IN THE EL PASO AREA.

RICHARD! I'M REALLY GLAD YOU CAME, SON!

KRAK

UT
BAM

KA-POW!

HAPPY HANUKKAH
MERRY CHRISTMAS
SO I SUPPOSE THERE'S A GOOD REASON YOU WANTED ME TO DRAG MYSELF DOWN HERE ON CHRISTMAS EVE?

YOU'RE NOT GOING ANYWHERE EXCEPT JAIL, CREEP.

ONE PUNCH! ONE PUNCH!
WHERE'S BATMAN WHEN YOU REALLY NEED HIM TO SEE SOMETHING?
I SWEAR I DIDN'T DO ANYTHING, MOM...
SUBJECT NO LONGER COHERENT.
I KNOW! I DIDN'T EVEN HIT HIM THAT HARD!

LOOK, I KNOW YOU DON'T WANT TO BE HERE, AND I KNOW I'VE BEEN A LOUSY DAD.
AND I KNOW THERE WERE PLENTY OF CHRISTMASES THAT I LET YOU DOWN...
JUST LIKE A LOT OF OTHER DAYS.

ALL MY LIFE I'VE BEEN MAKING EXCUSES. I'M DONE WITH THAT.
TODAY I JUST WANT TO TELL YOU WHY I THINK THINGS HAVE HAPPENED THE WAY THEY HAVE.

MY GRANDFATHER DONNIE FOUGHT THE FIRST BLUE BEETLE AND LOST.
MY FATHER FOUGHT THE SECOND BLUE BEETLE AND LOST.
AND YOU FOUGHT THE NEW BLUE BEETLE AND LOST?

NOT ONLY DID I GET BUSTED BY THE NEW BLUE BEETLE, I MOVED MY FAMILY ACROSS THE COUNTRY TO AVOID GETTING BUSTED BY THE BLUE BEETLE...
AND STILL GOT TAKEN DOWN BY HIM.
GREAT. A FAMILY OF THREE-TIME LOSERS. AT LEAST I'VE GOT THAT GOING FOR ME.
COLE

I'VE BUSTED YOU TWICE NOW, MAN, AND I HAVEN'T BEEN DOING THIS THAT LONG.
HAVE YOU CONSIDERED ANOTHER LINE OF WORK? YOU'RE JUST NOT THAT GOOD AT THIS ONE...

YOU'RE RIGHT, SON.

AND I JUST DON'T WANT YOU TO END UP LIKE US.

WHOA, DAD, THAT'S NOT HAPPENING TO ME. JUST BECAUSE YOU GUYS--

MY GRANDFATHER WAS A HARD MAN. MY OLD MAN WAS AN ABSOLUTE PSYCHO. THEY BOTH KNEW THE GAME THEY WERE PLAYING.

BUT I WASN'T MEANT FOR THIS KIND OF LIFE. I KNEW IT, I DIDN'T DO ANYTHING ABOUT IT, AND HERE I AM.
NOW, UNLIKE A LOT OF YEARS, I ACTUALLY HAVE SOMETHING FOR YOU THIS CHRISTMAS.

YOU'RE GOING TO START BEING A GOOD DAD NOW? FROM PRISON?

I'M GOING TO TRY.

SO WHAT'S THIS BIG SPECIAL PRESENT YOU HAVE FOR ME, DAD? A SHIV? A PACK OF SMOKES?

I WANT YOU TO WALK AWAY FROM ALL OF THIS. TAKE YOUR MOTHER IF YOU CAN, BUT GET YOURSELF OUT AND DO IT NOW.
YOU'RE NOT MEANT FOR THIS LIFE EITHER. EVEN IF YOU NEVER SEE ME AGAIN.
BUT I'M NOT--

I KNOW YOU'RE HANGING WITH VENDO'S CREW AND HE'S PLANNING A BIG JOB.
BUT HOW--

I HAVE FRIENDS. IT HASN'T GONE DOWN YET. YOU STILL DON'T HAVE A RECORD AND THAT'S WHY YOU STILL HAVE A CHANCE, RICHARD.

From "DC Universe Holiday Special" #1 © 2009 DC Comics. Used with Permission. BLUE BEETLE is ™ DC Comics.

I've always enjoyed writing comics and this was my first chance to do it for DC, so I was very excited. And pretty quickly I got the idea of how to involve the Golden Age, Silver Age and modern Blue Beetles in one story.

Once I had decided to do that and the editors had approved it, I also wanted to throw in real nods to the originals. So if you look on the fourth page of this story, you'll see that the Dan Garrett image recreates a close-up on *Mystery Men Comics* #8, the iconic Ted Kord image was inspired by *Blue Beetle* #1 (1986), and the Jaime Reyes image, which at the time was a lot more recent, was from *Blue Beetle* #1 (2006).

Pencil artist Lee Garbett, who has since gone on to do the best-selling *Batman: The Return of Bruce Wayne* story arc, and inker Trevor Scott seemed to really get into the spirit of it.

— *J.C. Vaughn*

IT'S A WHOLE NEW GUIDE!

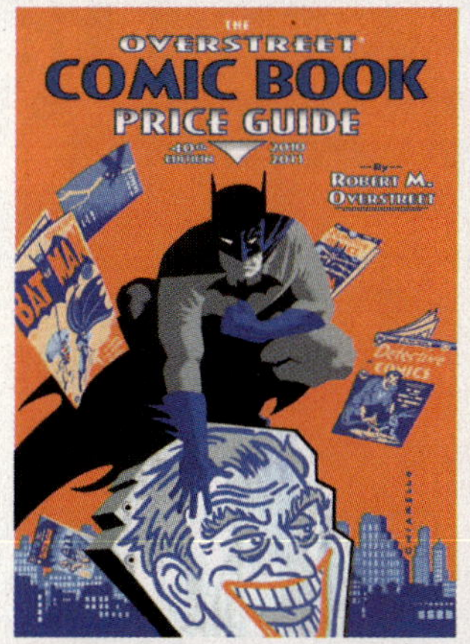
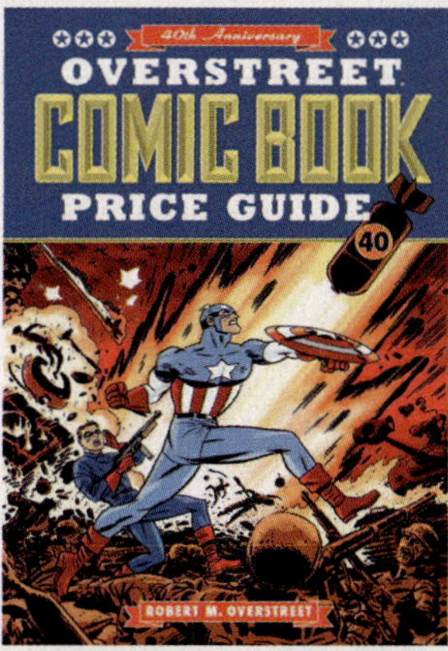

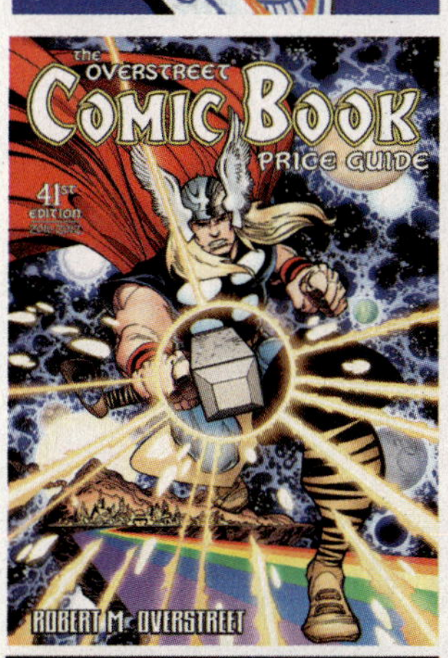

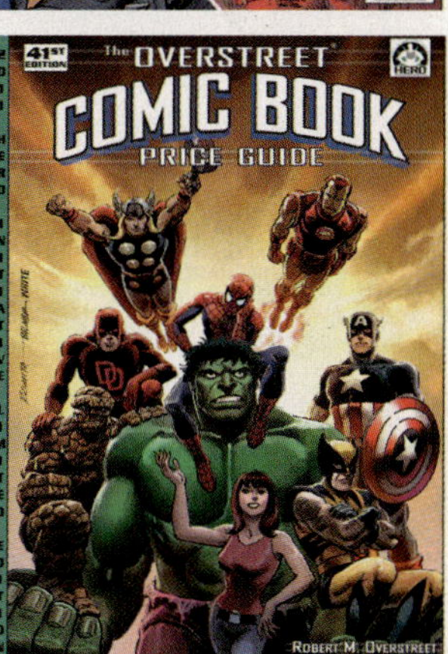

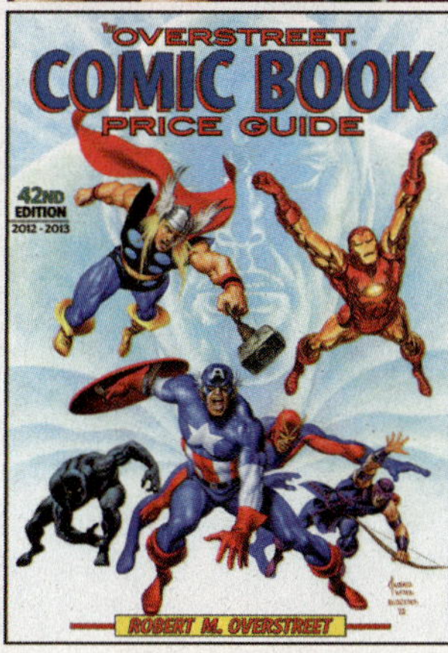
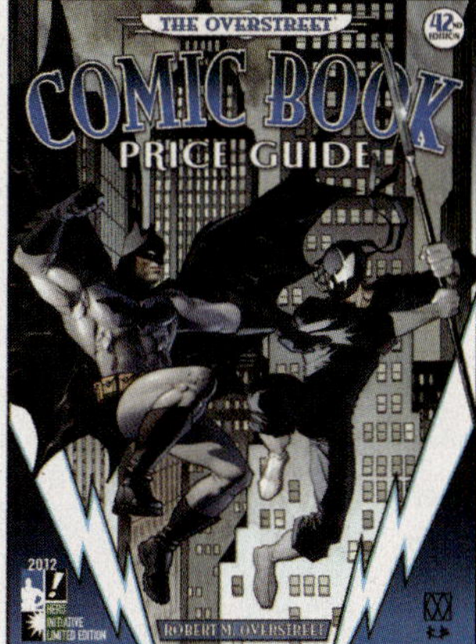

An Annual tradition since 1970!

www.gemstonepub.com

Collecting by Genre

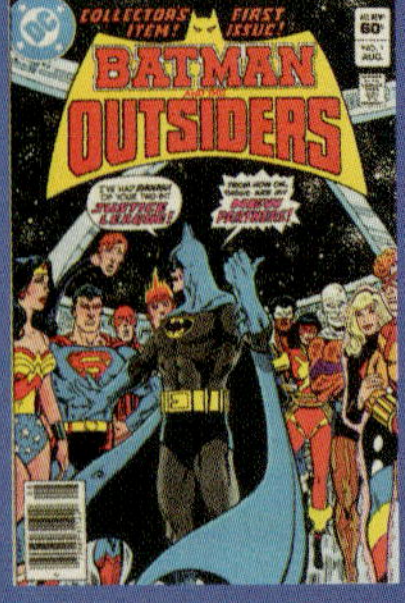

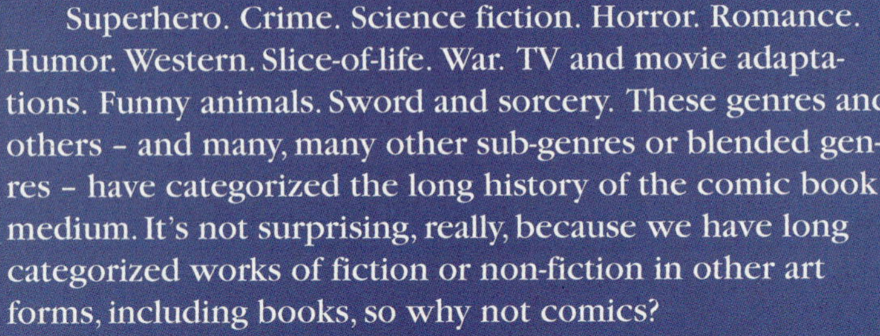

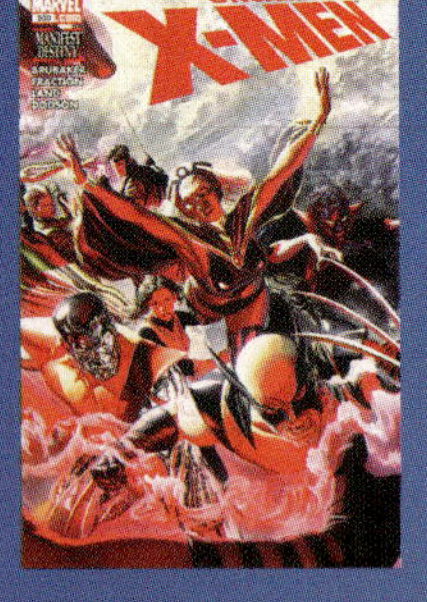

Superhero. Crime. Science fiction. Horror. Romance. Humor. Western. Slice-of-life. War. TV and movie adaptations. Funny animals. Sword and sorcery. These genres and others – and many, many other sub-genres or blended genres – have categorized the long history of the comic book medium. It's not surprising, really, because we have long categorized works of fiction or non-fiction in other art forms, including books, so why not comics?

Since "collecting everything" is left to kings and billionaires, the rest of us are left to segment our collections into manageable goals. Collecting by genre (or by sub-genre) offers one possible avenue for approaching comic book collecting.

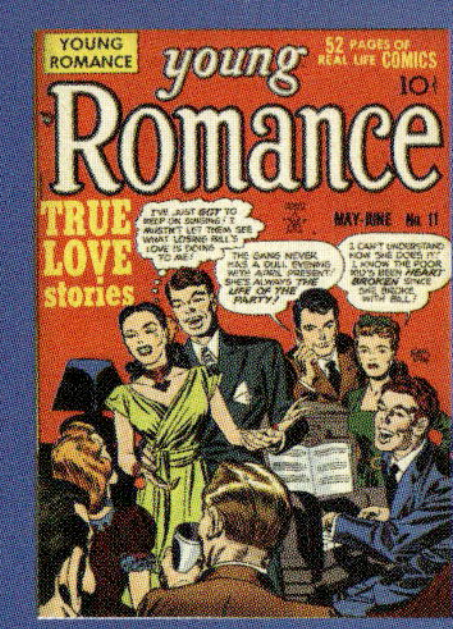

The biggest slice of the comic book market for the last few decades has been superhero comics. In its earliest days, Humor and slice-of-life titles were the best sellers. Neither category ever successfully locked up 100% of the market, thank goodness, so for most of the history of the medium there's been a variety of types of comics available.

Because superhero comics have been so dominant since the early 1970s, collecting all of them is an almost impossible ambition. Collecting sub-genes, such as Marvel's mutants or Avengers-related titles, collecting DC's Big Five War titles or the Romance comics of the 1950s, '60s and '70s.

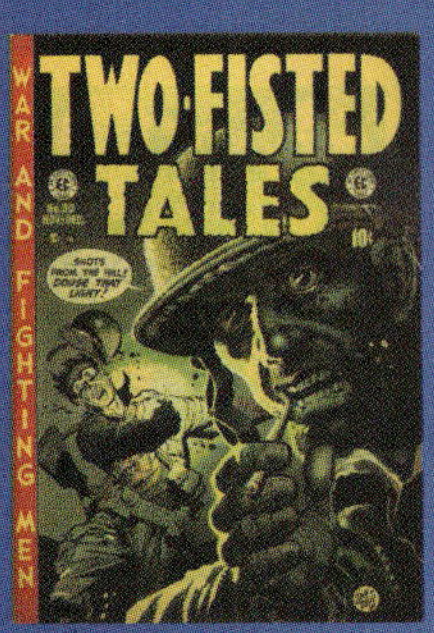

If you're already a superhero fan who is looking to expand, you'll find familiar creators have worked in these other genres, whether it's John Buscema's art in *Savage Sword of Conan*, Frank Miller's work in *Sin City*, Adam Hughes' early work on *Maze Agency*, or Jack Kirby and Joe Simon's ground-breaking Romance comics.

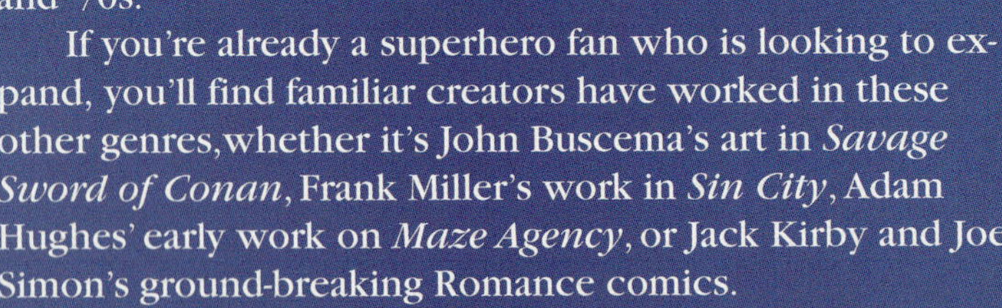

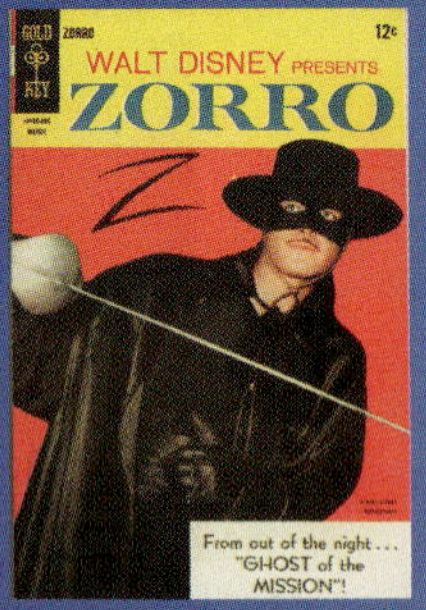

The post-World War II era saw a decade-long decline of the superheroes. That same period gave birth to the flying saucer craze, as well as new generations of movie monsters, military adventure, westerns and numerous other genres. All of them very quickly made their way into comics with lasting effect and remain great niches today.

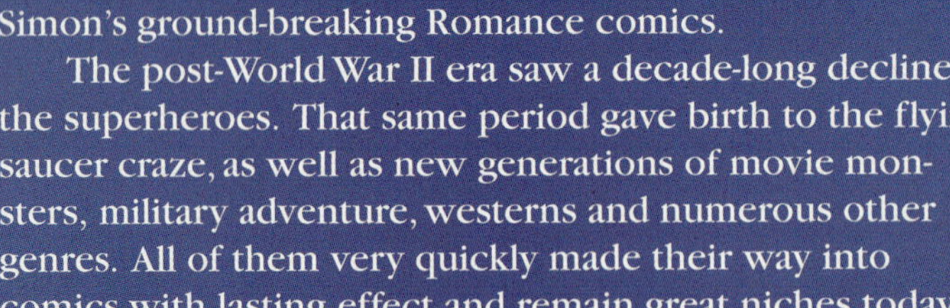

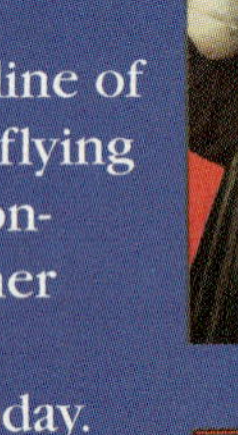

TV and movie adaptations, though they actually could be cross-listed in many other categories, can be considered a category to themselves, and Dell's title *Four Color* could keep someone pursuing this niche busy for a long time.

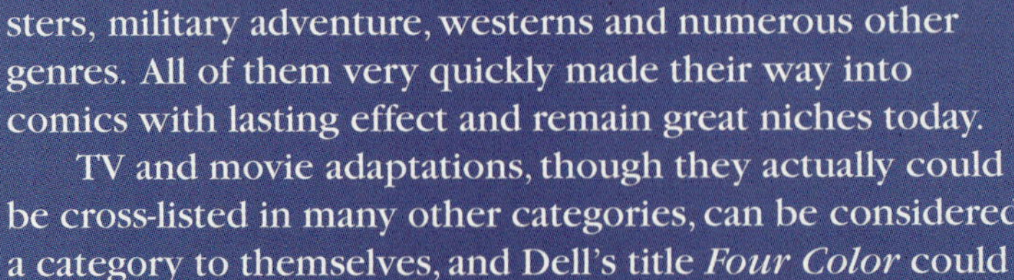

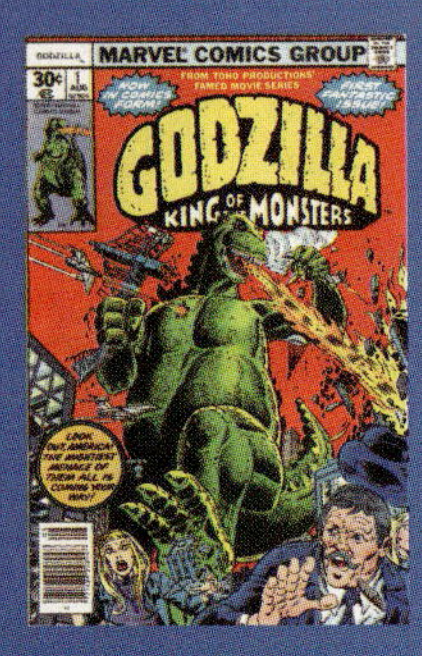

In the coming pages we'll take a brief look at two specific examples, War comics and Horror comics. As always, we're not telling you to collect these genres. Collect what you like. These are just examples (even if they're really, *really* good examples).

WAR COMICS

One of the longest-running and most actively collected genres is War comics. "Most actively collected," though doesn't refer to the number of collectors pursuing the various series, but instead it indicates the enthusiasm with which they collect. War comics collectors are among the most passionate collectors in the field, recognized for their dedication, subject knowledge, and frequently their camaraderie with each other (and given the subject matter they collect, that's sort of fitting).

Noted War comics collector and Overstreet Advisor Matt Ballesteros, who assembles the annual "War Report" section of the Market Reports in *The Overstreet Comic Book Price Guide* each year, said that like every other niche in comic book collecting, there are key series and issues which are more in demand than others.

"There are certainly a good number of prominent War comic titles and stand out characters," Ballesteros said. He said the most popular War books, and those garnering the heaviest attention are roughly as follows:

War Titles	War Characters
1) Our Army at War	1) Sgt. Rock
2) G.I. Combat	2) Sgt. Fury
3) Sgt. Fury	3) Haunted Tank and crew
4) Two-Fisted Tales	4) Unknown Soldier
5) Frontline Combat	5) Enemy Ace
6) Star Spangled War Stories	6) Gunner and Sarge
7) All American Men of War	7) Combat Kelly
8) Wings	8) The Losers
9) Battle	9) Mademoiselle Marie
10) Combat	10) Don Winslow

Ballesteros said that the debate over what are considered the toughest ones to get and why could engender a very long-winded response.

"It all depends on what you are interested in of course. For each publisher/title there are several issues that are just outright elusive. Factors include low print run and scarcity, age, key appearances, popularity and price," he said.

"For the sake of brevity, here's a cross-section sampling: *Our Army at War* #83; not surprisingly is considered a very tough book not only because it is Sgt Rock's first appearance and commands a high price, but there are just not many copies available on the market when compared to many comparable super hero titles. However, there are actually much tougher books to find. Try finding a *Don Winslow* #1 for instance, or a *Foxhole* #1. Not to mention entire comic lines where scarcity is abundant, like those War comics published by Atlas or Charlton. How about any of the first 30 issues of any DC War Big Five title? Those 10-centers are rather scarce all around. Here's one….The beautiful *Star Spangled War Stories* #81, it came out about the same time as the first Rock, yet there's only one lone copy on the CGC census. Tough!" he said.

He said the last decade has seen some significant changes in the marketplace.

"War comic collecting has always resided as a niche genre, which naturally garnered a dedicated but small number of collectors. However, the last decade has seen a massive spike in interest all around, particularly in the last five years. It can be assuredly stated that activity and popularity has substantially outpaced other focused categories such as Romance, Sci-Fi and Western comics. This could be credited to a combination of factors including, but not limited to the resurgence of quality War films in the early 2000s, the advent of social media (which provides a platform for the genre) and the rediscovery of the high caliber art and storytelling by the collective comic collecting community," he said.

Although there has been a recent track record of change, he said predicting the next few years isn't easy.

"If we knew that, we would be buying up investment copies of comics that show promise and dumping books that exhibit signs of slowing. One thing that we are fairly confident of, key titles should retain their prominence and interest," he said. "Another thing that seems probable is that a book's popularity will be increasingly subject to the quality of the art on the cover. With more and more certified comics, the genre will have a percentage of its sphere literally 'judged by its cover.' It will be interesting to see that play out over the next decade."

Through peaks and valleys, thick and thin, War comics collectors have waved the flag for their genre. What, though, has compelled them do it?

"There is no published demographic data, that we are aware of, that would substantiate support to anything specific," Ballesteros said. "However, it can be said with high confidence that art and story are the grand captivating elements of the genre. There is no disputing the high quality work by greats like Kubert, Heath, Kanigher, Glanzman, et al., and the influence they have had on the comic book hobby as a whole. With thousands of War books published, there are countless undiscovered treasures for new recruits and scores of comic worth revisiting for seasoned veterans."

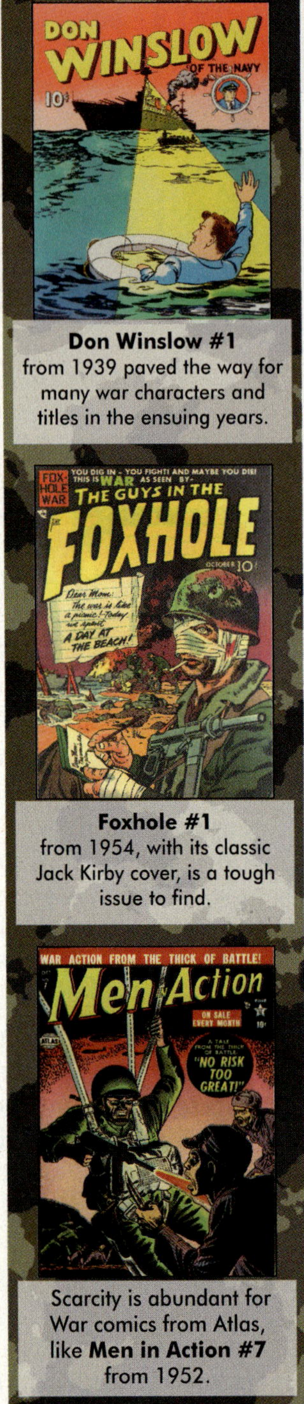

Don Winslow #1 from 1939 paved the way for many war characters and titles in the ensuing years.

Foxhole #1 from 1954, with its classic Jack Kirby cover, is a tough issue to find.

Scarcity is abundant for War comics from Atlas, like **Men in Action #7** from 1952.

THE MOST IMPORTANT WAR COMICS

AS VALUED IN *THE OVERSTREET COMIC BOOK PRICE GUIDE* 43RD EDITION

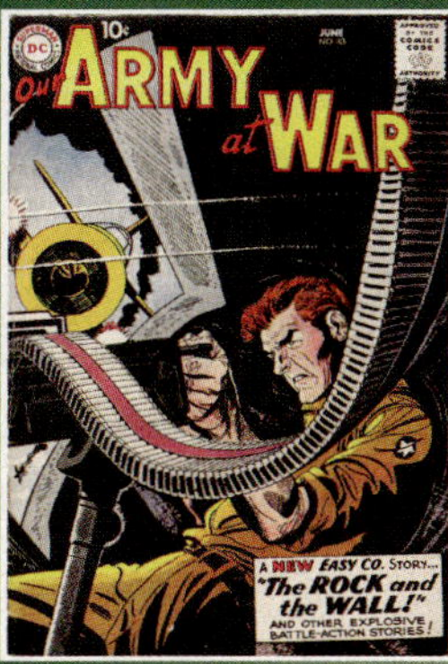

Our Army at War #83
June 1959
First Sgt. Rock app.
2013 *Guide* 9.2 Price: $12,000

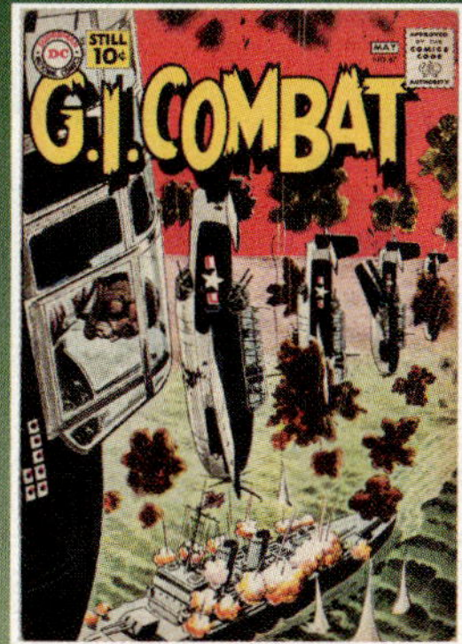

G. I. Combat #87
April-May 1961
First app. of The Haunted Tank
2013 *Guide* 9.2 Price: $3,800

Sgt. Fury #1
May 1963
First app. of Sgt. Fury
2013 *Guide* 9.2 Price: $9,000

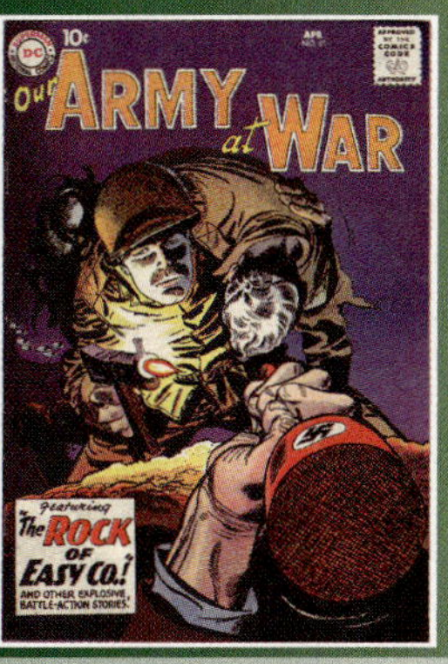

Our Army at War #81
April 1959
Sgt. Rock prototype
2013 *Guide* 9.2 Price: $8,200

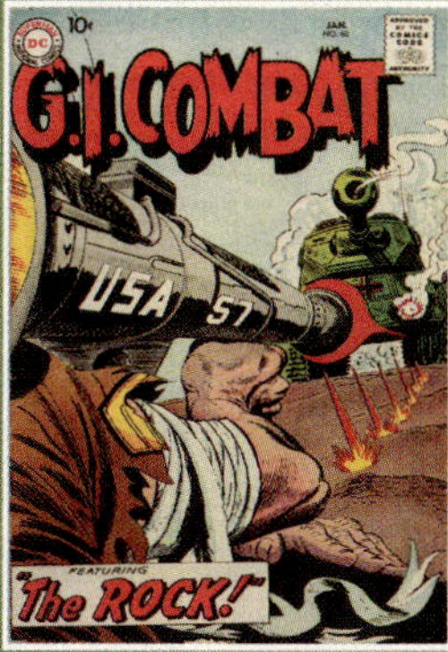

G. I. Combat #68
January 1959
Sgt. Rock prototype
2013 *Guide* 9.2 Price: $3,700

Our Army at War #82
May 1959
First app. of a Sgt. Rock
2013 *Guide* 9.2 Price: $2,500

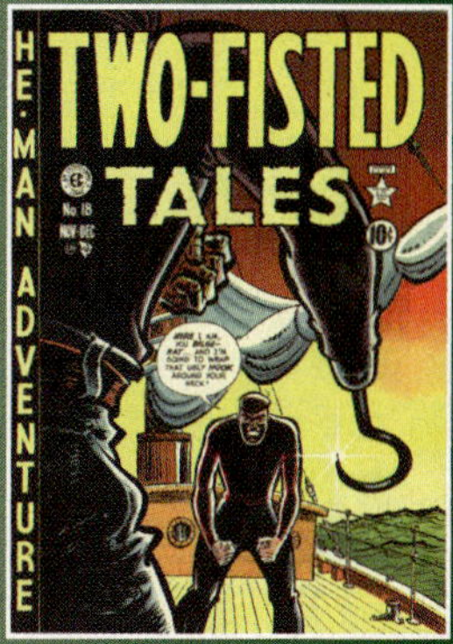

Two-Fisted Tales #18 (#1)
November-December 1950
Cover by Harvey Kurtzman
2013 *Guide* 9.2 Price: $1,700

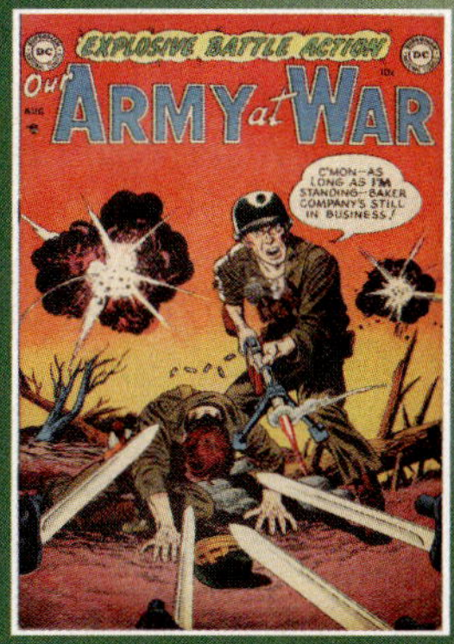

Our Army at War #1
August 1952
2013 *Guide* 9.2 Price: $5,500

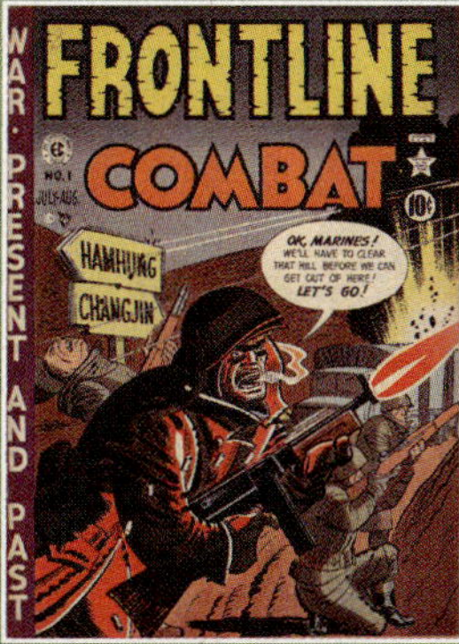

Frontline Combat #1
July-August 1951
Art by Severin & Kurtzman
2013 *Guide* 9.2 Price: $1,300

Our Army at War #90
January 1960
How Rock got his stripes
2013 *Guide* 9.2 Price: $1,500

**For the latest prices on these comics – and about 300,000 other issues –
check out the latest edition of *The Overstreet Comic Book Price Guide*.**

From the multiple printings in multiple formats hit *The Sandman* at DC/Vertigo to Stephen King's *The Stand* at Marvel, from *The Night Stalker* at Moonstone to *Rachel Rising* at Terry Moore's Abstract Studio, horror has a big place in comic books, and it's been that way since the late 1940s.

"Horror is an ancient art form. We have tried to terrify each other with tales which trigger the less logical parts of our imaginations for as long as we've told stories. From the ballads of the ancient world to modern urban myths, audiences willingly offer themselves up to sadistic storytellers to be scared witless, and they are happy to pay for the privilege. Theories abound as to why this is so; do we derive basic thrills from triggering the rush of adrenalin which fear brings, or do horror stories serve a wider moral purpose, reinforcing the rules and taboos of our society and showing the macabre fate of those who transgress?" wrote Karina Wilson on horrorfilmhistory.com. And while Ms. Wilson was essaying about films, her points are salient for horror in any format, including comics.

Often overshadowed by their superhero brothers and sisters, horror comics have a rich tradition and have often been created by some of the best practitioners of the comic book arts. Doubt it? Take a look at the line-up working for EC in the 1950s: Jack Davis, Graham Ingles, Johnny Craig, Reed Crandall, George Evans, Wally Wood… and so many others that it's no surprise the work still stands up today.

Like the genres of crime and science fiction, horror comics have always had their hardcore collectors, too. In fact, given Bob Overstreet's devotion to the EC line as a kid, it's easy to argue that *The Overstreet Comic Book Price Guide* would never have happened without horror comics. Throughout this issue, you'll find horror fans – including many current comic book creators and dealers – calling out their favorite horror comics (with some surprising results).

As with any genre, there have been peaks and valleys in the realm of horror comics, but taken as a whole, there have been some amazing high points. *Creepy, Eerie, Vampirella, Tomb of Terror, Chamber of Darkness, House of Mystery, House of Secrets, Tower of Secrets, Weird War Tales, Tomb of Dracula, Werewolf By Night, Twisted Tales, Tales of Terror, Swamp Thing, Hellblazer, From Hell, 30 Days of Night, Locke & Key, Desperadoes, Army of Darkness, The Wicked West, The Living and the Dead, Sight Unseen, Dead Irons* and so many others are ready to be discovered in the back issue bins and bookshelves.

We'll share with you our picks for the greatest – as well as those of others – but in the end it's *you* who have to decide what scares you…

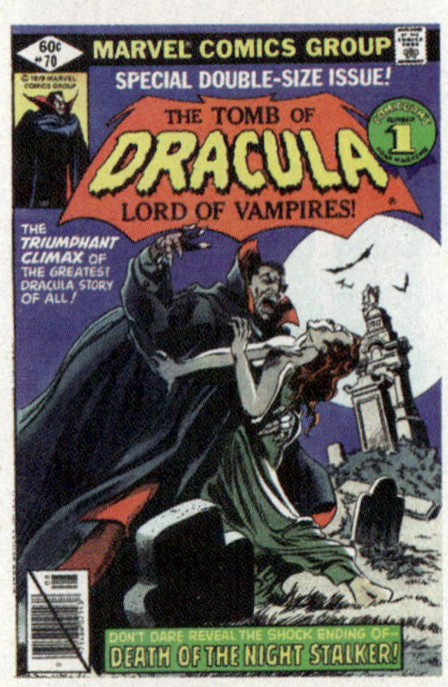

...A Six Pack Of...
HORROR

BY SCOTT BRADEN

Writer, comics historian, and former Gemstone Publishing
pricing editor Scott Braden talks with Previews editor
and noted horror fan Marty Grosser about what makes
these six series among the most notable in comics history.

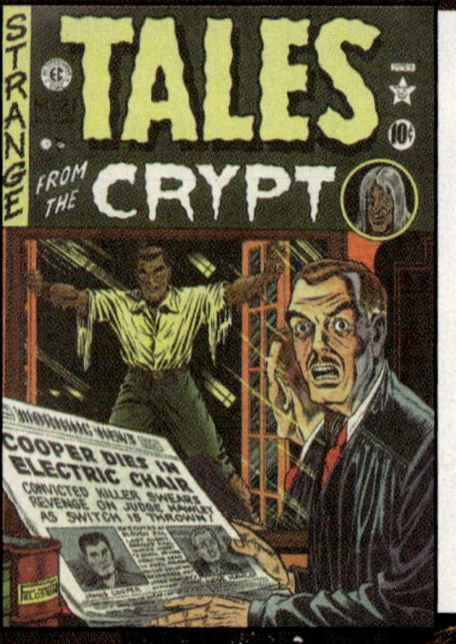

"*Tales from the Crypt* is the horror granddaddy of them all," said *Previews* Editor Marty Grosser. "That was publisher Bill Gaines doing his dark, classic morality tales with exceptional artwork and shock value. I don't think anything has ever matched it in its quality and excellence. *Tales from the Crypt* contains stories that still reach out to readers of today — since the majority of the stories are not dated. *Tales from the Crypt* and the other EC titles are timeless and their message still rings true to a modern audience."

Why It Was Great: Hall of Fame-caliber creators telling tightly knit stories.

Why It Is Still Great: Hall of Fame-caliber creators telling tightly knit stories never go out of style.

CREEPY

"*Creepy* was the 1960s and '70s answer to the famed horror comics of the 1950s from EC Comics. Jim Warren was the publisher of *Creepy* (and its sister mag, *Eerie*), and he got a lot of EC guys and others to work for him," Grosser said. "Talent like Joe Orlando, Grey Morrow, Johnny Craig, Steve Ditko, Richard Corben, Tom Sutton, Al Williamson, Alex Toth, Wally Wood, and Archie Goodwin, among others. They were going for — and I think they actually captured — the *Tales from the Crypt* formula. With a host — there was Uncle Creepy and Cousin Eerie — books like Warren's *Creepy* had morals to them, but weren't preachy or anything. Looking back now, a lot of the creators worked at Warren and the House of Ideas when the Marvel '70s explosion first started."

Why It Was Great: Hall of Fame-caliber creators telling tightly knit stories. Hey, it works!

Why It Is Still Great: Check out the *Creepy Archives* from Dark Horse, particularly stories by Archie Goodwin and/or Steve Ditko; then we suspect you'll get it.

TOMB OF DRACULA

There's very few readers that wouldn't agree that Marvel Comics' *Tomb of Dracula* was writer Marv Wolfman and artist Gene Colan's masterpiece. "Colan looked like he drew with smoke," Grosser said. "His images just coalesce on the page like smoke becoming solid. The series had a unique style that was probably closest to a Hammer horror film, but on paper. Colan was so atmospheric, fluid, and lifelike — we'll probably never see his like again. There was a wonderful kineticism about the book, and it was like you walked down the street and every-thing is moving around you and it's all full of life. At the same time, Marv Wolfman took what could have been a throwaway comic and turned it into something special.

"With Dracula, Wolfman gave you a villain that you could re-late to and understand his motivations. It's like Darth Vader and Hannibal Lecter. You know they are rotten to the core but you end up loving them because they are bad. It's a safe bad that you can watch play out at a safe distance and at the end of the day you walk away un-changed even though you're rooting for the bad guy.

"Wolfman also never created throwaway characters. You have the damaged Blade, the heroic Frank Drake, vampire detective Hannibal King, and the Van Helsings."

Why It Was Great: A superb blend of Dracula's nobility and villainy, and a truly awesome cast of characters.

What It Is Still Great: Marv Wolfman certainly wrote material that sold better, but these stories and characters may be the best of his career. It has stood up brilliantly.

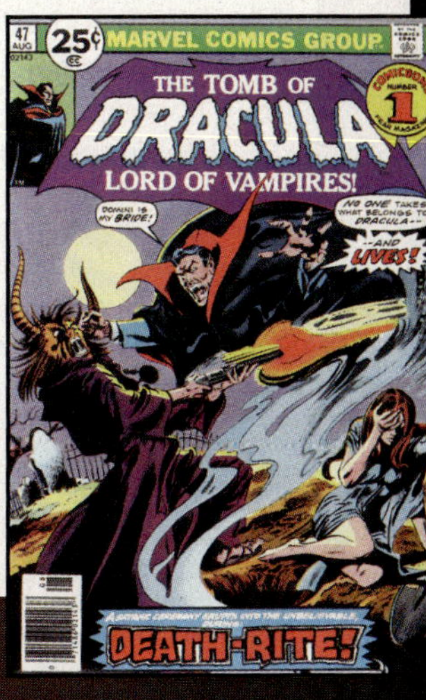

SWAMP THING

The monstrous-but-sympathetic Swamp Thing was Len Wein and Berni Wrightson's creation for DC Comics. But according to Grosser, "You can look back and see that the Heap, a classic comic book character from the 1940s, was the granddaddy of both Swamp Thing and his Marvel Comics' doppelganger, Man-Thing."

Nevertheless, it contained the seeds of greatness, and *Swamp Thing* was the book that brought writer Alan Moore to American shores in the 1980s. From his fan-fa-vorite "American Gothic" storyline, to all of the one-off stories that fell in-between, Moore transformed what was a fairly routine horror title into a work of great promise that is enjoyed by readers today.

Why It Was Great: The sympathetic monster done well always has appeal.

Why It Is Still Great: The monstrous and mysterious nature of Swamp Thing lends itself well to divergent in-terpretations by different creators.

Based on a hit TV show with a seriously hardcore following, the comic book series benefited from the tacit involvement of series creator Joss Whedon. It only truly came into its own when Whedon, who also created the *Buffy* spin-off *Angel* and the series *Firefly*, came on board as writer/producer of the Dark Horse Comics' series.

In print form he and other hand-picked writers told the stories of the never-made Season 8 (and now Season 9) of the TV show, which actually ended after Season 7. The comic book and its trade paperback collections continue to be popular.

Why It Was Great: A clever tweak on the old vampires vs. vampire hunter genre.

Why It Is Still Great: Not that it wasn't good before, but *Buffy* turned out to be the rarest of all licensed titles, one that gets *better* after the show that spawned it ended.

The Eisner Award-winning comic book series chronicles the adventures of zombie apocalypse survivors. But if you were to ask its readers, the book is much more than that. Delving into the lives of its characters, the series' readers get a book that is very action oriented, but also heartwarming and terrifying at the same time. No one is safe in *The Walking Dead* — any character could fall prey to the zombies, or some other threat, at any time. And with creator Robert Kirkman at the helm of both the comic book and the hit TV series, they do.

Why It Was Great: Because so many people thought a black & white comic wouldn't make it.

Why It Is Still Great: While there have been some major changes in pace and a few in the characters between the comic and the hit TV show it spawned, *The Walking Dead* continues to be accessible to new readers, of which we hope there's many.

TOP 10
HORROR COMICS

AS VALUED IN *THE OVERSTREET COMIC BOOK PRICE GUIDE* 43RD EDITION

Eerie #1
January 1947
First Supernatural Comic
2013 *Guide* 9.2 Price: $9,500

The Vault of Horror #12
April-May 1950
Tied for First Horror Comic
2013 *Guide* 9.2 Price: $8,700

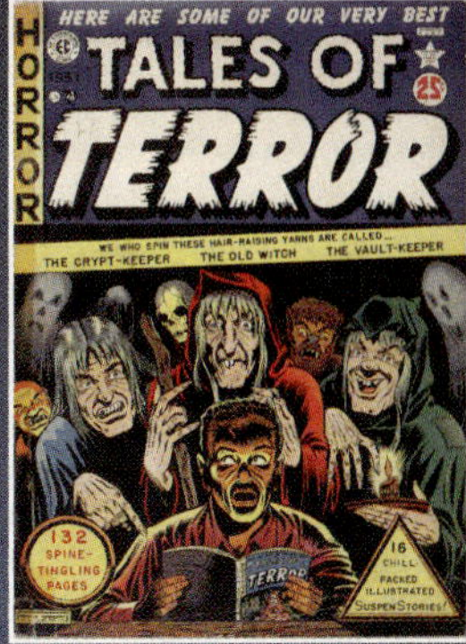

Tales of Terror Annual #1
1951
Cover by Al Feldstein
2013 *Guide* 8.0 Price: $7,600

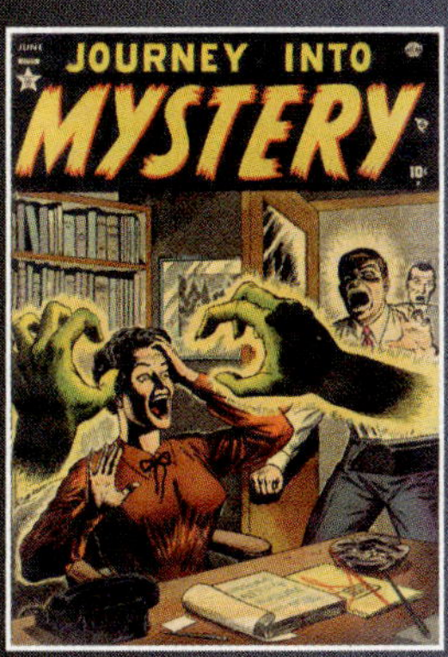

Journey Into Mystery #1
June 1952
Cover by Russ Heath
2013 *Guide* 9.2 Price: $6,700

Strange Tales #1
June 1951
2013 *Guide* 9.2 Price: $6,000

The Crypt of Terror #17
April-May 1950
Tied for First Horror Comic
2013 *Guide* 9.2 Price: $5,300

The Haunt of Fear #15 (#1)
May-June 1950
Cover by Johnny Craig
2013 *Guide* 9.2 Price: $5,200

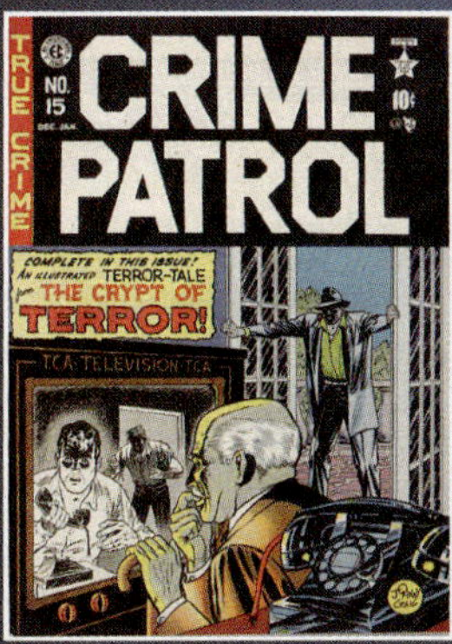

Crime Patrol #15
January 1947
First app. of the Crypt Keeper
2013 *Guide* 9.2 Price: $4,700

Tales To Astonish #1
January 1959
Cover by Jack Kirby
2013 *Guide* 9.2 Price: $5,200

House of Mystery #1
Dec. 1951-Jan. 1952
DC's First Horror Comic
2013 *Guide* 9.2 Price: $3,900

For the latest prices on these comics – and about 300,000 other issues –
check out the latest edition of *The Overstreet Comic Book Price Guide.*

THE BIRTH OF FOUR-COLOR HORROR

By Will Murray

Novelist, pulp author, radio writer and pulp culture historian Will Murray takes a look at the earliest successful horror titles in comics from the American Comics Group…

It seems amazing, but up until 1948, the comic book industry never offered a successful horror title until the American Comics Group released *Adventures into the Unknown* #1 that autumn. True, Avon had issued a one-shot called *Eerie* in 1947. It went nowhere. *Classics Illustrated* adapted *Frankenstein* and other supernatural classics, but those were exceptions.

The concept was the brainchild of Leo Rosenbaum, professionally known as Richard E. Hughes. He had scripted superheroes such as The Black Terror and Pyroman for Nedor during the early '40s, but by the close of the decade, superheroes were out. Comic publishers were groping for bold new directions.

In the ACG editorial saddle, Hughes had an idea. He was a fan of *Weird Tales*, and bought every Arkham House book being issued. Among his stable of writers was a survivor of the Lovecraft circle of writers, Frank Belknap Long, who was scripting comics in between writing horror and science fiction pulp stories.

With World War II over, and comic books no longer being sold through military PX newsstands in high quantities, the industry was fast losing the mature fan. Hughes wanted to hold onto those readers before they were lost forever. He convinced his publisher to take a chance on *Adventures into the Unknown.* Long scripted the entire first issue, which focused on the three main horror tropes—vampires, werewolves and haunted houses. The odd witch and zombie would later be added for variety. Edvard Moritz drew the moody first issue cover and some interior stories.

It was probably the worst time to launch such a project. Parents groups were already looking hard at the industry, upset over crime comics and associated violence. Predictably, after two issues, letters of complaints reached the desk of publisher Frederick Iger. Cancellation loomed for *Adventures into the Unknown.*

Frank Long reached out to Arkham House publisher August Derleth, asking him to pen a letter of praise about the at-risk title. Derleth did. It worked. Iger relented. The ghost would continue to walk.

As Long wrote to Derleth, "Extraordinary as it may seem, the magazine has sold *very well indeed!* It has vindicated the editor's judgment right up to the hilt. He believed that the real old-style ghost story, with the chill factor stressed to the utmost, would have a tremendous appeal to kids and adults alike. He felt

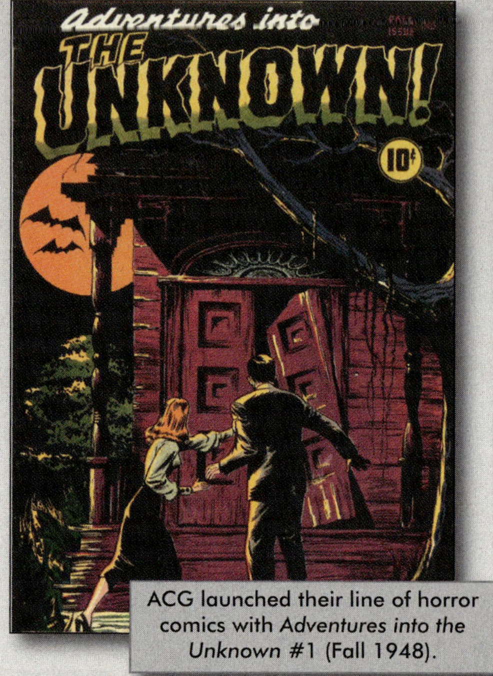

ACG launched their line of horror comics with *Adventures into the Unknown* #1 (Fall 1948).

that it would reach a much larger and slightly different audience, and was not deterred by the fact that pulp magazines in the weird field do not hit an impressive circulation high. He felt that straight ghost stories in pictures would appeal to kids—and apparently he was right, and how. There is a large audience for that sort of thing!"

It didn't take long for other publishers to jump in with imitations. Most were schlocky, but EC Comics raised the bar with their line of well-produced, well-written titles, beginning with *The Vault of Horror* and *Crypt of Terror* in 1950. Horror became a hot comics trend.

Too hot, as it turned out. By the time the Comics Code was implemented in 1954, most of the field was swept clean. With its restrained, traditional approach, the ACG line, which had grown to include *Forbidden Worlds,* managed to survive. Hughes was forced to abandon his formula of werewolves, zombies and vampires in favor of ghost stories and fantasy. He also ditched his writers, including Long and fellow *Weird Tales* contributor, Manly Wade Wellman. Readers howled for the return of raw vampirism and werewolfery, but Hughes was adamant. He had a new direction, and stuck to it, aided and abetted by star artist Ogden Whitney and others adept at portraying actual human beings, not malevolent monsters.

The stories produced during thus period borrowed as much from science fiction magazines as they did from *Weird Tales* or radio programs like *Inner Sanctum,* both fading from the scene as TV knocked out pulps and radio drama alike. Dinosaurs and time travel tales replaced the more extreme Code-forbidden creatures of the night. Witches were permitted, so they populated many issues. But ghosts in all varieties stepped into the spotlight and refused to be banished into the outer darkness.

Out of this era came a strange conceit. The ACG production department had been in the habit of coloring their apparitions a vapid green. Ghosts have to inhabit some realm, and since religion was a taboo topic in comics, Hughes—or one of his writers—cooked up an iron-gated community in the Great Beyond called the Unknown. It looked like a glorified cemetery, but came equipped with councils and overseers. As more and more stories delved into the afterlife and protagonists haunting or being haunted by their relatives, deceased or otherwise, all-knowing hooded specters symbolizing judgment represented the presiding powers in this non-denominational own. It was an intriguing concept that carried down through the final days of ACG.

Science fiction boomed in the days of the early space program, so for variety, tales of alien invasion, inter-species romance and other familiar concoctions grew more frequent as the 1950s progressed. Interwoven with those familiar fantasies, Hughes inserted, and probably scripted—numerous one and two-page supposedly true tales of supernatural experiences, culled from literature. Evidently, Hughes was no mere yarn-spinner, but a believer in the spirit world. And why not? He was making his living off it!

By the close of the 1950s, with sales flat but stable, Hughes began writing much of his own material under pen names like Ace Aquila and Lafcadio Lee. Curiously, this is when the true Golden Age of ACG

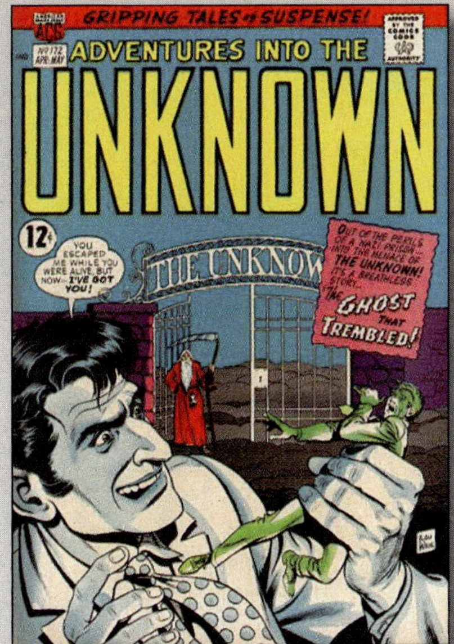

Adventures into the Unknown *#172 (April-May 1967) with a ghostly cover by Kurt Schaffenberger.*

came into being. The new editorial slant of sentimental human-interest supernatural and science fiction yarns brought forth such still fondly remembered classics as "There's a New Moon Tonight," "A Highly Localized Snowfall" and "A Machine Named Spotty," and the all-time reader favorite, "Heavenly Heavyweight." Most of these revolved around flawed or pathetic human beings caught up in moral dilemmas that could only be solved by an equal application of stern self-sacrifice and the supernatural. Letters poured in, praising Hughes under his many aliases. In 1960, he added a third title, *Unknown Worlds.* In practice, they were all interchangeable, but the best stories seemed to land in *Adventures into the Unknown* and *Forbidden Worlds.*

Drawing upon industry talents such as artists Kurt Schaffenberger, Chic Stone, Paul Reinman, Pete Costanza, Steve Ditko and others, Hughes kept his books reader-friendly and professional. DC and Marvel cranked up their Silver Age of superheroes, leaving ACG with its own little niche of casual but committed readers.

All seemed well until the rise of Batmania in the mid-60s. Readers with long memories began bombarding Hughes for the return of The Black Terror and other bygone superheroes. Hughes tried to hold the line, claiming his books were unique, and costumed heroes were a mere fad. He was half right. When he succumbed to publisher pressure to include two supernatural superheroes named Nemesis and Magicman into his top titles—preserving the relative purity of *Unknown Worlds*—sales spiked, then collapsed.

By the time Hughes restored the old formula, adding a new title, *Gasp!* the damage was done. Sales failed to rebound. The ACG line folded quietly in 1967, a victim of Batman. Hughes was forced to toil at answering complaint letters for a New York department store, while his top artist to the bitter end, Odgen Whitney, ended up in an asylum.

Adventures into the Unknown #27

Forbidden Worlds #11

Forbidden Worlds #103

Unknown Worlds #26

Pre-Code horror took a long time to be fully appreciated by collectors of vintage comics. Since the early collecting focus was on superheroes, the pre-Code years (1950-1954) were seen as an awkward interregnum between the two heroic eras that define the Golden and Silver Ages. And this 'excluded middle' was dominated (in theory…) by EC Comics, which were grudgingly admitted as a bright spot in a dark time.

Pre-Code collecting gained a lot of ground in the early 1990s: Ernie Gerber's *Photo Journal Guide to Comic Books* made hundreds of seldom-seen covers, horror and otherwise, available for adoring viewing at any time. And the fan magazine *Comic Book Marketplace* (begun in 1991) helped put pre-Code on the map. My monthly column, "Weird Words," had as an undeclared mission statement the goal of showing that other brands of pre-Code horror gave EC a real run for their money.

Far more comics were sold in the pre-Code era (around 70 million a month) than in any before or since. Not only were these the most popular years for comics, but during this time horror-fantasy-science fiction was the most popular genre. Fawcett Comics, whose Captain Marvel was a giant of the 1940s, often outselling Superman, put their spin on the genre with a group of titles that consistently delivered excellent entertainment. While most other companies offered four or five stories per issue with a strong emphasis on "twist" (and twisted!) endings, Fawcett horror books usually featured three longer stories, with the color and excitement of the narrative events themselves presented in greater detail. They are very 'reader friendly'.

As to the personnel involved, Sheldon "Shelly" Moldoff tops the list. He had pitched the idea of a horror host to Bill Gaines in the late 1940s while working for EC, but Gaines deferred, although as soon as Shelly was gone he ran with the idea on his own. That's not to slam Gaines, business is business,

Fawcett cross-promoted their horror titles with full-page house ads- often on both inside covers in black-and-white and on the back cover in color. This one shows 'The Mummy' holding court over some bizarre blobby sea-folk.

This Magazine is Haunted #12 (August 1953) Al Eadah turned in the job of a lifetime and chose wisely because the super script helped him achieve spectacular results, including great use of the Fawcett 'screentone' ghosts (some can be seen in the splash panel).

and ripeness is all, but what happened, happened. At any rate Shelly approached the editors at Fawcett in 1951, and they agreed, which resulted in the first Fawcett horror comic, *This Magazine is Haunted* #1 (Oct 1951) featuring Shelly's fleshless front man, Dr. Death. Shelly drew most of the covers for the title, and usually illustrated a story inside as well.

Other cover artists include Norman Saunders, George Evans, and Bernard Baily. On interiors, one less-well-known name, Bob McCarty, did a lot of excellent work, and the redoubtable Bob Powell contributed some classics, with Evans and Baily drawing on the insides too.

Fawcett's second horror book, *Worlds Beyond*, followed the next month (Nov 1951, retitled *Worlds of Fear* with #2), and in mid-1952 three more titles were added: *Beware! Terror Tales* (#1 May), *Strange Suspense Stories* (#1 June), and *Strange Stories from Another World* (#1 titled *Unknown World* - June). Although Fawcett tended to go with particular artists for each title's covers - Baily did a handsome run on *Beware!* - the stories inside were more homogenous. *Beware!* was their only other title to feature a horror host; stories were introduced and narrated by 'The Mummy'. Without the framing devices and occasional interpolations the stories in those two titles were much like the stories in the other books. Dr. Death also hosted tales in the last two issues of *Whiz Comics* (the anthology home of Captain Marvel) #154 April and #155 June 1953.

Highlights of Fawcett's five fantasy titles include two stories that were recently anthologized in a fifties horror retrospective (*Four-Color Fear* by Greg Sadowski) and the savvy editor picked them because they are two towering masterpieces. "The Slithering Horror of Skontong Swamp" is an eleven-page magnum opus of George Evans art whose lurid realism creates some of the most ghastly ghosts ever to slither, perfectly wedded to an elegant example of Fawcett's incident-rich story style. This landmark yarn was cover feature in *This Magazine is Haunted* #5 June 1952. And the eight-page "Wall of Flesh" where the always-pleasing Bob Powell outdoes himself in the service of a superb script is everything a weird story should be: it graced *This Magazine is Haunted* #12 August 1953. The #12 is notable in that it contains another classic story fully the equal of the two aforementioned, "The Door." This eleven-pager is a stellar performance by Al Eadah, who takes advantage of another really strong script. The wonderful full-page slash panel (a Fawcett fixture- especially on the lead story) is reproduced for your delectation.

Beware! Terror Tales #3 September 1952 has it all: nice Baily cover, Moldoff cooking on the opener, McCarty sizzling in the middle, and a fine finale. Awesome painted covers by Norman Saunders enhance all five issues of *Strange Stories from Another World*. The covers of #4 (Dec 1952) and #5 (Feb 1953) are particularly brilliant, and both issues each have solid stories drawn by Moldoff and McCarty at the top of their game. *Worlds of Fear* #10 (June 1953) features the famous "eyeballs" painted-cover classic by Saunders, and Dr. Death makes a title-jumping appearance as narrator inside.

The remaining issues (Fawcett published 42 horror comics) are readable and enjoyable - they always aimed to please and usually hit the mark. Many of the stories feature spectral figures drawn with a "screentone" effect, a nice trademark touch that unifies the works of various artists.

The Fawcett horror titles offered compelling product on magazine racks crowded with competition. The thing that set them farthest apart from the others was the manner of their demise. The pre-Code years boasted all-time-high sales because most everyone read comics back then, and it was the adult horror, crime, and war getting mixed in with kid stuff that fueled the brouhaha leading to the comics self-censorship (begun in late-1954) that decimated the industry. But in 1953 everyone from long-established publishers to little fly-by-nights wanted the party to go on as long as it could and were determined to stick around and get while the getting was good. However, Fawcett quit at the peak, with their last horror comic (mayhap their last comic as well) *This Magazine is Haunted* #14 dated December 1953.

Heretofore it has been surmised that the DC versus Fawcett, Superman versus Captain Marvel ongoing lawsuit was the main reason they bowed out of comics. But while it was a factor, an updated viewpoint can only praise the acumen and accuracy of their business decision. The wise realized the party would not last forever… And Fawcett at the time was riding the runaway success of their Gold Medal paperback line which featured original novels rather than the reprints that comprised most previous paperbacks. So seeing the writing on the wall, and having this other project an up-and-coming moneymaker, made the costs of the DC lawsuit an excuse to exit comics a little early. Certainly the impact Fawcett made with horror comics in their truncated pre-Code time frame surpasses that of most of the companies that stuck it out to the bitter end.

Pat Calhoun collects and writes about weird literature and figurines with an emphasis on ten-cent comic books. He lives in an old house full of stuff in Santa Rosa, California.

Strange Suspense Stories #3 (October 1952) George Evans contributed an effective cover and the 12-page lead story. The headless chap makes an appearance in "Port of Terror" with art by Bernard Baily.

This Magazine is Haunted #7 (October 1952) Here's some science gone awry on a cover that looks like Shelly's art: it certainly radiates that eerie atmosphere that we associate with pre-Code horror.

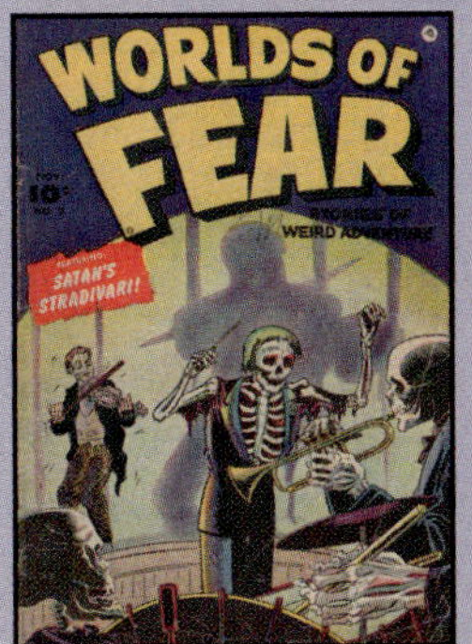

Worlds of Fear #7 (November 1952) Sheldon Moldoff comes through with some creepy composition and coloring on this engaging cover. Bob McCarty's art on the 12-page lead story, "Journey Into Chaos," helps make it a wild ride.

This Magazine is Haunted #9 (February 1953) A vivid sample of Bob McCarty's work, the "Devil's Mask" story is an utterly predictable chestnut, but the all-out effort on the art makes it a pleasure to read.

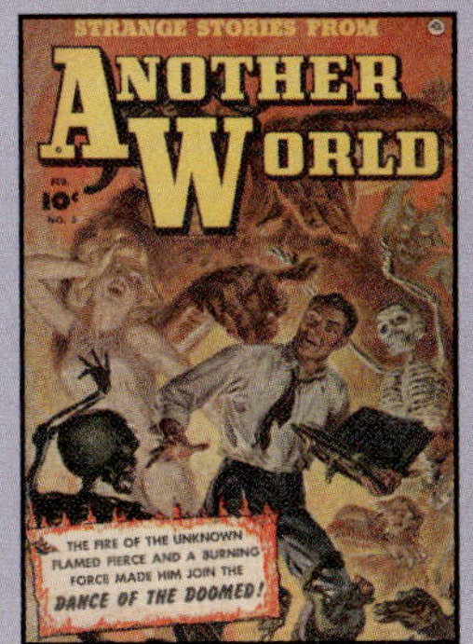

Strange Stories from Another World #5 (February 1953) This incredible painted cover by the great Norman Saunders speaks for itself… And there are some good stories inside too. The title ended on a high note, as this was the final issue.

By **Weldon Adams**

A fun way to collect comic books is to find a company that interests you and attempt to collect every issue they have published. Now, if you select this method, much like collecting by creator, there are some questions you have to ask yourself:

Do you want to collect a company that is still publishing today?

If so, you must be prepared to purchase everything new that they publish. That means that it may take you that much longer to amass their back issues. And, of course, as long as they keep publishing, you may never catch up.

That makes attempting to collect everything published by some companies all but impossible. So maybe a better choice for you would be to pick a company that is smaller, or even just collect a specific imprint of a larger company. Maybe you want all of DC Comics' Vertigo line or all of Ape Entertainment's Kizoic line, for instance.

Usually when someone collects by company, though, it's a company that is no longer in business. Here is a short list, certainly not inclusive, of companies that are no longer publishing and are very fun to collect and read:

Atlas-Seaboard

Not to be confused with the Atlas name used by Marvel from the 1950s, this is a company that published from 1974 to 1975. And although they published many titles, none of them went beyond four issues. So collecting the entire company's run is possible, however some specific issues are very rare and hard to find. There's a lot more about both Atlas publishers elsewhere in this book.

Capital Comics

In 1981, a comic distributor company named Capital City decided to get into publishing comic books as well as distributing them. The very first book

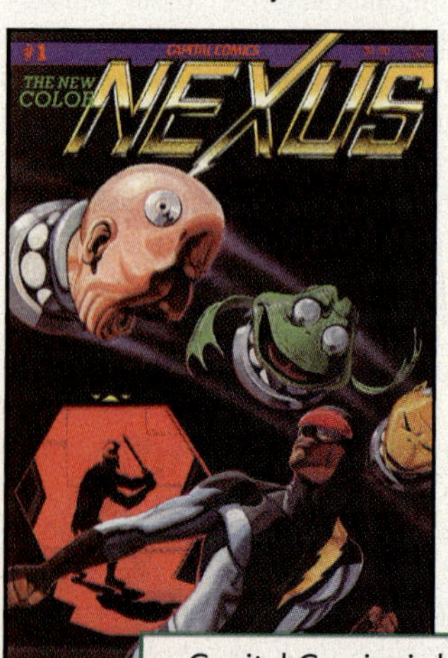

Capital Comics is best known for the early issues of *Nexus*.

they published was a black & white magazine named *Nexus*. They made only 3 issues before it went to a color comic book format in 1983, when they expanded their publishing to include 2 other color comics. In all, they published three issues of *Nexus* magazine, six issues of the *Nexus* comic book, four issues of *Badger*, and two issues of *Whisper*. So with only 15 issues, you have a complete collection!

Charlton Comics

Most known for their Silver Age contributions, Charlton Comics was actually founded in 1946. They published comics until 1985, so they do have a much larger bibliography than either of the previous two on the list. Charlton published something in almost every genre on the market including westerns, romance, funny animal, superhero, licensed TV show properties, and horror comics. Quite a few of their creators went on to make much larger names for themselves at Marvel and/or DC Comics, including Steve Ditko, Dick Giordano, Jim Aparo and others.

Comico: The Comic Company

Comico burst onto the publishing scene in 1982 with the publication of *Primer* #1, a black & white anthology. To call their first work sub-par may be kind. But with this unimpressive start, Comico would eventually give us *Grendel*, licensed *Robotech* comics, *Johnny Quest*, *Mage*, *Evangeline*, and *The Elementals*, among others. Truly great work, but not what you would expect from reading about *Slaughterman*, *Az*, and *Skrog*. This is a very collectible line.

Grendel #1 from Matt Wagner, a good starting place for a Comico collection.

EC Comics

The history of EC Comics is fascinating and could easily fill entire books on its own. In fact, it has! Not only did they give us an amazing line of science fiction, horror and crime comics, they also gave us *MAD* magazine, which started as a comic book as part of the EC line. EC published comics and magazines from the 1940s until 1956 when they cut back to essentially just *MAD*, but *Tales from the Crypt*, *Weird Science* and others they published still influence creators today. The Gaines File pedigree collection is highly sought after by collectors today (see the article elsewhere in this edition).

Eclipse Comics

Eclipse published its first book in 1978, and it was the first original graphic novel to be distributed through the new growing direct market of comic book specialty stores. It was called *Sabre*. They continued to publish groundbreaking comic books until 1993. Along the way, they gave us *Detectives, Inc.* by Don McGregor and Marshall Rogers, *Rio* by Doug Wildey (creator of Johnny Quest), *Static* by Steve Ditko, *Miracleman* by Alan Moore (later by Neil Gaiman), and *Ms. Tree* by Max Collins and Terry Beatty.

Other titles included *Airboy*, *Appleseed*, *Area 88*, *Axel Pressbutton*, and *Aztec Ace*. And that's only some of the titles that start with the letter 'A'. Their catalog list is huge. "Q" is in fact the only letter that they would not have any books filed under. (But look for *Reid Flemming, World's Toughest Milk Man* in the R's. It's worth it.) The line is readily collectible and features the first broad success of manga in the U.S. market.

Miracleman #3, from one of the most notable of the Eclipse titles.

First Comics

First Comics published from 1983 to 1991. They would give us *American Flagg!*, *Grimjack*, *Warp*, *Jon Sable, Freelance* and *Shatter* (the first all-digital comic book), the original graphic novel *Beowulf*, color reprint collections of the *Teenage Mutant Ninja Turtles*, and more. They also picked up the titles from Charlton (*E-Man*), Pacific Comics (*Elric*, *Starslayer*), Capital Comics (*Nexus*, *Badger* and *Whisper*), Marvel's Epic line (*Dreadstar*), among others. In addition, they revived the old Classics Illustrated comics with all new artwork by top talent in the field.

American Flagg #2 displaying one of Haward Chaykin's dynamic covers.

Trident Comics

Trident was a British based company from Leicester, UK. They published from 1989 until 1992. They published black and white comics featuring work from talent who would go on to reshape the comics industry just a few years later. Neil Gaiman, Grant Morrison, Eddie Campbell, Mark Millar, and Paul Grist were all published by Trident. Fans of Gaiman's work should look for the eponymous *Trident* anthology featuring "The Light Brigade." Likewise, fans of Grant Morrison and Paul Grist would be interested in the "St. Swithin's Day" story from that anthology. And Mark Millar fans should check out *Saviour*, his first published work, a six-issue series published by this company. All in all, Trident Comics published 29 books.

Valiant Comics

Here's one that you can collect several ways: The original Valiant Comics were published from 1992 until 1996. The Acclaim Comics were published from 1996 until 2002. While collecting a large percentage of their respective outputs is very easy, assembling complete runs should be considered challenging (particularly when one includes variant cover editions). Most recently a new company, Valiant Entertainment, has acquired the rights to the Valiant heroes and began publishing new adventures of their characters in May 2012.

In addition to the superhero comics for which they were mostly noted, during the Acclaim years, the company produced several high-quality crime-noir comics such as *The Grackle* and *Gravediggers*. Also, they acquired the rights to Classics Illustrated and began reprinting the originals in digest form with new text pieces in the back. There was also a high quality young-reader line of books, some featuring in-continuity stories set in the VH2 universe published by Acclaim.

The Grackle #1, one of the high-quality crime-noir comics from *Valiant's* Acclaim years.

These suggestions should help get you started. And remember that these are just a very small sample of the many wonderful companies out there to collect. We didn't even touch on DC's Milestone Media imprint (actually a separate company published by DC), All American Comics (a similar partnership with DC during the Golden Age), Defiant, or Malibu or Marvel's incarnation as Timely. We barely mentioned Pacific Comics, Marvel's Epic Comics line, their days as Atlas. In other words, there are lots of worlds to explore!

But the most important thing to remember, no matter what method of collecting you follow, is "Buy what you enjoy."

25 MILLION DOLLARS
IS WHAT WE'VE SPENT OVER THE PAST YEAR ON COMIC BOOKS & COLLECTIBLES!
NO ONE ELSE IN THIS BOOK CAN CLAIM THAT!
GET CA$H FOR COMICS!
WHEN YOU ARE READY TO SELL YOUR COMIC BOOKS & BE PAID TOP DOLLAR IN $ $ $ CA$H $ $ $
THERE'S ONLY ONE COMPANY TO CALL:
GETCASHFORCOMICS.COM
CALL OR EMAIL US TODAY!
1-866-461-0640 / BUYING@GETCASHFORCOMICS.COM

WWW.HAKES.COM

SOLD: $15,181

SOLD: $41,264

SOLD: $9,740

★ CONSIGN NOW ★
WWW.HAKES.COM

SOLD: $21,275

SOLD: $3,478

SOLD: $26,565

SOLD: $11,132

SOLD: $18,658

★ ORIGINAL ART WANTED ★ PROVEN RESULTS ★

SOLD: $11,500

SOLD: $9,740

SOLD: $3,452

SOLD: $2,932

SOLD: $8,222

If interested in consigning contact:
Kelly McClain at mkelly@hakes.com or call 866.404.9800 ext: 1636 or
Alex Winter at walex@hakes.com or call 866.404.9800 ext: 1632
Hake's Americana & Collectibles
PO Box 12001 - York, PA 17402
Toll Free: (866)404-9800

A DIVISION OF
GEPPI'S ENTERTAINMENT AUCTIONS

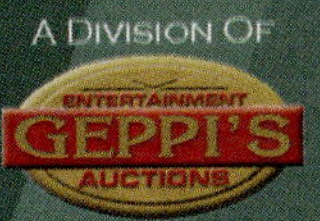

In the mid-1980s, Overstreet Advisor and ValiantFans.com founder Greg Holland was playing Little League baseball. Keeping up with his teammates, he ended up collecting baseball cards. Like many card shops in the early '90s, the place he shopped started carrying comics. Through price guide "top ten" lists he saw that Valiant was very popular and he found out for himself that their universe was very accessible and not laden with decades of continuity.

He attributes the growth of the internet and him joining eBay in 1997 as the sparks that eventually led to the creation of ValiantFans.com.

"I had also wondered what happened to Valiant, and it was clear that Acclaim (the video game company who purchased Valiant in 1994) had not continued the stories that I had enjoyed a few years before," Holland said.

"Wanting to know more about Valiant,

I checked for existing websites about Valiant. There were a few sites with information, but nothing that seemed to bring it all together. I registered ValiantComics.com in 1999 to try to consolidate reference information about Valiant," he said.

"I had a lot of help from other Valiant collectors who provided scans and information. Within a couple of years, I was being asked to add a message board to the site. In 2004, I registered ValiantFans.com to provide the message board with more stable webhosting. Valiant-Fans.com message board currently has more than 2,400 registered members, over 800,000 posts, and more than 17,000 unique visitors making 130,000 visits just in the past six months," he said.

He's seen Valiant collecting at its frenzied heights and also when only a loyal few were doing it.

"Valiant started small in 1991, but those comics were very, very good. By late-1992, Valiant was turning heads and gaining a lot of steam. The whole comic market was also seeing a huge increase in the number of books being printed. If all those books had been high-quality, and getting into the hands of fans, perhaps the industry would have sustained the growth. Unfortunately, I'm not sure if even 10% of those mid-1990s issues (from all publishers) were ever even opened, much less read and enjoyed. The earliest Valiant books were unobtainable for a lot of collectors, and the later books were everywhere for pennies on the dollar. The biggest valley for Valiant fans would have been during the late 1990s and early 2000s. Acclaim

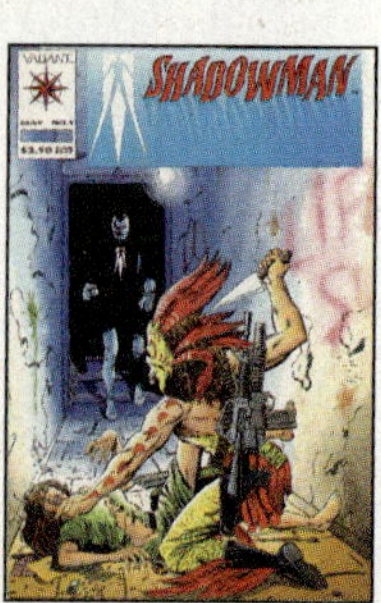

had taken what was best about Valiant and replaced it with whatever comics they thought might make a good video game. Before long, Acclaim had gone bankrupt. Many comic shops had closed, and although it was becoming possible to collect Valiant online, most Valiant fans probably assumed that Valiant was gone forever," Holland said.

"My site wasn't the first Valiant website, but it did seem to provide a beacon for Valiant collectors to find each other. The message board really let Valiant fans get to know each other, and the website gave us all an opportunity to see which books we were missing and what the real back issue market looked like, reflected in the price guide I compiled. Once the message board became a weekly, or even daily, destination for a lot of members, the discussion naturally expanded to other topics and also to discussions about what Valiant collecting was like in each member's local areas. Comic conventions became opportunities for Valiant fans to meet each other "in person," rather than remain anonymous online. Charity work became a regular activity on the website, primarily supporting the Cystic Fibrosis Foundation in honor of one member's daughter suffering from CF. Comic conventions allowed Valiant fans to organize panels with former Valiant artists, writers, and employees, allowing a combination of reminiscing and rejuvenating for the possibility that Valiant might return someday. One of the two buyers of the Valiant copyrights, a founder of the new Valiant Entertainment, was an active ValiantFans.com message board member first. He remembered Valiant fondly, as the comic book universe he could call his own, much like many of us remember Valiant. Marvel belonged to our fathers, and DC to our grandfathers. Valiant was our universe, even when it looked like it would never return," he said.

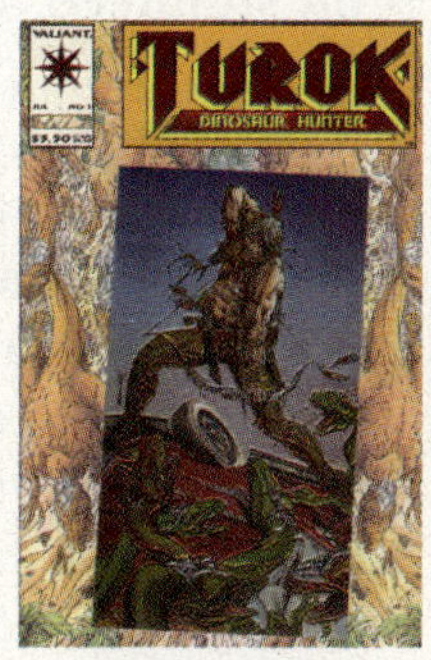

With multiple incarnations and many different variants, what are some of the different ways he's seen fans collecting Valiant?

"There are very few Valiant collectors who had the opportunity to collect all the variants as the books were released in the 1990s. The incentive books were next-to-impossible for most collectors to find or to afford," he said.

"Many collectors focus on being able to read all the stories, requiring only a single version of a book or even a trade paperback to serve that purpose. At the other end of the spectrum, some Valiant collectors want every possible Valiant variant and all possible Valiant products, from silver rings to cardboard store display items," he said.

Holland said some collectors are not satisfied with only a single pristine copy of their favorite books, while others are satisfied with any reader copy that has all its pages.

He said his personal favorites from his Valiant collection have changed over the years, ranging from high grade, CGC-certified Valiant issues and original artwork to production pieces, prototypes and a set of bound, hardcover volumes he purchased from former Valiant Editor-in-Chief Bob Layton.

What advice would he offer for someone who was just becoming a Valiant fan and wants to collect it all?

"Read them first! Being a fan means knowing what you like. Early 1990s Valiant comics were excellent comics! The continuity of the universe, the characters, artwork, stories… Valiant did those things very well. Who are your favorite characters? If you want to collect Valiant, focus first on what you like best. The new Valiant books being produced are also done very, very well. Valiant is taking what was best about the first Valiant and building a universe around those characters in today's world. The new Valiant books are made by people who love the first Valiant. Don't worry too much about spending top dollar for limited edition Valiant books the moment they're released. Do be sure to get a copy of each book to read. Open it up! Find out what you like. Collecting can be about quickly spending money and hurriedly marking items off a checklist, or it can be about discovering things as you go along. Valiant is back, and they're building a universe for us to enjoy," he said. "Let's make sure we take the time to enjoy it!"

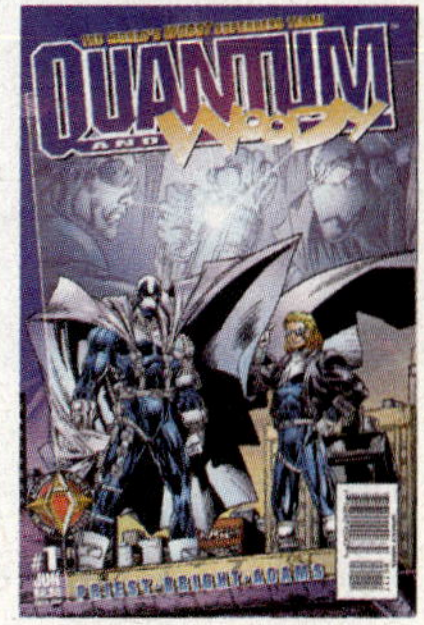

For more information about Valiant comics, you will find galleries, checklists, message boards, and a thousand other reference pages available online at www.ValiantFans.com.

Collecting

Dead Universes

Tower. VALIANT. Continuity. Eclipse. CrossGen. Triumphant. Milestone. DEFIANT. DC's Impact! line. Dark Horse's Comics Greatest World. Marvel's New Universe. Archie's Red Circle line. Deluxe Comics. Broadway Comics. Atlas-Seaboard.

For years it seemed like the collectors of these and numerous other "Dead Universes" were isolated in the loneliest outposts of comicdom. The development of internet communities, such as VALIANT-fans.com, though have swelled the ranks and given encouragement to those who not only collect the comics of bygone publishers or imprints, but who document every aspect possible.

Such fans often discover, scan and post previously forgotten advertisements, posters and other promotional items. They track down creators and editors and get inside information. They find rare variant covers and misprints.

And yet they dwell in a world of incomplete stories, tales which very often will never have an ending. What makes them do it?

After a long break from comics, Chris Scott stumbled upon a copy of the X-O Manowar trade paperback from VALIANT in a local comic shop. Remembering how much he had enjoyed the series and other material from the publisher, he picked it up and read it in one sitting.

"This started me on a quest to find all of the VALIANT Comics that I used to read. Eventually, I would own and read every book that VALIANT published from its beginning to its end. This was truly my first

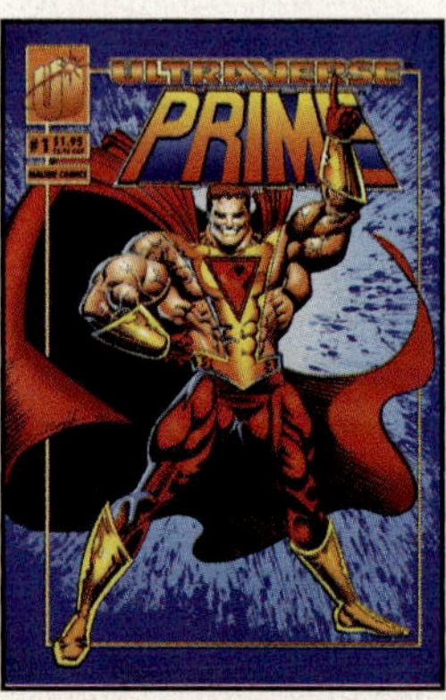

Dead Universe collection of comics. Once I had the VALIANT set completed, I realized that I really liked the writing of Jim Shooter and his work in the early days of VALIANT. This led me to collect his other works, namely DEFIANT and Broadway Comics," Scott said.

"This started me on the road to collecting comics that were no longer in print or their signature universe had died many years ago. I went on to collect Continuity, Malibu, Malibu's Ultraverse, Bravura, Marvel's New Universe, Impact!, CrossGen, Tekno, Event, Eclipse, Red Circle, Triumphant, Marvel's 2099, Virgin, Majestic, Future, Milestone, Atlas-Seaboard, Dagger, Tower and a few other universes," he said.

"I find the Dead Universe to be appealing for many reasons. The stories are fun to read. The number of issues in any said universe are finite. In many cases, the stories were left unfinished (a sad instance of this was the CrossGen universe). Trying to put these runs together is sometimes incredibly easy to do, which leads to another aspect of Dead Universe books in that the common issues are very inexpensive," he said.

On the other hand, he pointed out, there are some issues which are very hard to find, such as variant covers, premium comics and promotional or one-of-a-kind items.

Collector Robert McGinity echoed the appeal of the low cost average issues, but warned there can be a more serious commitment needed for some of the tougher ones.

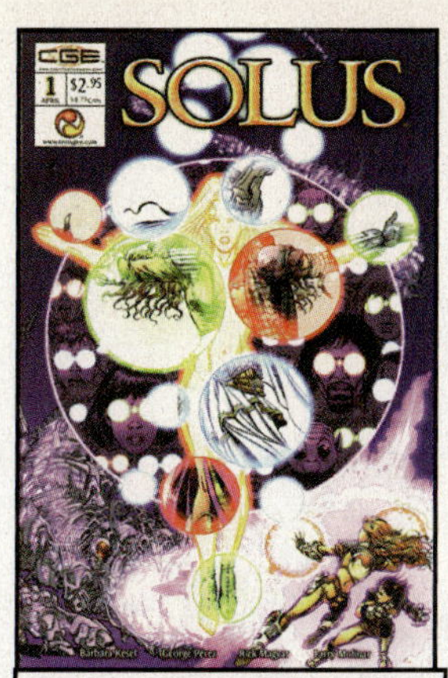
CrossGen's *Solus* #1 with art by George Pérez

"Sometimes I will have to buy 20 books just to get one that I want. That leads to storage issues, but it's nothing the occasional garage sale doesn't fix," McGinty said.

But it is, after all, supposed to be about the fun, getting some level of personal interest or satisfaction out of the activity.

"I think the enjoyment of collecting Dead Universes is the same for me as for most of the other collectors. It's a finite number of books to collect, you don't have to pay the high prices of new comics to collect them, and there are lots of great premium books that were tough to get back when they came out, but which now can often be found in bargain bins," said collector Joe Piechota. "We're also always finding new items that are not widely known."

And since we're talking about comics, where "dead" frequently doesn't have the meaning it does in the real world, not all Dead Universes stay that way.

Many of the Milestone characters such as Static and Xombi have come back at DC, as has Tower's *T.H.U.N.D.E.R Agents*. The Gold Key and VALIANT titles *Magnus, Robot Fighter*, *Doctor Solar, Man of the Atom* and *Turok, Son of Stone* were briefly revived by Dark Horse Comics (joined by Gold Key's *Mighty Samson*). Several of the Atlas-Seaboard titles from 1975, including *Phoenix* and *The Grim Ghost*, have seen recent rebirths at Ardden Entertainment. Marvel has revisited their New Universe. Dynamite revived Event's *Painkiller Jane*.

And no doubt others will follow…

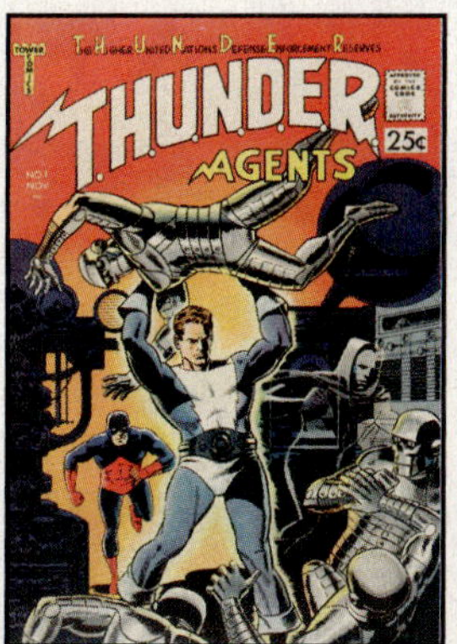

Art by Anthony Castrillo and colors by Thomas Mason.

THE BIG ATLAS SECTION

ATLAS AT LAST!

By J.C. Vaughn

From March 11, 2011 and throughout the remainder of the year, Geppi's Entertainment Museum (GEM) in Baltimore's historic Camden Yards sports complex played host to "Atlas At Last," the first exhibition focused on the Atlas-Seaboard line of comic books from 1974-1975.

In the years between the time of their founding in the late 1930s as Timely Comics and the 1960s when they became known by their current name, Marvel Comics was known as Atlas Comics (until the Marvel name stuck, there were actually many different corporate names on paper, but for back issue collectors and dealers, Timely and Atlas are the pre-Marvel names commonly used).

When founder Martin Goodman had sold Marvel in the late '60s and left the company in the early '70s, there didn't seem like any likely reason the Atlas name would return.

When Marvel's new owners reneged on an agreement to keep Goodman's son, Charles Goodman, on board, however, all that went out the window. In 1974 Goodman set in motion a new Atlas under the umbrella of a company called Seaboard-Periodicals.

As news of the upstart company filtered through fandom, it quickly was dubbed "Atlas-Seaboard," so as to quickly differentiate it from the original Atlas.

Their roster was populated with characters that were fresh and original, and with those who seemed like bad knock-offs of other genre favorites. Their cover design was clearly Marvel-esque. It probably didn't hurt that in addition to Goodman, Atlas had hired Marvel impresario Stan Lee's brother, Larry Lieber, as one of their editors, alongside editor-in-chief Jeff Rovin, who had come over from Warren Publishing.

The creators ranged from those at the top of their craft (one series boasted former Warren Publishing and DC Comics editor Archie Goodwin as writer, Spider-Man co-creator Steve Ditko on pencil art, and EC Comics veteran and *T.H.U.N.D.E.R. Agents* creator Wally Wood on inks) to up-and-comers like Larry Hama, who later for generations of kids would define the 1980s G.I. Joe characters.

Over a brief span, the company produced 72 full color comic books and black and white magazines. Their longest running titles hit four issues,

and then it all fell apart. Everything was shut down and Atlas disappeared.

Or rather, the company disappeared.

The issues lingered in back-issue boxes in comic book shops and at conventions. While many fans forgot about the characters and the line, others did not. In the 36 years since they closed shop, it's become increasingly difficult to track down high grade copies of their output (lower grade copies for most issues are plentiful, but a few of them now are hard-to-find in any grade).

Of course in the comic book world meeting one's demise is something more akin to setting up the next big story line. In the pages of comic books, death has a way of not being so permanent. The same, it seems, is true for comic book publishers.

It almost seemed to be out of nowhere, then, when right before October 2011's New York Comic Con and its 90,000 fans came together at the Jacob Javits Center, small publisher Ardden Entertainment announced that they were re-launching some of the Atlas characters with the participation of Jason Goodman, the grandson of Marvel's founder.

The companies rolled out two of the characters in new issues, *The Grim Ghost* #0 and *Phoenix* #0, and also announced a third project.

The Grim Ghost #0 and **Phoenix** #0

Almost following the original model, the creators lined up were a mix of top professionals and hot newcomers.

Ardden and Atlas subsequently announced that March 2, 2011 would be "Atlas Day," the day that would see their official debut with the launch of three new series based on their characters.

HISTORY REPEATS

It started, as these things do, with a lot of promise. It was 1974 and a brand new comic book publishing company offered creators high pay rates to write and illustrate an entire new universe full of characters. Atlas-Seaboard offered forms of creator ownership, a venue for trying new things, and a mix of established, seasoned professionals and hot newcomers.

The very existence of this firm challenged the big two in terms of retaining creators. If this new enterprise succeeded, Marvel and DC would have to either accept their losses or raise their own pay rates. Sure, going up against the big guys had been tried before, but this time it at least seemed different.

Marvel Comics founder Martin Goodman, who had sold Marvel a few years before, and his son Charles, started Seaboard Periodicals with the hope of rivaling Goodman's old company. To do this, they followed the Marvel formula of the day: superhero comics, barbarian comics, and black and white magazines. They even adopted the name Atlas, familiar to Silver Age fans as the name Marvel published under after Timely and before Marvel Comics.

The general look of the comic book covers was about as Marvel as one could get shy of using the Marvel logo. Creators including Steve Ditko, Wally Wood, Archie Goodwin, Howard Chaykin, Jack Sparling, Rich Buckler and others made the move to Atlas.

"In the late Summer of 1974, the comics press eagerly anticipated the arrival of the upstart Atlas/Seaboard (a moniker settled on by comic book historians to distinguish it from the 1950s line of Martin Goodman, though officially it was Seaboard Periodicals, parent company of the new Atlas Comics)," wrote comics historian Jon B. Cooke in *Comic Book Artist* #16.

"*Inside Comics* #3 (Fall 1974) speculated, 'Seaboard seems to be off on the right foot and, if their plans succeed, we may be in store for a real treat," he wrote, noting further advance praise from Jim Steranko's *Mediascene* #11 (Jan.-Feb. 1975) and in *The Comic Reader* #109 (Aug. 1974).

Original characters like Demon-Hunter (created and illustrated by Buckler) and The Scorpion (created, written and illustrated by Chaykin) were intermingled with a Hulk knock-off (*The Brute*), a sort of negative image version of Spider-Man (*The Destructor*), and a couple of seemingly Marvel-esque barbarians (*Ironjaw* and *Wulf the Barbarian*).

Several of the titles, though trite in concept, had a smattering of freshness due to the talent involved. *The Destructor*, for instance, featured the team of Archie Goodwin (writer), Steve Ditko (pencils) and Wally Wood (inks). The concept, young man headed down the wrong path until death of a loved one forces him to confront responsibility. Throw in a grave-side vow of righting wrongs, and you get the idea. Still, in his pre-hero days The Destructor is actually an anti-Peter Parker of sorts.

THE END…

Unfortunately the company was not successful in generating enough sales through newsstands or spinner racks, and there was not yet a specialty direct market for comic books yet, so the newsstand was life or death. In this case, it wasn't life.

"What the Goodmans did go out of their way to do

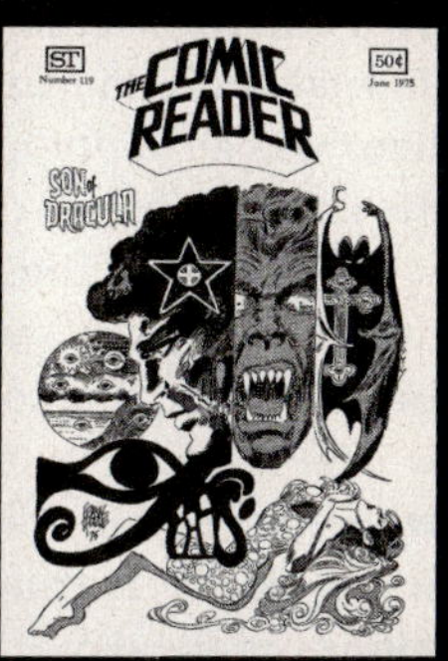

The Comic Reader, one of the most popular and long running fanzines, frequently covered the Atlas-Seaboard line.

was to tackle Magazine Management and Marvel head-on. The bitterness they felt about Chip's falling-out was clear not only in the similar nature of the Seaboard titles in production and on the drawing boards, but in the choice of Atlas as a name for the comics, Atlas having been a Marvel imprimatur during the 1950s," Rovin wrote much later in the pages of *The Comics Journal*. "Unfortunately, anger is a lousy reason to start a publishing company; not only are bad calls made in an effort to be vindictive or to recapture lost glories, but the angry party tends to lose interest when the anger fades and the bills continue to mount. That was to prove a fundamental problem at Atlas Comics."

In a profile several years ago in *Comic Book Marketplace*, Lieber recounted how he was on jury duty while awaiting the verdict on whether Atlas lived or died. The word came down, and that was that. The short-lived experiment was less than two years in duration with less than one full year of published product.

The promise of Atlas at the beginning was probably gone well before the end. Chaykin left over a dispute which resulted in *The Scorpion* #3 having little, if anything, to do with *The Scorpion* #1-2. From one of their few sparkling gems of originality, the title immediately became a bad Daredevil/Spider-Man sort of coagulation.

Larry Hama, writer-artist on *Wulf the Barbarian*, had also already quit. Pay rates were headed down and the seemingly arbitrary nature of the editorial decision-making accelerated the process. There was a fair amount of finger-pointing at the time and that hasn't changed in years since.

The legacy of the Atlas line as a entity unto itself is small, but in a way it is not insignificant. They were the first to challenge Marvel and DC in the '70s. The idea of offering a degree of creator ownership or control was still entirely foreign to the big two then, truly existing only in the undergrounds of the day.

Would Eclipse Comics or Pacific Comics have popped up when they did, or later First Comics if Atlas hadn't taken the plunge? The creator rights movement and other market forces practically guaranteed something would have happened sooner or later, but without Atlas there has to be at least a small question of whether it would have happened the way it did.

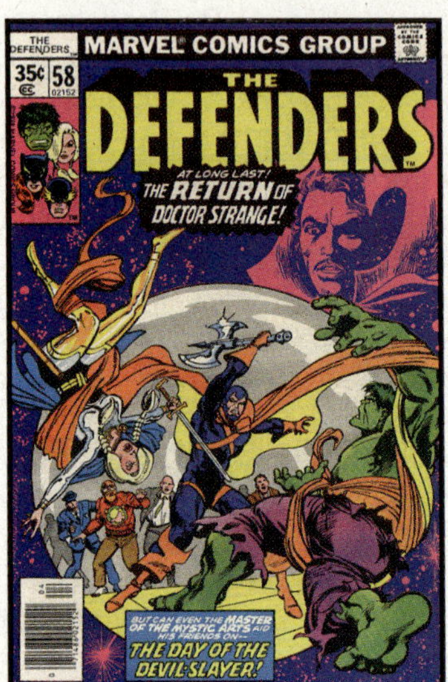

One of the post-Atlas appearances of Demon-Hunter as Devil-Slayer.

AFTERMATH

Martin and Charles Goodman got out of comics for good. Jeff Rovin has worked in the comics field and other media. Larry Lieber has illustrated a very long run on *The Amazing Spider-Man* newspaper strip scripted by his brother, Stan Lee.

The various creators employed by Atlas went many different directions. Some were never heard from in comics again. Some went on to become comics superstars.

Two of the characters also found employment with other publishers. Sure, it's not the first time a character has been picked up. The modern era of DC, for example, encompasses characters created at Fawcett, Charlton, Quality and elsewhere. The characters in question are Demon-Hunter and The Scorpion, and both of them landed at Marvel. Actually, Demon-Hunter landed in two places.

In his Atlas origin story (and only issue), Gideon Cross had renounced the demon cult which had granted him incredible powers and now stood opposed to them. Their goal was "Xenogenesis," the rebirth of a demon race on earth.

David Anthony Kraft (*Comics Interview*) wrote it and Rich Buckler plotted and illustrated it.

Meanwhile, over at Marvel, Buckler's "Deathlok The Demolisher" series in *Astonishing Tales* had been canceled mid-story. The story was to be more or less wrapped up in *Marvel Spotlight* #33 (1977), although it would also carry into *Marvel Two-in-One* #27 before fading into the great land of permanently dangling storylines. Again with Kraft writing and Buckler illustrating, Deathlok returned ostensibly for the wrap-up story. Only it was easily as much the origin story for Devil-Slayer.

Devil-Slayer was Eric Simon Payne. He had renounced the demon cult which had granted him incredible powers and now stood opposed to them. Their goal, and stop me if you've heard this before, was "Xenogenesis," the rebirth of a demon race on earth. His costume was blue with an orange cape where Demon-Hunter's was red with a blue cape, but otherwise it's the same guy.

Devil-Slayer went on to pop up in Kraft's *The Defenders* #58-60 (1978) for a three-part story entitled, not surprisingly, "Xenogenesis." He wasn't done there.

Well, Devil-Slayer was, as was Eric Simon Payne, but Gideon Cross wasn't.

Gideon Cross came back as Bloodwing, in the Buckler-published *Galaxia Magazine* (1981). This one didn't get as far as mentioning Xenogenesis, but there was mention of a demonic "Crimson Brotherhood." The character looked the same as his Marvel incarnation on the color cover (interiors were black and white), but the feel was a little more rough and tumble.

Since the early 1970s, Howard Chaykin seems to have been turning out intense characters with heavy doses of adventure, politics, sex and a generally cynical, rogue-ish behavior: Cody Starbuck, *The Scorpion*, *Dominic Fortune*, his version of *The Shadow*, *American Flagg*, and *Power & Glory*.

At Atlas, a falling-out over control of *The Scorpion* lead to Chaykin's departure before the ship had sunk. He showed up at Marvel where he, with Len Wein providing a script, came up with Dominic Fortune. The color of the outfits may be slightly different, but the attitude and presence of the characters is unmistakably the same. The result was two stories, one written by Wein and one by Chaykin himself, that appeared in *Marvel Preview* #21 under the "Bizarre Adventures" banner.

The background stories were different enough. *The Scorpion* was set in New York and the character was somehow long-lived and of unspecified age. He was, though, a mercenary for hire with the same attitude and demeanor as Dominic Fortune, who instead lived just off the west coast, near Los Angeles, outside territorial waters, on a rather large gambling ship. Both were set in the late 1930s and had elements of the approaching World War II looming in the background.

Missing from Fortune was the undefined extended life scenario, but otherwise their similarities overwhelm the differences. Chaykin has explored the theme of extended life in other stories, too, most notably his four-issue DC Comics *Shadow* mini-series (1980).

REVIVAL

The Atlas-Seaboard line had been dormant, but far less dead than most thought. For some years, Jason Goodman had been fielding inquiries about the properties. One of the queries came from Ardden

Entertainment Co-President Brendan Deneen.

"I've always had a soft spot in my heart for Atlas Comics. I found them all in back issue bins when I was a teenager and ate them up. At the time, I had no idea about the history behind the company; I just really enjoyed them for what they were: fun comics! Fast forward to about a year ago, I now co-owned a small comic book company and was in the middle of putting out critically-acclaimed re-launches of both *Flash Gordon* and *Casper the Friendly Ghost* (aka *Casper and the Spectrals*). A memory of Atlas Comics came rushing back to me one day while I was at work. I reached out to AtlasArchives.com (an amazing site), and they were kind enough to put me in touch with Jason. The rest, as they say, is history (in the making!)," Deneen said.

After releasing *The Grim Ghost* #0 and *Phoenix* #0 at the New York Comic Con in October 2010, Ardden and Atlas subsequently announced that March 2, 2011 would be "Atlas Day,"

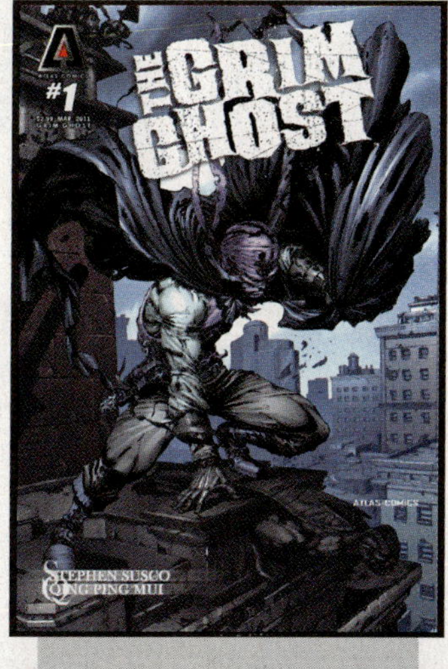

the day that would see their official debut with the launch of three new series based on their characters. In addition to Grim Ghost and Phoenix, their third revival is *Wulf* (details of which may be found in our interview with writer Steve Niles in this issue of *Comic Book Marketplace*).

"The relaunch of Atlas is something I have been wanting to do for quite awhile. It means a lot to me personally as Atlas was very important to Grandpa (Martin) and Dad (Chip). It is also more fun than you can imagine! My creative team and Brendan and his team at Ardden have been working hard and having a blast! The positive response we have been getting is amazing! The number of exclamation points I now feel the need to use is even more amazing!" Jason Goodman said with a laugh.

"We certainly intend to emulate Atlas 1.0 by telling great stories and working with supremely talented writers and artists! Atlas 2.0 will be more patient and methodical as it rolls out (re-introduces) titles and characters. We have no desire to flood the market with mediocre product, instead we will let existing stories play out more fully and add titles and releases when the time and talent is right," he said.

The new #1 issues of *The Grim Ghost* and *Phoenix*.

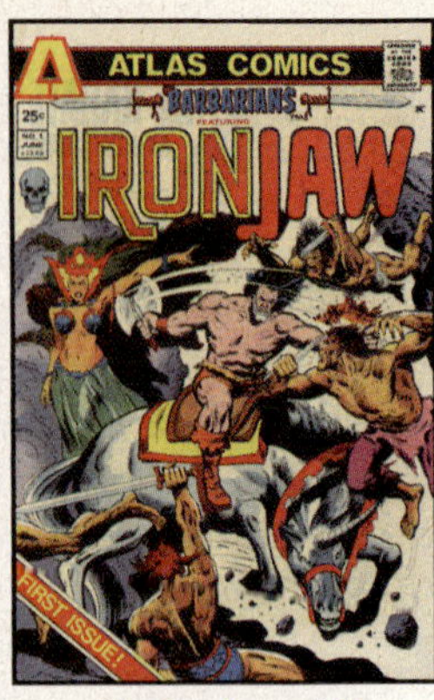

Barbarians #1
June 1975

Blazing Battle Tales #1
July 1975

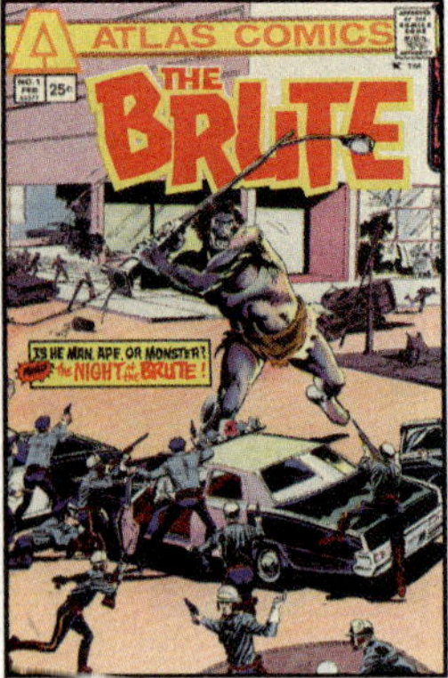

The Brute #1
February 1975

The Brute #2
April 1975

The Brute #3
July 1975

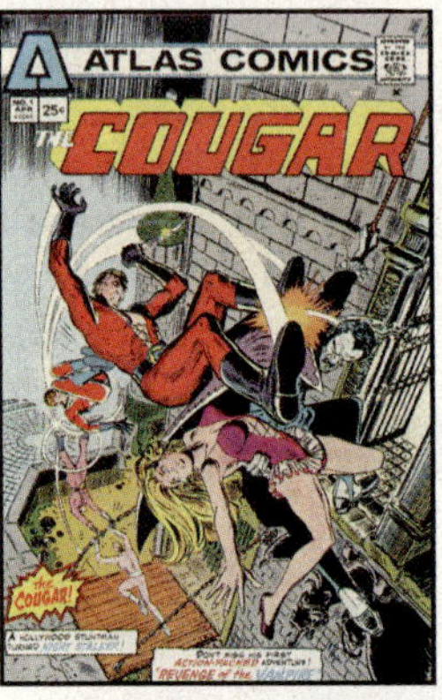

The Cougar #1
April 1975

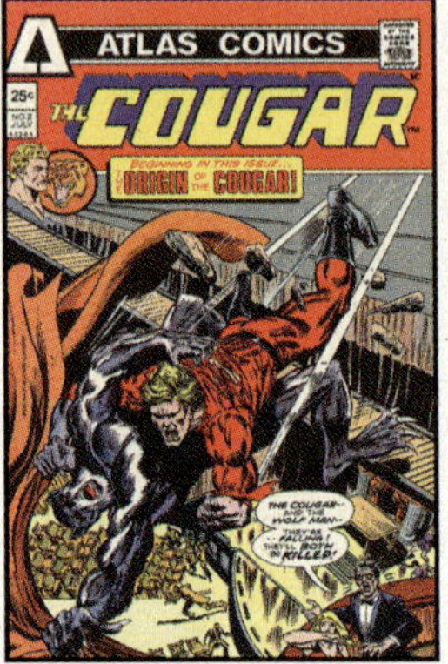

The Cougar #2
July 1975

Demon-Hunter #1
September 1975

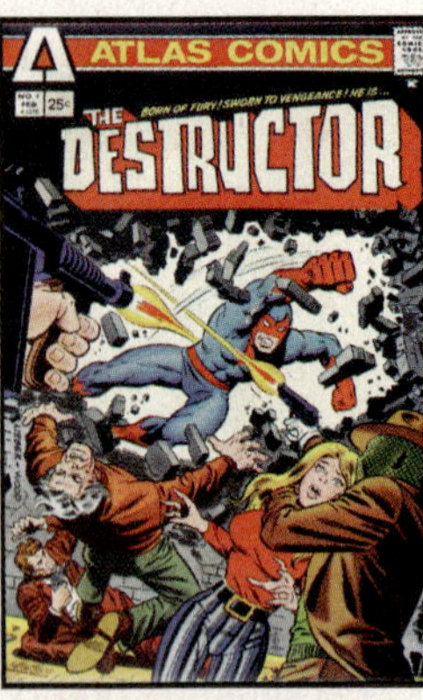

The Destructor #1
February 1975

The Destructor #2
April 1975

The Destructor #3
June 1975

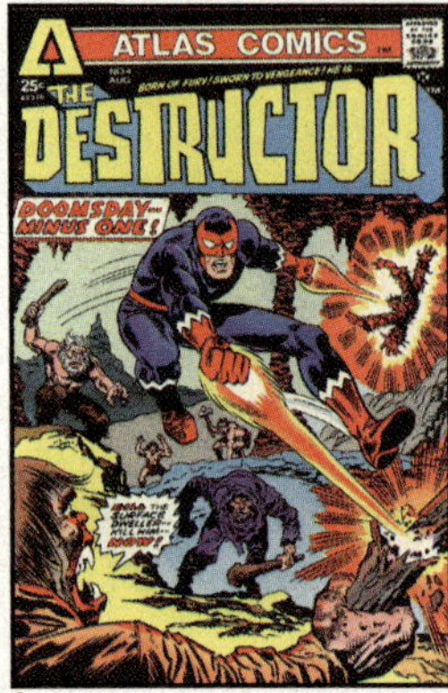

The Destructor #4
August 1975

Fright #1
August 1975

The Grim Ghost #1
January 1975

The Grim Ghost #2
March 1975

The Grim Ghost #3
July 1975

Hands of the Dragon #1
June 1975

Ironjaw #1
January 1975

Ironjaw #2
March 1975

Ironjaw #3
May 1975

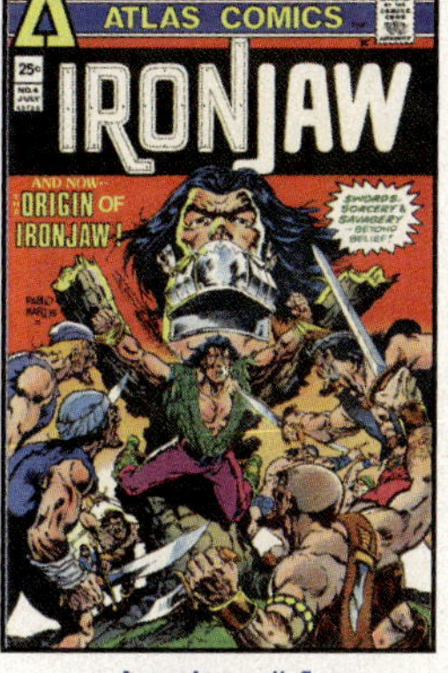

Ironjaw #4
July 1975

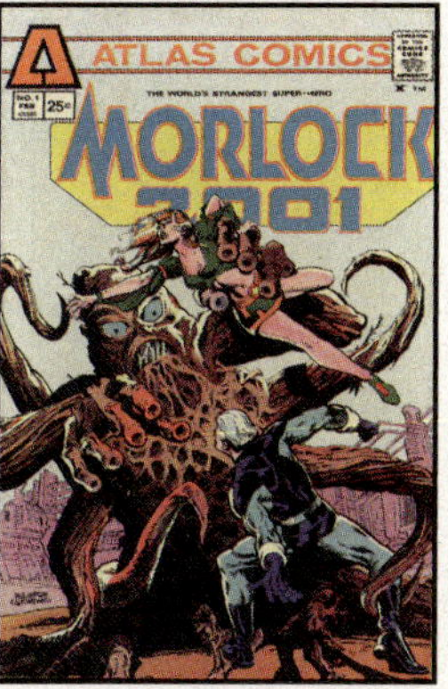

Morlock 2001 #1
February 1975

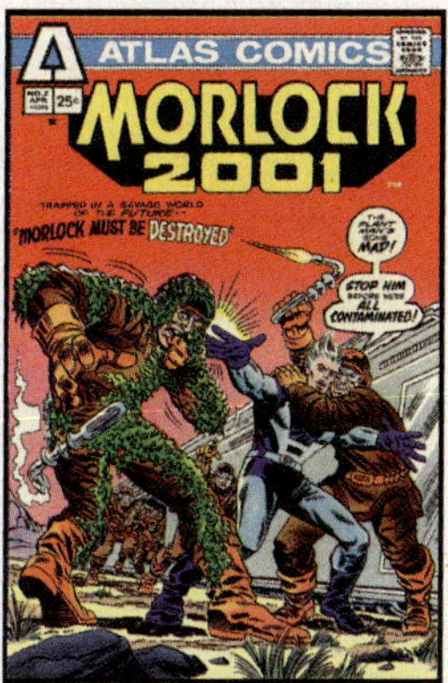

Morlock 2001 #2
April 1975

Morlock 2001 #3
July 1975

Phoenix #1
January 1975

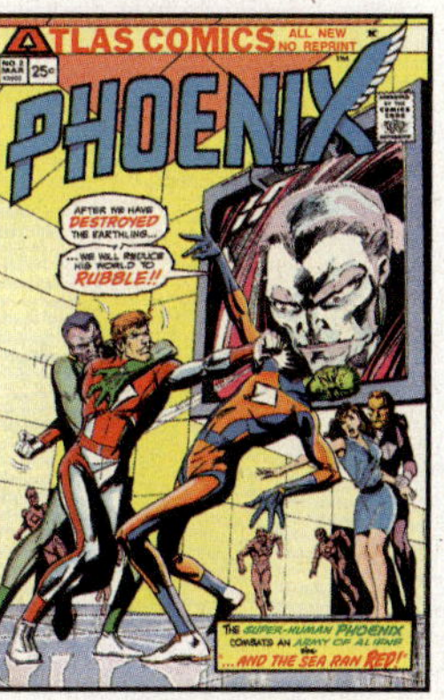

Phoenix #2
March 1975

Phoenix #3
June 1975

Phoenix #4
October 1975

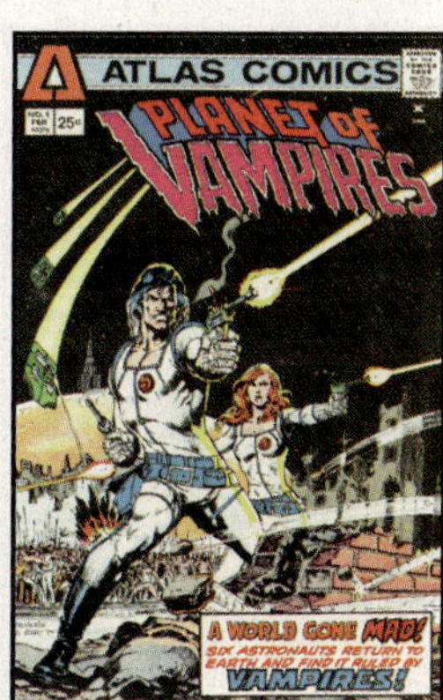

Planet of Vampires #1
February 1975

Planet of Vampires #2
April 1975

Planet of Vampires #3
July 1975

Police Action #1
February 1975

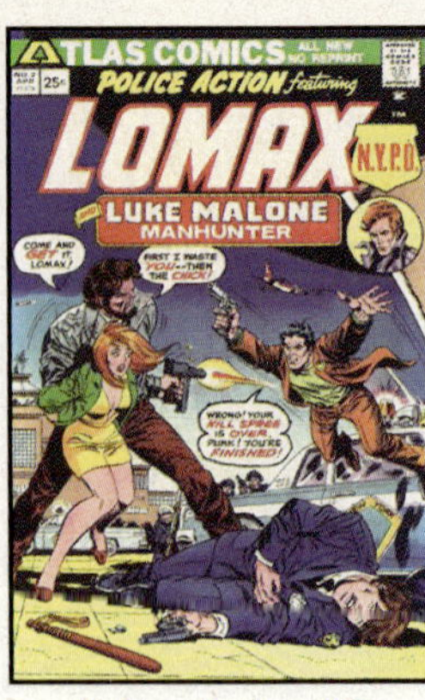

Police Action #2
April 1975

Police Action #3
June 1975

Savage Combat Tales #1
February 1975

Savage Combat Tales #2
April 1975

Savage Combat Tales #3
July 1975

The Scorpion #1
February 1975

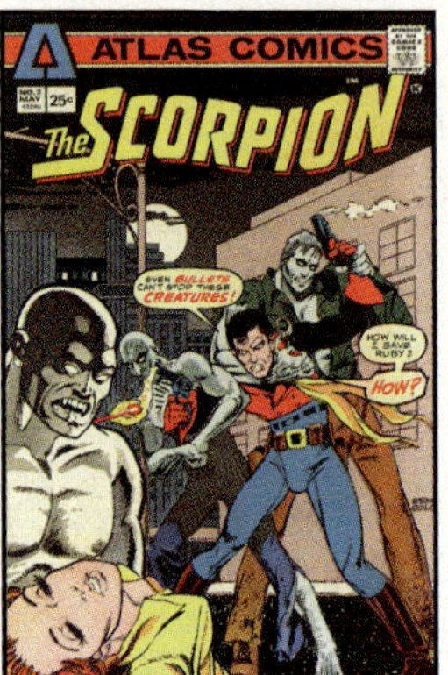

The Scorpion #2
May 1975

The Scorpion #3
July 1975

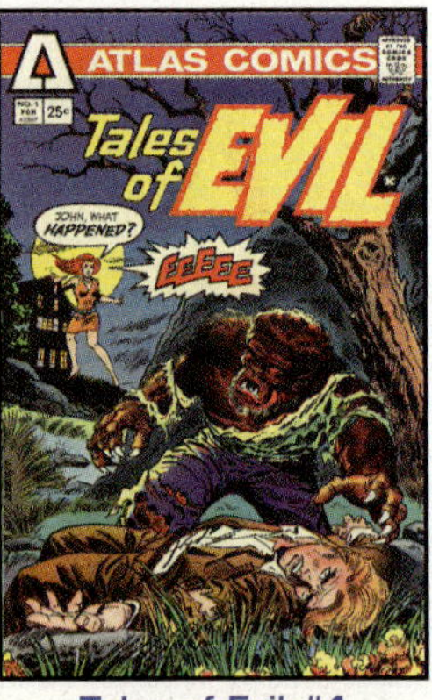

Tales of Evil #1
February 1975

Tales of Evil #2
April 1975

Tales of Evil #3
July 1975

Targitt #1
March 1975

Targitt #2
June 1975

Targitt #3
July1975

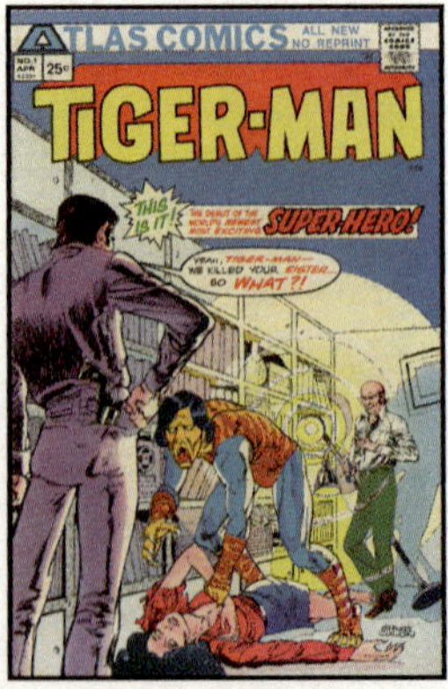

Tigerman #1
April 1975

Tigerman #2
June 1975

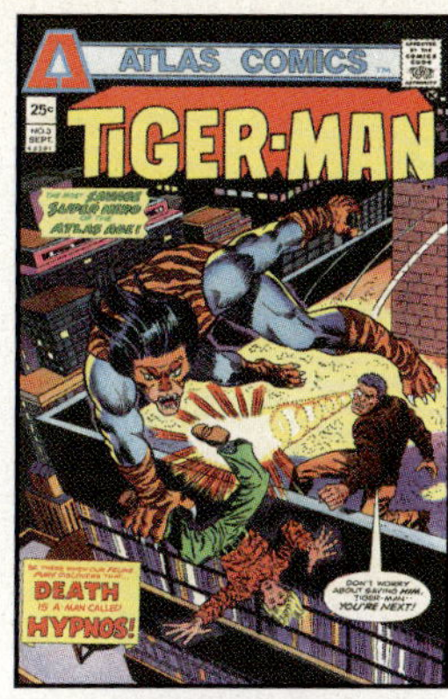

Tigerman #3
September 1975

Vicki #1
February 1975

Vicki #2
April 1975

Vicki #3
June 1975

Vicki #4
August 1975

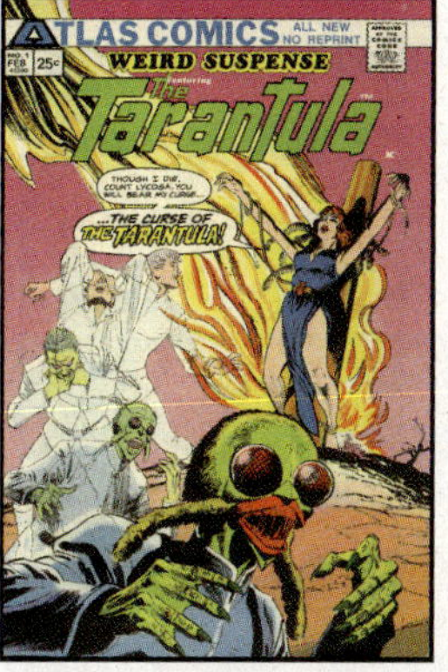

Weird Suspense #1
February 1975

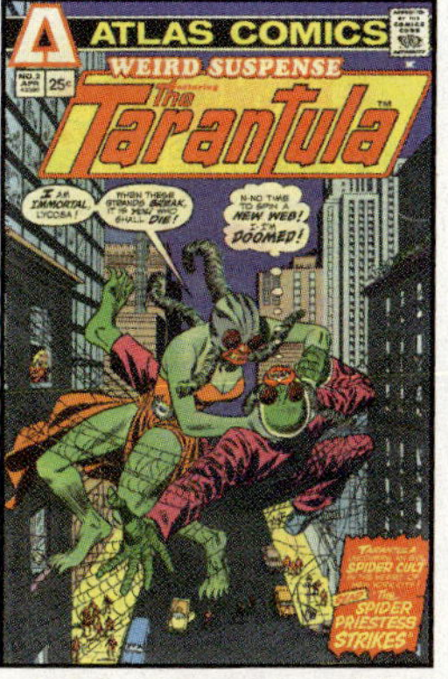

Weird Suspense #2
April 1975

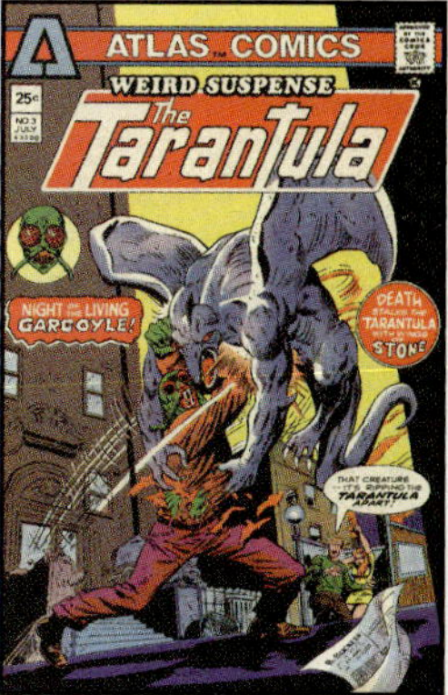

Weird Suspense #3
June 1975

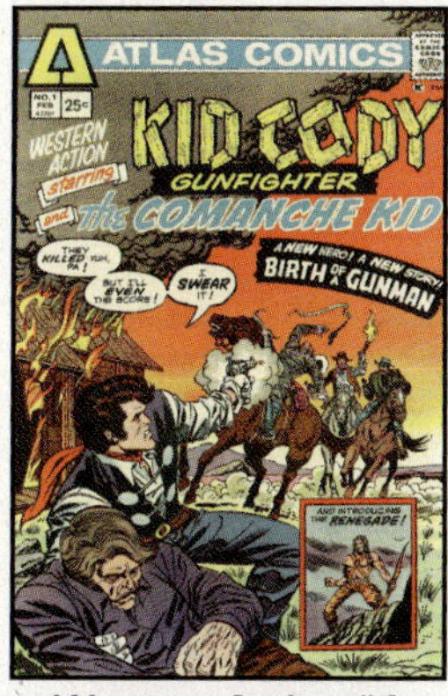

Western Action #1
February 1975

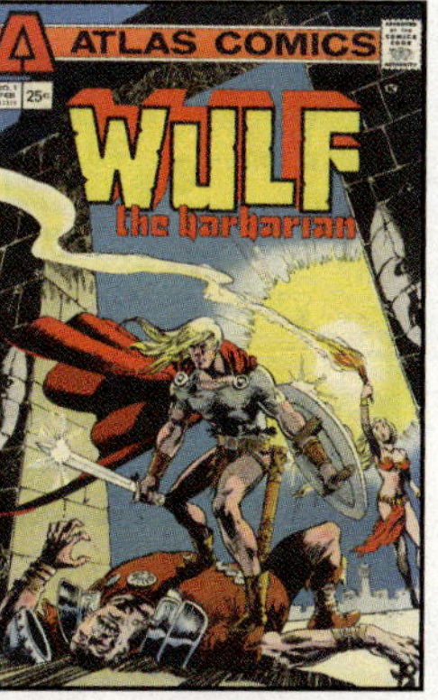

Wulf the Barbarian #1
February 1975

Wulf the Barbarian #2
April 1975

Wulf the Barbarian #3
July 1975

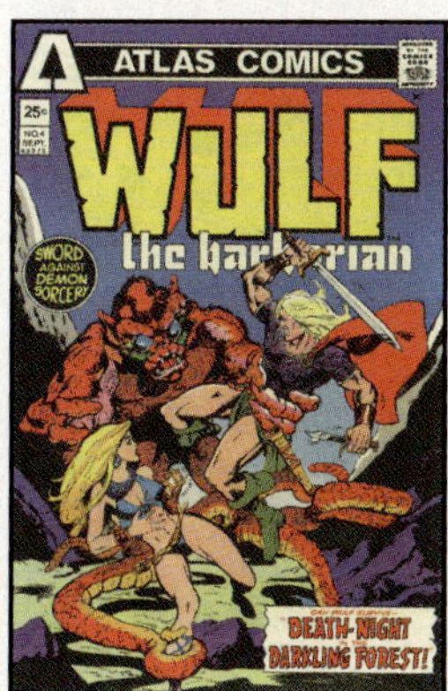

Wulf the Barbarian #4
September 1975

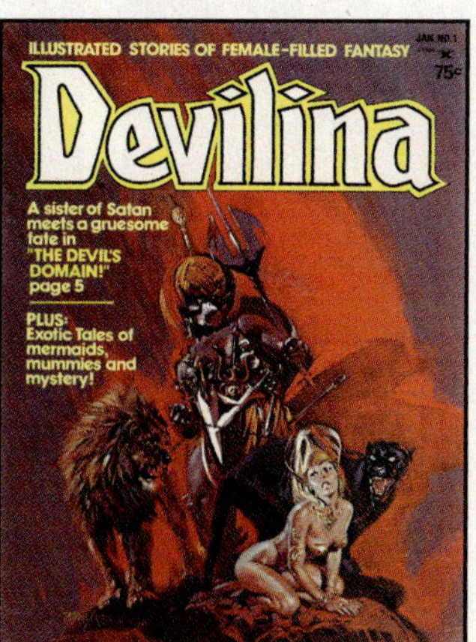

Devilina #1
January 1975

Devilina #2
May 1975

Gothic Romances #1
December 1974

Movie Monsters #1
December 1974

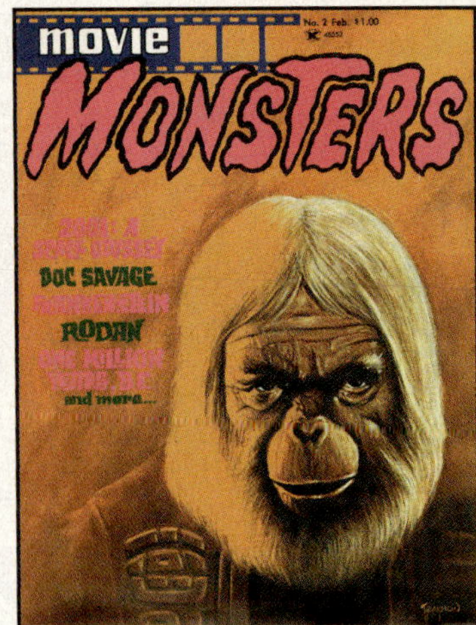

Movie Monsters #2
February 1975

Movie Monsters #3
April 1975

Movie Monsters #4
August 1975

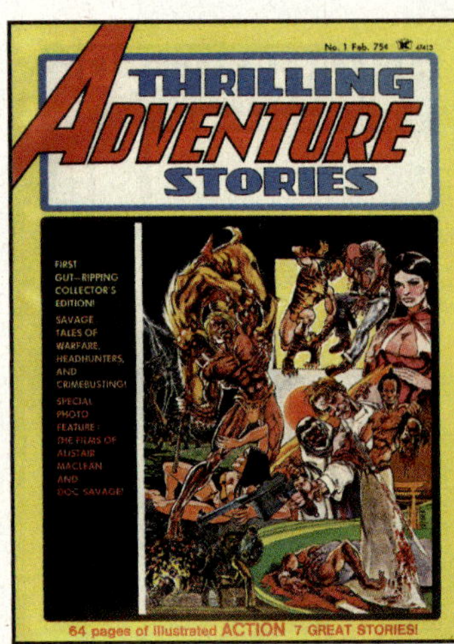

Thrilling Adventure Stories #1
February 1975

Thrilling Adventure Stories #2
August 1975

Weird Tales of the Macabre #1
January 1975

Weird Tales of the Macabre #2
March 1975

By J.C. Vaughn, Mike Wilbur and Michael Naiman

With creators such as Neal Adams, Howard Chaykin, Pat Broderick, Walter Simonson, Jeff Rovin, Frank Thorne, Pablo Marcos, Larry Lieber, Al Milgrom, John Severin, Alex Toth, Dick Giordano, Mike Sekowsky, Sal Amendola, Ernie Colon, Steve Ditko, Archie Goodwin, Larry Hama, Russ Heath, Mike Ploog, Rich Buckler, Wally Wood, Tom Sutton, Doug Wildey, and others, even some of the more obscure Atlas-Seaboard titles are worth investigating. Here is a quick, somewhat subjective run-down of each of the titles.

THE BARBARIANS

This first (and only) issue of Atlas' third Sword & Sorcery title was to begin an ongoing anthology series featuring "not only established brawlers like Ironjaw and Wulf, but also new concepts in swash-buckling heroics..."

Published between *Ironjaw* #3 and #4, the lead feature united Ironjaw with his new biographer Gary Friedrich (who assumed scripting duties with #4) and set a new direction for the character's own series. The backup in this issue was the story of Andrax, an Olympic athlete from 1976 kidnapped by a mad scientist and put in suspended animation to awaken 2000 years later in a desolate future.

BLAZING BATTLE TALES

A one shot war comic featuring Sgt. Hawk (sounds a lot like Rock...) and his killer Platoon. Set in WWII, we have potato mashers, damsels in distress, carnage and explosions... all typical of the genre. There's a couple  of bondage panels and the omnipresent Nazi devils.

The one redeeming feature is a John Severin two-page salute to American hero Private William Swanson closing out this less than memorable book.

THE BRUTE

The Brute was a sub-human cave dweller frozen during the last Ice Age and thawed "in the Spring of 1975" from the heat produced by a nuclear power plant built near his subterranean tomb. Hungry and confused, the Brute kills two young boys exploring his cave. A female scientist is awarded custody by the court, but her plans of study are ruined when the father of the murdered boys is killed trying to exact vengeance. From there, the series becomes a 

sub-human version of *The Fugitive*, with the woman scientist trying to save the Brute, even as police hunt him with orders to kill.

The third and final issue foreshadowed a change in direction, with the Brute speaking his first words, and the introduction of a costumed nemesis, Doom-stalker.

THE COUGAR

Stuntman Jeff Rand thrives on the danger of his chosen profession, known to his fellow stuntmen as The Cougar due to his cat-like speed and agility. Issue #1 has him battling a vampire and pretty standard supernatural fare all around. Issue #2 shows us his origin and continues the tale with the obligatory werewolf saga. Battling throughout the issue his heretofore unknown werewolf brother, we never discover what happens to the crippled Cougar and his shattered spinal cord as the issue wraps up.

DEMON-HUNTER

Created and plotted by Marvel veteran Rich Buckler, and written by David Anthony Kraft (best known for his run on *The Defenders*), Demon-Hunter was one of the most original titles published by Atlas-Seaboard (the character would later resurface as in two different incarnations.)

"What does a Demon-Hunter do?" read the opening page, "Everything he can to prevent Xenogenesis... the rebirth of a demon race here on Earth! His name? Gideon Cross. He is a telepath." 

Empowered by a cult seeking to bring about Xenogenesis, Gideon Cross was empowered with a shadow cloak and new abilities to serve their bidding. He turned against them, however, and became a one-man force against their evil. Unlike Dr. Strange or Dr. Fate, Demon Hunter was fighting a specific war against a specific evil.

THE DESTRUCTOR

One of the longest-lived Atlas-Seaboard characters started with the amazing team of Archie Goodwin (writer), Steve Ditko (pencils), Wally Wood (inks) and Larry Lieber (editing).

Jay Hunter was a low-life, young thug-in-training.

His father was a noble scientist trying to come up with a formula to expand man's senses, to create a super-hero. When Jay's crime lord boss marked him for death, both he and his father were mortally wounded. There was enough serum for one. His father gave it to him. He became the Destructor.

Almost an anti-Spider-Man, he was shunned by his high school crowd because he used to shake them down for money. Otherwise, this one stuck pretty close to the Spidey formula, down to the oath at the end of #1.

Goodwin stayed for three issues with Gerry Conway writing the fourth. Ditko handled the art on all four with Wood inking the first two and Al Milgrom inking the fourth.

FRIGHT

Featuring the Son of Dracula, this lone issue tells of the original Dracula's union with a female blood relative. Betrayed by Dracula following the birth of their son, the unnamed woman sends the baby to America with a foster mother, with instructions for his "protection". Furious, Dracula vows to one day reclaim his son.

Years later, in 1975, Columbia University professor Adam Lucard is horrified when his true nature reveals itself for the first time. Aware of his heritage, Lucard always takes nocturnal precautions passed down from his natural mother... but an intruder disturbs his rest and becomes his first victim.

THE GRIM GHOST

Recently hanged Revolutionary War highwayman Matthew Dunsinane is going to suffer the tortures of perdition, thanks to his new found buddy Satan... unless, of course, they can make a "deal." Lucifer wants Matthew to keep him supplied with souls for his domain since evil people deserve to die! Armed with a few parlor tricks supplied by Satan, the Grim Ghost is sent into the 20th Century to harvest his crop of evil-doers. He rides mounted atop a jet black steed laughing like a demon from the darkest pits of hell only to battle evil in our time.

THE HANDS OF THE DRAGON

Wu Teh was a twin raised by his grandfather in a mysterious Chinese monastery. Trained in the martial arts, the other twin, Ling, turned to evil. Wu Teh, also known as The Dragon, became a journalist and moved to America to seek out his evil brother, who worked for the Evil Dr. Nhu. Not just Dr. Nhu, Evil Dr. Nhu. The story was convoluted, but probably could have been straightened out if it has taken place over two issues. A second issue, though, this book would never have.

IRONJAW

The first of the Atlas sword-slinging characters, Ironjaw roams the world in Earth's distant, post-apocalyptic future. He's a violent, amoral wanderer who lives for battle. Hired by rebels to help overthrow a tyrannical king, Ironjaw discovers his true heritage.

When he was an infant, his mother's lover killed Ironjaw's father, the true king, and ascended to the throne himself. With the complicity of the queen, the new king ordered the infant killed, since he would inherit the throne and depose the usurper upon reaching adulthood. A soft-hearted stablehand abandoned the infant on a snowy mountainside, rather than kill him.

After killing the tyrant-king, Ironjaw, identified by a distinctive birthmark as the true heir to the throne, is crowned king. Upon discovering to his dismay that "...a king cannot fight, or hunt, or steal or chase wenches...," Ironjaw chooses to slip away in the middle of the night, abandoning his new kingdom to resume his wanderer's ways.

After a personality-altering interlude in *The Barbarians* #1, Ironjaw returns in his 4th and final issue with the first part of his long-awaited origin story; the tale of how the abandoned infant became the warrior.

MORLOCK 2001

The year is 2001 A.D., a time when life as we know it has become hideously transformed. A rigid totalitarian regime holds the people in an iron grip, and mankind's greatest truths have been declared "inoperative." Professor Kroschell, the "mad botanical professor" has been conducting illegal botanical experimentations when he is gunned down by the jack-booted police. They confiscate a gigantic pod that holds a male human within its leaves.

Outwardly appearing human yet structurally a plant, we are introduced to Morlock. When transformed into his plant-like form his mind is clouded with the bestial preoccupation for finding food.

Only to later find out that the mad scientist was planning to develop an army of Plant Men to overthrow the dictatorship, Morlock continues his fight against oppression in 2001. Beware the touch of Morlock! He'll turn everyone into fungus creatures.

The saving grace is issue #3, which is drawn by Steve Ditko and inked by Berni Wrightson. Clearly one of the best issues in the entire Atlas comic book run.

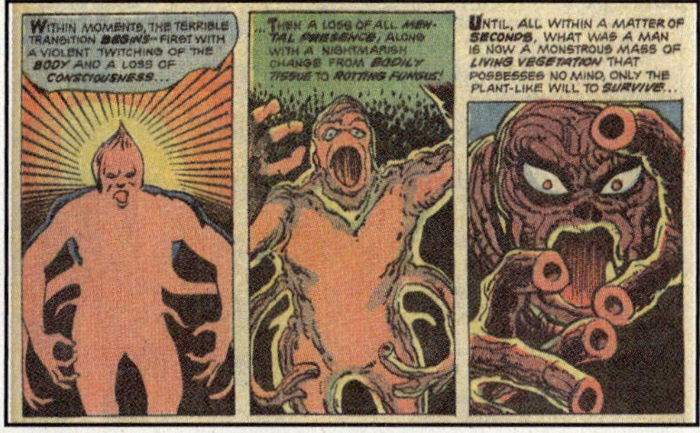

THE PHOENIX

Near death, the sole survivor of the destruction of an orbiting space station is rescued by a group of aliens who observe Earth from a secret sub-Arctic base. The aliens have been monitoring human evolution, which they claim to have initiated millions of years ago through the deliberate mutation of prehistoric apes.

Incorporating some of the aliens' technology into his flight suit, the astronaut escapes from his captors. On the run, he stops to use his stolen powers to aid a disaster-stricken Reykjavik, Iceland... thus alerting the aliens to his location. A battle ensues, and the aliens' installation is destroyed in an atomic explosion. Reykjavik is leveled by the shockwave.

On a rampage of revenge, the alien survivors set about the task of destroying all human life on earth, which they have now deemed a failed experiment. Beginning (of course) with New York City.

In issue #4 (with new writer Gary Friedrich at the helm) the title changes to *Phoenix...The Protector*. Blaming himself for the alien attacks on Reykjavik and New York, and despairing of any hope for the future of mankind now that the aliens are on the warpath, Phoenix carves a tombstone for planet Earth and launches himself into space at full power, planning to burn himself up in the atmosphere.

Rescued by yet another group of aliens (The Protectors) Phoenix is given a choice. Revealing themselves to be the masters of the previous group of aliens, the Protectors offer Phoenix the opportunity to prevent the termination of all human life on Earth by proving they are "worthy" of life. Given a new costume, new identity and new powers, Phoenix has become The Protector.

PLANET OF VAMPIRES

Playing on that era's popular post-apocalyptic sub-genre of science fiction, *Planet of Vampires* manages to incorporate elements of *Planet of the Apes*, *Omega Man*, and *Buck Rogers* into a very interesting concept.

Launched in 2010, a manned Mars mission returns to Earth after a five-year journey. The six astronauts aboard are tense, arguing with each other, and they can't raise Mission Control. They're forced to make a water landing just outside of New York, a city they find in ruins.

Following a nuclear war, society has split in two. Those who live in a protective dome, and the savages outside it. The folks from the dome rescue the astronauts (well, five of them anyway) and present themselves as

the saviors of mankind. Only the savages are actually the good guys, the "domies" have been mutated into vampires who prey on humans.

Two great Pat Broderick-Neal Adams covers were followed by a Russ Heath cover.

POLICE ACTION

Big City cops are used to violence from petty heists to wholesale slaughter. But when one of their own ends up in pieces over a hundred foot area, that's when NYPD's Sam Lomax gets called! Plenty of .38 Special gun play in these pages. Mike Ploog adds his Sam Spade-esque San Francisco based gumshoe, Luke Malone, as the back-up feature. The artistic contrasts are striking. What we ended up with is a bi-coastal police drama that had seen it's day before it was published!

SAVAGE COMBAT TALES

This features Sgt. Ben Stryker and his Death Squad. Rescuing his band of war-hardened combat-happy commandos from certain death, Stryker assembles his group made up of unhappy US Army prisoners Lee Shigeta, judo expert (and of Asian origin), Duke Ripley, circus acrobat, Turk Ankrum, behemoth pro wrestler, and Ice Marko, gangster (and of course, his last name ends in a vowel). They start out as jailbirds and end up as heroes. By issue #3, the convicts get pardoned for their heroic exploits and wonder how they'll spend the rest of the war in retirement.

THE SCORPION

Probably the Atlas title with the most break out potential was *The Scorpion*, written and illustrated by Howard Chaykin. At least the first two issues.

The Scorpion was a man presently called "Moro Frost," but who had many different identities over many different generations. Using themes he would continue to explore over the next 15 years, Chaykin created a pulp-type adventure hero set in the days just before World War II.

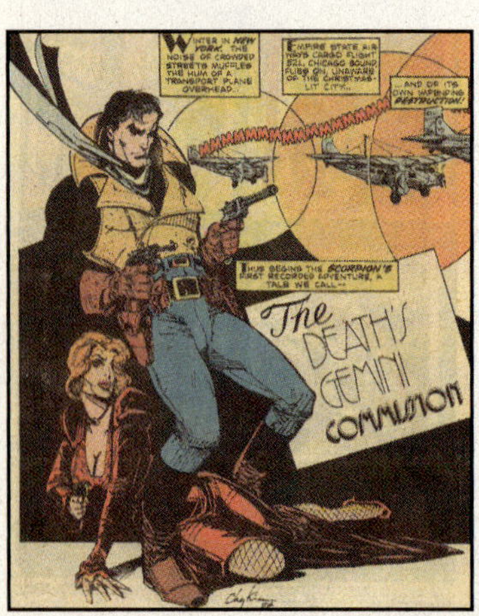

The second issue saw art assists from a veritable Who's Who of artists: Berni Wrightson, Michael Kaluta, and Walter Simonson among them.

The third issue has just about nothing to do with the first two. Chaykin quit over issues of control regarding his character. With a Gabe Levy/Jim Craig story set 30 years later and the main character now a Daredevil-like costumed crime fighter, only the logo remained.

TALES OF EVIL

A horror anthology series with no regularly featured characters, *Tales of Evil* included stories of a demon conjuror, a werewolf, and a vampire in its inaugural issue. The second issue starred the Bog Beast, backed up with a ghost story and another werewolf story.

The final issue stars The Man-Monster, a conceited playboy mutated into an amphibious form by an unknown substance unearthed by an offshore oil rig. The Man-Monster, incidentally, battles a costumed villain named Hell-Blazer. The story concludes with the note "to be continued in the first exciting issue of the Man-Monster." Also appearing in this issue is a second tale of the Bog Beast.

TARGITT

A candidate for the most neurotic title of the line. It starts like a typical guy-with-a-gun-gets-revenge-for-slain-family story complete with thugs, drugs, teenage killers, and the mob. Then the action gets... well, cartoony. Slapstick. He blows a guy's head off and the panel looks more like an Archie comic. A few pages later, Modesy Blaise would fit right in. And that's just the first issue. In the second issue, he gets a costume just like Daredevil's foe, Bullseye, and it's a rocket sled downhill from there.

TIGER-MAN

After injecting himself with an experimental serum derived from tiger chromosomes, a young doctor working in a clinic in Zambia acquires the strength, speed and keen senses of a tiger. After his sister is murdered, Tiger-Man uses his enhanced abilities to track down and exact vengeance on her killers. Feeling unfulfilled after dispatching the murderers, Tiger-Man resolves to hunt down all criminals who prey on others.

VICKI

We have a teen blonde bombshell and her dark-haired female friend, Tommy the red-haired boyfriend and his dark-haired rival, and a large slow moving character named Tiny. Add them all up, drop them in Centerville, USA and you have Archie... er, Tippy Teen.... er, Vicki, Atlas' contribution to the teen scene.

Issue #1 is a 68 pager, but the oddball of the entire Atlas line is probably *Vicki* #2, the only Atlas square bound comic of all the line's issues! On top of it all, there is nothing even printed on the spine of this, likely the rarest comic Atlas ever produced, certainly so in high grade.

Once again we have cartoon teen hi jinx set in the high school background of Anywhere, USA. Enjoyable for just about any pony-tailed youngster between the ages of 10 and 15.

All issues are reprints of Tower Comics' *Tippy Teen*. Many characters were slightly redrawn to reflect the more contemporary clothing and hair styles of the day. Tower Comics published 26 issues of *Tippy Teen* (25 regular issues and 1 Special Collectors Edition) from November 1965 thru October 1969.

WEIRD SUSPENSE

The Dark Ages in Europe finds the soon-to-be-burned-at-the-stake Spider Princess of the Tarantula Cult placing a curse on the male descendants of her captor, Count Lycosa. They will be doomed to wander the countryside in quest of victims to appease their spider's lust.

Count Eugene Lycosa, the 11th in line to bear the heinous curse, has vowed to use his tarantula powers for some practical purpose. It is the duty of the Avenging Arachnid to protect the helpless and prey on evil wherever it may flourish. Issue #2 finds the High Priestess back from the grave seeking vengeance against the Count Eugene Lycosa, only to again end up on the short end of the battle.

The last issue finds our spider-buddy fighting a turban-topped swami who has the power to control inanimate matter. Peter Parker has nothing to fear from this fly-headed webman.

WESTERN ACTION

A "must have" for any serious western fan! Larry Lieber writes the "Kid Cody" story that is illustrated by *Jonny Quest* creator Doug Wildey! Better than average story and great art. The backup feature (by Steve Skeates and, incredibly, Jack Abel) features the Comanche Kid.

WULF THE BARBARIAN

"...On a nameless world in a forgotten time..." there lived a man called Wulf. Orphaned 10 years ago when his parents, the king and queen, were slain in an ambush staged by trolls in the service of an evil sorcerer, Wulf has spent the last decade training for the day he would return to claim his birthright.

After his trainer/mentor is killed by the same troll who killed his mother 10 years earlier, Wulf avenges his mother's death, reclaims his father's sword from the slain troll, and begins his long awaited trip home. As Wulf rides homeward with the intent to raise an army to raid the evil sorcerer's lair and free his hereditary kingdom, he encounters many magic-induced obstacles conjured by his foe.

DEVILINA

The only Atlas-Seaboard B&W magazine with a regularly featured character, Devilina is sort of a cross between Vampirella and Marvel's Santana.

The sister of Satan, Devilina is transported through time, along with her mother, from the Biblical "time of the casting out" to modern day New England. There, under the watchful eye of her mother, the infant Devilina grows to womanhood in a mansion guarding "the secret entrance to Hell.

Shortly after arriving at college, Devilina is contacted by Satan, who invites her to join him in ruling Hell. She refuses and is allowed to return home.

Years pass and Devilina pushes family concerns out of her mind as she pursues her studies. After her date to the graduation ball is killed in a fire triggered by Satan, she vows a war of vengeance on her brother.

The rest of the book is an anthology of horror stories featuring women in the lead roles, including a tale of the reanimated mummy of Queen Nefertiri.

GOTHIC ROMANCES

The real oddball of the Atlas-Seaboard line and probably the rarest they ever published. What red-blooded male teen would possibly buy this magazine in 1974? Check out the ads for teeth whitening, convertible nude bras, weight loss miracles and wig sales! While certainly reminiscent of covers from DC's romance comics (and maybe even *House of Mystery*), the only redeeming virtue once you get by the overbearing text content is the spot artwork by the likes of Howard Chaykin, Ernie Colon... and even Neal Adams.

MOVIE MONSTERS

A large magazine format 8" x 10 3/4 " devoted to television and movie sci-fi and monsters. This black and white magazine utilizes movie stills and studio photos to illustrate this look at horror and space operas similar to the style of *Famous Monsters of Filmland*.

THRILLING ADVENTURE STORIES

These two issues (in particular the second), are worth the hunt it will take to find them. The first features a Tiger-Man story (a prequel to the series) and several other stories which would have been at home in any Warren title of the time. The first issue includes a beautiful Frank Thorne-illustrated version of "Lawrence of Arabia" and an article on the films of Alistair Maclean.

The second issue is probably one of the all-time gems of black and white publishing. Starting with the Neal Adams cover (semi-obscured with copy), the issue contains an Archie Goodwin/Walter Simonson samurai story (circa their Manhunter collaboration) and additional pieces by Jack Sparling, Russ Heath, John Severin, and Alex Toth. It also includes a Warren-like article on *The Towering Inferno*.

WEIRD TALES OF THE MACABRE

With covers by Jeff Jones and Boris Vallejo, respectively, the two issues of this series would have fit right in with the horror material being produced by Warren or Marvel at the time. Some beautiful work from artists including Pat Boyette, Ernie Colon, Leo Duranona, and John Severin. Bog Beast, seen in *Tales of Evil*, also appears in #2.

....

ANNOUNCED, BUT NEVER PUBLISHED

Among the projects announced but never published included *Midnight Madness* #1 (this is a black humor magazine, and features a satire of the Night Stalker with a cover by Tom Sutton), *The Barbarians* #2 (Wulf the Barbarian stars in "Death Night in the Darkling Forest" by Gary Friedrich and Jim Craig, which did see print in *Wulf the Barbarian* #4), *Hands of the Dragon* #2 ("Operation Dragonkill" by Ed Fedory and Jim Craig), *The Cougar* #3 (The Cougar fights a fellow stuntman who has a skull of steel. He also gains a new costume and new powers as the book heads off in a new direction in "Claws of the Crippled Cougar" by Gary Friedrich, Alan Kupperberg and Frank Giacoia), *Planet of Vampires* #4 (Mike Friedrich and Pat Broderick present "Revenge of the Vampires" with a cover by Pablo Marcos), *Fright* #2 (The Son of Dracula stars in "He Stalks the Streets in Silence" by Gary Friedrich and Frank Springer, with a cover by Frank Thorne), *Tales of Evil* #4 (The Scorpion stars in a ten page lead "The Graffiti Killer" by Gabe Levy and Keith Pollard, with an untitled Bog Beast story as the backup), *Iron Jaw* #5 (Soran the Sorceress dies in "The Sword and the Sorceress" by Gary Friedrich and Pablo Marcos), *Vicki* #5, *Man-Monster* #1 (This issue would have featured Atlas' first team-up as the Man-Monster fought Demon-Hunter, written by Dave Kraft and Jim Lawrence, pencilled by "The Mean Machine" [Rich Buckler, Keith Pollard and Aubrey Bradford] and inked by Wayne Howard, Dan Greene and Frank Giacoia). Also announced but never appearing, Steve Ditko was scheduled to write and draw a spy/super-hero series called *Wrecage*.

Special thanks to AtlasArchives.com

DISCOVER
WHAT'S GONE BEFORE

www.gemstonepub.com

GEMSTONE
PUBLISHING

BACK ISSUES NOW AVAILABLE
The Overstreet Comic Book Price Guide • Overstreet's FAN
Comic Book Marketplace • Overstreet's Comic Book Monthly
Overstreet's Golden Age & Silver Age Quarterly
Hake's Price Guide To Character Toys • The Overstreet Comic Book Grading Guide
Overstreet's FAN Edition Comics • And much more!

THE ORIGINAL ATLAS
AN OVERVIEW

By Pat Calhoun

Martin Goodman began work in the publishing industry around 1930 as a salesman for Independent News. Soon he was publishing his own pulps: an early example, *Ka-zar* (1936) was typical of his approach: Tarzan was hot so he offered a clone thereof. Ka-zar also appeared in the first of Goodman's comic books, *Marvel Comics* #1 (1939), which introduced two key characters, The Human Torch and the Submariner. 'Subby' was an anti-hero with appealing art, and the 'Torch' was an android without much emotional depth, but the fiery streak he made soaring across the sky was one of the great visual signatures of comics' vibrant Golden Age.

With the introduction of Captain America in 1941 Goodman had a trio of four-color superstars and parlayed them into a healthy list of titles, usually referred to publisher-wise as Timely Comics.

Occasionally in the mid 1940s an issue would appear (such as *Captain America Comics* #36, March 1944) with a new logo on the cover: a little globe with a banner draped across it labeled 'Atlas.' In so few words and realizing that this chapter really gets underway in the late 1940s: Atlas is Goodman's attempt at not just a successful publishing company, but an empire that included self-distribution.

From the vantage of today it is hard to comprehend how important books and magazines were in the pre-TV post-WWII world.

And as comics history has been obsessed with chronicling superheroes, a mistaken impression of the late 1940s sees them as some kind of decline as that genre did decline. But all other genres were exploding as publishers began catering to older audiences as well as kids with the goal of selling more comics. And they did with each year into the 1950s topping the last.

In 1949 Goodman closed down the superhero titles and began ramping up the genres. As the 1950s got underway the Atlas empire (embracing a plethora of sub-publishers) was in full swing. Offerings included at least a dozen mostly monthly titles each of fantasy (*Strange Tales*, *Journey Into Mystery*, *Marvel Tales*, *Mystic*, *Menace*, etc), western (*Kid Colt*, *Black Rider*, *Two-Gun Kid*, etc), war (*Battle*, *Combat Kelly*, *Battlefront*, etc), girl and romance (*Millie the Model*, *Patsy Walker*, *Love Romances*, *Lovers*, etc), a fair amount of crime and funny animal, some satire and jungle titles, and plenty of miscellaneous.

Editor Stan Lee presided over great staff artists and also employed a large group of talented freelancers. Much wonderful work was produced, with Bill Everett, Joe Maneely, and Russ Heath notable standouts on both covers and interiors. (Many artists would return in the 1960s to lend their hands to the Marvel age.)

Goodman's pulps through the early 1950s were a large handful of crime, western, and romance - with a few fantasy and sports titles mixed in. As the pulp format faded, he

Uncanny Tales #2 (August 1952) A colorful intrusion of the 'uncanny' into everyday life: this kind of scene was a staple of the Atlas fantasy covers. Lurid, pellucid, and perfectly framed, this one shows why Joe Maneely is revered by collectors.

launched a paperback line (Lion Books) and pumped his men's magazines (*Stag, Male,* etc) into big sellers along with his popular true crime titles.

Month after month the newsstands were flooded with colorful paper entertainment, a fair amount of it from Goodman. Superheroes had pushed comic sales up to 20 million a month in the WWII years. In the early 1950s the number climbed to an amazing 70 million a month. But comics were headed for a fall.

It's hard to say how much of the trouble was really about censorship (with the crime and horror comics available to kids), but the brouhaha led to a senate investigation which urged the publishers to clean up their act….or else!

In late 1954 a Comics Code was adopted and many horror, crime, and war titles and publishers vanished seemingly overnight. By 1957 sales had plummeted to 12 million a month, and they kept sliding down to five million a month by 1960. Of course television's ever-increasing domination can't be overestimated when calculating the decline of print media.

On top of that Atlas Comics had a second problem. They had weathered the censorship war pretty well, even adding a few titles and artists as smaller publishers fell by the wayside. But Goodman, in a rare instance of market mistiming, contracted with American News for distribution just before that company lost a big court case and went bankrupt.

This also made bad blood between Goodman and the wholesalers, so that going back to self-distribution was removed as an option. Goodman had to eat crow and go with the company owned by rival DC Comics, Independent News, where they cut him down to eight titles a month.

The last Atlas logo appeared in late 1957.

How he made a comeback while under their thumb, first revamping his fantasy titles and then introducing a new generation of superheroes, is of course a Marvelous story…

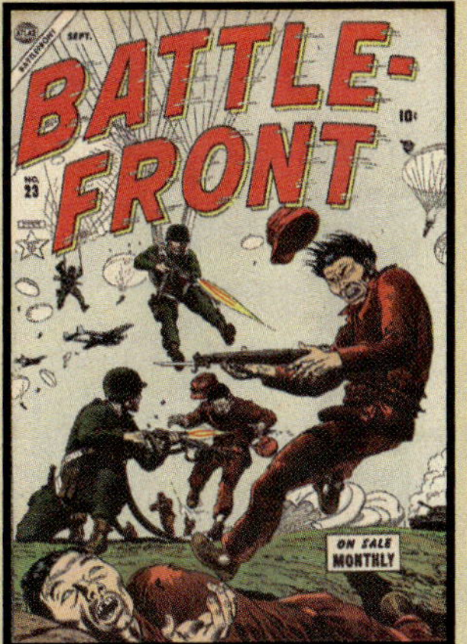

Battle-Front #23 (September 1954) Paratroopers land into red-hot action on this dynamic cover by Russ Heath. Recent speculation has suggested that the war comics were one of the main targets of the censorship movement.

Two-Gun Kid #11 (November 1953) Syd Shores produced a lot of solid art (like this cover), and as Timely art director was a key figure in the transition to Atlas. Two-Gun Kid ran for another 24 years with the last issue (#136) dated April 1977.

Adventures Into Weird Worlds #28 (April 1954) Nice creepy cover by Harry Anderson who did a lot of excellent work for Atlas in the early and mid 1950s. Goodman killed this title with issue #30 because "Weird" was a buzz word that the coming Comics Code would ban.

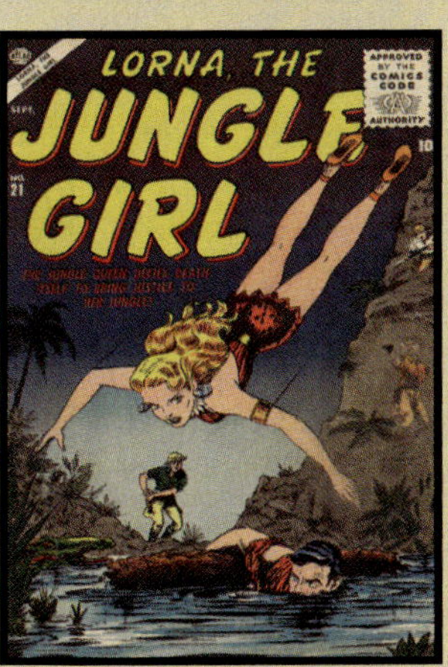

Lorna, the Jungle Girl #21 (September 1956) Bill Everett didn't draw many jungle covers, but this one makes you wish he had! This issue came out just before the premiere of the *Sheena* TV series, making 1956 a banner year for Jun-Gals.

Collecting By
TITLE RUNS & SETS

By Weldon Adams

One frequently overlooked but nonetheless valid way to collect comics is to collect by "title runs" or by sets that are actually specific subsets or groups within other titles. This differs from collecting a title because the goal is not to collect every single issue of that title. And it differs from collecting by creator, although in many cases a run on a title was marked the work of a specific creator's input. The difference here is that you may not collect everything that person does, just this one run on this one book. There are many other ways to define title runs or sets. In the case of team books, you may just want the issues where a specific group of characters are on the team at the same time.

Want to do your own research to find out what issues are included? How about the JLA Satellite era, Frank Miller's first or second run on *Daredevil*, the pre-Venom black costume Spider-Man stories, the Huntress backups in *Wonder Woman*, Marvel Comics with Marvel Value Stamps in them, Walter Simonson's run on *Thor*, Jack Kirby's "Fourth World" titles at DC, the "Project Pegasus" story from *Marvel Two-In-One*, or "Zatanna's Search" from various DC titles?

Those are just a few ideas – there are almost as many of them out there as there are comic books in the first place.

How about some more specific suggestions? Here are some examples of title runs and sets that are fun to collect:

Wonder Woman's "White Period"

In 1968, sales on *Wonder Woman* were not doing well. And not surprising, as in the previous 12 issues, she had fought a villain made of newspaper, a giant egg, a human centipede (don't ask), and been turned into a gorilla. In an effort to revitalize sales and to help the character to connect with a more modern audience, some radical changes were introduced. Wonder Woman gave up all of her Amazonian powers and her costume so she could stay on Earth when the Amazons retreated to a different dimension. She became a regular mortal woman. No powers…No costume…She was just Diana Prince now.

In fact, the new logo said "*Diana Prince: Wonder Woman.*" And the world knew she had lost her powers and was just mortal Diana Prince. So now the emphasis was on the woman, and not the wonder. The new creative team turned her into a woman in charge of her own life. She began studying Karate from an older Chinese man and the title took on a very 'spy adventure' feel for most of this run. This was at a time that the British TV show *The Avengers*, starring Diana Rigg, was very popular. Rigg's character on the show wore very modern clothing and could fight as well as any of the men on the show.

Some of the creators on *Wonder Woman* during this time have cited that as an inspiration for Diana Prince's transformation. Diana Prince began dressing in very similar, modern clothing. And very soon, her gimmick was that whatever she wore was all white, hence the reason this is referred to as her 'White Period'. (Note: This was not Diana Rigg's only contribution to comics' lore. One of Rigg's well-remembered outfits from the *Avengers* TV show, with the cut-out side panels, would also become the inspiration for Saturn Girl's new costume in the *Legion Of Super-Heroes*.)

Wonder Woman's 'White Period' ran from an ad in the back of issue #177 until issue #204. At the end of issue #185, she puts on her first set of white street clothes. This becomes her trademark for the rest of this run. This period also includes a few guest appearances. She appeared in *Superman's Girlfriend Lois Lane #93*, *World's Finest #204*, and *Brave & The Bold #87 & #105*.

Wonder Woman was published bi-monthly at the time. So this period actually lasted from August 1968 (Issue #177) until February 1973 (Issue #204). That is just shy of five years! There is no other change in any other comic book characters' status quo that was as radical of a departure and lasted as long as this one.

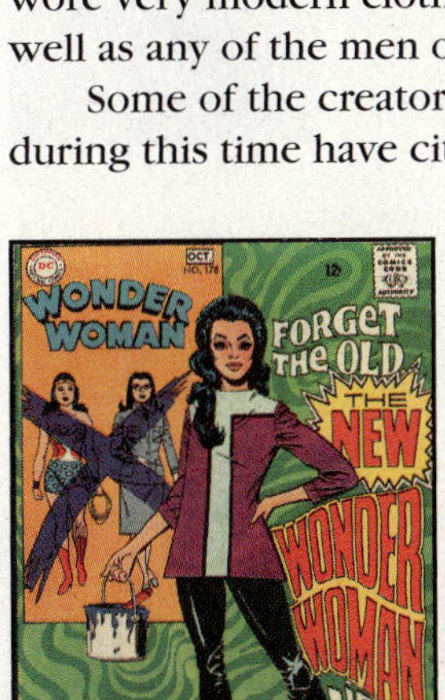

Wonder Woman #178
Sept.-Oct., 1968

Wonder Woman #200
May-June, 1972

Wonder Woman #203
Nov.-Dec., 1972

World's Finest #204
August, 1971

JLA/JSA Team-Ups

Another interesting set to collect are all of the Justice League of America/Justice Society of America crossover stories. By the early 1960s, DC Comics had a winning formula on their hands. They were reviving and updating their old Golden Age heroes. They had even created a then-modern (what we now call the Silver Age) version of the original team, the Justice Society Of America (which appeared in *All Star Comics*). After initial appearances in *Brave and The Bold*, this new team book was titled the *Justice League Of America*.

Naturally there were fans of the original versions of those characters who missed them. After all, *Showcase #4* (featuring the first Silver Age Flash appearance) appeared on the sales racks in 1956, only five and a half years after the last appearance of the Golden Age Flash in *All Star Comics*, home of the original JSA.

So by 1961, DC had found a way to make those fans happy. They had the Silver Age Flash meet the Golden Age Flash in *Flash #123*. And then again in *Flash #129*, only this time there was a flashback to an old JSA case from *All Star Comics #57* (their last appearance). And finally in *Flash #137*, we are given the first full appearance of the JSA in the Silver Age of comics. So if the two Flashes had met, and the JSA was shown to be active again, it was only a matter of time before the JSA met the new JLA. And that is exactly what happened in *Justice League Of America #21*. This started an annual summer crossover event that ran for twenty-two years! Typically it would be a two-issue story or at least a double-sized issue, but several were three issues and one was a massive five-issue story. In later years the stories would begin to feature other teams joining the JLA and JSA.

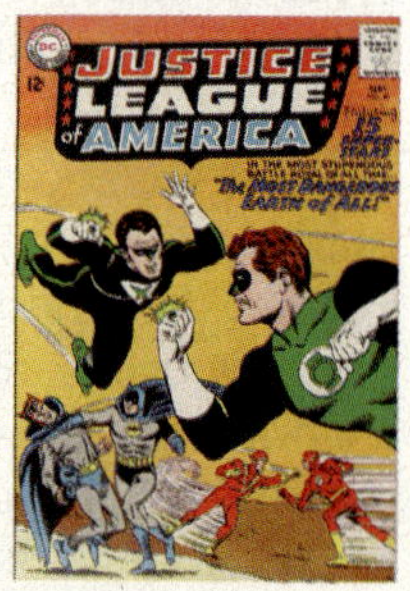

The team-ups are in the following issues…

Issues:	Year:	Teams:	Notes:
JLA #21 & 22	1963	JLA/JSA	First team-up for these two teams.
JLA #29 & 30	1964	JLA/JSA	Introduces 'Earth-3' and the Crime Syndicate
JLA #37 & 38	1965	JLA/JSA	"Crisis on Earth-A"
JLA #46 & 47	1966	JLA/JSA	
JLA #55 & 56	1967	JLA/JSA	First appearance of grown up Robin in the JSA
JLA #64 & 65	1968	JLA/JSA	Introduces Red Tornado android to JSA
JLA #73 & 74	1969	JLA/JSA	Black Canary moves from Earth-2 to Earth-1
JLA #82 & 83	1970	JLA/JSA	
JLA #91 & 92	1971	JLA/JSA	
JLA #100 - 102	1972	JLA/JSA/Seven Soldiers of Victory	First three-issue team-up
JLA #107 & 108	1973	JLA/JSA/Freedom Fighters	Introduces Earth-X
JLA #113	1974	JLA/JSA	100 page special issue. Full story plus reprints.
JLA #123 & 124	1975	JLA/JSA	Writers Cary Bates and Elliot S! Maggin travel from Earth-Prime
JLA #135 - 137	1976	JLA/JSA/Fawcett characters	Introduces Earth-S with the Marvel Family.
JLA #147 & 148	1977	JLA/JSA/LSH	Features the 30th century Legion of Super-Heroes
JLA #159 & 160	1978	JLA/JSA/???	Features characters from DC's past: Jonah Hex, Viking Prince, Enemy Ace, Miss Liberty
JLA #171 & 172	1979	JLA/JSA	Mr. Terrific murdered on the JLA satellite!
JLA #183 - 185	1980	JLA/JSA/New Genesis	Features Kirby's Fourth World characters.
JLA #195 - 197	1981	JLA/JSA	
JLA #207 - 209 and *All-Star Squadron* #14 & 15	1982	JLA/JSA/All-Star Squadron	Five-issue story
JLA #219 & 220	1983	JLA/JSA	Attempt to re-explain Black Canary's origin.
JLA #231 & 232	1984	JLA/JSA	
JLA #244 and *Infinity, Inc.* #19	1985	JLA/JSA/Infinity, Inc.	Leads directly into *Crisis On Infinite Earths*.

There were more cross-overs eventually, but without the 'Earth-1/Earth-2' dynamic, it just wasn't the same.

If that wets your whistle, then be aware that the JSA characters made many other appearances in other DC titles outside of the JLA during this time. Titles such as *Flash*, *Atom*, *Green Lantern*, *Showcase*, and *Brave and The Bold* all had guest appearances by Earth-2 characters. And there are many other books as well.

Go-Go Check Covers

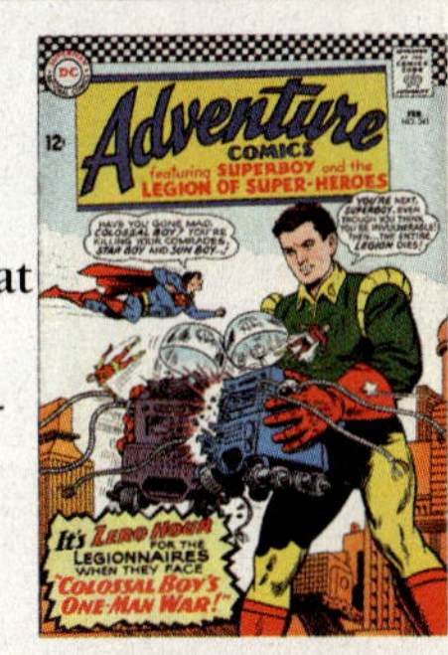

Another DC Comics subset that has received attention over the years is the Go-Go Check covers: In February of 1966, DC decided to add a row of "Go-Go" checks to the tops of all of their comics to make them stand out better on the spinner racks and fall racks used by newsstands, drug stores and grocery stores at the time. Many have viewed this as response to the increasing success that Marvel was having at the time, but the reason or reasons they did it don't really matter. It made them distinct from the issues that came before or after them. They did this until September of 1967.

Action Comics #333-352
Adventure Comics #341-358
Adventures of Bob Hope #98-106
Adventures of Jerry Lewis #93-101
All-American Men of War #114-117
Aquaman #26-34
Atom #24-32
Batman #179-193
Blackhawk #218-234
Brave and The Bold #64-72
Capt. Storm #12-18
Challengers of the Unknown #49-57
Detective Comics #348-365
Doom Patrol #102-112
Falling In Love #82-92
Flash #159-171
Fox and the Crow #96-104
G.I. Combat #117-124
Girls' Love Stories #117-128
Girls' Romances #115-126
Green Lantern #43-54
Hawkman #13-20
Heart Throbs #100-108
House of Mystery #157-168
House of Secrets #77-80
Inferior Five #1-3
Justice League of America #43-54
Metal Men #18-26
Metamorpho #5-13
Mystery in Space #106-110
Our Army at War #165-183
Our Fighting Forces #98-108
Plastic Man #1-5
Sea Devils #28-35
Secret Hearts #110-120

Showcase #61-69
Star Spangled War Stories #126-133
Strange Adventures #185-202
Sugar and Spike #64-71
Superboy #127-140
Superman #185-198
Superman's Girlfriend Lois Lane #63-75
Superman's Pal Jimmy Olsen #91-103
Swing with Scooter #1-7
Tales of the Unexpected #94-101
Teen Titans #2-10
Tomahawk #103-111
Wonder Woman #161-171
World's Finest Comics #156-167
Young Love #54-62
Young Romance #141-148

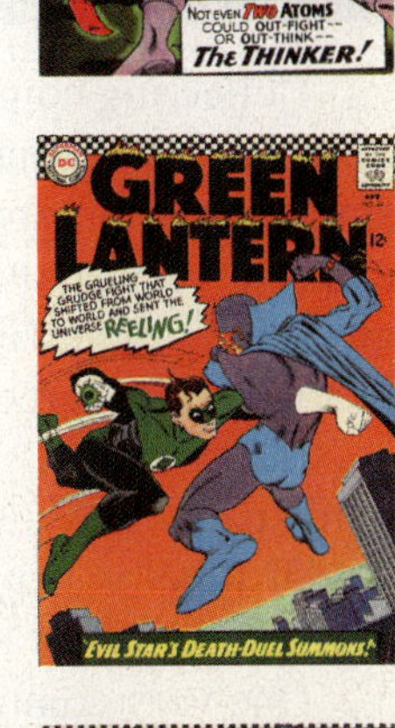

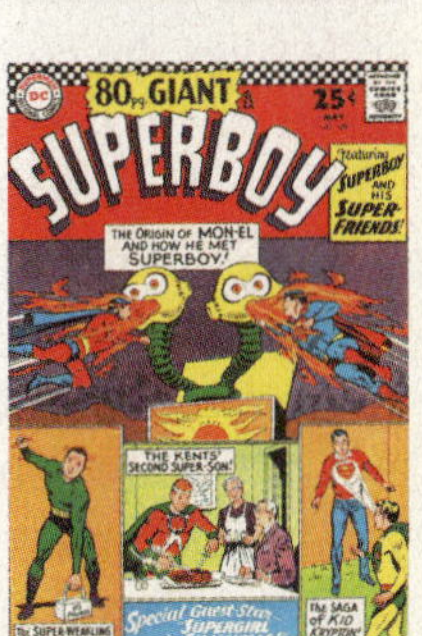

Again, these are just a few suggestions. You could pursue "The 12-Labors of Wonder Woman," which ran in *Wonder Woman* #212 to #222, the Rose & Thorn backups which ran in *Superman's Girlfriend, Lois Lane* from #105 through #130 (skipping only a few issues), The Avengers "Kree/Skrull War" from *Avengers* #89-97, *The Avengers* Wonder Man-Beast era lasted several years. (*Avengers* #136-151 with Beast, and #152-211 with both Wonder Man and the Beast), the *Green Lantern* "Relevant" era of #76-89 (another high-water mark in comic book history), or so many others.

We hope you try collecting some title runs. It can be very rewarding!

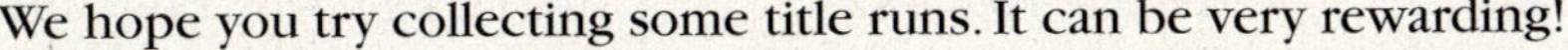

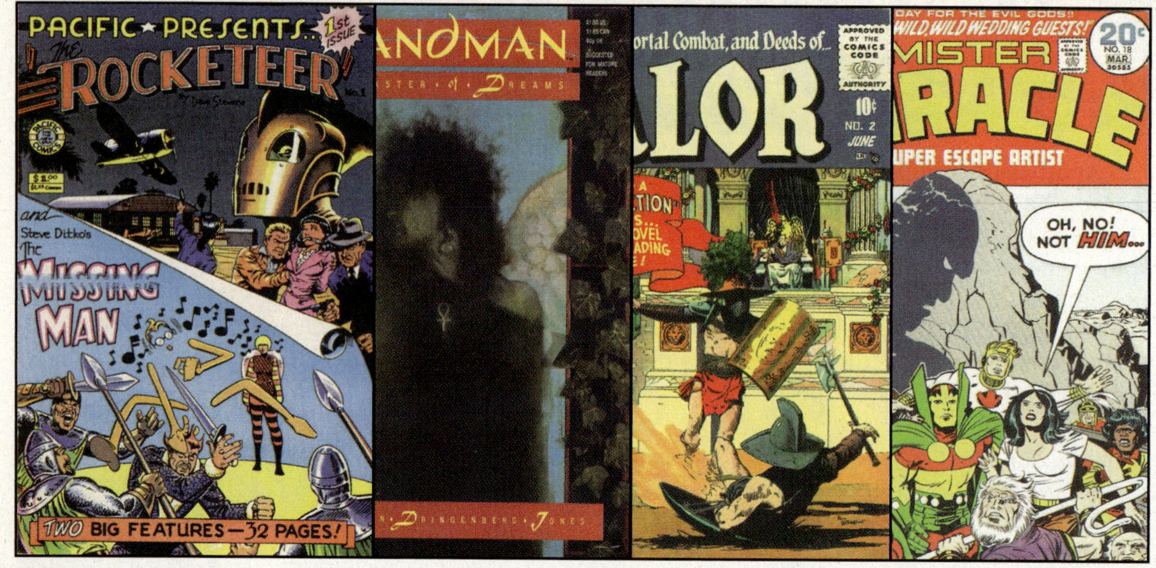

Collecting By Creator

By Weldon Adams

Collecting comic books isn't just any one thing. There are many ways to collect beyond simply randomly buying what catches your eye at any given moment. Not that there is anything wrong with that, all collectors do that to some degree, to be sure.

But many collectors find something that really captivates them and then they pursue it. And that helps shape the collection that they end up with.

One very common method of collecting is to find a creator that you really like, and then follow their work from book to book and from company to company. One of the real joys of collecting this way is that you can piece together the progression of someone's artistic style over the course of their career, even if you were not there as these books were coming out new.

If you decide to collect the works of a specific creator, there are some questions you should answer so you know what you are doing and

The Kirby collector can't go wrong focusing on 1960s Marvels like *Fantastic Four #52*.

where it will take you: How prolific is this creator? Do you want to collect everything they have ever done, or just everything they have done for a specific company? In the case of a creator spanning decades, you might even want to narrow it to only work during a specific time period of their career.

When collecting by creator, one of the biggies that always comes up is Jack Kirby. Kirby was so prolific that it is actually very difficult to collect *everything* he ever did. Many people start with a sub-genre of Kirby comics, such as Kirby's 1960s Marvel work. That can be pricey, but they are some of the most outstanding gems in the industry to be sure. Jack Kirby had a hand in creating almost every cornerstone character at Marvel Comics. As a result, there are more 'key issues' with Kirby's name on them than almost any other creator, with the exception of Stan Lee. In the first 50 issues of *Fantastic Four* alone we get the first appearances of The Fantastic Four, the

Skrulls, Doctor Doom, the Watcher, Kang (as "the Pharaoh"); the Inhumans, the Silver Surfer, and Galactus! You also get the first Marvel Comics Silver Age crossover (with the Hulk) and the revival of the Golden Age Sub-Mariner… Not to mention that Jack Kirby and Stan Lee even appear in one of the stories as themselves! These key issues are by their very nature going to cost more.

However, many (but not all) of those stories have been reprinted in other books over the years. So you can even set about collecting the reprint runs. Those will be cheaper than the original appearances. *Marvel Collectors' Item Classics* and *Marvel's Greatest Comics* reprinted many of these early appearances. *Fantastic Four* #4 (Sub-Mariner revival), *FF* #12 (the first Silver Age cross-over story), *FF* #36 (first Medusa of the Inhumans), *FF* #44 (first appearance of many of the other Inhumans), *FF* #45 (first Black Bolt of the Inhumans), *FF* #48 (first Silver Surfer & Galactus) were all reprinted in one of those titles.

But maybe a more recent creator could be a better place for you to start. Someone very influential, but not quite as far ranging as Jack "King" Kirby. How about John Byrne? …A name even to this day synonymous with the "All-New/All-Different" *X-Men*. But beyond his run of classic *X-Men* stories from #108 through #143, Byrne has had many amazing runs on other titles, some are even very obscure.

Just staying with Marvel Comics for the moment, it is worth mentioning Byrne's run on the *Avengers* (#164-166, #181-191), and his run on *Captain America* (#247-255). Although brief, both are noted as high-points in those titles' runs. The fact that they are relatively short runs makes them much easier to collect. And both of

You can also focus your collecting on reasonably priced reprints of classic issues.

those runs were produced during the same time period he was working on the *X-Men*, so his artwork is relatively the same.

Byrne later did his longest continuous run on a title on *Fantastic Four* (#209-293). And again it is remembered as a high water mark for that title, second in many collectors' eyes only to the Lee-Kirby era itself.

But part of the joy of collecting by creator isn't just finding their most outstanding and influential work. Part of it is to go backwards and find some of their earliest work. And in the case of John Byrne, that will lead you to *Iron Fist*. This was a title from Marvel in 1975 that ran only fifteen issues, but Byrne worked on all fifteen. And that short run contained the first appearance of Sabertooth! Sabertooth would later go on to become a major player in the background of Wolverine, but he first appeared in *Iron Fist* #14. And issue #15 guest-starred the *X-Men*, a prelude to Byrne switching over to that title. Wolverine is even wearing the "Fang" costume that he had just gotten in a then current issue of the *X-Men*.

But you can go back even further to get earlier pre-Marvel work by John Byrne if you like. How about his Charlton Comics work? His first work for them featured ROG-2000, a character that he had created years earlier. Rog appeared in *E-Man* and the CPL fanzine. Byrne also did *Doomsday + 1*, *Space: 1999*, *Emergency!*, and *Wheelie And The Chopper Bunch*. (The last three being TV show licenses) In addition, Byrne had work in all but one issue of the 5 issue *Charlton Bullseye* magazine.

But why start there when you could begin with his very first professional comics work, Skywald Publications' *Nightmare* #20 from August of 1974? From the Golden Age (and earlier) to the present, there are

Some of John Byrne's early work can be found in Charlton's *Space: 1999* (#5 shown).

artists whose work is definitely worth considering as a collecting subject. Take a look at comics by George Pérez, Marc Silvestri, Frank Frazetta, Al Williamson, Neal Adams, Joe Kubert, Adam Kubert, Andy Kubert, Billy Tucci, Gene Colan, Doug Wildey, Matt Wagner, Joe Quesada, Jimmy Palmiotti, David Mack, Don Heck, Jim Lee, Wally Wood, Walter Simonson, Todd McFarlane, Nick Cardy, John Buscema, J.G. Jones, John Romita, Sr., John Romita, Jr., Dave Stevens, Dave Sim, P. Craig Russell, John K. Snyder III, Jack Davis, Jamal Igle, Ethan Van Sciver, or Graham Ingles, just for starters. There's an artist out there for every taste.

The same, of course, is true for writers. Neil Gaiman, Robert Kirkman, Mark Waid, Roger Stern, Brian Michael Bendis, Stan Lee, Jim Shooter, Frank Miller, Archie Goodwin, Larry Hama, Chris Claremont, James Robinson, Jim Krueger, Don McGregor, Paul Jenkins, J. Michael Straczynski, James Kuhoric, Ed Brubaker, Joe Gill, John Jackson Miller, Scott Snyder, Mike Baron, Jack Burnley, and so many others represent a diverse group of writing styles and approaches to stories.

As an example, one writer that crosses genres, eras and companies is Steve Englehart. It would take an entire article's worth of space just to list his writing accomplishments without even getting into why they are worthy of collecting, but his run on the *Avengers* is another high point for that title in almost anyone's book. You would also find his work in *Detective Comics* at DC, *Scorpio Rose* at Eclipse (and later Image), *Coyote* at Marvel's Epic imprint,

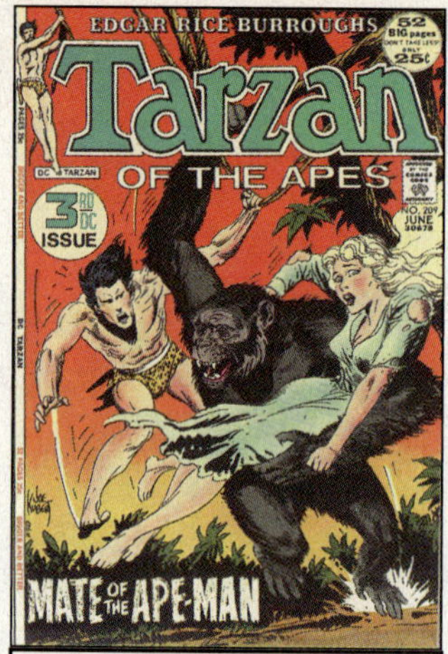

Joe Kubert's artistic output stretched from the Golden Age to the present.

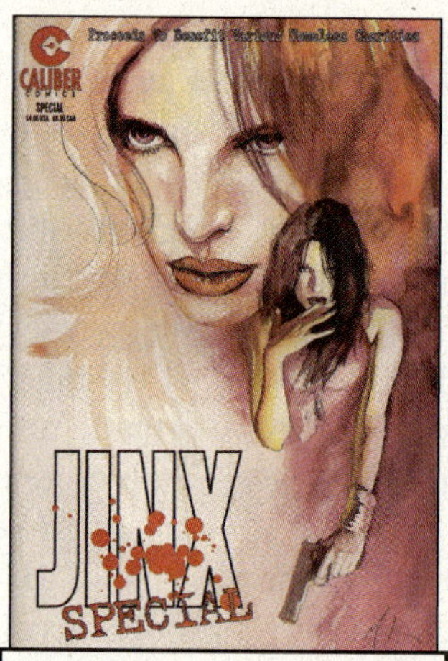

Writers, like Brian Michael Bendis, are just as interesting as artists when considering a collecting subject.

St. Swithin's Day (April 1990) shows the earliest work of artist Paul Grist.

The Strangers in Malibu's Ultraverse, *T.H.U.N.D.E.R. Agents* at Deluxe, and many, many other titles.

But maybe you would like to start with a contemporary creator, just so there is not so much to hunt down. How about Paul Grist? Paul is a British writer-artist. His first published work was written by Grant Morrison. (*St. Swithin's Day*, published by UK based publisher Trident Comics) He also did a story that appeared in the UK's *Crisis* magazine #55-59 in 1991. Later he self-published his own work *Kane*, and *Jack Staff*, and republished and continued his creation *Burglar Bill* (originally from Trident as well). Both *Kane* and *Jack Staff* were picked up and continued by Image Comics, where he also published *Mudman*. Grist's work is very different from the typical superhero fair, but his story telling skills (particularly in *Jack Staff*) are amazing. He can break an entire issue down into three-page story segments, each separate, but then tie them all together at the end.

Again, though, these are just two examples. Don't take our word for it. Find a creator whose work you really like and try something else they've worked on!

Collecting by a specific creator can be fun and rewarding. The upside is that if they have a lot of work out there, you can watch as their skills progress and change. The downside might be that you will need to hunt down smaller runs from many different titles and/or publishers. But one of the things that draws people to this type of collecting is that if you enjoy a creator's work, you will usually get what you expect out of them.

The OVERSTREET
HALL OF FAME

-- An Introduction --

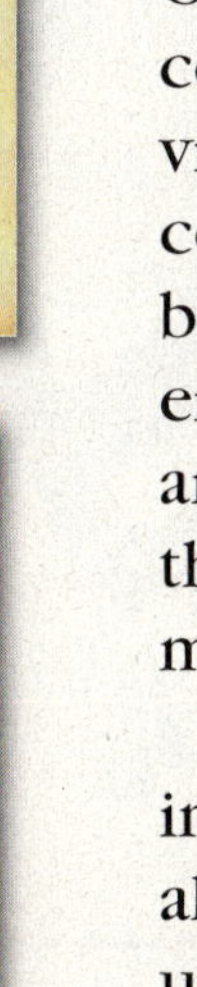

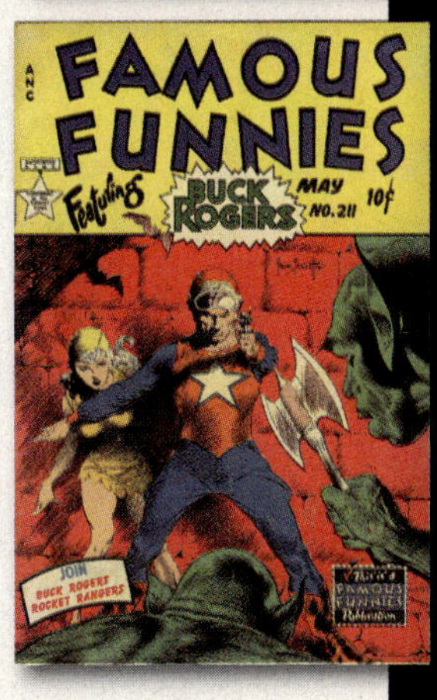

First announced in 2006 with a class that included Murphy Anderson, Jim Aparo, Jim Lee and Mac Raboy, The Overstreet Hall of Fame was conceived to single out individuals who have made great contributions to the comic book arts. This includes writers, artists, editors, publishers and others who have plied their crafts in insightful and meaningful ways.

While such evaluations are inherently subjective, they also serve to aid in reflecting upon those who shaped the experience of reading comic books over the years. Membership in The Overstreet Hall of Fame also denotes creators whose work is definitely worth investigating, whether one is thinking of collecting by creator or not.

New additions are made annually in the pages of *The Overstreet Comic Book Price Guide*.

NEAL ADAMS

Neal Adams is one of the greatest artists our medium has ever known. He is also the single most influential artist in the history of comic book publishing. An amazing number of artists, including many whose styles are nothing like Neal's, many you'd never guess, started out trying to emulate Neal. He has personally trained a small army of artists. Not only a master of the visual, Neal writes as well, and also does, it seems, whatever else he wishes to with ease and grace. His brilliance extends beyond the printed page. He works with light, motion and sound. He creates three-dimensionally. *Any* medium is his medium.

And, everything he does, he does with rare excellence. He brings insight to any endeavor. Most importantly, he *truly* creates. New ideas. Original thoughts. Genesis! Beyond that, he has always been a force in the industry – a righter of wrongs, a bringer of change, a leader. Neal is a genius and a giant who has lifted up us all.

- Jim Shooter

INDUCTED 2009

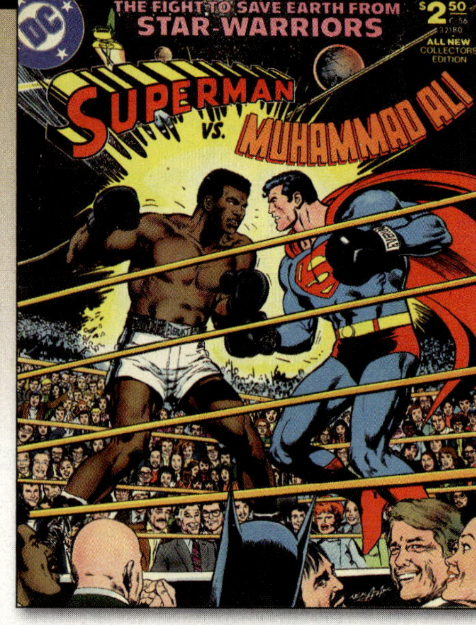

ALL-NEW COLLECTORS' EDITION C-56
1978. © DC

GREEN LANTERN #86
October-November 1971. © DC

AVENGERS #96
February 1972. © MAR

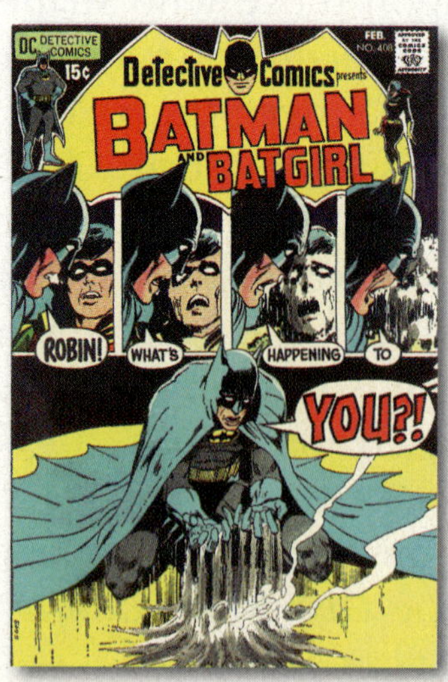

DETECTIVE COMICS #408
February 1971. © DC

X-MEN #58
July 1969. © MAR

BRAVE AND THE BOLD #61
August-September 1965. © DC

MURPHY ANDERSON

Born July 9, 1926 in Asheville, North Carolina, Murphy Anderson began his life-long career in comic books in 1944 working at Fiction House, where he pencilled and inked for several years. Beginning in the Golden Age, he worked steadily for a number of companies in the industry, including Ziff-Davis, and DC Comics (where he would become a mainstay with work spanning five decades).

He worked also on newspaper strips, notably including taking over the reins of the *Buck Rogers* strip from creator Dick Calkins, and he also produced the military's *P.S. Magazine* (following Will Eisner and preceding Joe Kubert, both also Overstreet Hall of Fame members).

Anderson helped to propel the Silver Age of DC Comics with work on such characters as Adam Strange, The Atom, Flash, Green Lantern, Hawkman, and many others, including his inks over artists Curt Swan and Carmine Infantino.

Widely regarded as a gentleman of the old school, Murphy Anderson was a member of the first class inducted into The Overstreet Hall of Fame in 2006.

JUSTICE LEAGUE OF AMERICA #3
February-March 1961. © DC

INDUCTED 2006

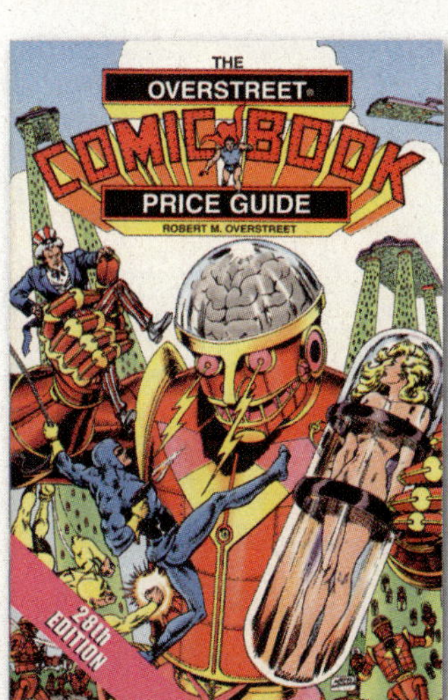

OVERSTREET C.B.P.G. #28
1998. © DC

SHOWCASE #60
January-February 1966. © DC

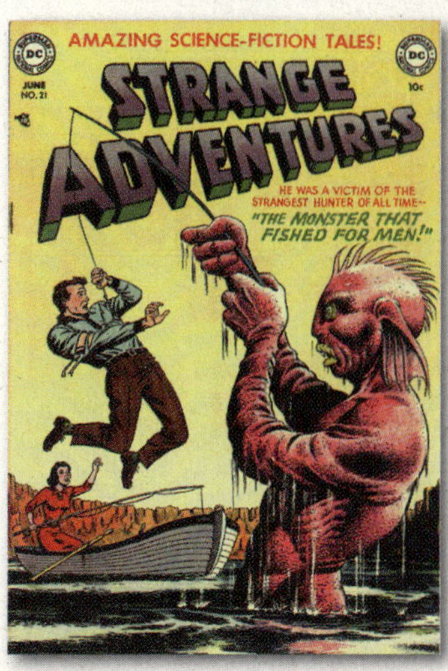

STRANGE ADVENTURES #21
June 1952. © DC

JIM APARO

Jim Aparo was considered to be "the definitive Batman artist" by a generation of comic readers, but he also left his mark on numerous other characters. In a career spanning 1966 to early 2000s, he created memorable portrayals of Aquaman, The Spectre, The Phantom Stranger, Green Arrow, The Outsiders and the guest stars of the *Brave and the Bold*.

His comics career started in 1966 at Charlton Comics working on "Miss Bikini Luv" in *Go-Go Comics*. Brought to DC Comics by editor Dick Giordano, Aparo began work on Aquaman and The Phantom Stranger before landing the regular assignment on *The Brave and the Bold* starting with #100 and lasting until the title's end with #200. During that time, he also contributed art for the Spectre in *Adventure Comics* and short mystery stories. His Batman work in the late 1980s included the story that killed off the second Robin, Jason Todd. He continued to work until his retirement in the early 2000s.

Jim Aparo passed away on July 19, 2005 but his artistic legacy won't soon be forgotten.

INDUCTED 2006

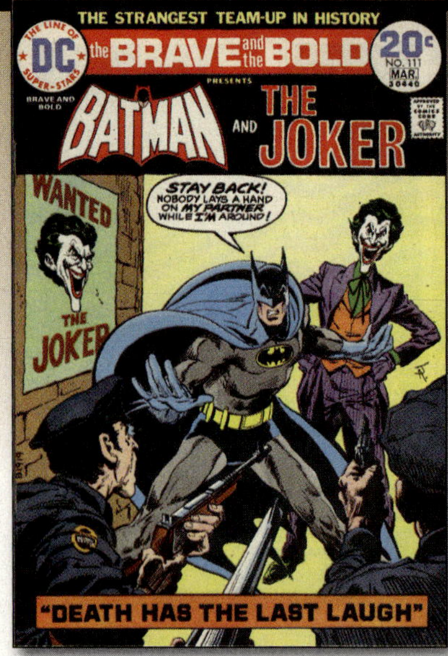

BRAVE AND THE BOLD #111
February-March 1974. © DC

Panel from BATMAN #428
December 1988. © DC

ADVENTURE COMICS #432
April 1974. © DC

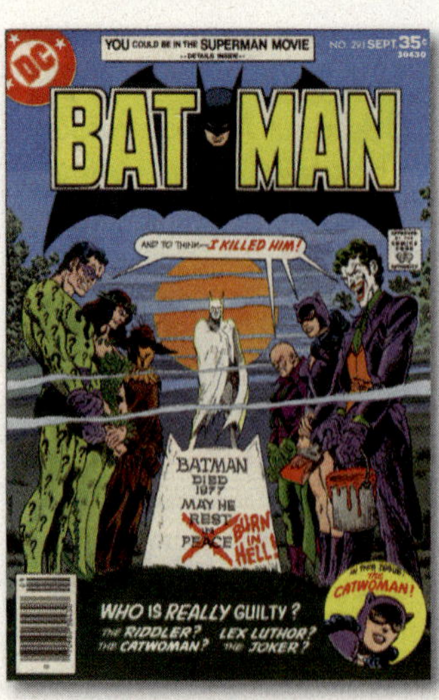

BATMAN #291
March 1977. © DC

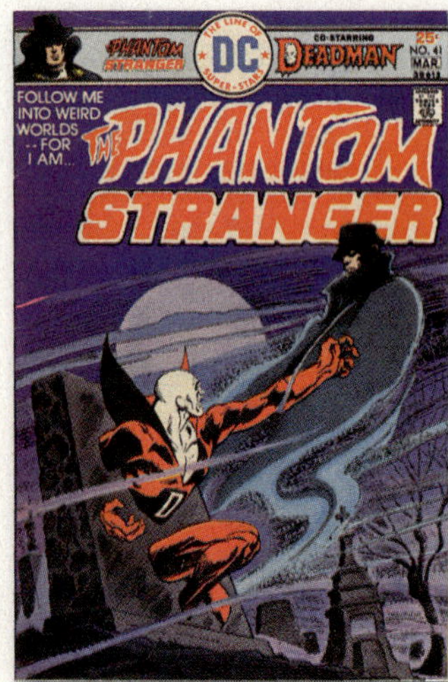

PHANTOM STRANGER #41
February-March 1976. © DC

SERGIO ARAGONÉS GROO THE WANDERER #60
December 1989. © Sergio Aragonés

SERGIO ARAGONÉS

Who knew that all those gutters could be so funny? Sergio Aragonés (1937-) never let panel borders get in the way of telling quick and delightful comic stories, and his margin cartoons ("marginals") in the pages of *MAD Magazine* not only raised doodling to a high art but packed the periodical with laughs in every conceivable corner. Thanks to the marginals and his "A *Mad* Look At…" features, Aragonés – often called "The World's Fastest Cartoonist" – has been a beloved fixture of the magazine since 1963. In 1982 he also introduced us to *Groo*, a lovable and seriously inept barbarian that has an insatiable love of cheese dip and an unerring knack for getting into, or causing, trouble. In all of his work, Aragonés' melodic, hyper-detailed style is instantly recognizable (as is his trademark moustache), and his joy in sharing humor with the world is evident in every line.

- Dr. Arnold T. Blumberg

INDUCTED 2010

DC SUPER-STARS #13
March-April 1977. © DC

SERGIO ARAGONÉS DESTROYS DC #1
June 1996. © DC

SERGIO ARAGONÉS MASSACRES MARVEL #1
June 1996. © MAR

MATT BAKER

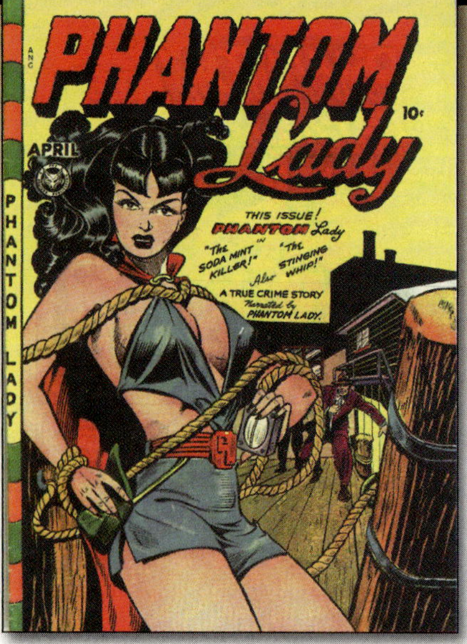

PHANTOM LADY #17
April 1948. © FOX

One of America's first major African American cartoonists, Matt Baker (1921-1959) is best known for his "good girl" comics and his romance comic work. He is considered by many to be a master in drawing the female form. He clearly adored women and enjoyed drawing them and all their beauty.

Not just a pin-up artist, his attention to detail and his ability to use the background details to help set a scene was something very few of his peers were doing at the time. Educated at Cooper Union in New York City, he got his start with Iger Studios in the mid-1940s, providing art for St. John, Fox, Fiction House, Quality and Atlas. His work included the genres of Westerns, Romance, and Jungle Adventure, but he is mostly remembered for his work on the *Phantom Lady* series. So provocative for the day, one of his *Phantom Lady* covers was used in Fredrick Wertham's book on the ill effects of comic books on America's youth, *Seduction of the Innocent*.
- Amanda Sheriff

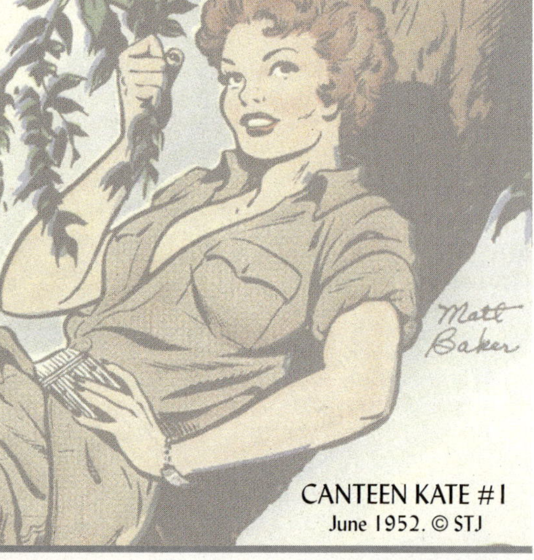

CANTEEN KATE #1
June 1952. © STJ

INDUCTED 2009

GIANT COMICS EDITIONS #15
1950. © FOX

SEVEN SEAS COMICS #4
1947. © Universal Phoenix Feature

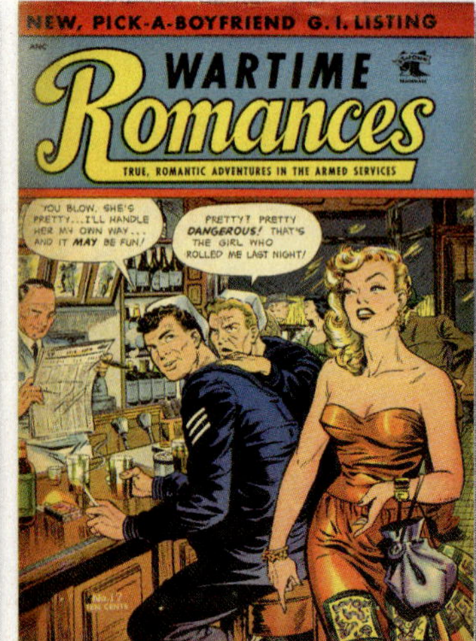

WARTIME ROMANCES #17
September 1953. © STJ

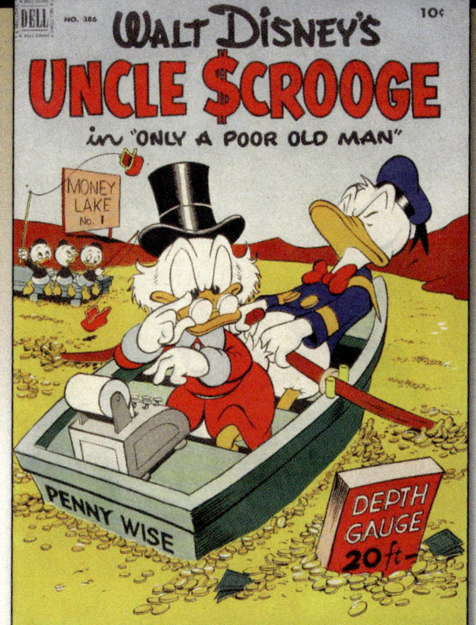
FOUR COLOR COMICS #386
First Uncle Scrooge issue. March 1952. © DIS

CARL BARKS

Originally known to fans only as "The Good Duck Artist," in 1935, Carl Barks went to work for the Disney Studios and storyboarded cartoons such as *Donald's Nephews* and *Donald's Cousin Gus*. In 1942, Western Publishing asked him to work on the comic story "Donald Duck Finds Pirate Gold," and then to rewrite and draw a 10-page Donald story for *Walt Disney's Comics and Stories* #31. Soon, he became a regular contributor, lasting 25 years in the position, until his retirement in 1967. After retiring, though, Barks kept active. In 1971 he obtained permission from Disney to produce and sell oil paintings based on the Duck characters. In 1976 Disney withdrew permission, but in 1982 Another Rainbow Publishing, which had just secured a license from Disney to produce lithographs of Barks' paintings, commissioned him to paint two new oils per year. In 1995, Barks finally retired for real. He died on August 25, 2000, just shy of 100 years old.

OVERSTREET C.B.P.G. #7
1977. © Warner Brothers

INDUCTED 2008

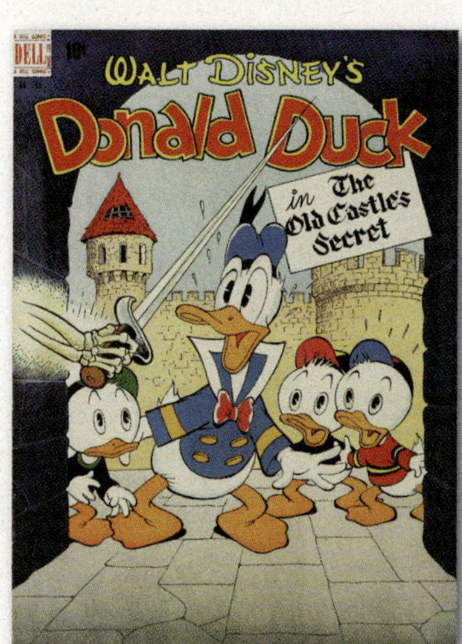
FOUR COLOR COMICS #189
Barks' first cover. June 1948. © DIS

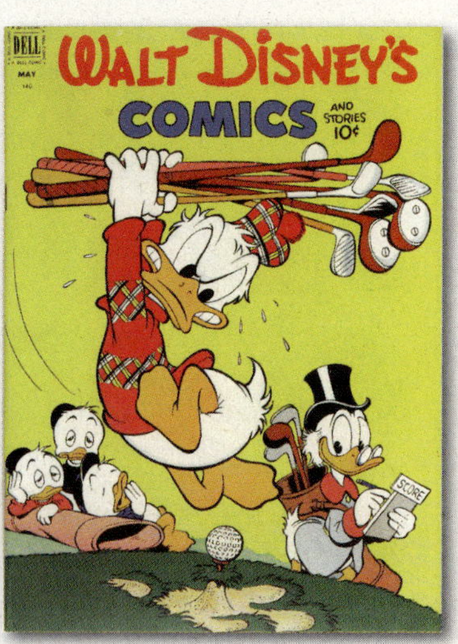
WALT DISNEY'S COMICS AND STORIES #140
First WDC&S cover with Scrooge. May 1952. © DIS

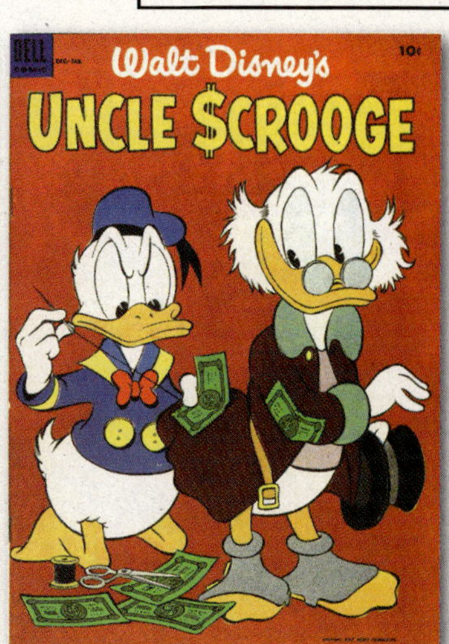
UNCLE SCROOGE #4
December 1953. © DIS

JOHN BUSCEMA

AVENGERS #58
November 1968. © MAR

Inspired by the work of Hal Foster, Alex Raymond, and Burne Hogarth, John Buscema began his career at Marvel Comics in 1948, when it was still Timely Comics. He stayed on staff there for a year and a half, afterward freelancing for a number of companies. After leaving the comics field to go into advertising in 1958, Buscema returned to comics — and Marvel in particular — in 1966, when his old boss Stan Lee brought him back to the "House of Ideas." His Silver Age output could be seen within the pages of *Avengers*, *Conan the Barbarian*, *Fantastic Four*, *Nick Fury: Agent of S.H.I.E.L.D.*, and *Silver Surfer*, among others. He also co-wrote *How to Draw Comics the Marvel Way* with Stan Lee. His final published comics work was DC Comics' *Just Imagine Stan Lee with John Buscema Creating Superman*. His is a talent that is greatly missed, but lives on in myriad four-color tales.
– Scott Braden

SILVER SURFER #4
February 1969. © MAR

INDUCTED 2012

FANTASTIC FOUR #112
July 1971. © MAR

SAVAGE SWORD OF CONAN #40
May 1979. © Conan Properties Inc.

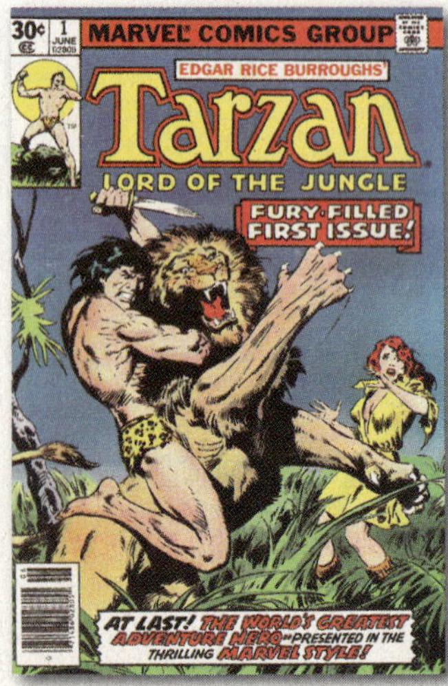

TARZAN #1
June 1977. © ERB

From the typewriters and drawing boards of our Hall of Famers came forth some remarkable creations. The most desirable issues now reach remarkable prices in the comic marketplace. Here are a few of the top sellers.

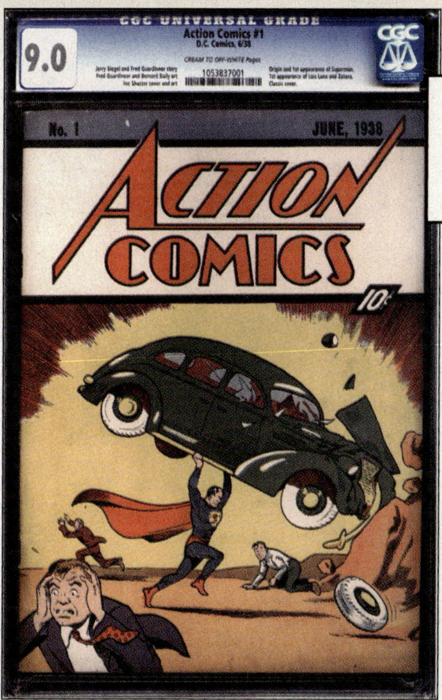

ACTION COMICS #1, CGC CERTIFIED 9.0
Sold for $2,161,000
by ComicConnect.com
in November 2011. © DC

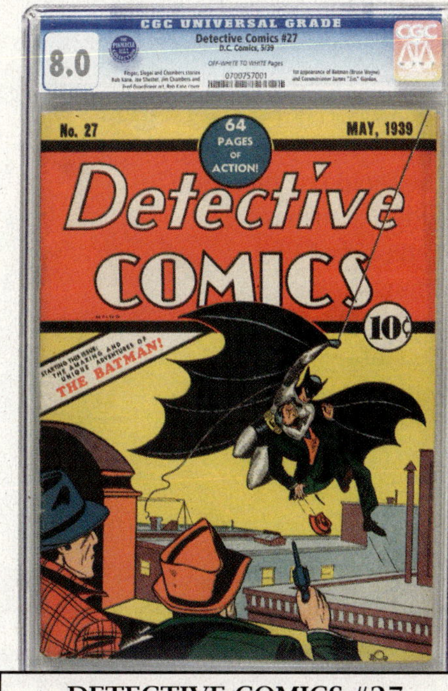

DETECTIVE COMICS #27,
CGC CERTIFIED 8.0
Sold for $1,075,500
by Heritage Auction Galleries
on February 25, 2010. © DC

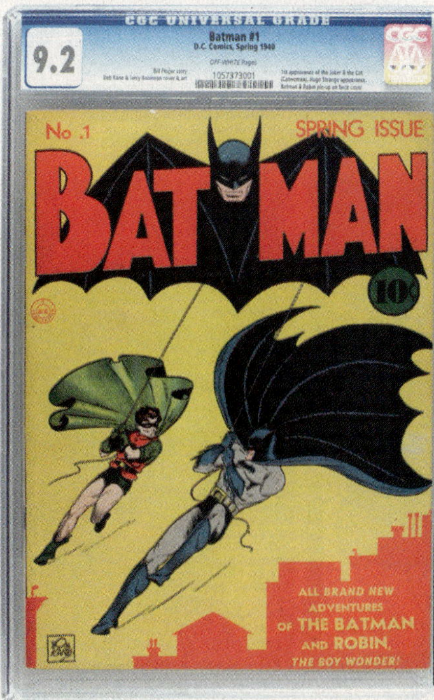

BATMAN #1, CGC CERTIFIED 9.2
Sold for $850,000
by Heritage Auction Galleries
in May 2012. © DC

CHRIS CLAREMONT

Chris Claremont has written many wonderful things. He's passionate about everything he writes. Especially notable, of course, is his work on the X-Men. Chris gets a good deal of credit for the success of the X-Men, but not nearly as much as he deserves. Not only did he do an outstanding job as writer, he built the team that built the team. He recruited artists when needed. He made sure the lettering and coloring were consistent and top drawer. He spent time, effort and money out of his own pocket to insure the quality of the book. He sweated the details. He fought like a Wolverine to defend the integrity of his vision, his work, his words. If there's a Hall of Fame for Caring, Trying and Outworking Everyone, he should be there, too. Babe Ruth didn't create the Yankees and Chris Claremont didn't create the X-Men, but each of them built the house.

-JS

INDUCTED 2009

X-MEN #100
August 1976. © MAR

X-MEN #141
January 1981. © MAR

IRON FIST #14
October 1977. © MAR

MARVEL GRAPHIC NOVEL #4
1982. © MAR

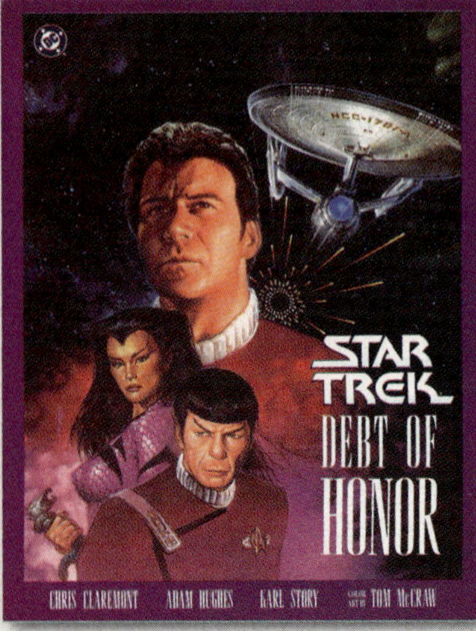
STAR TREK: DEBT OF HONOR
Graphic novel. 1992. © Paramount

X-MEN #94
August 1975. © MAR

DAVE COCKRUM

Dave Cockrum began his career in comics as an assistant to artist Murphy Anderson (another Overstreet Hall of Fame member), who was at the time responsible for various DC titles starring Superman and Superboy. This included *Superboy*, which featured back-up stories of The Legion of Super-Heroes, which Cockrum took over and redefined with his style and sequential storytelling.

Marvel's *Giant-Size X-Men* #1 hit the stands with the debut of the new team of X-Men, including Cockrum's co-creations, Storm, Nightcrawler and Colossus. Since then, it has become one of the most sought after comics of the Bronze Age. Working initially with writer Len Wein and then Chris Claremont, he helped re-launch the regular title, *Uncanny X-Men*, with issue #94. He continued on the series through issue #107, working with writer Chris Claremont, and then returned for another run (#145-163). After his second stint with the X-Men, Cockrum produced *Marvel Graphic Novel #9: The Futurians*. It became a short-lived series for Lodestone and was published as a collection by Eternity.

Cockrum passed away in 2006.

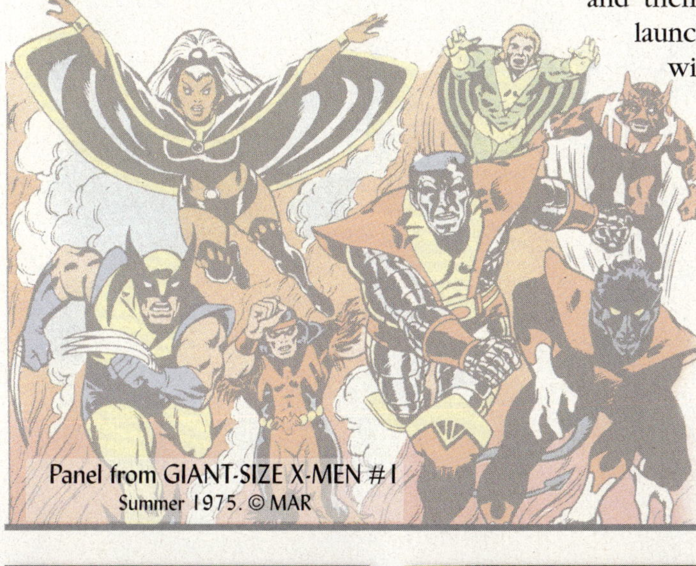
Panel from GIANT-SIZE X-MEN #1
Summer 1975. © MAR

INDUCTED 2007

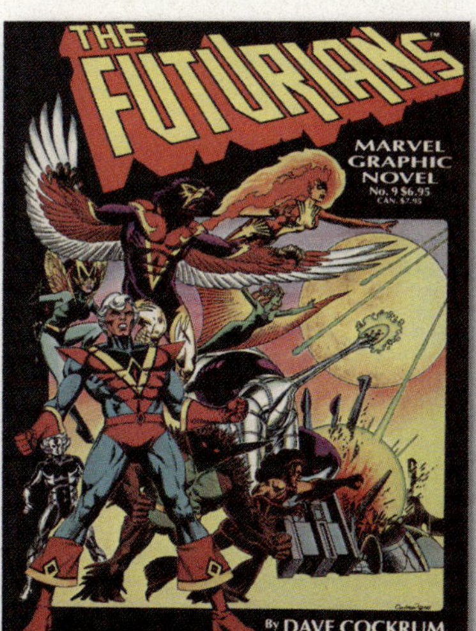
MARVEL GRAPHIC NOVEL #9
1983. © Dave Cockrum

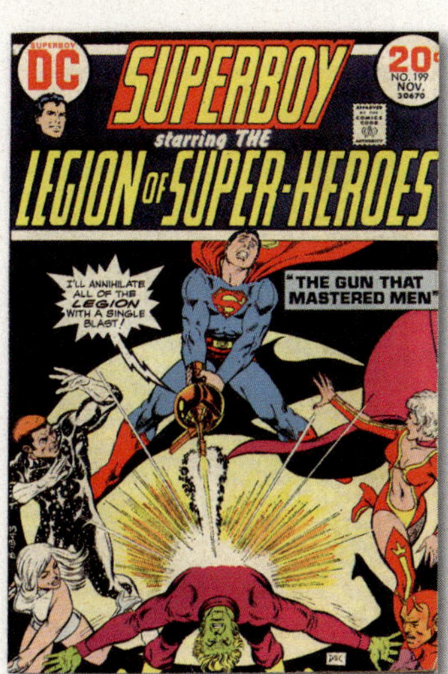

SUPERBOY #199
November 1973. © DC

UNCANNY X-MEN #145
May 1981. © MAR

PALMER COX

Palmer Cox (April 28, 1840 – July 24, 1924) was a Canadian-born cartoonist whose best known work revolutionized the world of comic characters and comic character merchandise. As the creator of The Brownies, Cox can be credited with the first successful recurring characters, the first internationally successful characters, and with developing a principled road map for producing character-themed merchandise for children. Appearing in serialized form in *St. Nicholas* magazine, the fairy- or pixie-like characters had special powers, appeared only to the virtuous, and were collected for the first time in *The Brownies, Their Book* (1887). The Kodak Brownie camera featured the characters on its box, and items ranging from sheet music to candle holders were offered, creating a road map followed regionally by The Yellow Kid and internationally by Mickey Mouse and Superman.

INDUCTED 2009

THE BROWNIES THEIR BOOK
Hardcover book. 1887. © The Century Co.

PALMER COX SIGNATURE CARD
1902.

PALMER COX PHOTO
Frontis page from "The Brownies and Prince Florimel" hardcover book. 1918. © The Century Co.

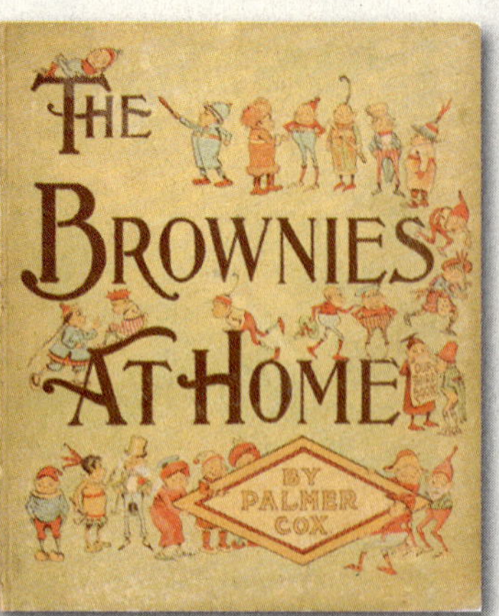
THE BROWNIES AT HOME
Hardcover book. 1893. © The Century Co.

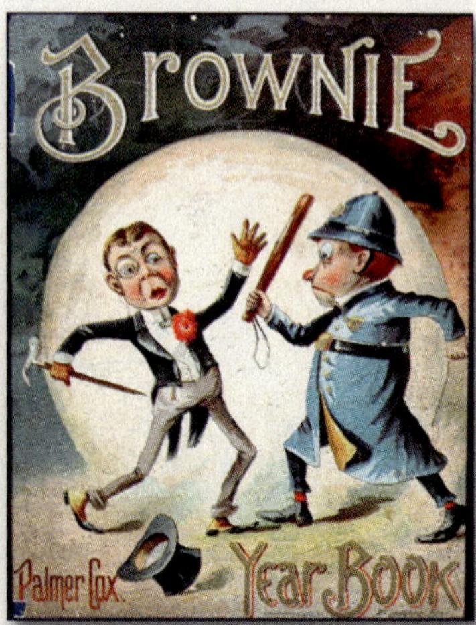
BROWNIE YEAR BOOK
1895. © McLoughlin Bros.

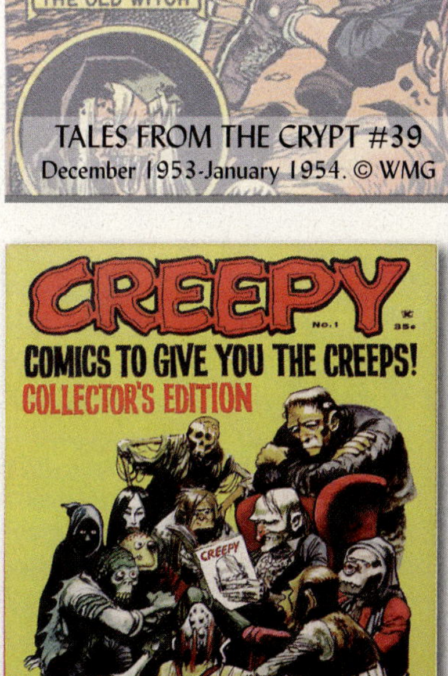

TWO-FISTED TALES #30
November-December 1952. © WMG

JACK DAVIS

The general public might recognize his style from his covers for *TV Guide* and *Time* or his movie poster and promotional work for such films as *It's a Mad, Mad, Mad, Mad World*, *Viva Max!* and *Kelly's Heroes*, but comic book fans have long known the distinctive art of Jack Davis in a variety of genres. At EC Comics, his horror stories included appearances in *Tales from the Crypt*, *The Haunt of Fear*, *The Vault of Horror*, *Crime SuspenStories*, and *Shock SuspenStories* and later the "Picto-Fiction" series *Terror Illustrated*. His action-adventure work appeared in *Frontline Combat*, *Two-Fisted Tales* and *Piracy*, and his material was also seen in *Incredible Science-Fiction*. As much as he won fans for all of his work (including Westerns for Atlas such as *Rawhide Kid*), though, it was in humor where he defined himself. His work appeared in almost all the early issues of *MAD* (and many later ones, too), all 12 issues of *Panic*, as well as *Trump*, *Humbug*, *Help!* and even *Cracked*.

TALES FROM THE CRYPT #39
December 1953-January 1954. © WMG

INDUCTED 2011

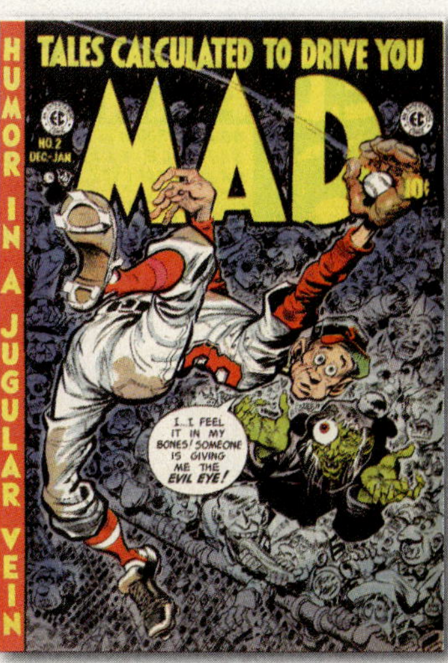

CREEPY #1
1964. © WARREN

INCREDIBLE SCIENCE FICTION #30
July-August 1955. © WMG

MAD #2
December 1952-January 1953. © WMG

DAN DeCARLO

Born on December 12, 1919, Dan DeCarlo established the visual house style of Archie comics for the modern age. DeCarlo created Sabrina the Teenage Witch, Cheryl Blossom, and Josie and the Pussycats (he named Josie after his wife) for the company in addition to his work on the various other Archie titles.

He broke into the four-color medium working for Timely Comics in 1947, drawing such classic titles as *Millie the Model*. He also freelanced for *The Saturday Evening Post*, *Argosy*, and the Humorama line of pin-up cartoon digests. He won the National Cartoonists Society Award for Best Comic Book in 2000 for *Betty & Veronica*.

The prolific artist has also been cited to be a strong artistic influence on *Love & Rockets* creators Jaime and Gilbert Hernandez, among others, and his work can be seen in a new line of "best of" hardcovers from Archie and IDW Publishing.

– SB

INDUCTED 2012

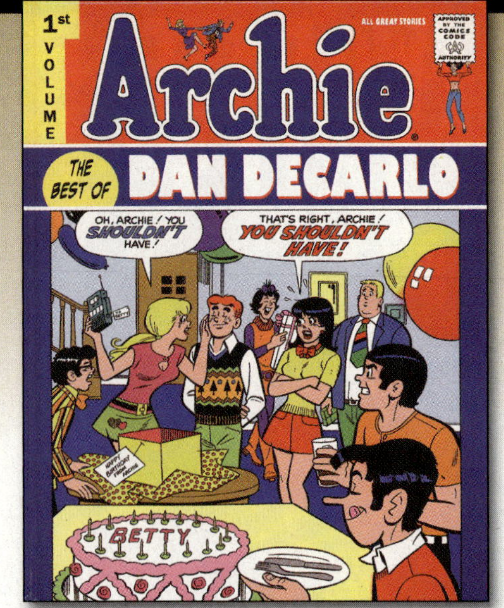

ARCHIE: THE BEST OF DAN DECARLO Vol. 1
May 2010. © AP

JOSIE AND THE PUSSYCATS #45
December 1969. © AP

CHERYL BLOSSOM #1
September 1995. © AP

JOSIE #1
February 1963. © AP

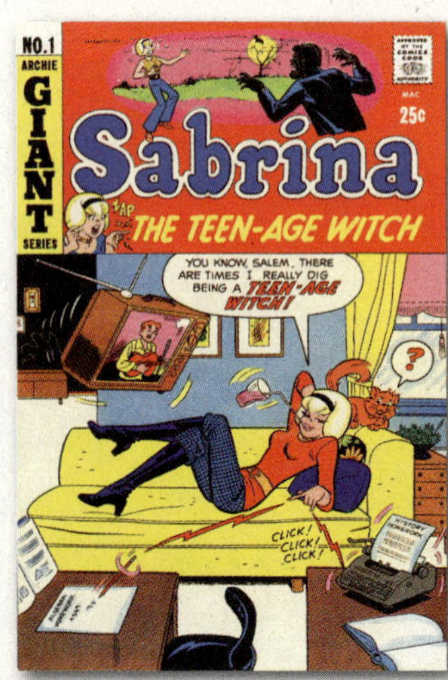

SABRINA, THE TEEN-AGE WITCH #1
April 1971. © AP

AMAZING SPIDER-MAN ANNUAL #2
1965. © MAR

STEVE DITKO

No artist other than Jack Kirby had as much influence on the formative years of the Marvel Comics universe as Steve Ditko. Although he was not as prolific as Kirby, the style, substance and mood of his artwork defined Spider-Man, Doctor Strange and numerous other characters for the publisher. His work debuted in *Black Magic* Vol. 4 #3 and *Captain 3-D #1* at about the same time in 1953. He worked for Marvel predecessor Atlas on horror, monster and science fiction stories. *Tales of Suspense*, *Journey Into Mystery*, *Amazing Adventures*, and *Tales to Astonish*, all featured his work at Marvel, but it was *Amazing Fantasy #15* and his subsequent 38-issue run on *Amazing Spider-Man* and his Doctor Strange stories in *Strange Tales* that made him a fan favorite. At Charlton, he worked on Captain Atom, Blue Beetle, The Question, and other characters, and at DC he created Shade The Changing Man, among other works.

INDUCTED 2007

AMAZING SPIDER-MAN #14
July 1964. © MAR

BLUE BEETLE #2
August 1967. © CC

FANTASTIC GIANTS Vol. 2 #24
September 1966. © CC

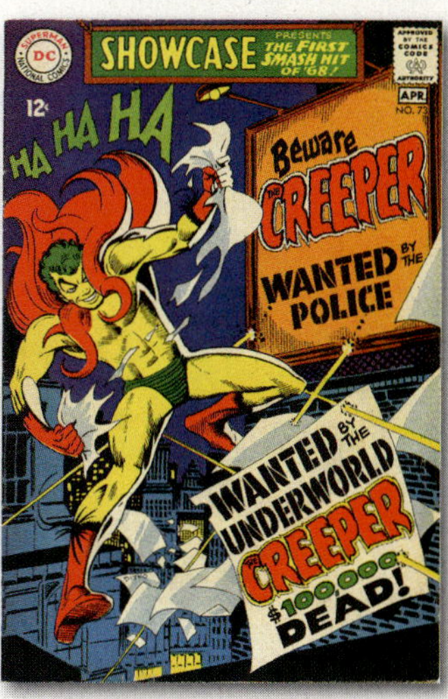

SHOWCASE #73
March-April 1968. © DC

WILL EISNER

Considered by many to be the father of the American graphic novel, Will Eisner was a writer, artist, master storyteller, and businessman. In a career that spanned eight decades, he created The Spirit, John Law, Lady Luck, Mr. Mystic, Uncle Sam, Blackhawk and numerous other characters.

He co-founded the Eisner – Iger Studios, then created *The Spirit* sections which were issued weekly in newspapers across America, and developed and packaged *P.S. Magazine* for the U.S. Army.

His book *A Contract With God* is widely regarded as the first American graphic novel (it wasn't, but it was an early and significant work in the format), and he continued to produce numerous other important works well into his 80s with the quality for which he was known. His innovative panel design and artistic choices seemed always to be in service to the story, rather than simply demonstrating his impressive skills. At one Harvey Awards ceremony at the Pittsburgh Comicon, he received honors for works produced 60 years apart (*The Spirit* and *Last Day in Vietnam*).

Eisner passed away in 2005 following heart surgery, but he left an almost immeasurable legacy.

INDUCTED 2008

THE SPIRIT NEWSPAPER SECTION
August 25, 1940. © Will Eisner Studios

THE SPIRIT NEWSPAPER SECTION
October 6, 1946. © Will Eisner Studios

A CONTRACT WITH GOD
1978. © Will Eisner Studios

DROPSIE AVENUE: THE NEIGHBORHOOD
1995. © Will Eisner Studios

THE SPIRIT #20
April 1950. © Will Eisner Studios

DAREDEVIL #1
Everett & Kirby cover. April 1964. © MAR

BILL EVERETT

As the creator of Namor, the Sub-Mariner, Bill Everett (1917-1973) was responsible for one of Timely Comics' three main characters (the other two were Captain America and The Human Torch). Namor was likely the first very successful anti-hero in the comic book world, since he was nearly constantly at war with the surface-dwelling humans. *Motion Picture Funnies Weekly* #1 featured the character's first appearance, which was then expanded for *Marvel Comics* #1. He wrote and drew the character in a number of different titles for the publisher both before and after his service in World War II. During the 1950s, he illustrated Marvel Boy, Venus and the first appearance of Simon Garth, The Zombie, among other work. Timely had become Atlas and then Marvel Comics when he illustrated the first issue of *Daredevil*. His last lengthy work in comics was a 1972-1973 run on his original character, *Sub-Mariner*.

Panel from MARVEL COMICS #1
October 1939. © MAR

INDUCTED 2009

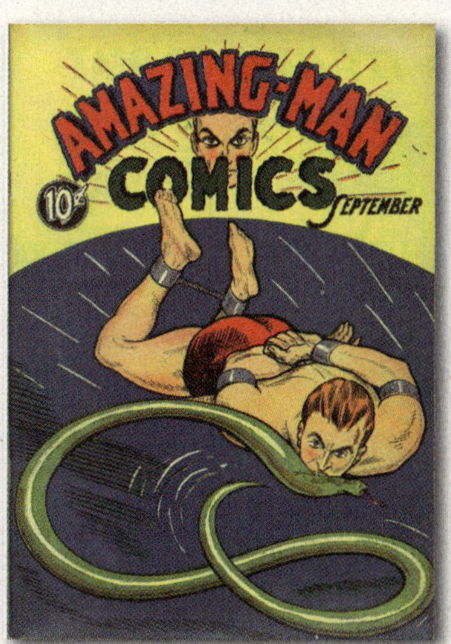

AMAZING-MAN COMICS #5
September 1939. © CEN

STRANGE TALES #148
September 1966. © MAR

SUB-MARINER COMICS #33
April 1954. © MAR

AL FELDSTEIN

WEIRD SCIENCE #13 (#2)
July-August 1950. © WMG

As an editor with EC Comics, Al Feldstein created, wrote, illustrated and edited titles in one of the most influential comic book lines in history. With a body of work ranging from horror (*Tales from the Crypt*) to science-fiction to crime and suspense, his contributions have been reprinted numbers of times over the years. They also stood up to the harshest critic: time. In 1955, he became editor of *MAD*, which had started as part of EC's comic book line-up and survived the demise of its sister publications by graduating to magazine format. Under his editorship, the magazine's circulation steadily increased from 375,000 to almost 3 million. Using his own pen name, he christened Alfred E. Neuman, *MAD*'s trademark character, and made short work of many social conventions. In 1984, Feldstein retired from *MAD* to devote his time to painting, something he continues in his Montana home.

OVERSTREET C.B.P.G. #30
2000. © WMG

INDUCTED 2008

SHOCK SUSPENSTORIES #9
June-July 1953. © WMG

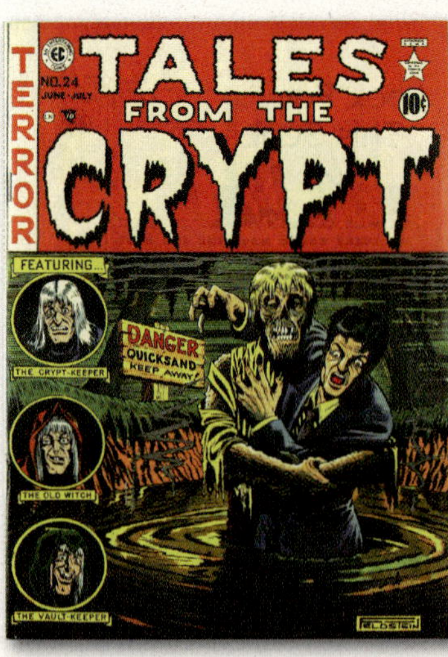

TALES FROM THE CRYPT #24
June-July 1951. © WMG

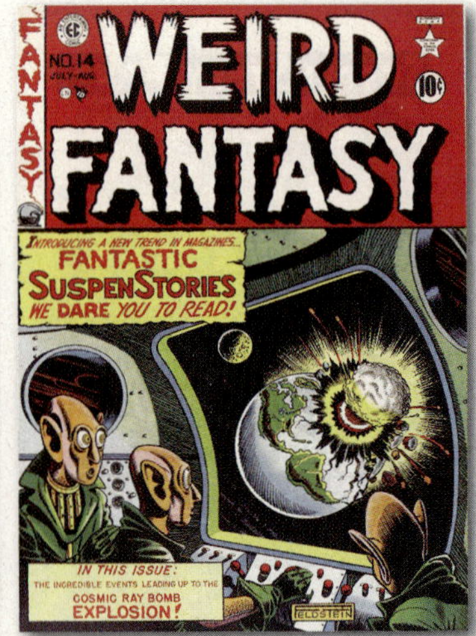

WEIRD FANTASY #14 (#2)
July-August 1950. © WMG

FRANK FRAZETTA

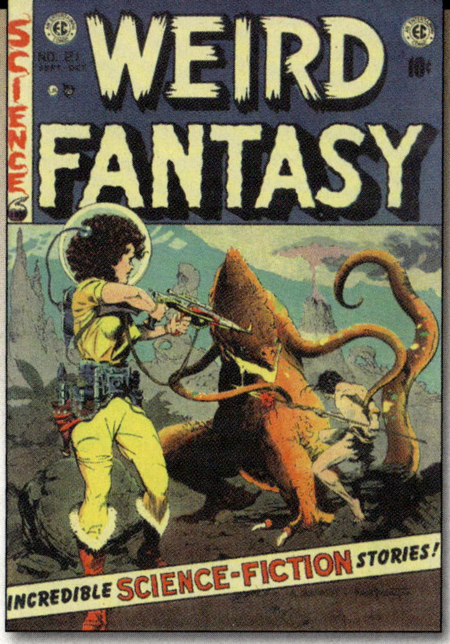

WEIRD FANTASY #21
September-October 1953. © WMG

Frank Frazetta started illustrating comic books and comic strips with a wide variety of themes before becoming the almost universally lauded master fantasy illustrator he became. He worked in the western, mystery, humor, and other genres including stories for EC Comics, National's Shining Knight, Avon and other publishers (his collaborations with EC's great Al Williamson and the talented Roy Krenkel are particularly noteworthy). His work on *Buck Rogers*, *Famous Funnies*, *Li'l Abner*, *Flash Gordon* and Johnny Comet still shine, but when he turned his hand to a series of Conan book covers he found a depth and a serious connection to a legion of fans. From the 1960s to the 1990s, he illustrated more than a dozen movie posters. His own characters, such as the Death Dealer, have taken on lives of their own on posters, album covers, and in comic books. He is truly a legend whose true impact on the artists who follow him is yet to be fully felt.

- Robert M. Overstreet

WEIRD SCIENCE-FANTASY #29
May-June 1955. © WMG

INDUCTED 2009

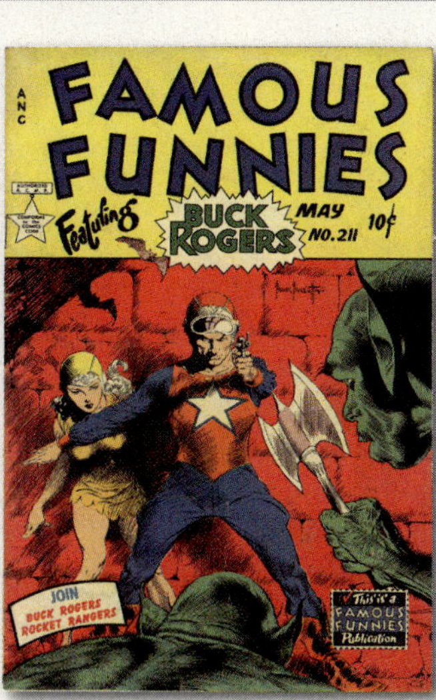

BLAZING COMBAT #2
January 1966. © WP

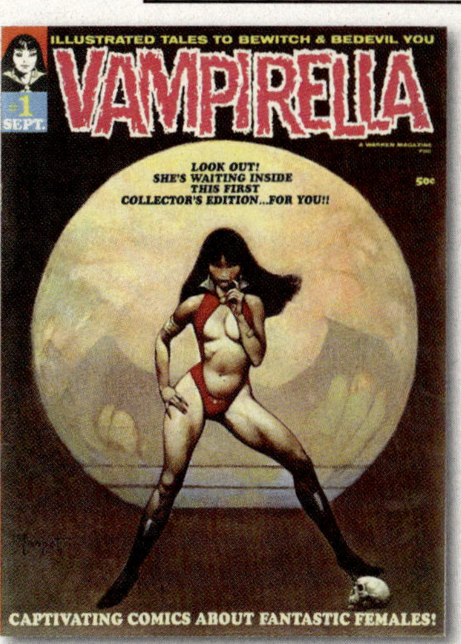

FAMOUS FUNNIES #211
May 1954. © EAS

VAMPIRELLA #1
September 1969. © WP

NEIL GAIMAN

SANDMAN #1
January 1989. © DC

Even though they thought they had something special, when DC Comics released *Sandman* #1 in 1989, it would have been impossible for them to know what they had on their hands since it really hadn't happened before. By the time the series ended with *Sandman* #75 (March 1996), it had given birth to DC's Vertigo imprint (*Sandman* #47), introduced or re-introduced the comic book world to a number of exceptional artists, and established Neil Gaiman as one of the medium's most distinct voices. Lyrical, moody, sensitive, and painterly, his ability to take readers to the world in which his characters lived captured and kept readers from beyond the normal fan base. With spin-offs such as *Death: The High Cost of Living*, he rounded out that world and soon began carving out others, in comics, novels, and other media.

Popular world wide, his *Sandman* has never been out of print since it debuted, finding success in multiple formats.

Panel from SANDMAN #8
August 1989. © DC

INDUCTED 2009

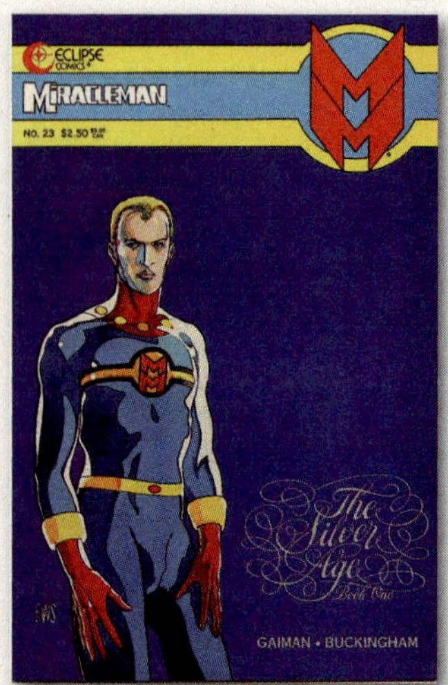

MIRACLEMAN #23
June 1992. © ECL

NEIL GAIMAN AND CHARLES VESS' STARDUST
Softcover. 1998. © Neil Gaiman & Charles Vess

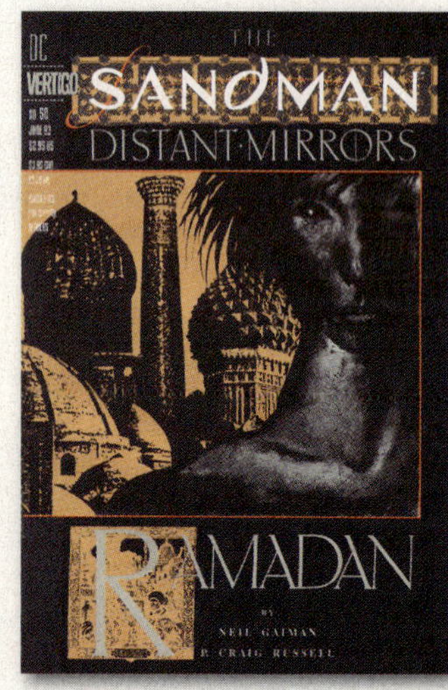

SANDMAN #50
June 1993. © DC

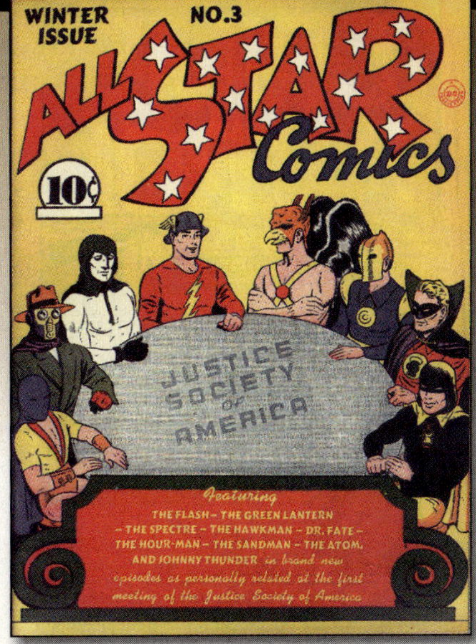

ALL STAR COMICS #3
Winter 1940. © DC

M.C. GAINES

Pioneer, publisher, promoter and advocate Maxwell Charles Gaines is known for creating the idea in 1933 of repackaging the Sunday newspaper comic strip into the format we recognize as modern comic books and distributing them to the newsstand. Comic strips had been collected into books since the 1800s, but he felt by folding a full tabloid page of eight or sixteen pages down twice to produce a 32-page or a 64-page comic magazine that it could be sold for 10¢, even during the Great Depression.

He tried first with *Funnies On Parade*, then with *Famous Funnies, A Carnival of Comics*, both done as promotional comics. *Famous Funnies*, Series 1, was the following step. The next issue, also #1, dated July, 1934 was distributed as the first newsstand comic magazine. The series lasted until 1955.

In 1938 Gaines (with Jack Liebowitz) started All-American Publications, which was a separate company co-marketed with DC Comics. In 1944, DC bought out Gaines, who then started a new line, Educational Comics (EC). He died in a boating accident in 1947.

– RMO

INDUCTED 2010

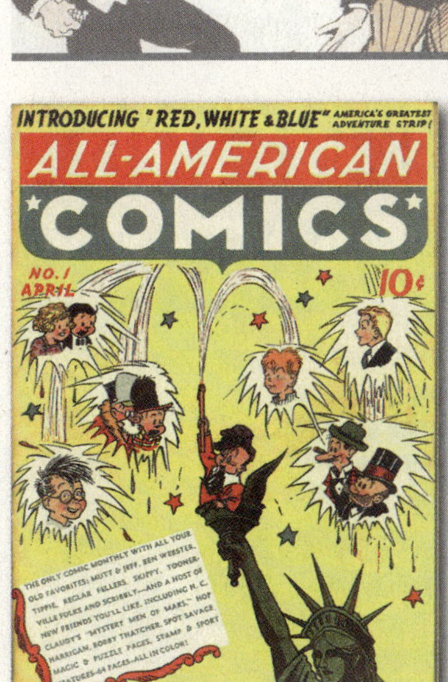

FUNNIES ON PARADE
1933. © EAS

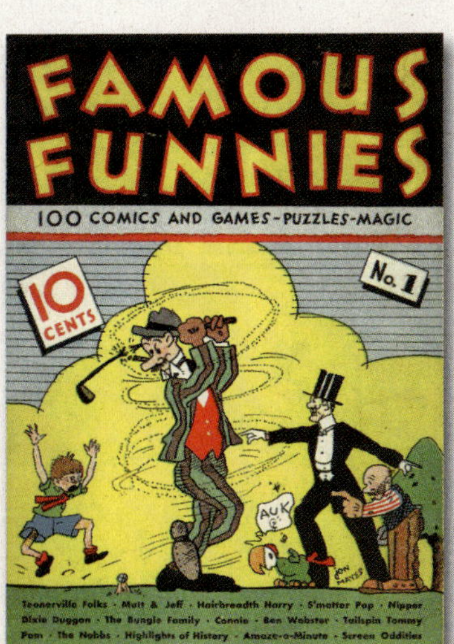

ALL-AMERICAN COMICS #1
April 1939. © DC

FAMOUS FUNNIES #1
July 1934. © EAS

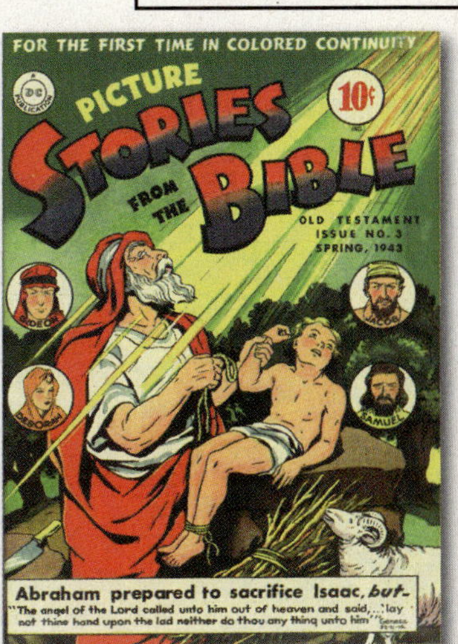

PICTURE STORIES FROM THE BIBLE #3
Spring 1943. © DC

WILLIAM M. GAINES

Best known on the national stage as the founder and publisher of *MAD* magazine, Bill Gaines suddenly found himself in charge of a floundering comic book company after the accidental death of his father, industry pioneer M.C. Gaines. Over the course of the next few years and in the course of trying to capture the latest trends, the younger Gaines published westerns, romances, and thrillers. Along the way, though, he began assembling an unparalleled roster of contributors, starting with writer-editor-artists Al Feldstein and Harvey Kurtzman and including Al Williamson, Jack Davis, Graham Ingles, Johnny Craig, Reed Crandall, George Evans, Wally Wood, John Severin and many others. With titles like *Tales From The Crypt*, *Weird Science*, *Two-Fisted Tales*, and *Shock SuspenStories*, in just a few years Gaines and company created titles that still influence other creators today. *MAD*, of course, became a cultural icon and did its own brand of influencing.

INDUCTED 2009

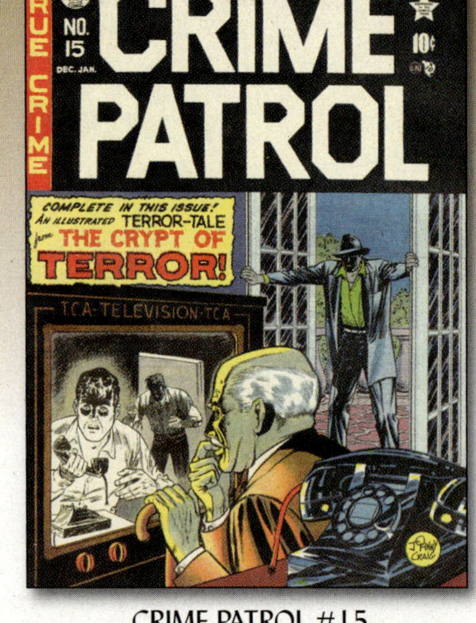
CRIME PATROL #15
1st appearance of the Crypt Keeper.
December 1949-January 1950. © WMG

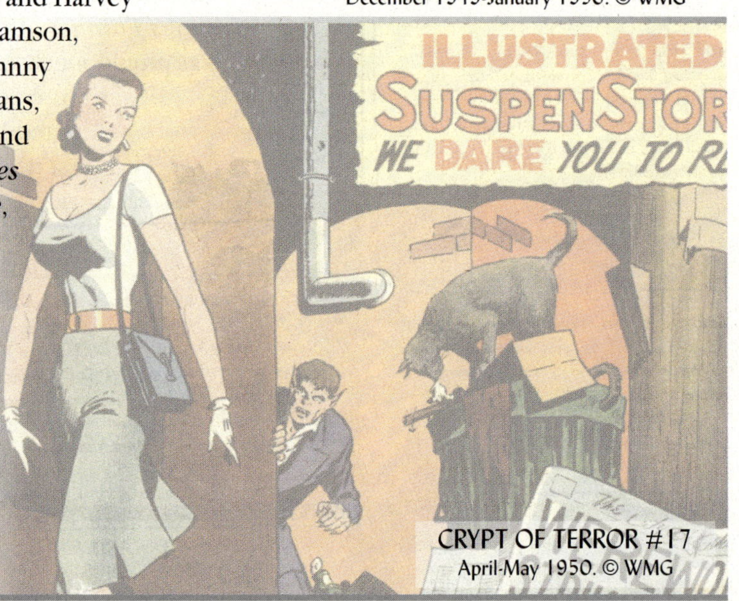
CRYPT OF TERROR #17
April-May 1950. © WMG

HAUNT OF FEAR #15 (#1)
May-June 1950. © WMG

WAR AGAINST CRIME #10
December 1949-January 1950. © WMG

WEIRD FANTASY #13 (#1)
May-June 1950. © WMG

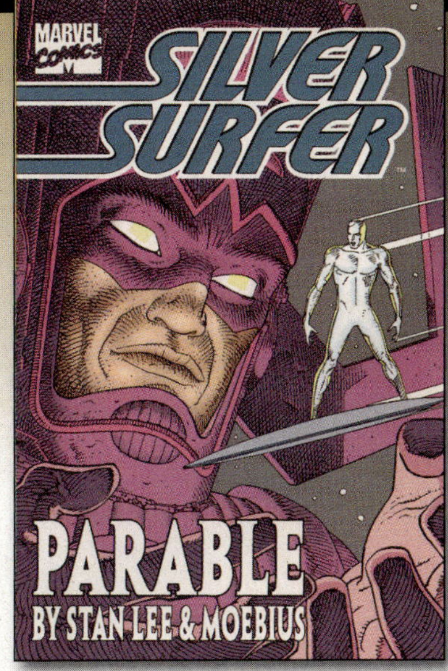

SILVER SURFER: PARABLE
February 1998. Reprint of graphic novel. © MAR

JEAN GIRAUD (MOEBIUS)

The term "visionary" is bandied about almost as much as the word "classic," but even in an era in which the meaning of the expression has been diluted through overuse, Jean Giraud was an edge-pushing pioneer, an artistic leader, and a true visionary. The French writer-artist passed away on Saturday, March 10, 2012 at the age of 73 after a long battle with cancer. Many American fans got to know his work through reprint collections published in the U.S. and through his collaboration with Stan Lee on *The Silver Surfer*, a two-part mini-series published in 1988-89. His range of topics was vast, and his impact equaled their scope. "The life of a storyteller like Jean Giraud cannot be evaluated simply by his prolific output or the elegance of his art or even by his commitment to his craft. Instead, in an earthly sense, we can only gauge his time among us by the impact he and his work had on others. In that sense, his effect is probably the definition of immeasurable," said Melissa Bowersox, Executive Vice-President of Geppi's Entertainment Museum.

INDUCTED 2012

EPIC GRAPHIC NOVEL
MOEBIUS 1 - UPON A STAR
1987. © Starwatcher Graphics

BLUEBERRY #1
1989. © Starwatcher Graphics

IRON MAN POSTER ART
1980s. © MAR

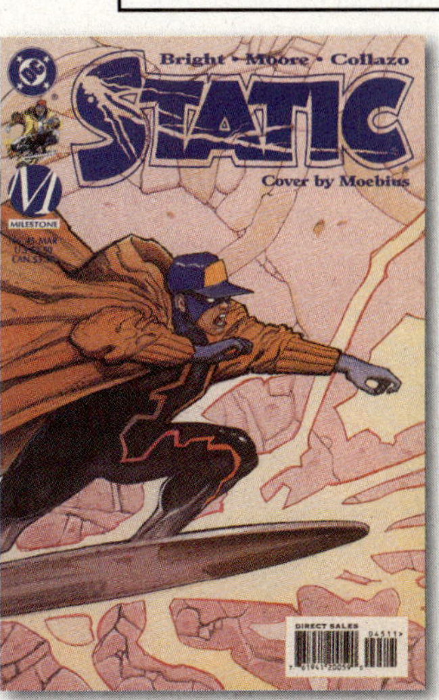

STATIC #45
March 1997. © Milestone Media

MARTIN GOODMAN

In 1931 Martin Goodman joined with future MLJ Magazines (Archie) co-founders Louis Silberkleit and Maurice Coyne to start pulp magazine publisher Columbia Publications. In 1932 he started his own business. His first publication was *Western Supernovel Magazine*, which premiered in May 1933, and he began building a variety of publishing companies from there. Under his umbrella came *Mystery Tales*, *Real Sports*, *Star Detective*, *Marvel Science Stories*, *Ka-Zar* and others.

In 1939, he contracted with Lloyd Jacquet's Funnies, Inc. to provide the content for what became *Marvel Comics* #1, which featured the Human Torch and the Sub-Mariner. With that comic as a hit, he hired his own staff, starting with writer-artist-editor Joe Simon. Timely Comics was born. A few years later, he hired his nephew by marriage, Stan Lee, as editor.

Eventually Timely Comics became Atlas Comics, and Atlas Comics became Marvel Comics. After selling Marvel in the late 1960s, he started a new Atlas line in 1974. While it didn't last at the time, it has recently been revived by his grandson, Jason Goodman.

INDUCTED 2011

MARVEL COMICS #1
November 1939. © MAR

ALL WINNERS COMICS #4
Spring 1942. © MAR

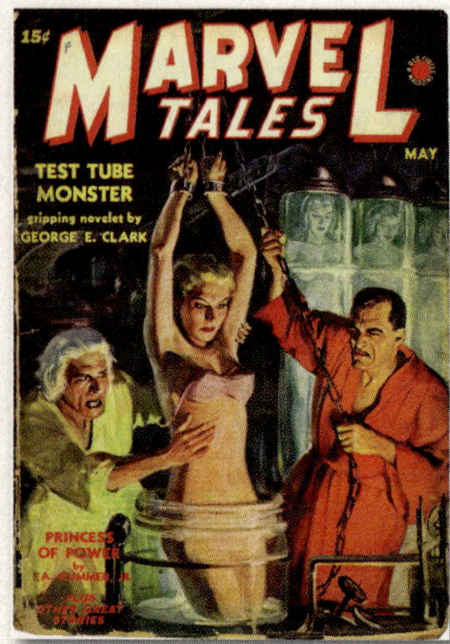

MARVEL TALES nn
Pulp magazine. May 1940. © MAR

TALES OF SUSPENSE #1
January 1959. © MAR

WEIRD TALES OF THE MACABRE #2
March 1975. © Atlas-Seaboard

EPIC ILLUSTRATED #1
Spring 1980. © MAR

ARCHIE GOODWIN

Ask the average fan to name the greatest creators in the history of comics and the name Archie Goodwin will not leap to the minds of many, because so much of Archie's brilliant work was behind the scenes or flew under the mainstream radar. But ask the creators with whom he worked! Ask other all-time great writers, artists, editors and creators! Gather the elders, the best of the best and ask them! His name will be among the first mentioned. Archie Goodwin was an amazing writer with outstanding story sense, penetrating insight, a gift for dialogue, an effortless knack for character, a flair for drama and utter mastery of the art of delivering the payoff. His sheer creativity ranks with the best ever. He was an all-time great editor and teacher. He made everyone he worked with better. On top of that, Archie Goodwin was a fine, wonderful, noble and honorable soul, loved and respected by everyone because he deserved it. This industry may never see his like again. How sad. He is desperately missed.

- JS

INDUCTED 2010

BLAZING COMBAT #1
October 1965. © WP

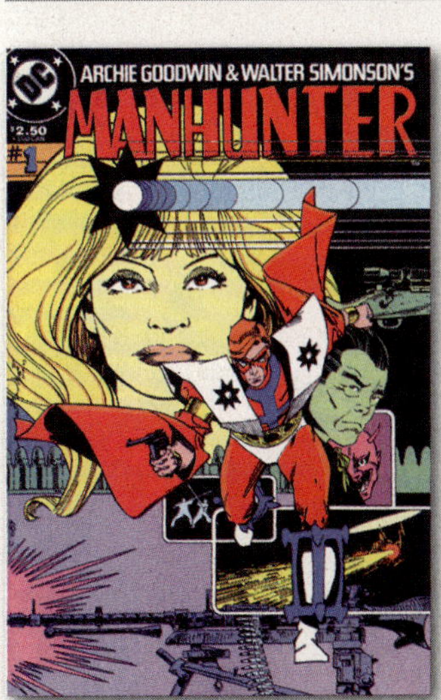

MANHUNTER #1
1984. © DC

STAR WARS HC COLLECTION
Reprints of newspaper strips. 1991. © Lucasfilm

VAMPIRELLA #100
October 1981. © WP

LARRY HAMA

G.I. JOE, A REAL AMERICAN HERO #1
June 1982. © Hasbro

Writer-artist-editor Larry Hama began his long association with the comic book incarnation of *G.I. Joe* almost immediately following then Marvel Comics editor-in-chief Jim Shooter's meeting with Hasbro. "It was Larry's book all the way," Shooter said. And in the minds of many fans, that's how it has remained. During the title's 155-issue run at Marvel, subsequent appearance at Devil's Due Publishing, and revival at IDW Publishing, Hama's portrayal of the characters defined many of them permanently for their fans. He has, however, been far from all *G.I. Joe*. He broke into comics as an assistant for Wally Wood, served as editor for Marvel's *Conan* line and *The 'Nam*, created *Bucky O'Hare*, wrote such titles as *Kitty Pryde, Agent of SHIELD*, *Punisher: War Zone* and *Weapon X*, among others. He has also written video games, consulted for G.I Joe in feature films, and even appeared as a actor on *M*A*S*H*, but it's his work on *G.I. Joe* – including the acclaimed "Silent Interlude" in *G.I. Joe* #21, which he wrote and penciled – that continues to demand attention.

G.I. JOE, A REAL AMERICAN HERO #21
March 1984. © Hasbro

INDUCTED 2012

CONAN THE BARBARIAN #162
September 1984. © Conan Properties Inc.

THE 'NAM #1
December 1986. © MAR

PUNISHER: WAR ZONE #25
March 1994. © MAR

RECORD SETTERS

AMAZING FANTASY #15
CGC CERTIFIED 9.6
Sold for $1,100,000
by ComicConnect.com
in March 2011. © MAR

TALES OF SUSPENSE #39
CGC CERTIFIED 9.6
Sold for $375,000
by ComicLink
in April 2012. © MAR

X-MEN #1
CGC CERTIFIED 9.8
Sold for $492,937.50
by Heritage Auctions
in July 2012. © MAR

BRUCE HAMILTON

A towering figure in the history of American comic books, Bruce Hamilton was publisher of Gladstone Publishing, a comics historian, and an early fan activist. Known around the world for the licensed line of Disney comics he lovingly published, Hamilton was a central figure in detailing the history of the medium. Possessed of an imposing stature, a radio announcer's voice, and a fiery drive, Hamilton helped get the comics industry organized, first as a dealer in Golden Age comics, then in other collectibles such as original art, movie posters, and cartoon cels. He was among the first to suggest that classic material be repackaged into deluxe formats. He began a 20-year relationship with The Walt Disney Company in 1980 when he and Russ Cochran acquired a license to produce The Fine Art of Walt Disney's Donald Duck, a collection of Carl Barks' Disney-based oil paintings. He passed away June 18, 2005.

INDUCTED 2007

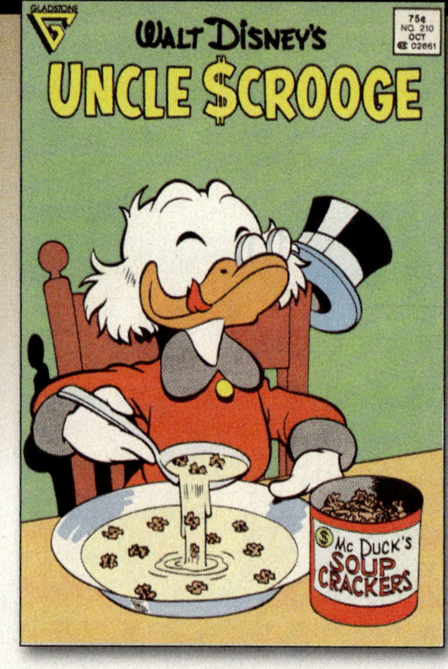

WALT DISNEY'S UNCLE SCROOGE #210
October 1986. © DIS

WALT DISNEY'S MICKEY MOUSE IN COLOR
Fall 1987. © DIS

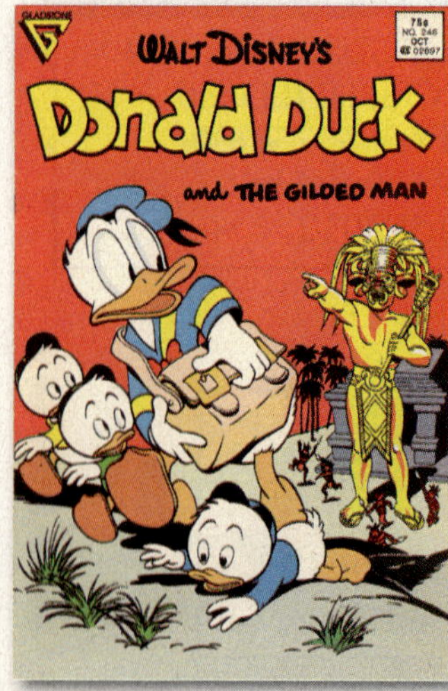

DONALD DUCK #246
October 1986. © DIS

MICKEY MOUSE #219
October 1986. © DIS

WALT DISNEY'S COMICS AND STORIES #511
October 1986. © DIS

CARMINE INFANTINO

AMAZING WORLD OF DC COMICS #8
September-October 1975. © DC

As a youngster, Carmine Infantino struggled to break into comics around the demands of his school schedule, making a number of sales and working on a variety of titles for different publishers including Hillman Periodicals, Fawcett, Holyoke, and DC Comics. He also worked for Joe Simon and Jack Kirby's Prize Comics during his early days. When editor Julius Schwartz paired him with writer Robert Kanigher on a revival of the Golden Age superhero The Flash in *Showcase #4*, though, lightning struck more than just the main character. Showing his illustration and design talents on characters ranging from the science fiction adventurer Adam Strange to serious superhero Batman to somewhat silly hero Elongated Man, Infantino became DC's Art Director, Editorial Director and eventually Publisher, supervising among other things the first Marvel - DC crossover, *Superman vs. The Amazing Spider-Man*. Following his staff tenure, he returned to work as a freelancer, illustrating *Star Wars*, *Nova*, and *Spider-Woman* for Marvel and various others for DC.

DETECTIVE COMICS #359
January 1967. © DC

INDUCTED 2009

BATMAN #183
August 1966. © DC

FLASH #135
March 1963. © DC

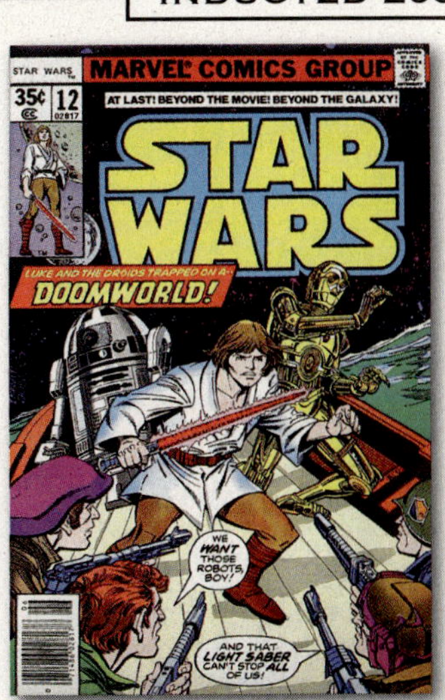

STAR WARS #12
June 1978. © Lucasfilm Ltd.

JACK KIRBY

A creative dynamo given human form, for many Jack Kirby defined with his work the very idea of what comic books should be. In his art and stories, the obvious brash doses of daring design and explosive action were infused with something more unexpected in the eras in which he worked: an equally bold excitement for the cerebral, philosophical and spiritual. Whether working with partners such as Joe Simon (with whom he co-created Captain America, the Fighting American, Boys Ranch, and many would say the romance comics genre) and Stan Lee (co-creating the Fantastic Four, Thor, and the Silver Surfer, among others), or on his own (DC's "Fourth World" titles such as *The New Gods*, *Mister Miracle*, *The Forever People*, or his creator-owned *Captain Victory* and *Silver Star*), Kirby worked as much in metaphor as he did in pencil. The number of creators and fans he influenced will never be known.

INDUCTED 2009

AVENGERS #4
March 1964. © MAR

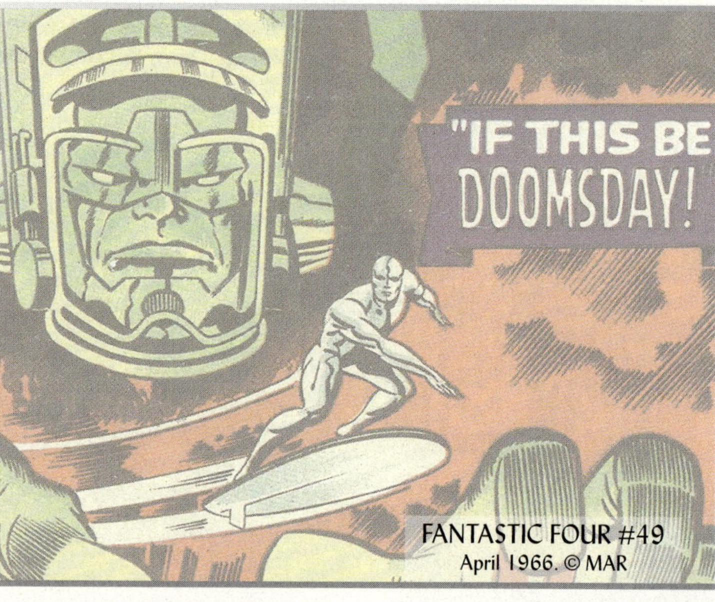

FANTASTIC FOUR #49
April 1966. © MAR

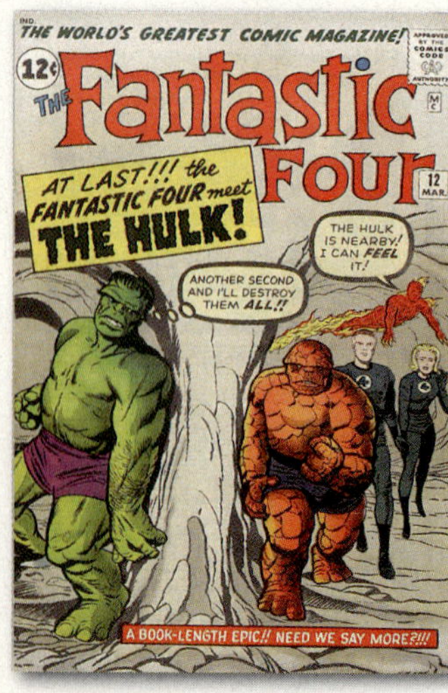
FANTASTIC FOUR #12
March 1963. © MAR

KAMANDI, THE LAST BOY ON EARTH #1
October-November 1972. © DC

STRANGE TALES #89
October 1961. © MAR

JOE KUBERT

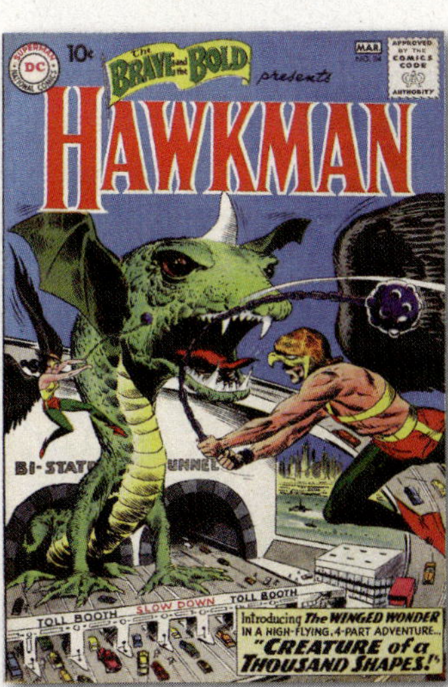

OUR ARMY AT WAR #112
November 1961. © DC

I don't know any other words that will as quickly put a fellow artist into that zone that exists between pure fandom and the cold sweats as the mention of writer, artist, editor, and educator Joe Kubert. In an industry predisposed to overuse words like 'legend,' Mr. Kubert truly is one. He started working in the business at age 11 in 1938 and for the rest of his career looked for ways to push himself and the medium for all its worth. While he is no doubt best known for his work on Sgt. Rock, he also poured his efforts into DC's other iconic war titles such as *G.I. Combat*, *Our Army at War* (and characters like Enemy Ace and the Haunted Tank), his art also graced titles like *Hawkman* and *Tarzan*, all of which would be enough for any artist. Not him. He founded the Joe Kubert School of Cartoon and Graphic Art in 1976, wrote and illustrated *Tor*, *Abraham Stone*, *Fax from Sarajevo*, *Yossel: April 19, 1943*, and still has more on the way. To put it bluntly, he is my biggest influence and my comic book hero!

- Billy Tucci

OVERSTREET C.B.P.G. #5
1975. © ERB

INDUCTED 2009

BRAVE AND THE BOLD #34
February-March 1961. © DC

ONE MILLION YEARS AGO
1st app. of Tor. September 1953. © STJ

STAR SPANGLED WAR STORIES #138
April-May 1968. © DC

HARVEY KURTZMAN

MAD #4
April-May 1953. © WMG

Harvey Kurtzman was a cartoonist, writer, editor, artist and master storyteller. Best known as the founding editor of *MAD* in its original comic book form at EC Comics, Kurtzman was also the driving force behind EC's *Two-Fisted Tales* and *Frontline Combat*. He also created *Hey Look!*, *Trump*, *Help!*, and *Humbug*. Throughout his career, he worked with artists such as Will Elder, Jack Davis, Wally Wood, John Severin, and Russ Heath, among others, but his method of scripting and providing page layouts had the impact of making a Harvey Kurtzman story come out looking like a Harvey Kurtzman story no matter who illustrated it. His war comics are generally considered among the best the genre has ever experienced even though they clearly portray the high cost of war on individuals rather than more typical war stories. The long-running comic book industry Harvey Awards are named in his honor.

MAD #6
August-September 1953. © WMG

INDUCTED 2008

FRONTLINE COMBAT #9
November-December 1952. © WMG

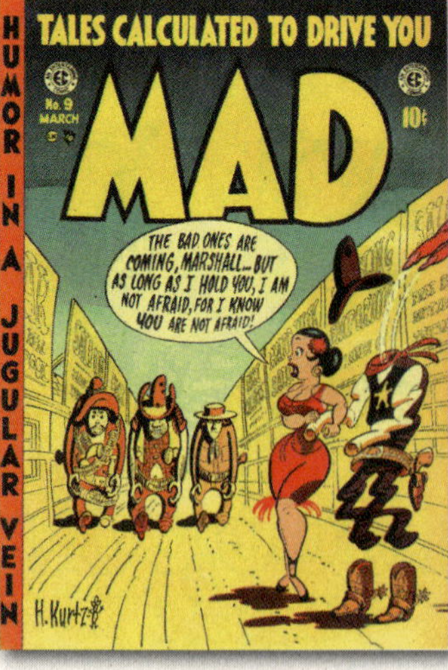

MAD #9
February-March 1954. © WMG

TWO-FISTED TALES #27
May-June 1952. © WMG

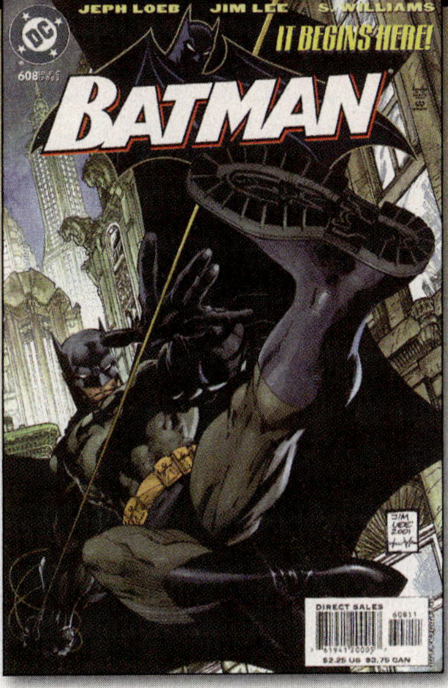

BATMAN #608
December 2002. © DC

Over the past twenty years, Jim Lee has created many of the classic comic book images with his sense of style and attention to composition garnering plenty of fans. A native of Seoul, South Korea, he started his comics career in 1989 drawing *Uncanny X-Men* before helping to launch the record-breaking *X-Men* with co-writer Chris Claremont.

In 1992, Lee joined fellow comic creators in the founding of Image Comics, creating and co-creating new characters under his WildStorm Productions imprint including *WildC.A.T.s* and *Gen13*.

In 1998, Lee sold WildStorm to DC Comics. While he continued to work with the company he founded, he also began working on DC's iconic characters as well. He illustrated the 12-issue story arc "Hush" in the pages of *Batman* with writer Jeph Loeb, followed by a run on *Superman*. Much of his time has been spent closely developing the look of the characters and settings in DC's new online game with Sony.

In 2010, Lee was appointed co-publisher of DC Comics with Dan DiDio, succeeding Paul Levitz.

X-MEN © MAR

INDUCTED 2006

INFINITE CRISIS #2
January 2006. © DC

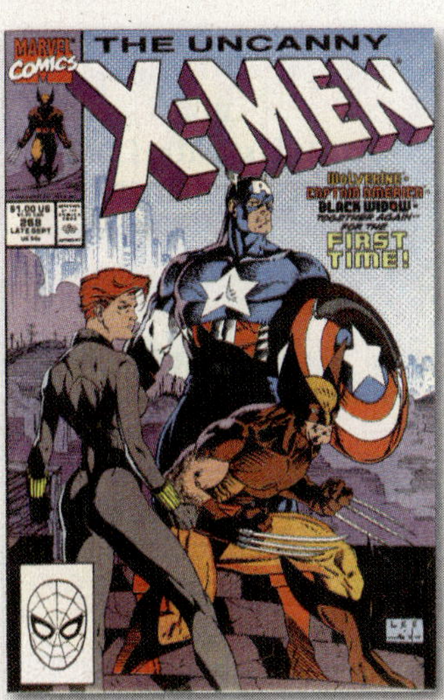

UNCANNY X-MEN #268
September 1990. © MAR

WILDC.A.T.S #5
November 1993. © WSP

STAN LEE

FANTASTIC FOUR #51
June 1966. © MAR

"Captain America Foils the Traitor's Revenge," a text piece in *Captain America Comics* #3 (May 1941) might not have been the most auspicious debut in the history of the comics, but it is nonetheless an important event. It marked the first published comic book work of young Stanley Martin Lieber, better known as Stan Lee, the writer, editor, creator, co-creator, publisher and pitchman who developed and relentlessly promoted the identity of Marvel Comics. After two decades in which Lee was forced to do comics as others wanted them done, he finally he tried them his way. The Fantastic Four, Spider-Man, Thor, The Avengers, The X-Men, The Incredible Hulk and others were the result. Eventually moving to the west coast to spearhead the company's Hollywood ambitions, this entertainment icon has lived to see many of his favorite creations hit the silver screen as Hollywood special effects finally caught up to his imagination of 40 years ago.

AMAZING SPIDER-MAN #23
April 1965. © MAR

INDUCTED 2008

CAPTAIN AMERICA COMICS #3
May 1941. © MAR

INCREDIBLE HULK #1
May 1962. © MAR

X-MEN #4
March 1964. © MAR

LEGION OF SUPER-HEROES #294
December 1982. © DC

ADVENTURE COMICS #462
March-April 1979. © DC

PAUL LEVITZ

He started out as a fan, established a broad base of historical and contemporary knowledge about the field, developed as a writer, and eventually became the leader of one of the two biggest comic book companies. After writing and co-publishing the long-lived fanzine *The Comic Reader*, Paul Levitz could have called it a day and still been lauded for his contributions to the four color world. Good thing for us, though, he didn't stop there. As a writer, he's known for writing the Earth II adventures of the Justice Society of America in the revived *All Star Comics* in the 1970s, a period in which he co-created The Huntress. In the 1980s, he wrote a lengthy run on *Legion of Super-Heroes*, and he recently returned to scripting for a run of *JSA*. He's probably best known, though, as the President and Publisher of DC Comics, where he has worked tirelessly to promote their characters as well as the history and future of the medium.

–Stephen A. Geppi

INDUCTED 2009

DC SPECIAL #29
August-September 1977. © DC

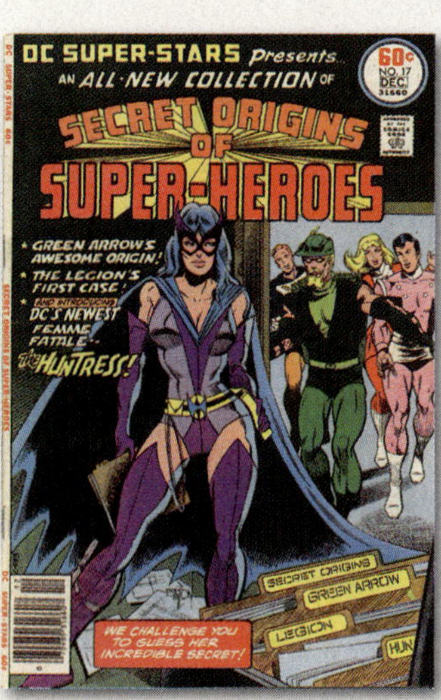
DC SUPER-STARS #17
November-December 1977. © DC

TEEN TITANS #44
November 1976. © DC

RUSS MANNING

MAGNUS, ROBOT FIGHTER #5
February 1964. © Random House

Whether one knows his work from his long run on the *Tarzan* newspaper strip, a too-brief stint on the *Star Wars* newspaper strip, or creating the comic book series *Magnus Robot Fighter*, the illustrations of Russ Manning (1929-1981) pack clean, crisp line work and solid storytelling into every panel. With a design sense dictated by the stories (His *Star Wars* or *Magnus* are substantially different than his *Tarzan*), he became influential with comic artists, even though his work was never published by Marvel or DC.

In recent years, Dark Horse has reprinted many of his Tarzan stories in collected editions, sharing them with new generations of fans. Each year The Russ Manning Most Promising Newcomer Award is an award presented at Comic-Con International: San Diego to a comic book artist whose first professional work appeared within the previous two years. In 1982 the first recipient was the late Dave Stevens, who had worked as an assistant of Manning's.

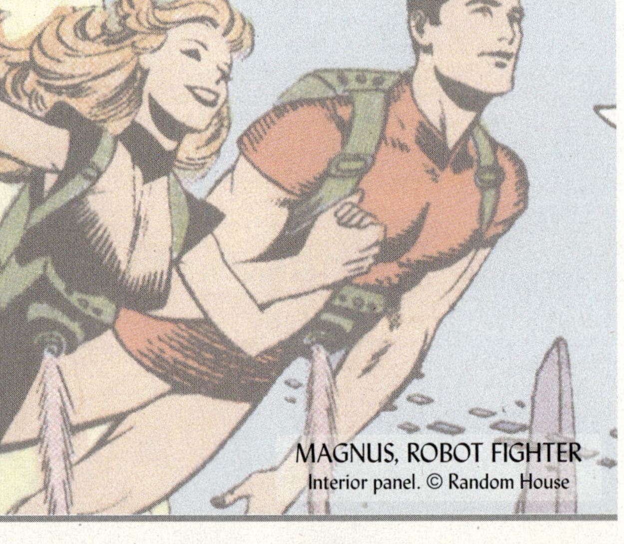

MAGNUS, ROBOT FIGHTER
Interior panel. © Random House

INDUCTED 2009

THE ALIENS #1
September-December 1967. © WEST

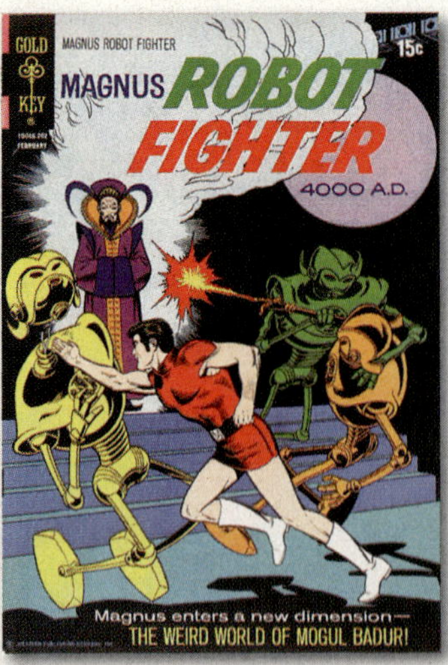

MAGNUS, ROBOT FIGHTER #30
February 1972. © Random House

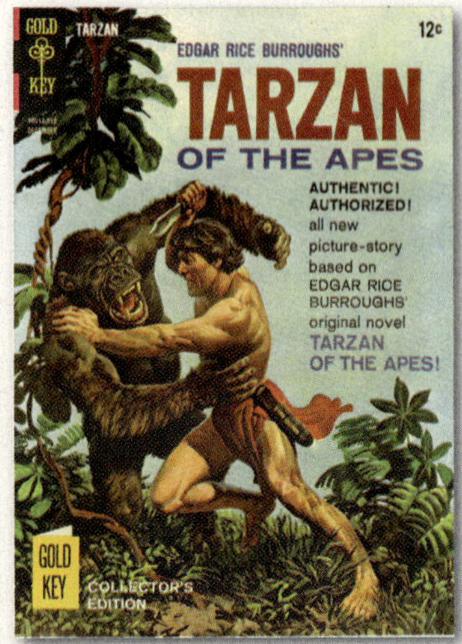

TARZAN #155
December 1965. © ERB

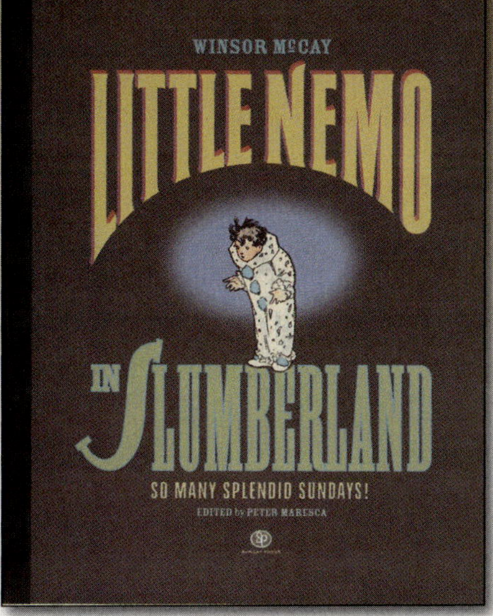

LITTLE NEMO IN SLUMBERLAND
SO MANY SPLENDID SUNDAYS!
2005. © Sunday Press

It's a daunting task to bring the world of dreams to vivid, waking life, but Winsor McCay (1867-1934) managed to do that for newspaper readers every week through his landmark artistic achievements, the ground-breaking strips *Dreams of a Rarebit Fiend* and *Little Nemo in Slumberland*. Chronicling the nighttime adventures of a little boy as he navigated a wonderland of imagination from 1905-1927, McCay's *Nemo* was a powerful exploration of childlike discovery and lush, expressive art. As an animator, McCay was a pioneer that introduced the world to *Gertie the Dinosaur* in 1914 and employed vaudevillian techniques to blend live-action and animation long before Roger Rabbit was born. His work in comic strips and cartoons inspired the likes of Walt Disney, Bill Watterson, Maurice Sendak and many more. It is absolutely fair to say that without McCay, the world of comic characters as we know it would simply not exist.

- ATB

LITTLE NEMO
IN SLUMBERLAND
Undated print.

LITTLE NEMO
IN SLUMBERLAND
Bisque statues from 1914

INDUCTED 2010

GERTIE THE DINOSAUR
Animation drawing. 1914.

LITTLE SAMMY SNEEZE
December 1905. © NY Herald Co.

TODD McFARLANE

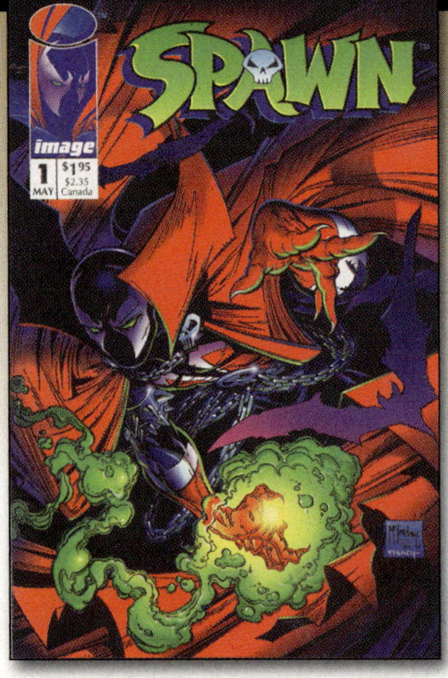
SPAWN #1
May 1992. © TMP

Writer, artist, toy designer, businessman. All of these titles and others apply to Todd McFarlane, the former Spider-Man writer-artist who capitalized on incredible sales in 1992 and co-founded Image Comics. Following a back-up story in *Coyote*, which was then published by Marvel's Epic imprint, McFarlane began quickly making a name for himself. After illustrating *Batman: Year Two* and *Infinity, Inc.* at DC Comics and *Incredible Hulk* at Marvel, he landed the art duties on *Amazing Spider-Man*. After 28 issues on that series, he launched a new one, simply *Spider-Man*, which he wrote and illustrated. He parlayed the overwhelming sales for that series into the launch of Image Comics, where he wrote and illustrated his own series, *Spawn*, and created many others. McFarlane has built his McFarlane Toys into a serious force in the toy business, and continues to work in various areas in entertainment in addition to comics.

AMAZING SPIDER-MAN #316
June 1989. © MAR

INDUCTED 2009

DETECTIVE COMICS #577
August 1987. © DC

INCREDIBLE HULK #340
February 1988. © MAR

SPIDER-MAN #1
August 1990. © MAR

MIKE MIGNOLA

HELLBOY: SEED OF DESTRUCTION #1
March 1994. © Mike Mignola

Having worked for both Marvel and DC on titles like *Daredevil*, *Incredible Hulk*, *Batman: A Death in the Family* and *Gotham by Gaslight* (which launched DC's "Elseworlds" line), artist Mike Mignola blended his love of Lovecraft-like horror and pulp/B-movie monster mashes, tinkering at his table like a latter-day Frankenstein until the bulky, huge-handed, nearly hornless, bright red paranormal crusader known as Hellboy leapt from the pages of Dark Horse Comics in 1994. Broadening his accomplishments to include scripting many of Hellboy's tales, Mignola's distinctive artistic style mixed Jack Kirby-like intensity with a darker layer of expressionistic shadow and shape. Mignola has also brought his artistic eye to Hollywood with conceptual work on Coppola's *Bram Stoker's Dracula* and the forthcoming *Lord of the Rings* prequel, *The Hobbit*. He also had the rare opportunity to help usher his own creation onto the silver screen via Guillermo del Toro's two *Hellboy* feature films.

- ATB

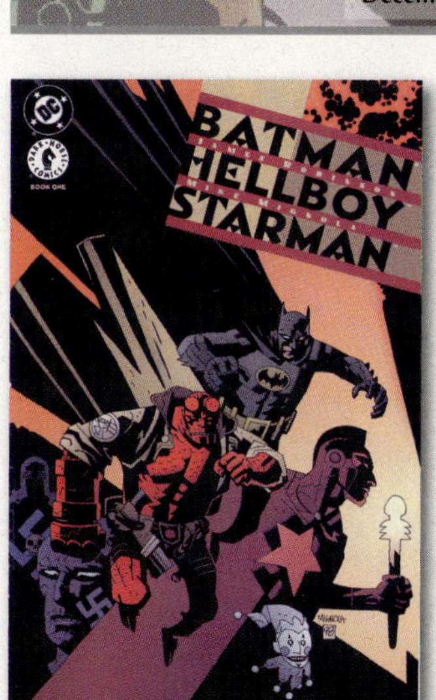

JOHN BYRNE'S NEXT MEN #21
December 1993. Next Men © JB / Hellboy © Mike Mignola

INDUCTED 2010

BATMAN/HELLBOY/STARMAN #1
January 1999. © DC, DH & Mike Mignola

COSMIC ODYSSEY #1
1988. © DC

GOTHAM BY GASLIGHT #1
1989. © DC

FRANK MILLER

After illustrating a few stories for Gold Key's *The Twilight Zone* and DC's *Weird War Tales* and *Unknown Soldier*, and following a story in Marvel's *John Carter: Warlord of Mars* #18, Frank Miller landed a two-part fill-in job on *Peter Parker, the Spectacular Spider-Man* #27–28, which guest-starred Daredevil, a character who he would define and which in return would define his early success. Miller took over as regular artist on *Daredevil* #158. By the time Elektra was featured on the cover of *Daredevil* #168, he was writing it as well. With inker Klaus Janson, he turned it into one of Marvel's most popular titles.

He also illustrated the first *Wolverine* mini-series, unleashed *Ronin*, and then turned his attention to Bruce Wayne's future with *Batman: The Dark Knight Returns,* which became a perennial best seller in its collected edition. Subsequently he wrote another run on *Daredevil* and *Batman: Year One*, both with artist David Mazzuccheli, before turning to creator-owned projects such as *Sin City* and *300*. He continues to create in both film and comics.

BATMAN THE DARK KNIGHT RETURNS #1
March 1986. © DC

WOLVERINE #1
Mini-series. September 1982. © MAR

INDUCTED 2010

DAREDEVIL #169
January 1981. © MAR

SIN CITY: A DAME TO KILL FOR #3
February 1994. © Frank Miller

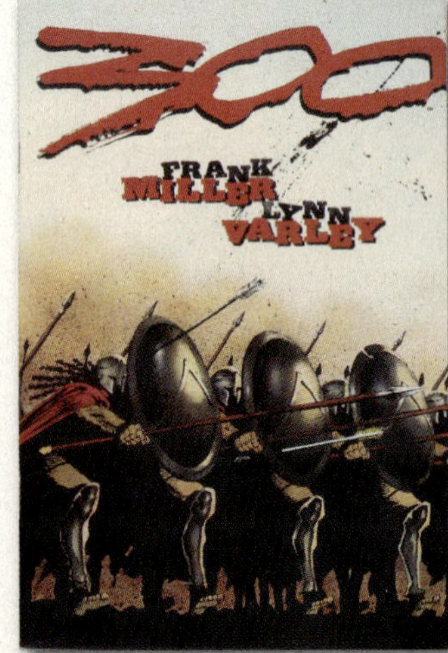

300 #1
May 1998. © Frank Miller

DEAN MULLANEY

ECLIPSE MAGAZINE #6
July 1982. © ECL

THE COMPLETE TERRY AND THE PIRATES
VOLUME ONE: 1934-1936
September 2007. © Tribune Media Services

In 2007, Dean Mullaney created IDW Publishing's archival imprint The Library of American Comics, which he edits and designs. Almost immediately his efforts began to usher in a new Golden Age of classic comic strip reprint collections, significant in both the material itself and the manner in which it is presented. In its first four years, LoAC has been nominated for nine Eisner awards and other accolades, and it has been called "the gold standard for archival comic strip reprints."

Under his guidance, Milton Caniff's *Terry and the Pirates*, Alex Raymond's *Rip Kirby*, Chester Gould's *Dick Tracy*, Harold Gray's *Little Orphan Annie*, Archie Goodwin and Al Williamson's *Secret Agent Corrigan*, Chic Young's *Blondie* and other strips have been showcased for seasoned fans and new readers alike.

In 1978, he launched Eclipse Comics when he published Don McGregor's *Sabre*, the first graphic novel created for the comics specialty market. Eclipse championed creator ownership and the first line of Japanese manga in English translation, and had the first digitally-colored comic book.

INDUCTED 2011

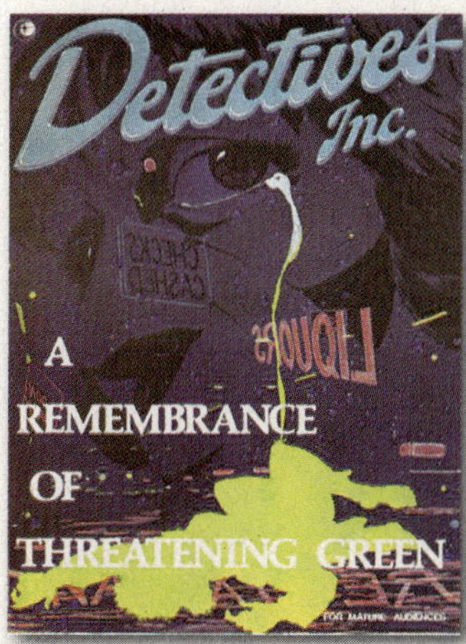

DETECTIVES, INC.
May 1980. © Don McGregor

ECLIPSE GRAPHIC ALBUM SERIES #1
October 1978. The 1st direct sale GN.
© Don McGregor

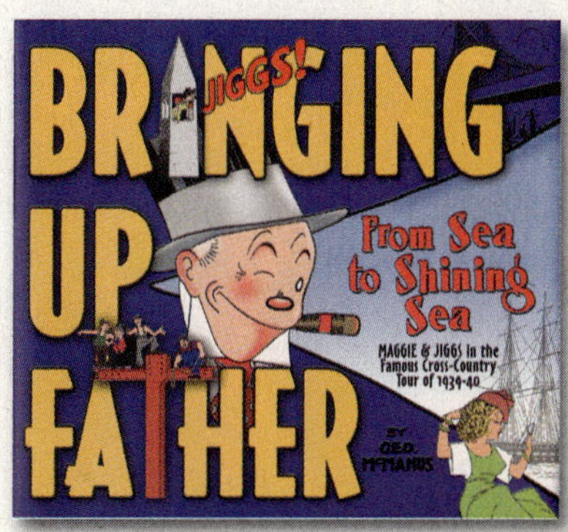

BRINGING UP FATHER:
FROM SEA TO SHINING SEA
December 2009. © King Features Syndicate

MART NODELL

GREEN LANTERN #3
Spring 1942. © DC

Martin Nodell was one of the shining lights of the Golden Age of comics. Best known as the creator of the Golden Age superhero the Green Lantern, Nodell took the character to All-American Publications, and his Green Lantern made his debut in the July 1940 issue of *All-American Comics* #16. The character proved popular and received its own title in the Fall of 1941. Nodell went on to illustrate for other publishers including Timely Comics, including cover art for *Captain America Comics* #74 and *Marvel Tales* #93.

In 1965, Nodell accepted an art director position at Leo Burnett Agency where he was a member of the design team that created the Pillsbury Doughboy which would go on to be another iconic character.

Starting in 1980, Nodell began attending various comic book conventions along with his wife, Caroline to meet the many fans and collectors who the Green Lantern and its creator had touched.

Panel from ALL-AMERICAN COMICS #20
November 1940. © DC

ALL-AMERICAN COMICS #31
October 1941. © DC

CAPTAIN AMERICA'S WEIRD TALES #74
October 1949. © MAR

MARVEL TALES #93
August 1949. © MAR

OVERSTREET C.B.P.G. #1
1970. © Gemstone

Editor's note: In celebration of the 40th anniversary of The Overstreet Comic Book Price Guide *and his contributions to comic book collecting, the Gemstone staff was very proud to induct Robert M. Overstreet into The Overstreet Hall of Fame.*

It started humbly with exposure to his older brother's Golden Age copies of *Captain Marvel*, *Daredevil* and the funny animal title *Fox And The Crow*, but when Bob Overstreet discovered EC Comics, look out! He began travelling to put together a full set of the EC titles, always searching for better copies and any bit of data he could find on them. A veteran coin collector, he quickly realized that what comics needed was a price guide. In 1970, after a lot more research, he published the first edition of *The Overstreet Comic Book Price Guide*. While some early fans thought the prices were way too high, time has proven him - and the *Guide* - right pretty frequently.

- SAG

INDUCTED 2010

OVERSTREET C.B.P.G. #12
1982. © EC

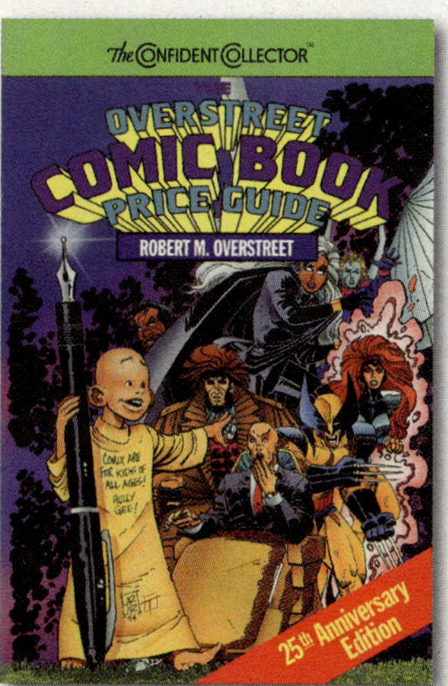
OVERSTREET C.B.P.G. #6
1976. © Will Eisner

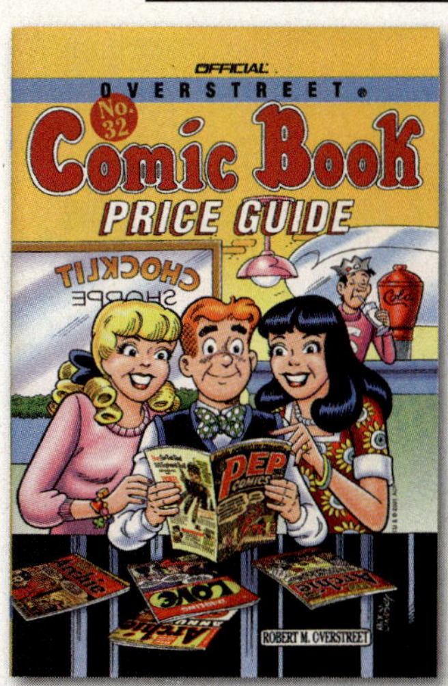
OVERSTREET C.B.P.G. #25
1995. © MAR

OVERSTREET C.B.P.G. #32
2002. © AP

GEORGE PÉREZ

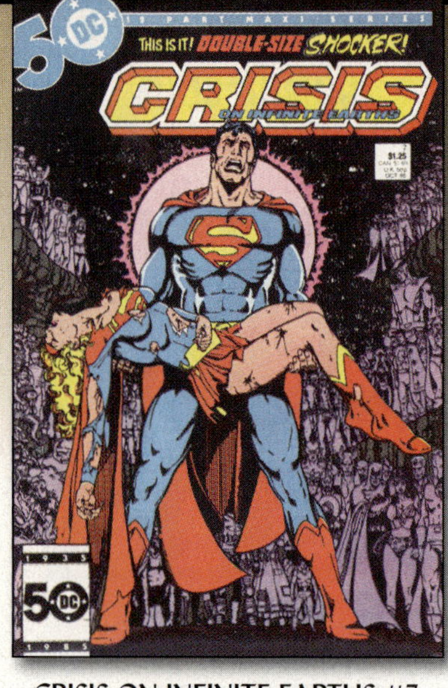

CRISIS ON INFINITE EARTHS #7
October 1985. © DC

George Pérez is arguably one of the greatest comic book artists to ever hold a pencil. He began his career working on a serialized action-adventure strip called *Sons of the Tiger* in Marvel's *Deadly Hands of Kung-Fu*. From there, Pérez moved on to work on Marvel premiere superhero team, *The Avengers* (beginning with issue #141) and soon took over artistic duties on Marvel's First Family, *The Fantastic Four*.

After tackling two of Marvel's flagship books, Pérez jumped ship and moved over to work on *Justice League of America* at DC Comics. Soon after, he teamed up with writer Marv Wolfman to streamline the DC Universe in the epic maxi-series, *Crisis on Infinite Earths* (1985).

Pérez, at one time or another during his illustrious career has drawn every major character from both the Marvel and DC Universe, many of whom were featured in *JLA/Avengers* (2003), a crossover that was 20 years in the making.

OVERSTREET C.B.P.G. #35
2005. © DC

INDUCTED 2007

AVENGERS #161
July 1977. © MAR

JLA/AVENGERS #1
September 2003. © DC

WONDER WOMAN #14
Second series. March 1988. © DC

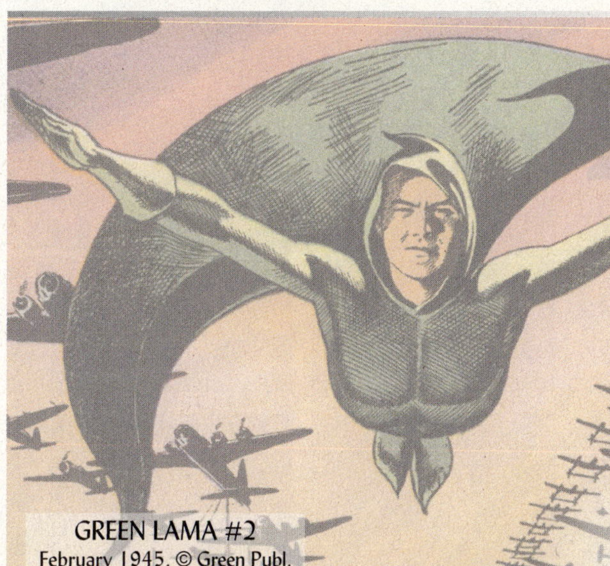

MASTER COMICS #30
September 1942. © FAW

MAC RABOY

Emanuel "Mac" Raboy began his comic book career in 1940 working for the Harry A Chesler studio, which was known for completing work for a variety of comic publishers. He also notably used his artistic talents at Fawcett Publications on many of the company's classic titles including *Captain Marvel, Jr.*, *Captain Midnight*, and *Master Comics*.

His art carries a classic feel that can be easily identified by his use of composition and perspective. Mac later left Fawcett in 1944 and used his abilities on the comic book *Green Lama*. From 1948 until his death in 1967 Mac Raboy worked as the illustrator on the *Flash Gordon* comic strip for King Features Syndicate.

GREEN LAMA #2
February 1945. © Green Publ.

INDUCTED 2006

BULLETMAN #2
Fall 1941. © FAW

CAPTAIN MIDNIGHT #9
June 1943. © FAW

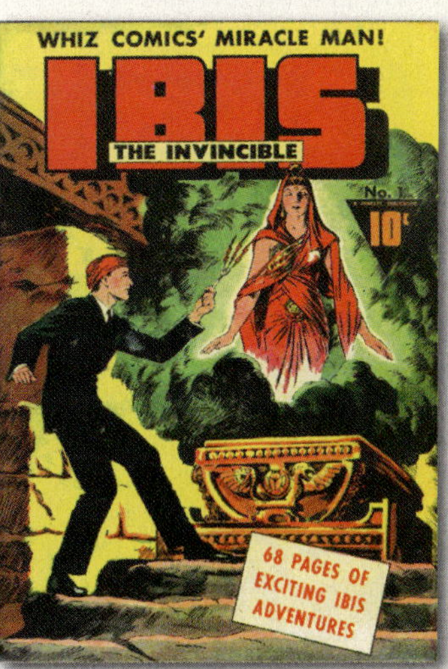

IBIS, THE INVINCIBLE #1
January 1943. © FAW

MIKE RICHARDSON

When Mike Richardson launched Dark Horse Comics in 1986 with *Dark Horse Presents* #1, very few could have predicted the events of the next 24 years. Even when *Concrete* #1 started garnering critical acclaim (the series would eventually win 26 Eisner Awards during its run), no one really knew what an independent powerhouse Richardson was building in Milwaukie, Oregon. They soon would.

Whether acting as the creator of projects like *The Mask*, *The Secret*, *Living with the Dead*, and *Cut*, co-authoring non-fiction books such as *Comics Between the Panels* and *Blast Off!*, developing comic book-inspired films, or championing the work of other creators, he said he founded the company with the goal of establishing an ideal atmosphere for creative professionals.

Over time, creators such as Frank Miller, Geoff Darrow, Dave Gibbons, Stan Sakai, Sergio Aragonés, Arthur Adams, Harlan Ellison, Matt Wagner, Mike Allred, Mike Mignola, Mike Baron, Steve Rude, Jim Shooter, and Dave Stevens, and licensed properties such as Aliens, Predator, Conan, and most notably Star Wars have made their home at Richardson's company with dazzling results.
- SAG

INDUCTED 2010

DARK HORSE PRESENTS #51
June 1991. © DH

COMICS BETWEEN THE PANELS
1998. © Duin & Richardson

CONCRETE #1
March 1987. © Paul Chadwick

RETURN OF THE GREMLINS #1
March 2008. © DIS

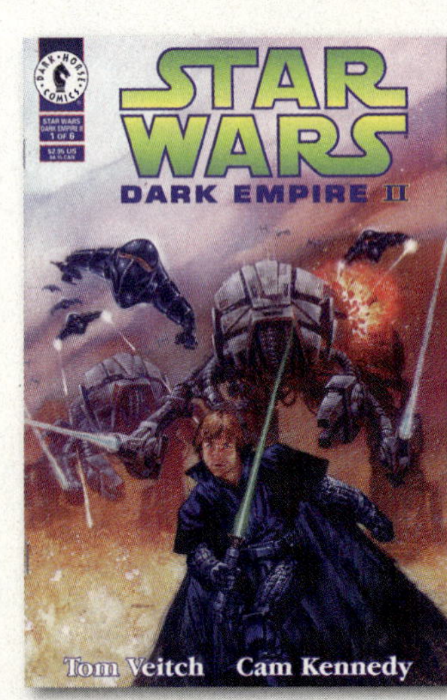

STAR WARS DARK EMPIRE II #1
December 1994. © Lucasfilm

JERRY ROBINSON

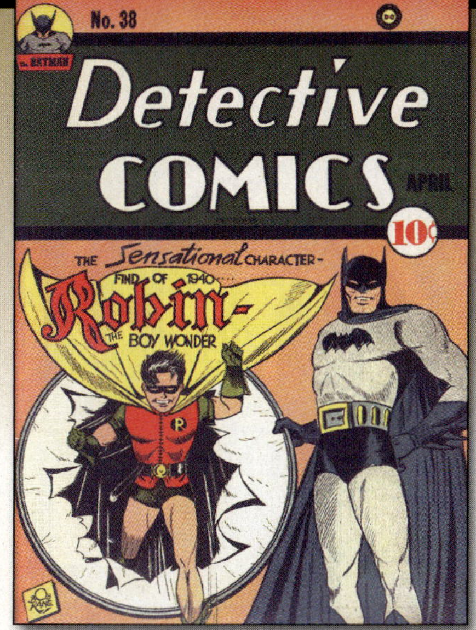

DETECTIVE COMICS #38
April 1940. © DC

Jerry Robinson was a Columbia University student when he met and began working for Batman creator Bob Kane in 1939. He started out working on backgrounds and lettering, teamed with Kane and writer Bill Finger. He quickly became the main inker for the character. When Kane and Finger discussed adding a sidekick for Batman while preparing for *Detective Comics* #38, Robinson suggested Robin, drawing inspiration from N.C. Wyeth's illustration of Robin Hood. In time for *Batman* #1, he (along with Finger) is unofficially credited with creating the Joker as well.

After working for Kane, then on staff at DC and illustrating comic books for others, Robinson had a highly successful career in newspaper comic strips and editorial cartooning. He served as President of the National Cartoonists Society and the Association of American Editorial Cartoonists, founded the Cartoonists & Writers Syndicate. He, along with Neal Adams and others, championed the cause of Superman creators Jerry Siegel and Joe Shuster receiving royalties for their creation.

He passed away on December 7, 2011 at the age of 89.

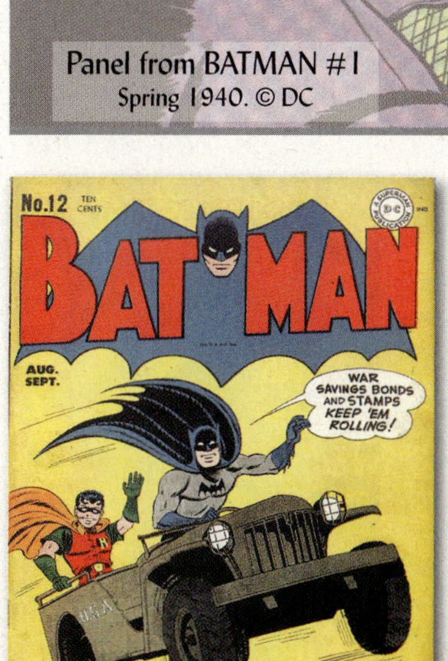

Panel from BATMAN #1
Spring 1940. © DC

INDUCTED 2010

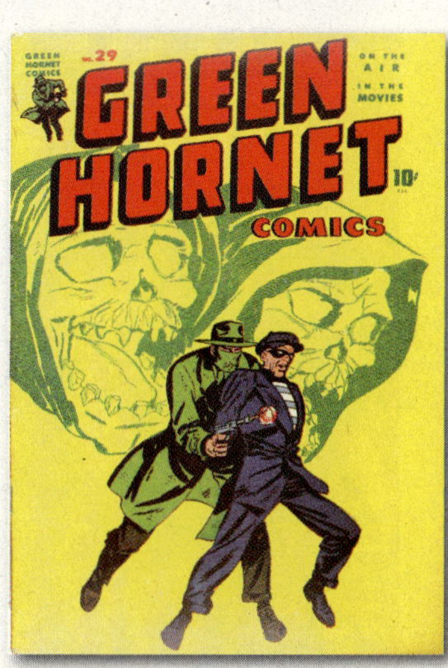

BATMAN #12
August-September 1942. © DC

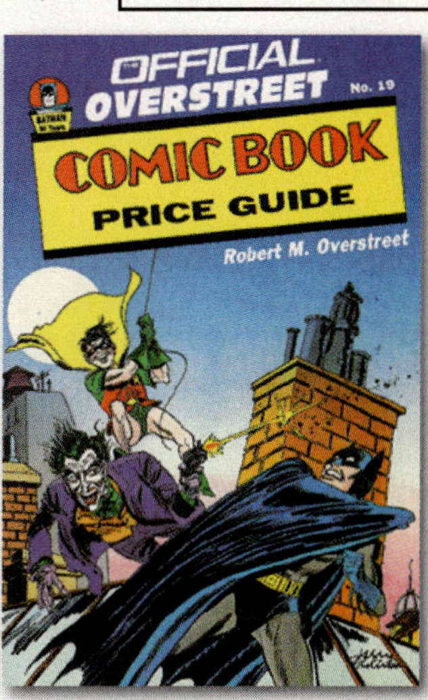

GREEN HORNET COMICS #29
March 1946. © HARV

OVERSTREET C.B.P.G. #19
1989. © DC

MARSHALL ROGERS

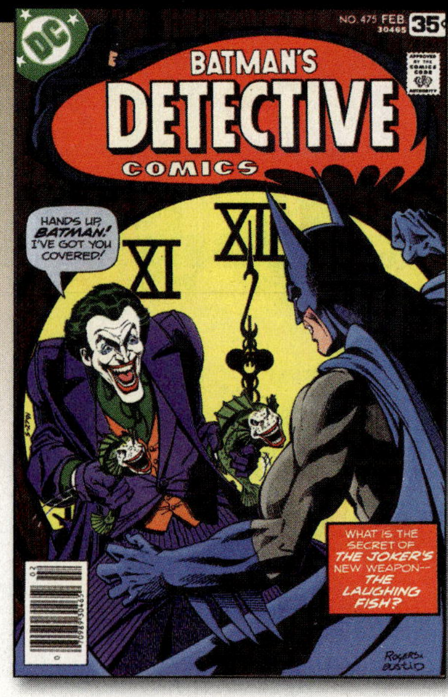

DETECTIVE COMICS #475
February 1978. © DC

Marshall Rogers visually defined Batman for a generation of fans. Teamed with writer Steve Englehart and inker Terry Austin, Rogers delivered the lead stories in a highly praised run on *Detective Comics* in the 1970s which introduced mob boss Rupert Thorne, Bruce Wayne's love interest Silver St. Cloud, and the Joker Fish. He simultaneously drew a memorable run of *Mister Miracle*. Rogers also worked with Englehart on *Coyote* in serialized form in the pages of *Eclipse Magazine*, *Madame Xanadu*, *Scorpio Rose*, *Silver Surfer* and later, again with Austin inking, on the mini-series *Batman: Dark Detective*. Rogers also illustrated a run on *Doctor Strange* and teamed with writer Don McGregor on the original *Detectives, Inc.* graphic novel. His work also appeared in *G.I. Joe*, *Howard The Duck*, *Green Lantern: Evil's Might*, *Batman: Legends of the Dark Knight*, and his own creation, *Cap'n Quick and a Foozle*. He passed away unexpectedly at the age of 57.

BATMAN: STRANGE APPARITIONS
TPB. 1999. © DC

INDUCTED 2008

DETECTIVES INC. #1
April 1985. © McGregor & Rogers

DOCTOR STRANGE #52
April 1982. © MAR

MISTER MIRACLE #20
October 1977. © DC

JOHN ROMITA, SR.

AMAZING SPIDER-MAN #100
September 1971. © MAR

SPECTACULAR SPIDER-MAN #2
Novenber 1968. © MAR

Even if they have never seen a comic book, anyone who saw the visual imagery in the first two Spider-Man feature films has seen the work of John Romita, Sr. (credited simply as John Romita for a good portion of his career). Imagery based on his strong, distinctive, character-rich comic book work permeated just about every important scene in those movies. He worked in the industry for years before he took over the art duties on *Amazing Spider-Man* from Steve Ditko, but his dynamic style and fluid linework put his stamp on Spidey almost immediately, forever associating him with the character. His influence on successive generations of Marvel Comics artists was foreseen by Stan Lee, who hired him as Art Director for the company. Although he is officially retired, his work still pops up from time to time, always to smiles from his fans and fellow professionals.

INDUCTED 2008

BRING ON THE BAD GUYS
Fireside Book Series. 1976. © MAR

DAREDEVIL #16
May 1966. © MAR

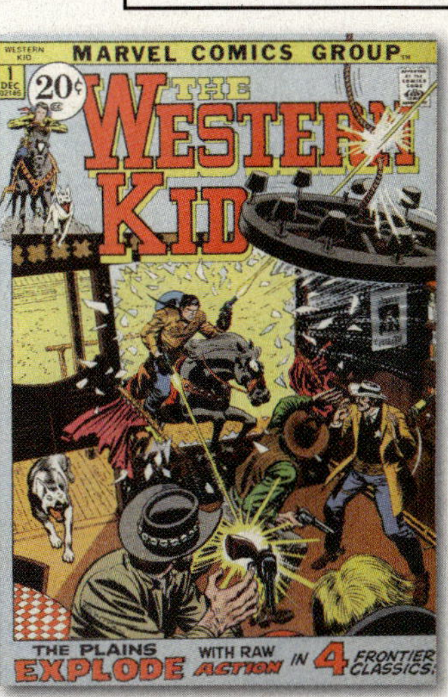

THE WESTERN KID #1
December 1971. © MAR

JOHN ROMITA, JR.

AMAZING SPIDER-MAN #508
July 2004. © MAR

After making his American comics debut in the pages of *Amazing Spider-Man Annual* #11, John Romita, Jr. quickly established himself as a popular artist with a healthy run on *Iron Man*. He then launched into his first run on *Amazing Spider-Man*, the series that had made his father a fan favorite. He followed this with stints on *Uncanny X-Men*, *Daredevil*, *Daredevil: Man Without Fear*, *Star Brand*, *Punisher War Zone*, *Cable*, *The Mighty Thor*, a second run on *Iron Man*, *Wolverine*, a second run on *Amazing Spider-Man*, *The Black Panther*, *The Sentry*, *The Eternals*, and the "World War Hulk" event. He illustrated the *Punisher-Batman* crossover and his creator-owned *The Gray Area*, which was released by Image Comics. He has worked with John, Sr. on a number of special occasions, always to the delight of the comic-buying public, but has clearly worked to develop his own style, sometimes sharing only a commitment to great storytelling with his father.

AVENGERS #1
July 2010. © MAR

INDUCTED 2008

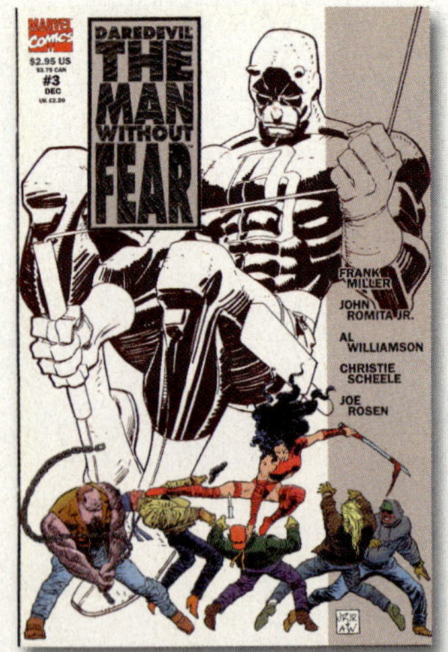

DAREDEVIL THE MAN WITHOUT FEAR #3
December 1993. © MAR

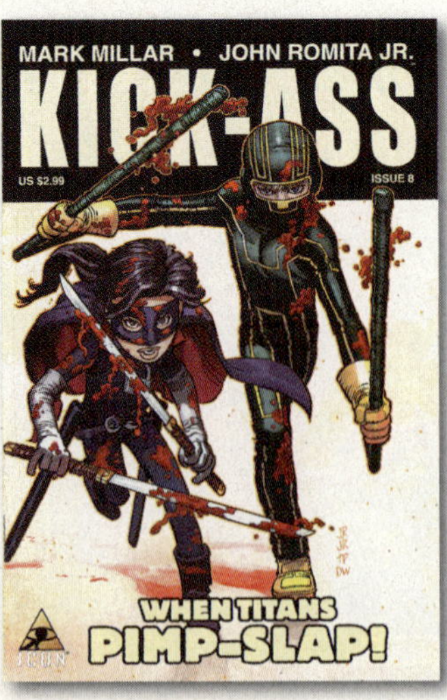

KICK-ASS #8
March 2010. © Millar & Romita, Jr.

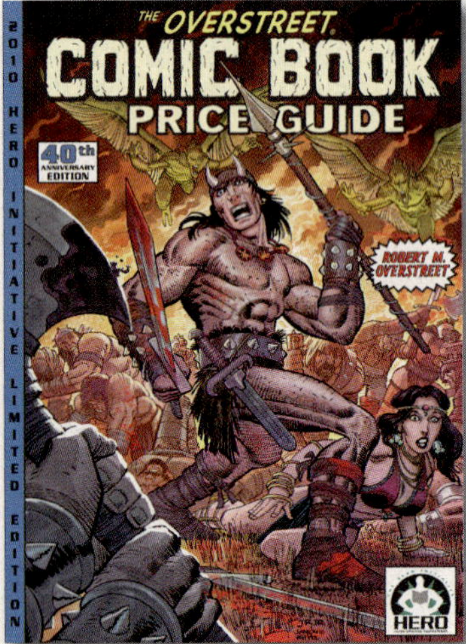

OVERSTREET C.B.P.G. #40
2010. © Conan Properties Int. LLC

THE LIFE AND TIMES OF SCROOGE McDUCK
Trade paperback. 2005. © DIS

DON ROSA

Born in Louisville, Kentucky in 1951, Don Rosa developed a love of Carl Barks' Uncle Scrooge tales from early childhood. That led Rosa to the creation of his own Barks-inspired comics and characters, notably "The Pertwillaby Papers" for his college newspaper. After graduation, Rosa divided his time between self-created comics, comics fanzine work, and his family's tile company. In the mid-1980s Rosa began writing and drawing his first Duck stories. "The Son of the Sun" (*Uncle Scrooge* #219) marked the start of many years' active work with Scrooge and Donald: first for Gladstone, then for Sanoma and Egmont in Europe.

Perhaps Rosa's most celebrated achievement is his 12-part epic, "The Life and Times of Scrooge McDuck," which has been repeatedly anthologized around the world and is regarded as one of Disney comics' great milestones.

With numerous beloved, highly intricate Scrooge McDuck adventures to his name and an international fan following, Don Rosa ranks among today's most significant Disney comics creators.

- JCV & Leonard (John) Clark

INDUCTED 2009

WALT DISNEY'S UNCLE SCROOGE #219
Rosa's first Duck story. July 1987. © DIS

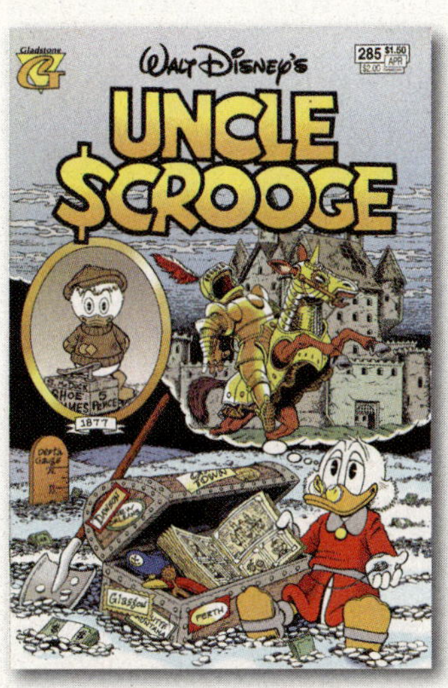

WALT DISNEY'S UNCLE SCROOGE #285
April 1994. © DIS

WALT DISNEY'S UNCLE SCROOGE #319
July 2003. © DIS

KURT SCHAFFENBERGER

The Marvel and Superman Families seldom looked better when handled by the skilled hand of Kurt Schaffenberger. Tackling the Big Red Cheese in the Golden Age for Fawcett Comics and the Bronze Age for DC Comics, the talented artist was also recruited by Otto Binder in 1957 to work on the *Superman* family of titles. He continued to work at DC for the next three decades, where he was the lead artist on *Superman's Girl Friend, Lois Lane* for the entirety of its first decade. It's been said that Schaffenberger's rendition of Lane became the "definitive" version of the character, and the artist was often asked by DC editor Mort Weisinger to redraw other artists' depictions of her in other DC titles in which she appeared. He retired from comics in the 1980s soon after penciling the second chapter of Alan Moore's pre-*Crisis Superman* tale, "Whatever Happened to the Man of Tomorrow?" Schaffenberger passed away on January 24, 2002.

– *SB*

INDUCTED 2012

AMAZING WORLD OF DC COMICS #2
September 1974. © DC

THE MARVEL FAMILY #41
November 1949. © FAW

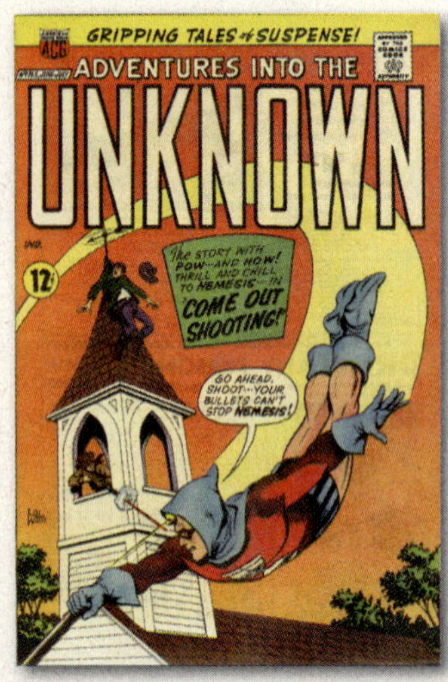

ADVENTURES INTO THE UNKNOWN #165
June-July 1966. © ACG

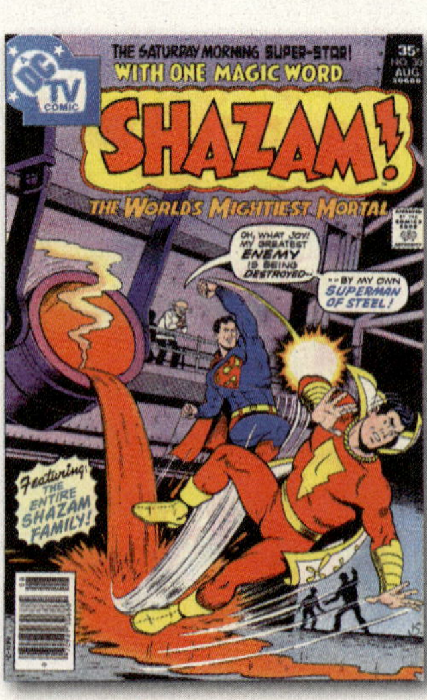

SHAZAM! #30
July-August 1977. © DC

SUPERMAN'S GIRLFRIEND LOIS LANE #73
April 1967. © DC

AMAZING WORLD OF DC COMICS #3
November 1974. © DC

JULIUS SCHWARTZ

It's difficult to measure the impact Julius "Julie" Schwartz had on the comic book world. In fact, as we observed at the time of his passing, we would probably need to invent a new unit of measurement just to begin to cover it. He was Ray Bradbury's first agent and an important voice in science fiction before he ever joined All-American Comics in 1944. Working with writers such as John Broome and artists like Gil Kane, Murphy Anderson, Carmine Infantino, and Joe Kubert, he began the underpinnings of what would become the resurgence of superhero comics in the 1950s and '60s.

After re-introducing and revamping characters such as Flash and Green Lantern, he helped develop DC's "multi-verse" by having the then-current incarnations of characters meet their predecessors, kicking off one of the best-loved eras in the company's history. He was continually a force for reinvention of characters and served as a goodwill ambassador after his retirement.

INDUCTED 2008

SHOWCASE #4
September-October 1956. © DC

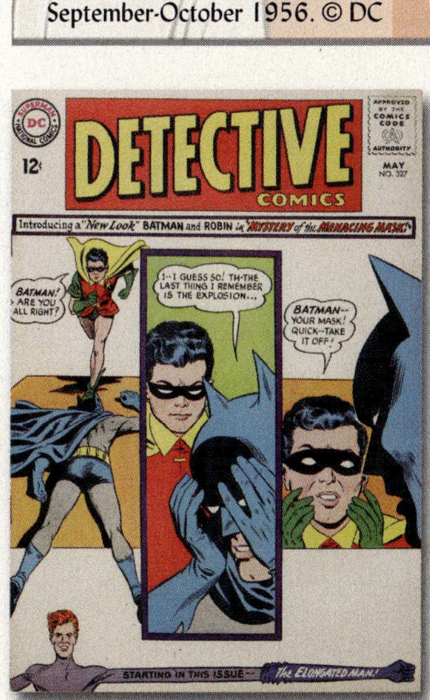

DETECTIVE COMICS #327
May 1964. © DC

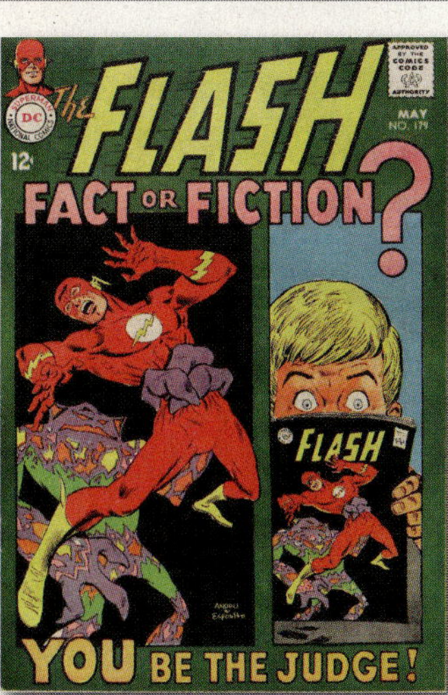

THE FLASH #179
May 1968. The Flash first meets
Julius Schwartz on Earth-Prime. © DC

SUPERMAN #233
January 1971. © DC

JOHN SEVERIN

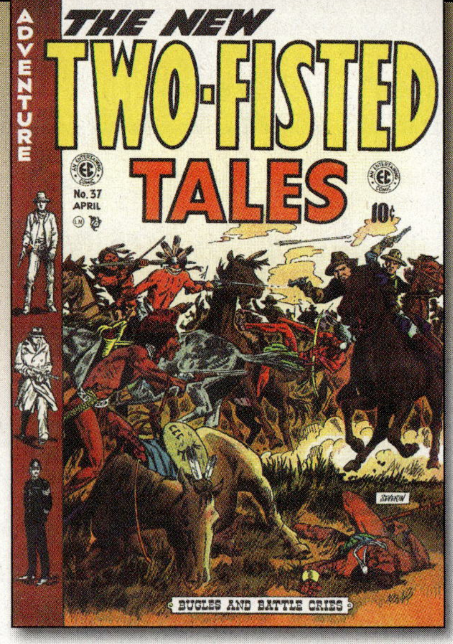

TWO-FISTED TALES #37
April 1954. © WMG

Rarely has an individual been known for two so distinctly different genres of work in the field of comic art, but John Severin is known equally for illustrating action-adventure tales and humorous stories. From his days as one of the original artists on EC's *MAD* (often with Will Elder providing the inking) to a lengthy run at *Cracked*, Severin became one of the prime send-up artists working in the business. Due to the wider circulation of *MAD* and *Cracked* compared to many comic books, it's safe to think that many know him for that work rather than the action-adventure genre, but comic book fans have had a deep appreciation for his westerns, war stories, horror, and other pieces in *Two-Fisted Tales*, *Blazing Combat*, *Creepy*, *King Kull*, *The 'Nam*, *Sgt. Fury*, and *Conan*, setting standards whether providing pencil art, inking, or supplying both. Most recently he had illustrated *Desperadoes: Quiet of the Grave* and *Bat Lash*.

He passed away on February 12, 2012

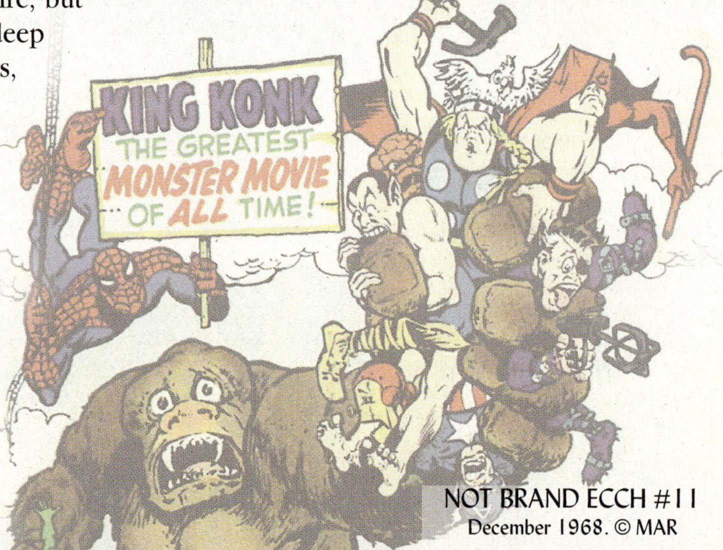

NOT BRAND ECCH #11
December 1968. © MAR

INDUCTED 2009

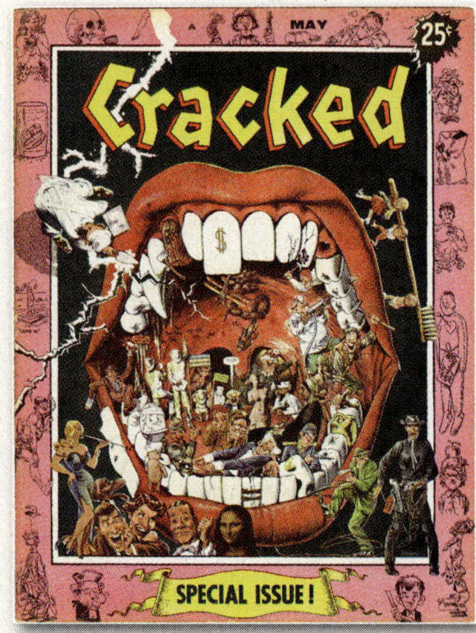

CRACKED #2
May 1958. © Major Magazines

TOMB OF DRACULA #2
May 1972. © MAR

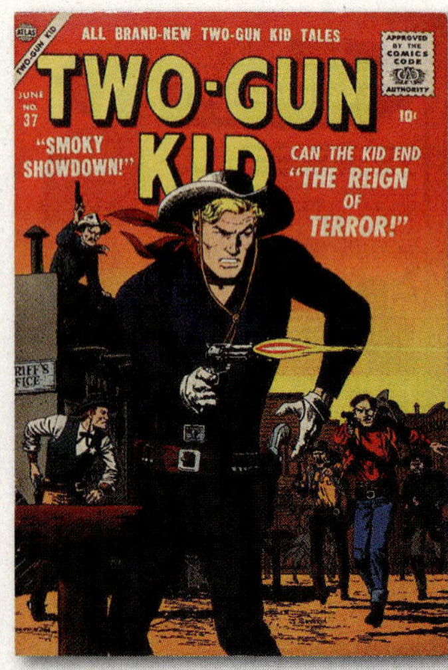

TWO-GUN KID #37
June 1957. © MAR

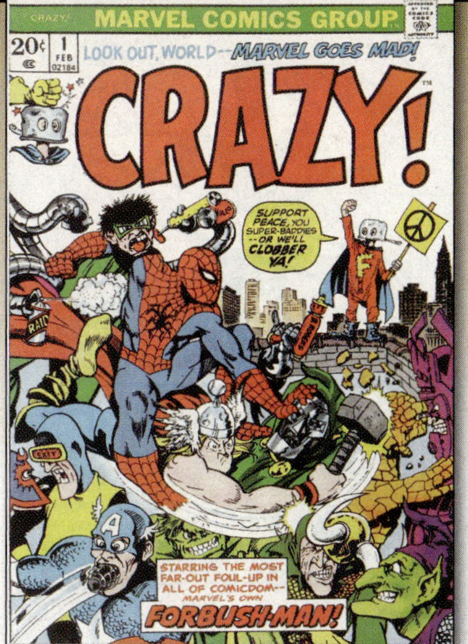

CRAZY #1

February 1973. © MAR

MARIE SEVERIN

Beginning with coloring *A Moon, a Girl... Romance* #9 (October 1949), Marie Severin became a highly regarded contributor to EC Comics. There she labored on the company's whole line, including the horror, action-adventure, science fiction and humor titles ranging from *Crime SuspenStories* to *MAD*, often working closely with her brother, artist John Severin, and writer-artist-editor Harvey Kurtzman. While noted as a colorist, she became highly capable in most artistic roles, including penciling, inking and lettering. When EC closed down, she worked at pre-Marvel Atlas before the industry took a downturn and she left. She reentered the business shortly before Atlas became Marvel and was there for the Silver Age growth. While continuing to color and deal with production issues, she illustrated *Captain America*, *Captain Marvel*, *Daredevil*, *Strange Tales* (taking over Doctor Strange from Steve Ditko), *Sub-Mariner*, *Tales to Astonish*, and *X-Men*. Her EC background (and perhaps her work with Kurtzman) influenced her wonderful stint on Marvel's self-parody series *Not Brand Ecch!*

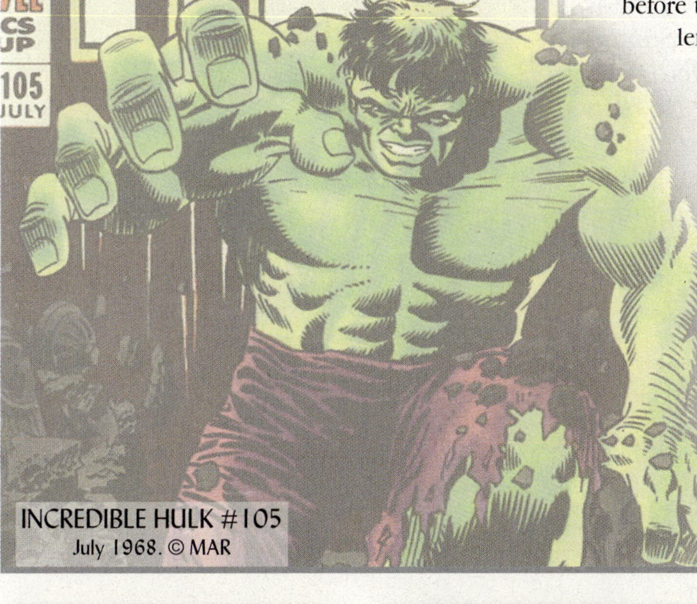

INCREDIBLE HULK #105

July 1968. © MAR

INDUCTED 2011

CAPTAIN AMERICA ANNUAL #1

January 1971. © MAR

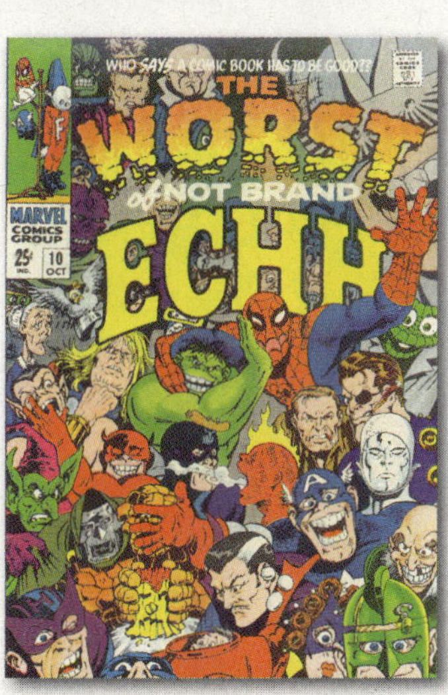

NOT BRAND ECHH #10

October 1968. © MAR

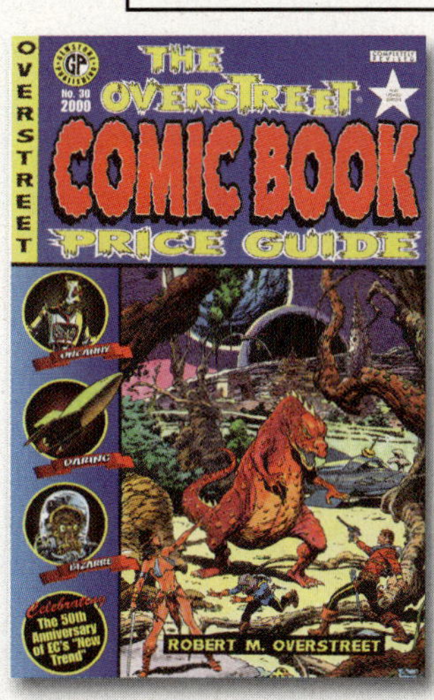

OVERSTREET C.B.P.G #30

2000. Coloring over Al Williamson art. © Gemstone

JIM SHOOTER

MARVEL SUPER-HEROES SECRET WARS #1
May 1984. © MAR

It's perhaps fitting that a career punctuated by sensational successes and seemingly crushing defeats began with a spectacular misperception. Jim Shooter began writing comics when he was 13 years old. The editors, thinking he was older, called to accept the stories and ended up having to negotiate with his mother. Over the next four decades, he put a distinctive stamp on the Legion of Super-Heroes in *Adventure Comics*, helped propel *The Avengers* to the top of the Marvel Comics universe, and his stint as Editor-in-Chief at Marvel launched such notable runs as Frank Miller's *Daredevil* and Walter Simonson's *Thor*. He wrote *Marvel Super-Heroes Secret Wars*, which is still a best-seller. He helped develop and launch Marvel's recently re-suscitated New Universe, then founded Valiant, Defiant, and Broadway Comics. In 2009, Dark Horse Comics hired Shooter to relaunch Gold Key's *Magnus, Robot Fighter, Doctor Solar, Man of the Atom, Turok, Son of Stone, Mighty Samson*, and *Doctor Spektor*, among others.

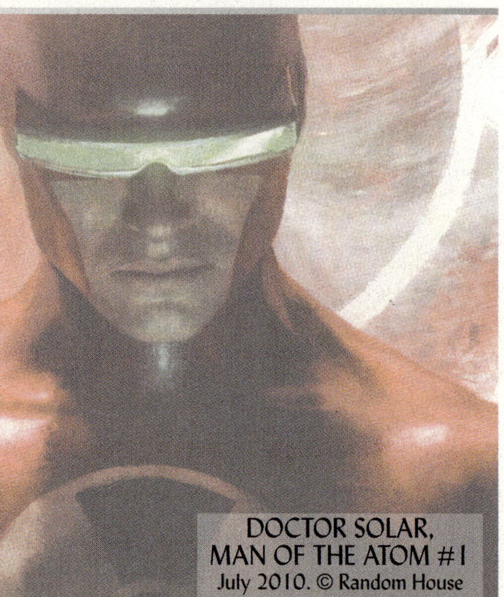

DOCTOR SOLAR, MAN OF THE ATOM #1
July 2010. © Random House

INDUCTED 2007

ADVENTURE COMICS #346
July 1966. © DC

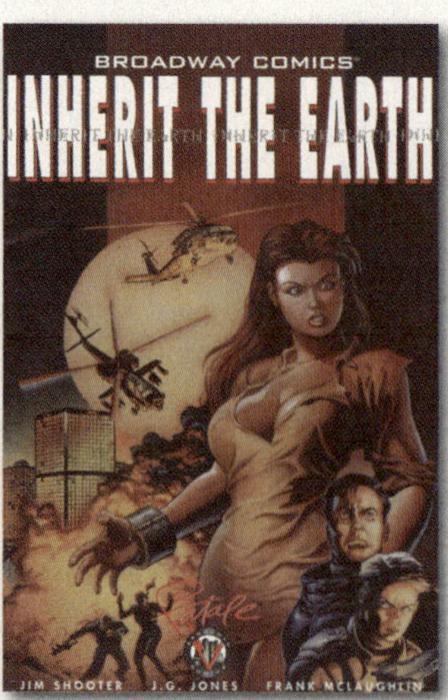

FATALE: INHERIT THE EARTH
1996. © Broadway Comics

MAGNUS ROBOT FIGHTER #0
1992. © Random House

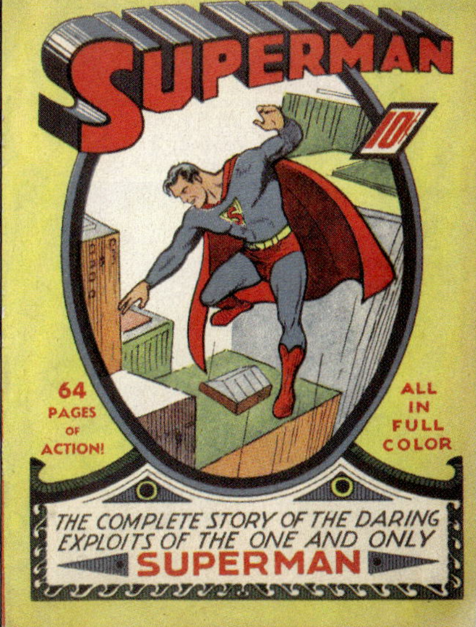

SUPERMAN #1
Summer 1939. © DC

By the time his greatest creation had become a worldwide sensation in the late '30s and early '40s, he was already beginning to lose his eyesight, but artist Joe Shuster (1914-1992) had vision to spare when working with partner and writer Jerry Siegel to craft the quintessential hero – Superman. Based on a mutual love of science fiction and pulp adventure shared by the Cleveland teens, the Man of Steel debuted in 1938 in *Action Comics* #1 (DC) with Shuster's hand shaping the dynamic look that would remain more or less intact for the next 70 years. Although marginalized by the industry in later years, Shuster eventually earned permanent credit for his role in Superman's creation thanks to a crusade spearheaded by the likes of industry star Neal Adams. Today every Superman comic and production still proclaims: "Superman created by Jerry Siegel and Joe Shuster." For a man that saw the future clearly even through fading sight, there is no better epitaph.

- ATB

ACTION COMICS #7
December 1938. © DC

INDUCTED 2010

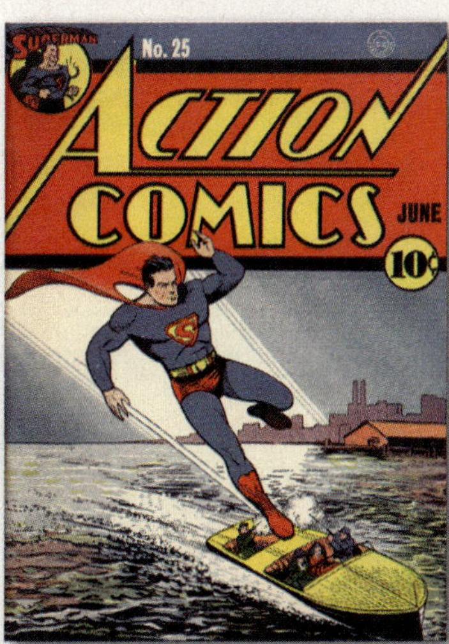

ACTION COMICS #25
June 1940. © DC

ADVENTURE COMICS #111
December 1946. © DC

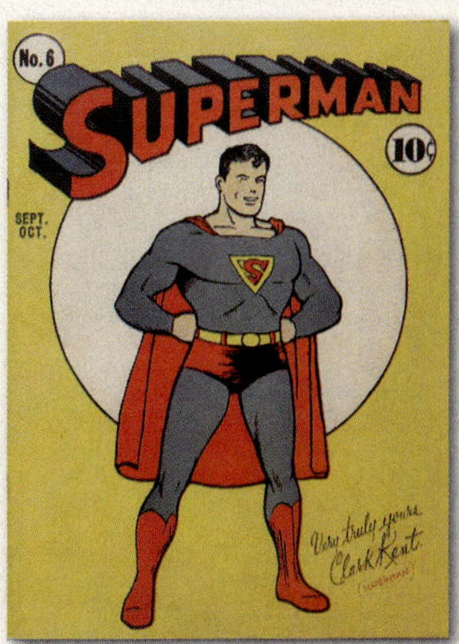

SUPERMAN #6
September-October 1940. © DC

JERRY SIEGEL

He was a Jewish kid from Cleveland with big dreams and a knack for writing high-flying adventure. Together with his friend, artist Joe Shuster, Jerry Siegel (1914-1996) created a character that would become the definitive comic book superhero for the next 70 years. Superman was a worldwide multimedia hit within a few years of his debut in *Action Comics* #1 in 1938, and although Siegel also created the creepy crusader known as the Spectre, it was the Man of Tomorrow that would cement Siegel's name in the annals of pop culture. Sadly, much of Siegel's later life was consumed more with legal battles than flights of fantasy as he (and later his family) fought to wrest control of his super-successful creations from DC. The ongoing courtroom saga has often obscured Siegel's accomplishments as one of the architects of the Golden Age and our modern mythology.
- ATB

INDUCTED 2010

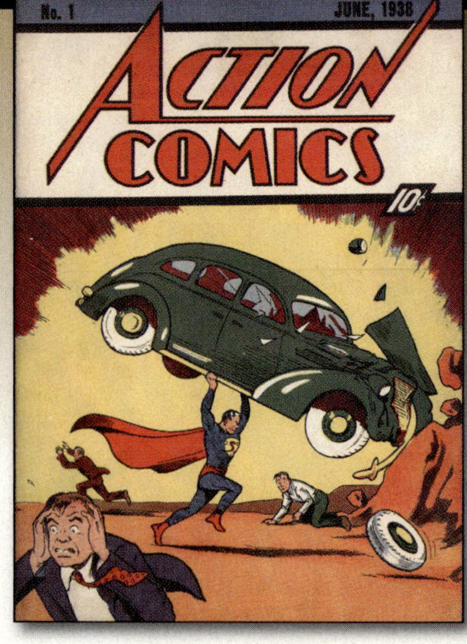

ACTION COMICS #1
June 1938. © DC

SUPERMAN NEWSPAPER PAGE
1941. © DC

ADVENTURE COMICS #340
January 1966. © DC

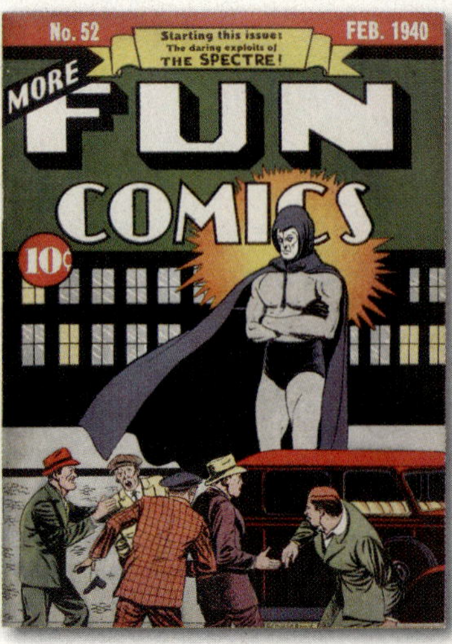

MORE FUN COMICS #52
February 1940. © DC

SUPERMAN #2
Fall 1939. © DC

ELEKTRA: ASSASSIN HC
1987. © MAR

Boleslav Felix Robert "Bill" Sienkiewicz is best known for his dynamic style of comic book and graphic novel illustration beginning with Marvel's Moon Knight in the pages *The Hulk* #13, later graduating with the character from the magazine to his own comic book series. Sienkiewicz grew up in rural New Jersey, taught himself anatomy to better his sketches, and worked construction to put himself through the Newark School of Fine and Industrial Arts. Starting his career on Marvel Comics' at the age of 19, he illustrated Moon Knight for several years, including its jump being available exclusively in the Direct Market only. Initially his work showed the strong influence of Neal Adams, but as he moved from assignment to assignment, it grew more expressionistic. It continued to evolve in the pages of *New Mutants*, *Daredevil: Love and War* (*Marvel Graphic Novel* #24), and *Elektra:Assassin*, as well as his acclaimed graphic novel *Stray Toasters*. He also has created advertising material, book art, CD covers, and film designs, among other projects.

– SB & JCV

NEW MUTANTS #21
November 1984. © MAR

INDUCTED 2012

MOON KNIGHT #1
November 1980. © MAR

SAVAGE SWORD OF CONAN #102
July 1984. © Conan Properties Inc.

TRANSFORMERS #1
September 1984. © Hasbro

JOE SIMON

Though best known as the co-creator of Captain America or as half of the Simon and Kirby team (with Jack Kirby), Joe Simon's prolific career as a writer, artist, editor and publisher has few parallels in comic book history. After freelancing for *True Story* and magazines, Simon reportedly came to the attention of Lloyd Jacquet, whose company, Funnies, Inc., packaged comic book material for publishers. A short while later, he met Kirby. They began working together on the second issue of *Blue Bolt* and became one of the most influential teams in the medium's history. They worked together until 1955, when comic sales nose-dived and Simon sought work outside the field. During that time, they produced *The Fighting American*, westerns such as *Boys Ranch*, and many others. They are credited with creating the romance comics genre with *Young Romance Comics*. Among the projects he later took on, he spent a decade working with *Sick*, a *MAD*-inspired humor magazine.

Joe Simon passed away on December 14, 2011 at the age of 98.

INDUCTED 2009

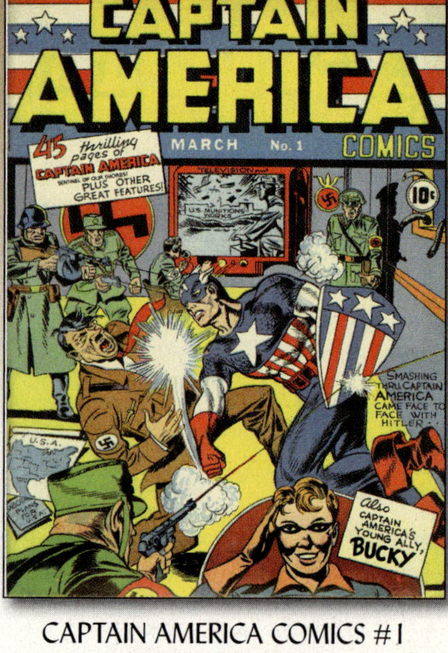

CAPTAIN AMERICA COMICS #1
March 1941. © MAR

BOY COMMANDOS #1
Winter 1942. © DC

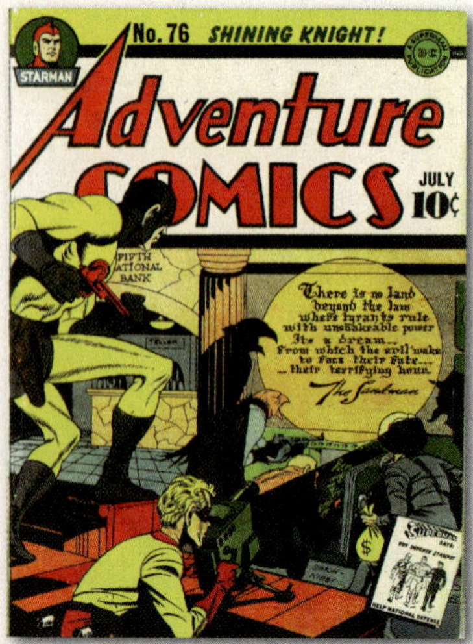

ADVENTURE COMICS #76
July 1942. © DC

FIGHTING AMERICAN #2
July 1954. © PRIZE

YOUNG ROMANCE #11
May-June 1949. © MAR

WALT SIMONSON

OVERSTREET C.B.P.G #42
2011. © MAR

While attending the Rhode Island School of Design, writer-artist Walt Simonson created *Star Slammers*, a different version of which years later would become *Marvel Graphic Novel #6* and later a *Star Slammers* series from Malibu's Bravura imprint. Between those two periods he established himself as a creative force, chiefly with the award-winning Manhunter back-up feature in *Detective Comics*, on which he collaborated with writer Archie Goodwin. Following work on DC's *Metal Men* and *Hercules Unbound* and Heavy Metal's *Alien* adaptation (again with Goodwin), he made his way to Marvel. Beginning with *Thor #337*, Simonson wrote and illustrated a definitive run on the title, eventually ending with Thor #382. Over the years, his other Marvel work included *Battlestar Galactica*, *Star Wars*, *Fantastic Four*, *The Avengers*, *X-Factor* (with wife Louise Simonson) and others. At DC, among other work, provided covers for *Jack Kirby's Fourth World*, wrote and illustrated 25 issues of *Orion*, illustrated *Elric: The Making of a Sorcerer*, and wrote the Catwoman and The Demon strip in *Wednesday Comics*.

THOR #337
November 1983. © MAR

INDUCTED 2011

BATMAN #366
December 1983. © DC

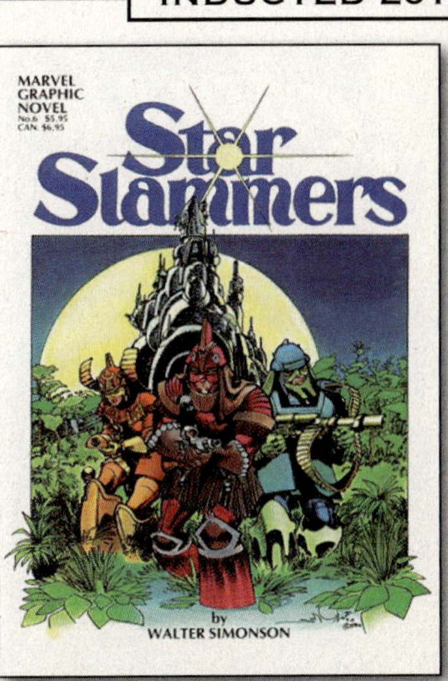

ORION #1
June 2000. © DC

MARVEL GRAPHIC NOVEL #6
1983. © Walt Simonson

JIM STERANKO

NICK FURY, AGENT OF S.H.I.E.L.D. #1
June 1968. © MAR

His covers for Marvel's *Captain America*, *Incredible Hulk*, and *Nick Fury, Agent of S.H.I.E.L.D.* are some of the most iconic and innovative pieces of pop art from the 1960s. Jim Steranko (1938-) was, perhaps auspiciously, born the year the Golden Age began, but he is far more than just one of the most influential artists of the Marvel Age. His *Chandler: Red Tide* helped to define the very meaning of the term "graphic novel," his conceptual artwork for *Raiders of the Lost Ark* breathed life into Indiana Jones – the man whose name was synonymous with adventure – and his two-volume *The Steranko History of Comics* offered a unique insight into the development of the medium during the Golden Age. Today the award-winning Steranko stands as one of comicdom's living legends with awards and honors that serve as testament to his indelible contributions.
- ATB

INCREDIBLE HULK ANNUAL #1
October 1968. © MAR

INDUCTED 2010

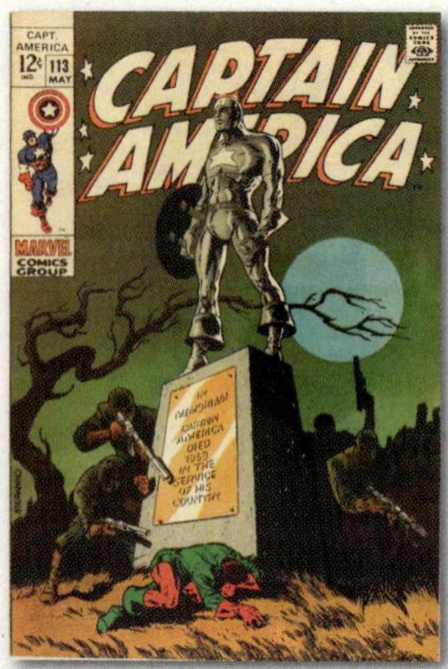

CAPTAIN AMERICA #113
May 1969. © MAR

HISTORY OF COMICS VOL. 2
1970. © Jim Steranko

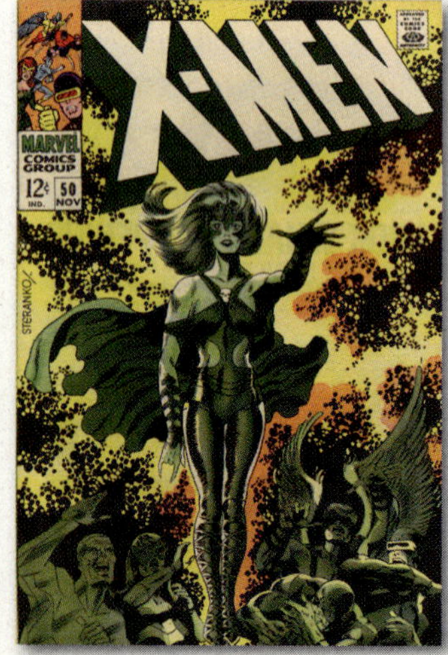

X-MEN #50
November 1968. © MAR

THE ROCKETEER: THE OFFICIAL MOVIE ADAPTATION
1991. © DIS

DAVE STEVENS

Dave Stevens, whose first comic work was inking Russ Manning's pencils for the Tarzan daily, made a splash in the comic book world with the introduction of The Rocketeer as a back-up feature in *Starslayer* #2 from Pacific Comics. The character jumped from there to *Pacific Presents* to his own comics from a number of publishers, and eventually onto the silver screen. His story and art were steeped in the styles and history of the 1930s, and they drew praise for their historical accuracy as well as their breathtaking imagery.

For a relative small comic book output, Stevens was widely considered "an artist's artist." He received the first Russ Manning Award in 1982, and played a key role in reviving interest in Bettie Page. While he illustrated numerous other covers (including *Alien Worlds*, *Bettie Page Comics*, and *Jonny Quest*, among others), Dave Stevens remains best known for high-flying pilot Cliff Secord, The Rocketeer.

He passed away in 2008.

THE ROCKETEER ADVENTURE MAGAZINE #1
July 1988. © Dave Stevens

INDUCTED 2007

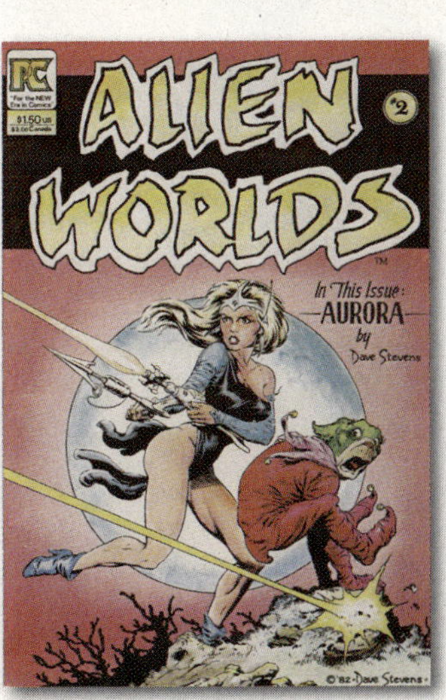
ALIEN WORLDS #2
May 1983. © Dave Stevens

BETTIE PAGE COMICS #1
March 1996. © Bettie Page

STARSLAYER #2
Back cover. April 1982. © Dave Stevens

CURT SWAN

SUPERMAN #423
September 1986. © DC

Douglas Curtis Swan, the artist most associated with Superman during the Silver Age of comics, produced hundreds of covers and stories from the 1950s through the 1980s. Following World War II and a stint on *Boy Commandos*, he began to pencil pages, leaving the inking to others, including famed inker Murphy Anderson (the pair's collaborative artwork came to be called "Swanderson" by fans). His first job pencilling the iconic character was for *Superman* #51. Swan felt, however, that his breakthrough came when he was assigned the art duties on *Superman's Pal, Jimmy Olsen*, in 1954.

Over the years, Swan was a remarkably consistent and prolific artist, often illustrating two or more titles per month. The artist illustrated the first chapter of the 1986 "last Silver Age" *Superman* story, "Whatever Happened to the Man of Tomorrow?" written by Alan Moore. Swan's last published story was five pages published posthumously in the 1996 special *Superman: The Wedding Album*.
– SB

INDUCTED 2012

SUPERMAN #161
May 1963. © DC

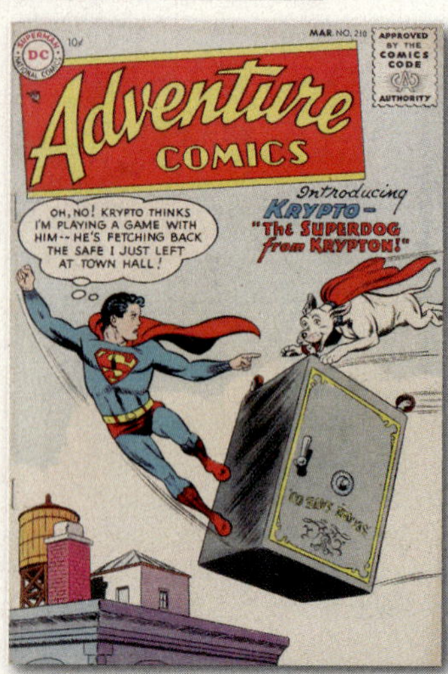

ADVENTURE COMICS #210
March 1955. © DC

SUPERMAN #200
October 1967. © DC

SUPERMAN'S PAL JIMMY OLSEN #99
January 1967. © DC

ALTER EGO #70
July 2007. © Roy Thomas

ROY THOMAS

Besides being Stan Lee's first successor as Editor-in-Chief of Marvel Comics, Roy William Thomas, Jr. has made enjoyed a long career as a writer, editor and comics historian. He is possibly best known for introducing the pulp magazine hero Conan the Barbarian to American comic book audiences. With *Conan The Barbarian* and *Savage Sword of Conan*, he added to the storyline of Robert E. Howard's character and helped launch a sword and sorcery genre in comics. Thomas is also known for his championing of Golden Age superheroes to new audiences by creating *The Invaders* at Marvel and a short while later the *All-Star Squadron* and *Infinity Inc.* at DC.

Thomas also enjoyed distinctive, key runs on *The X-Men*, *The Avengers*, *Wally Wood's T.H.U.N.D.E.R. Agents* among other titles, and continues his invaluable contributions in the pages of his award-winning magazine, *Alter Ego*, which explores comics history (though generally not the history he made himself).

- SB

CONAN THE BARBARIAN #1
October 1970. © Conan Properties Inc.

INDUCTED 2012

ALL-STAR SQUADRON #1
September 1981. © DC

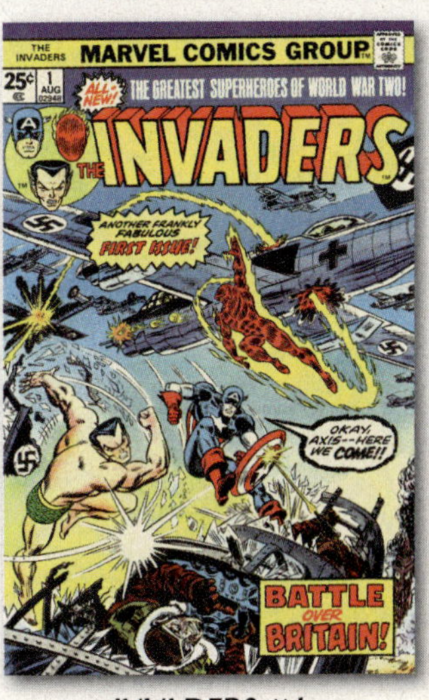

AVENGERS #87
April 1971. © MAR

INVADERS #1
August 1975. © MAR

ALEX TOTH

Beginning his career at the young age of 15, and quickly rising to be one of the most iconic artists in both the world of comics and animation, Alex Toth inspired a generation of fans through his body of work, both as an artist and writer. Throughout the mid-1940s and early 1950s, Toth worked for such companies as DC, Famous Funnies, Atlas, Marvel and Visual Edition (Standard). His portfolio included work on *Green Lantern*, *Mystery in Space*, *Strange Adventures*, *Unseen*, *World's Finest,* and *Zorro*. After serving a tour of duty in the US Army, Toth began to work for Hanna-Barbera doing storyboards for *Space Ghost*, *Challenge of the Superfriends*, *Fantastic Four*, *Herculoids*, *Birdman* and *Jonny Quest*. In addition to his work in animation, Toth continued to draw comics and write columns for *Alter Ego* and *Comic Book Artist*. He passed away in 2006.

LIMITED COLLECTORS' EDITION C-41
December 1975-January 1976. © DC

ZORRO
© Zorro Productions

INDUCTED 2007

ALL-AMERICAN WESTERN #105
January 1949. © DC

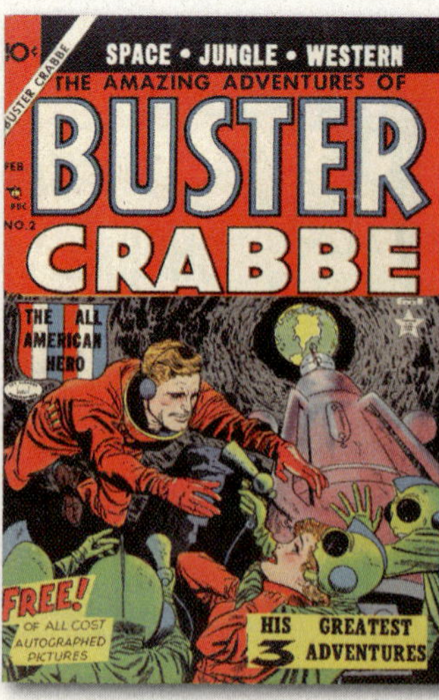

BUSTER CRABBE #2
February 1953. © LEV

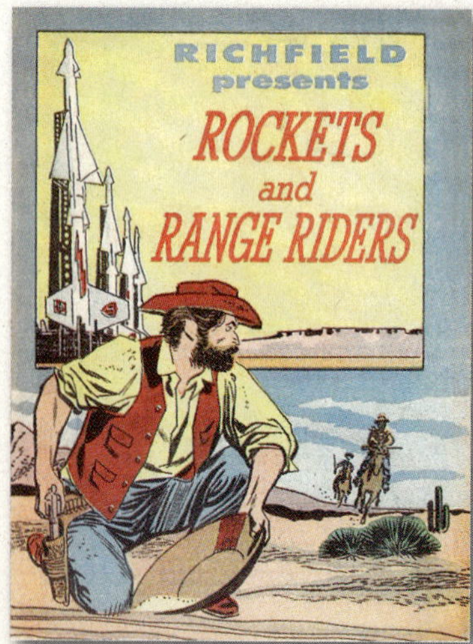

ROCKETS AND RANGE RIDERS
May 1957. © Richfield Oil

MICHAEL TURNER

WITCHBLADE #6
June 1996. © TCOW

Michael Turner began his career as a comic book artist in 1994 as a background artist working under Marc Silvestri at Image Comics' Top Cow Productions imprint. While there, Turner helped co-create Top Cow's *Witchblade* in 1995, which has been the company's longest running book. Following his success on *Witchblade*, he went on to create his first creator-owned property, *Fathom* in 1998.

In late 2002, Turner founded his own studio, Aspen MLT, Inc. where he brought *Fathom* and also launched *Soulfire*, *Cannon Hawke* and *Ekos*.

Turner was one of the most sought-after cover artists working in the industry, having done covers for both DC and Marvel Comics, as well as dozens of Independent Press books.

Tragically, he passed away in 2008 at age 37, following a long but brave battle against cancer.

INDUCTED 2007

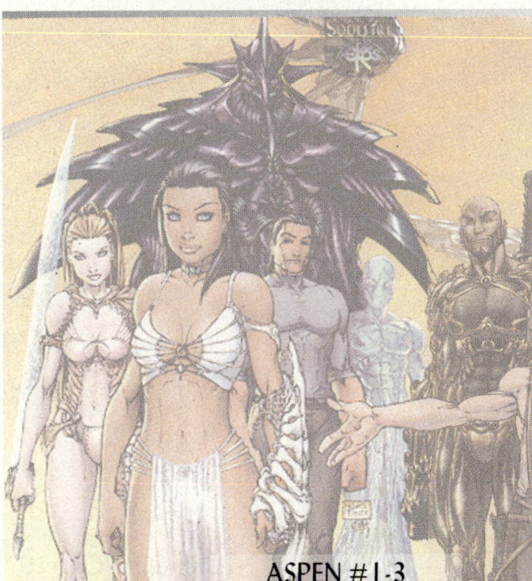
ASPEN #1-3
2003. © Michael Turner

CIVIL WAR: X-MEN #1
September 2006. © MAR

FATHOM #12
July 2000. © Michael Turner

SUPERMAN/BATMAN #13
October 2004. © DC

MAJOR MALCOLM WHEELER-NICHOLSON

NEW FUN COMICS #1
February 1935. The start of DC Comics. © DC

Honored in 2008 with a posthumous Eisner Award for his contributions to the comic book industry, Major Malcolm Wheeler-Nicholson might have become the forgotten titan of comic book history, except for the efforts of comics historians. The former soldier, adventurer and inventor was also a successful and prolific author and in the 1920s he made a solid living from writing novels and short stories, often for the pulp magazines. When the Great Depression forced him and his family to move back to New York from Europe, he turned his attention to a new enterprise.

Comic books had, of course, been around in one form or another, for more than 90 years, but they had almost exclusively been collections of reprinted newspaper comic strips and priced for adults. Wheeler-Nicholson not only wrote and commissioned original content, he priced them at 10¢. In 1934, he launched *New Fun Comics*. DC Comics – and with it a new form of the comics business – was born.

NEW ADVENTURE COMICS #19
September 1937. © DC

INDUCTED 2011

NEW COMICS #1
December 1935. © DC

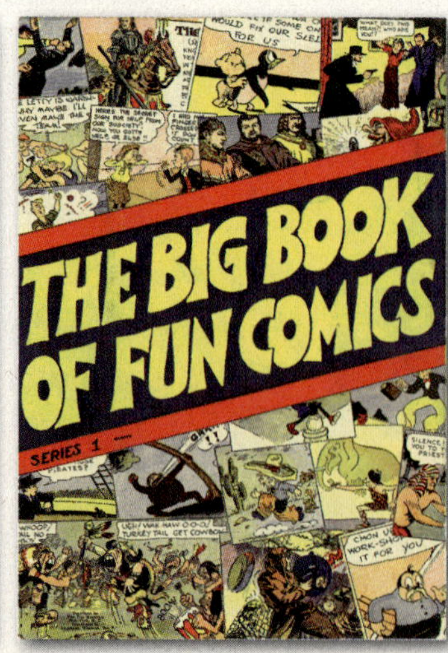

THE BIG BOOK OF FUN COMICS #1
March 1936. © DC

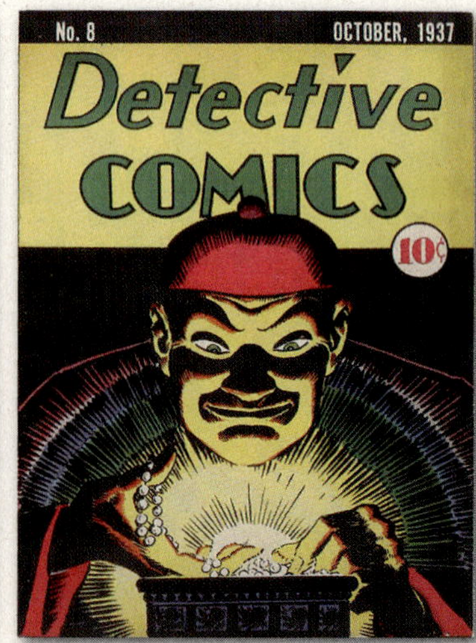

DETECTIVE COMICS #8
October 1937. © DC

RECORD SETTERS

GREEN LANTERN #76,
CGC CERTIFIED 9.8
Sold for $37,343.75
by Heritage Auctions
in November 2010. © DC

GOBBLEDYGOOK #1,
(First appearance of the
Teenage Mutant Ninja Turtles)
in VF+ condition
Sold for $11,352.50
by Heritage Auctions
in February 2011. © MIRAGE

INCREDIBLE HULK #181
CGC CERTIFIED 9.9
Sold for $150,000
by ComicLink
in February 2011. © MAR

MIKE WIERINGO

Also known as "Ringo," artist Mike Wieringo was best known for his work on DC Comics' *The Flash*, Marvel Comics' *Fantastic Four*, and *Tellos*; the creator-owned fantasy series he developed with friend and writer Todd DeZago. In an era in which many artists rely on shock or over-the-top style, his clean, deceptively simple linework captured the heroism superheroes are supposed to embody and earned the artist a strong fan following.

Born in Venice, Italy in 1963, he joined writer Mark Waid on DC's *The Flash* with issue #80 in 1993; during their run the two co-created the character Impulse. Wieringo also illustrated *Robin* at DC, *Sensational Spider-Man* (with DeZago) at Marvel, and then created *Tellos*. He also illustrated stints on *Adventures of Superman* and (again with Waid) on *Fantastic Four*, and *Spider-Man and the Fantastic Four*, among other projects. Sadly, Wieringo passed away suddenly on August 12, 2007 at age 44.

INDUCTED 2008

FANTASTIC FOUR Vol. 3 #60
October 2002. © MAR

SPIDER-MAN AND THE FANTASTIC FOUR #1
June 2007. © MAR

THE FLASH #92
July 1994. Debut of Impulse. © DC

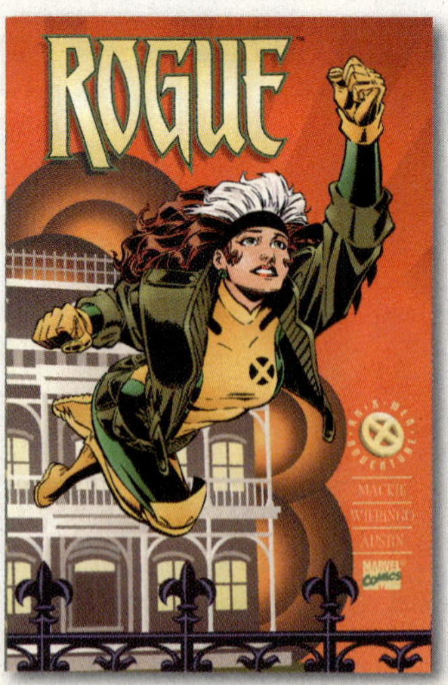

ROGUE TPB
1995. © MAR

SENSATIONAL SPIDER-MAN #8
September 1996. © MAR

AL WILLIAMSON

WEIRD SCIENCE-FANTASY #25
September 1954. © WMG

Fans and historians know Al Williamson for his highly evocative art over the last fifty years, ranging from penciling and inking stories in EC's *Weird Science-Fantasy* in the '50s to inking John Romita, Jr. on *Daredevil* for Marvel in the '90s, or newspaper work including a highly respected run on the daily and Sunday *Star Wars* strip.

Al Williamson is one of only a handful of top rated comic creators who have spent their entire careers working in our industry. Too often our very best talents are lured away by promises of fame and fortune in other venues. I think that Al stands as a shining example of the lifelong craftsman who works constantly to improve his already considerable talents; by the entire scope of his career he announces to every other person in the industry that this is a field fully worth the commitment of a lifetime of creations.

He passed away in 2010.

– Mark Wheatley

INDUCTED 2009

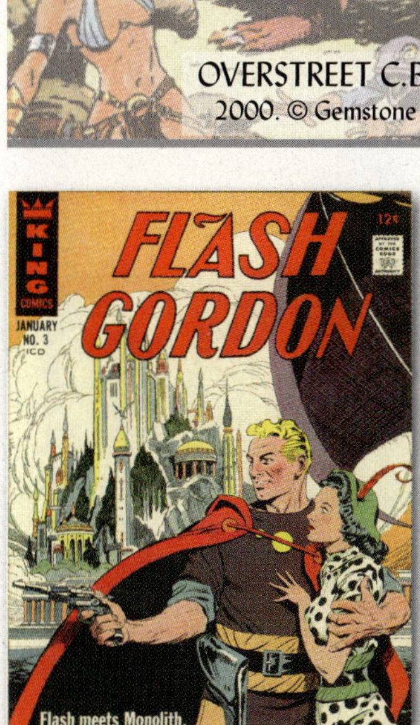

OVERSTREET C.B.P.G #30
2000. © Gemstone Publishing

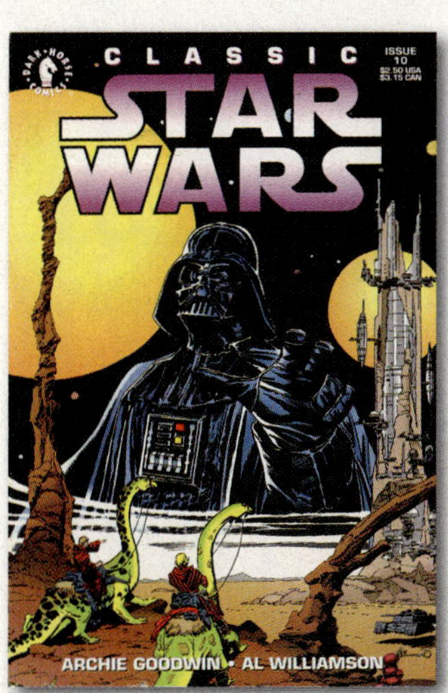

CLASSIC STAR WARS #10
July 1993. © Lucasfilm Ltd.

FLASH GORDON #3
January 1967. © KING

VALOR #2
May-June 1955. © WMG

WALLY WOOD

Wallace A. Wood landed his first comic work with Will Eisner as a back-up artist on The Spirit in 1948. He also began lettering for Fox Features Syndicate, then drew stories for their love and western titles. Over the next few years he worked for Avon, Better-Standard, EC, Fawcett, Fox, Kirby Publishing Co., Youthful Magazines and Ziff-Davis.

After trying multiple genres with EC, he soon found his niche in science fiction. His work on EC's *Weird Fantasy* and *Weird Science* followed covers on Avon's *Attack On Planet Mars*, *Flying Saucers*, *Earth Man on Venus*, *Space Detective* and *Strange Worlds*. No one could draw spaceship interior instrumentation and machinery like him.

He became the first Marvel Comics artist to get a cover blurb when Stan Lee touted Wood's arrival on *Daredevil* #5. In the years that followed, he continued to produce beautiful work for DC, Charlton, Gold Key, Harvey, Tower (where he launched the *T.H.U.N.D.E.R. Agents*), Warren and Atlas-Seaboard, as well as a number of self-published projects. Wood took his own life in 1981.
- RMO

INDUCTED 2010

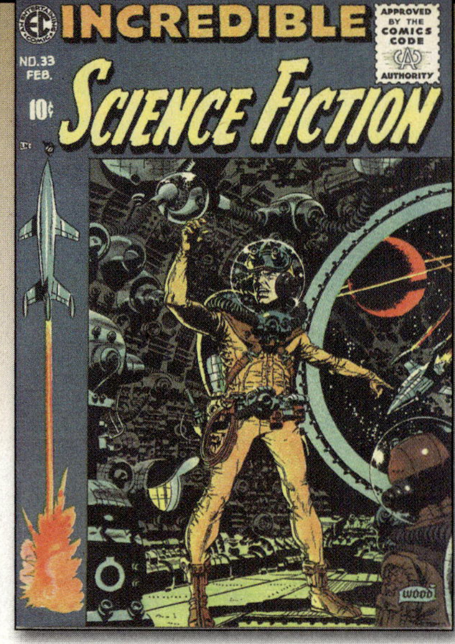

INCREDIBLE SCIENCE FICTION #33
January-February 1956. © WMG

OVERSTREET C.B.P.G. #9
1979. © Gemstone

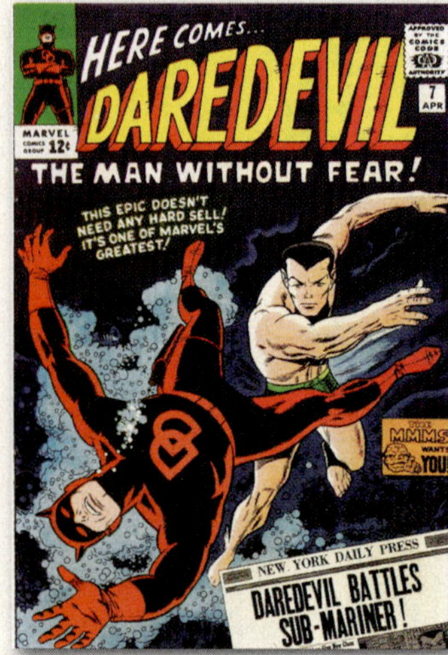

DAREDEVIL #7
April 1965. © MAR

HEROES, INC. PRESENTS CANNON
1969. © Wally Wood

SPIRIT NEWSPAPER SECTION #1
August 3, 1952. © Will Eisner Studios

THE HERO INITIATIVE

By Charles S. Novinskie

Microsoft was started by Bill Gates during a recession, proof positive that a great idea is truly recession-proof. Comparisons can be made to the late 20th century when the comic book industry was in something akin to a recession, but most frequently referred to as the near death of the comic book industry. Comic companies were closing their doors and creators were left without steady employment.

Enter comic journalist Jim McLauchlin and the then-owner of Crossgen Comics, Mark Alessi. Like many great ideas, this one started with two like-minded folks sharing a vision, in this case the desire to help comic creators that have toiled at their trade for decades with no pension, no benefits, no way to support themselves later in life.

Helping creators in need became the focus of the Hero Initiative as they shouted to one and all, "Everyone deserves a Golden Age!", a reference to the organizations original desire to help creators that worked during the Golden Age of Comics, a period from the 1930s through the late 1950s.

A Commitment to Our Roots (ACTOR, as Hero was first known) was born in October of 2000, becoming the first-ever, federally chartered not-for-profit corporation dedicated strictly to helping comic book creators in need.

In reality, anyone that meets the criteria of ever having worked in the comic book industry as a freelance writer, penciller, inker, colorist or letterer for a minimum of 10 years is eligible. Over the past ten years, as the economy worsened, more and more creators needed assistance to stay afloat. The reality was so bad that ACTOR had to change their name in July of 2006 because out of work Hollywood

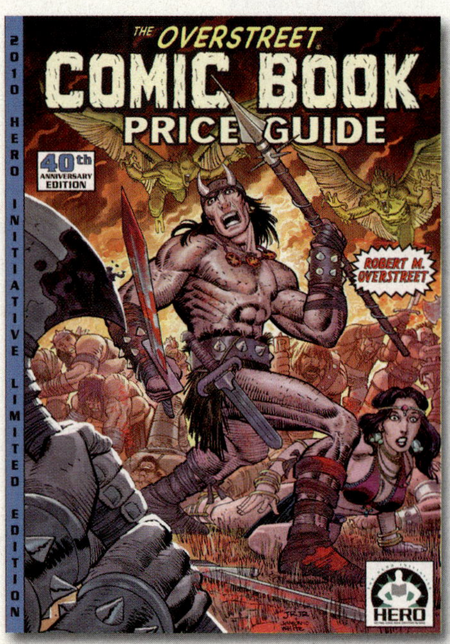

The 40th edition of *The Overstreet Comic Book Price Guide* sported this variant cover to benefit the HERO Initiative.

actors were applying for assistance based on the ACTOR acronym (true story). To date, The Hero Initiative has provided grants of over $400,000 to numerous comic book creators in need. Hero has also provided short-term, non-interest loans to creators that were between assignments.

While Hero respects the privacy of creators and keeps disbursements confidential, some creators have allowed us to share their stories to help promote the cause: Bill Messner-Loebs was provided assistance when he needed a place to live, Lea Hernandez was helped out after a devastating house fire, and Jim Sanders was provided assistance when all other sources of help were exhausted.

To date over 40 creators have been aided through everything from rough patches to costly, life-saving operations. Some have intimated that without Hero's intervention, suicide might have been their next step without intervention.

The real beauty is that with the exception of one full-time and one part-time paid employee, the entire organization is run by volunteers. Donations to Hero come from fans, creators, retailers, publishers, distributors and printers. While the need is great, the organization continues to grow and expand in the form of auctions, benefit books and the overall kindness and generosity of people that have a true love for this industry and want to give back and help any way they can.

Governed by a Fund Raising Committee and a Disbursement Committee, The Hero Initiative has board members from the comics industry: the Disbursement Committee (comprised of Walt Simonson, Denny O'Neil, John Romita Sr., Jim Valentino, George Pérez, Howard Chaykin, Roy Thomas, Jim McLauchlin and Charlie Novinskie) votes on disbursing funds and evaluates each creator's situation on a case-by-case basis. The Fund Raising Committee (Jim McLauchlin, Steve Borock, Mike Malve, Brian Pulido, Joe Quesada, Beth Widera, and Mark Waid) finds revenue streams that keep positive cash flow coming in so that Hero can provide for the needs of the ever growing list of creators in need. Many creators and retailers have donated their services, time, and talents for the cause. Poker matches, softball games, creator lunches and even green "Excelsior" wrist bands endorsed by Stan Lee have all contributed to promoting The Hero Initiative cause.

If you'd like to donate or volunteer your time, or know a creator in need, please don't hesitate to contact The Hero Initiative at www.heroinitiative.org.

Charlie Novinskie, an Overstreet Advisor, has been with The Hero Initiative since the early years.

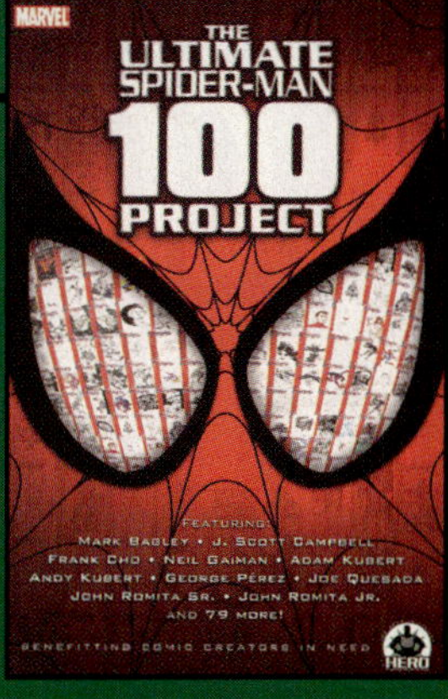

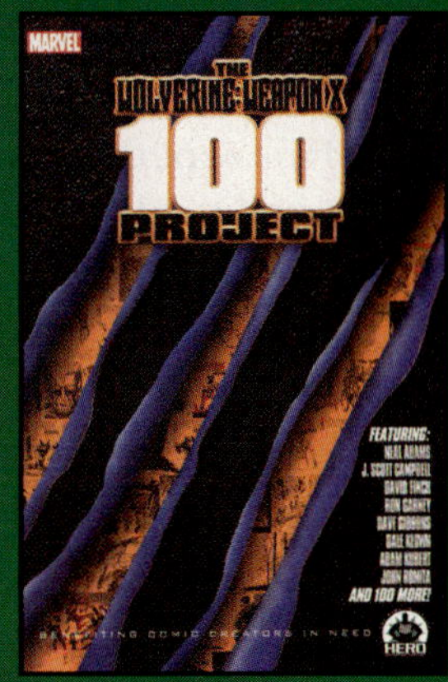

Creators donate their talents in various ways to help.

The COMIC BOOK LEGAL DEFENSE FUND

By Brady Bonney

The Comic Book Legal Defense Fund serves the comics community by defending the First Amendment rights of retailers, creators, and readers when those rights are threatened.

The CBLDF is a grassroots organization that exists because of the generous support of the comics community. The donations of individuals and small businesses add up to make CBLDF the first responder to First Amendment emergencies when they arise.

The CBLDF was founded in 1986 by artist and publisher Denis Kitchen to help store manager Michael Correa of Friendly Frank's, a shop in Lansing, Illinois. Correa was found guilty of distributing obscene material, fined, and sentenced to one year of court supervision after local law enforcement purchased 15 comics from him. The comics included titles now regarded as classic, including *Elektra: Assassin, Love & Rockets, Elfquest, Heavy Metal,* and *Omaha the Cat Dancer*.

As the publisher of *Omaha*, Kitchen felt a responsibility to help Correa. He said, "*Omaha* contained adult content, without question. But *Omaha* was also an artistic and literary success, having received high critical praise internationally. I also knew that the other titles seized could not qualify as pornographic. More importantly, Michael Correa was not charged with selling any of the titles to a minor. The police arrested the manager simply for having 'obscene' books on display."

Kitchen took action by rallying artists including Will Eisner, Robert Crumb, and Frank Miller to create a portfolio of prints to raise money towards an appeal. The appeal was successfully argued by pioneering First Amendment lawyer Burton Joseph, and Correa was a free man. Afterwards, Kitchen had several thousand dollars remaining. Feeling that this would not be an isolated incident, he used it to establish the CBLDF as a permanent institution.

Over the years, the CBLDF has led the charge in dozens of defense cases on behalf of many, including: Paul Mavrides, artist of the *Fabulous Furry Freak Brothers* against the State of California's Board of Equalization; cartoonist Kieron Dwyer against Starbucks; publisher Top Shelf Productions against U.S. Customs; and DC Comics creators Joe Lansdale, Timothy Truman and Sam Glanzman against the Winter Brothers. The Fund also squelches dozens of small incidents in retail stores and libraries every year by helping defuse situations before they can become a case. Full details on all of these cases can be read at cbldf.org.

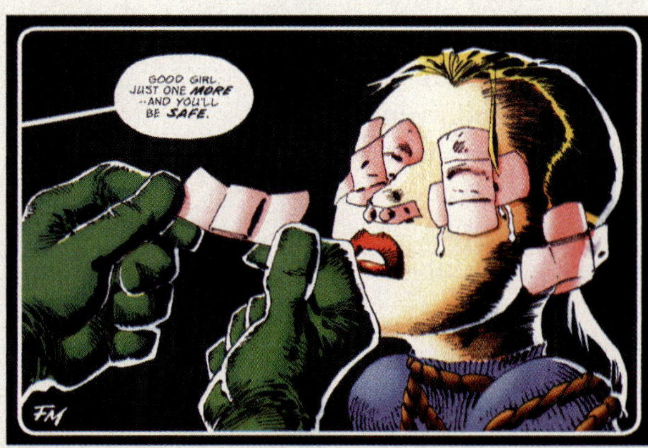

Frank Miller provided this chilling image used on promotional materials.

Most recently, CBLDF claimed a victory in a case that cost over $100,000 defending Gordon Lee, owner of Rome, Georgia store Legends, against baseless and inflated charges that took three years to resolve. Were it not for the CBLDF, Lee says he almost surely wouldn't still be in business today.

Lee participated in a local Halloween event where he handed out comics left over from Free Comic Book Day instead of candy. One of the comics in his overstock was *Alternative Comics* #2, a Free Comic Book Day title that included an eight page selection of Nick Bertozzi's graphic novel *The Salon*, a biographical work about the life of Pablo Picasso, where, for a short scene, Picasso appeared painting in the nude. Even though nudity was present in the book, it was not sexual in nature. A copy of *Alternative Comics* #2 was allegedly given to a minor at the Halloween function, but instead of being confronted with the accusation and given the opportunity to apologize, Lee was arrested under two felony charges, and five misdemeanor charges.

The Fund hired Begner & Begner, the best obscenity firm in Georgia, to manage the case. Over the course of three years, the firm fought for Lee, first knocking out the felony charges. On the eve of trial, 18 months into the case, prosecutors dropped all charges and then refiled the next day, because they claimed they had named the wrong victim. That morning, CBLDF litigator Alan Begner said, "I have never—as a criminal trial lawyer for thirty years—seen a complete changing of the facts like this. The dismissal of the charges ... reflects the prosecution's admission that everything that was presented as evidence before was untrue." In November 2007, after three years, prosecutors were still unable to prove their accusations against Lee, and created a mistrial during opening statements. District Attorney Leigh Patterson eventually agreed to drop all charges against Lee. Were it not for the CBLDF, Lee would have had to plead guilty to a crime he didn't commit or risk bankruptcy defending himself.

Many of the CBLDF's retail members express that they see their membership as an insurance policy, which they hope never to need. The CBLDF assures that whenever there is a First Amendment emergency, they'll be the first to respond. To learn more about any of the CBLDF's cases, or to make a contribution to the cause, visit CBLDF.org.

The first and second issues of Liberty Comics, an anthology of short stories by top creators, about the protection of free speech rights.

CBCA
COMIC BOOK COLLECTING ASSOCIATION

By Mark S. Zaid, Esq.

The Comic Book Collecting Association is a nonprofit international organization made up of comic book enthusiasts who share an appreciation for the history, artistic merit, and significance of the comic book medium as an important element of popular culture. The CBCA is guided by its founding principles of Fellowship, Education and Ethics.

The organization's Mission Statement "*is to promote the comic book art form and hobby of comic book collecting for people of all ages by encouraging fellowship among comic book enthusiasts, providing information and education to the public, and helping to facilitate the buying, selling, and trading of comic books and related material in an environment of trustworthiness and integrity*."

CBCA is modeled after prominent organizations from other hobby communities such as the American Philatelic Society and the Universal Autograph Collectors Club. A Code of Ethics was adopted that is patterned after industry best practices while being tailored to the hobby of comic collecting. For example, "CBCA members are expected to exercise common sense and courtesy in dealing with each other and with the general public. Members must share in the responsibility of furthering mutual trust and respect between the hobby and the public by conducting their comic book and comic-related business with fairness and integrity." The complete Code of Ethics can be read at http://www.comiccollecting.org/page/code-of-ethics/.

Our Board of Advisors includes some of the most prominent members of the comic community who have chosen to lend their names in support of CBCA's efforts: Doug Braithwaite (British Comic Book Artist), Dan Cusimano (Flying Donut Trading Co.), Steve Eichenbaum (CEO, Certified Collectibles Group/CGC), Danny Fingeroth (former Marvel editor, comic writer), Jamie Graham (Graham Crackers Comics), John Haines (John Haines Rare Comics), Tracey Heft (restoration expert, Eclipse Paper), Dave Kapelka (North Coast Nostalgia), Steve Korte, Historian, DC Comics Licensed Publishing, John Jackson Miller (comic book writer/commentator), Josh Nathanson (ComicLink), James Payette (Rare Books and Comics), Dave Reynolds (Dave's American Comics), Wayne Smith (VP, Warner Bros. Entertainment, Inc.), John Snyder, Jr. (past President, Geppi's Entertainment), Jim Steranko (comic book writer, artist, historian), Bob Storms (HighGradeComics.com), Doug Sulipa (Doug Sulipa's Comic World), Ted Van Liew (Superworld Comics), J.C. Vaughn (Associate Publisher & Executive Editor, Gemstone Publishing), Joe Vereneault (JHV Associates) and Vincent Zurzolo (Metropolis Collectibles).

Members are able to participate in many exciting and new educational programs through CBCA's web site, message board, Comic Book Quarterly newsletter, and programming such as grading and collecting seminars and visits to the Library of Congress' comic book and original art collection.

Annual membership is $20.00 and numerous perks are provided that more than cover the cost. Additional information, including an application, can be found at www.comiccollecting.org.

Mark S. Zaid, Esq. serves on the Board of Directors and handles Marketing for CBCA, and is the president of www.EsquireComics.com.

JOIN THE NEWEST SUPER TEAM IN FANDOM..
CBCA
ComicCollecting.org
COMIC BOOK COLLECTING ASSOCIATION
Learn to be a smarter collector
Collectors and dealers who pledge to buy & sell with ethics and integrity
CBCA member events, educational programs & convention seminars
"Your mission expresses an ideal that I believe in and have promoted ever since the early issues of Comic Book Marketplace."
- Gary M. Carter, former Editor, Comic Book Marketplace
To learn more or join, visit our web site and message board at
comiccollecting.org
Fellowship -- Education -- Ethics
All Characters © 2010 Respective Copyright Holders. All Rights Reserved.

Museum Times
TALES FROM GEPPI'S ENTERTAINMENT MUSEUM

I CAN'T THINK OF ANYTHING TO DO THIS WEEKEND...

LET'S GO TO GEPPI'S ENTERTAINMENT MUSEUM!

GREAT IDEA!

WO !

LOOK AT ALL THE COMICS!

OOOOHH!

I HAD THAT WHEN I WAS A JUVENILE.

COOL!

TOYS!

I BOUGHT US A MEMB WE CAN VIS AS MANY T WE

WOO-HOO!

GEPPI'S ENTERTAINMENT MUSEUM
HOME OF POP CULTURE

THE JOURNEY FROM FAN TO COMIC BOOK PROFESSIONAL

So, you're a comic book fan, a fan with a passion for the four-color world, a passion that goes far beyond a general sort of enthusiasm. You *love* comics. In fact you love them so much you'd like to make part or all of your living working in or around the comic book business.

There are great examples of those who have done it, and their achievements cover the spectrum from retailers and reviewers to writers and artists to editors and publishers. Whether selling that long-sought back issue or eagerly awaited new comic book, publishing that first critical review that brought readers to a new project, creating new properties, revitalizing old ones, or just making the comic book creative process work, the practitioners of these jobs have helped their fellow fans in many ways.

Take for instance the paths of Ed Catto and Joe Ahearn. Now friends and partners, their affection for collecting began in earnest with the debut of Captain Action.

The original superhero action figure first arrived on the scene in 1966 with the ability to change into a fantastic range of other incredible heroes, including Superman, Batman, Captain America, Spider-Man, the Lone Ranger, Buck Rogers, and the Green Hornet. He took on their costumes and personas and fought the forces of evil in their places. Produced by the Ideal Toy Company and developed by Stan Weston, who had been involved in the genesis of Hasbro's G.I. Joe just two years before, Captain Action enjoyed a fairly brief shelf life. The last of Ideal's original production runs ended in 1968.

In that short time, though, the 12-inch action figure had also doubled for Aquaman, Flash Gordon, the Phantom, Steve Canyon, Sgt. Fury, and Tonto. He had a sidekick, Action Boy (who became Superboy, Aqualad and Robin the Boy Wonder) and a blue-skinned, bug-eyed alien arch foe named Dr. Evil (obviously years before Austin Powers fought another Dr. Evil). There were playsets, vehicles, a headquarters, flicker rings, playing cards, a Ben Cooper Halloween costume, and a fondly remembered five-issue series from DC Comics that included contributions from such legends as Wally Wood, Jim Shooter, and Gil Kane.

As the years followed, Captain Action became the purview of the collecting community. A thriving secondary market developed and kept interest in the character alive within its ranks. In 1998, thirty years after the original production run ended, Playing Mantis brought Captain Action back to the world of new toys. Although their tenure with the toy line would also end after two years, it greatly fanned the flames of interest in the character and the original collectibles.

That led eventually to the formation of Captain Action Enterprises, none other than longtime collectors Catto and Ahearn. They relaunched the character in comic book form and eventually worked their way to a major toy release. Together they realized a dream held by many collectors by becoming the owners of one of their favorite characters.

Captain Action also has a tie to the creator of perhaps our favorite story about breaking into the business, that of the first Captain Action comic book writer and former Marvel Comics Editor-in-Chief Jim Shooter. His first work is famous. When he was just a teenager, he wanted to help out his parents financially. He didn't know that a kid couldn't write the adventures of the Legion of Super-Heroes, so he did it and made comics history.

In this section, we'll give you some examples of all these job categories and some of those who have turned their love of comics into their careers.

BY ART CLOOS

VINCENT ZURZOLO

Vincent Zurzolo was born in Brooklyn, NY and grew up in Rockaway Beach, Queens. He majored in marketing with a minor in international studies from St. John's University, also in Queens, where he graduated summa cum laude. He is married and lives in Manhattan. Today he is best known as the Chief Operating Officer of Metropolis Collectibles and ComicConnect.com.

When did you discover comics?

Vincent Zurzolo (VZ): I have loved comic books since back before I could even read. I had two older brothers who collected so I got to see their books. The first *Incredible Hulk* issues I read were #180-182, first *X-Men* were #95-100 and *Giant-Size X-Men* #1, you get the picture: Make Mine Marvel! I collected with my friends in school and neighbors. We all loved comic books. I remember we were into *Teen Titans* and the *Wolverine* miniseries. It was a fun time to be collecting. John Byrne was a god and we all loved *X-Men*.

What was your first comic show?

VZ: I recall going to a show in Manhattan. My mom and godmother dropped me off to go to the con all by myself. I think it was at the Roosevelt Hotel. There was an escalator that took you up to the main room. When I got off the escalator it was like reaching heaven. I had never seen so many comics in my life. I think I had $5.00 to my name that day and I ended up buying *Marvel Fanfare* #1 and 2. I am pretty sure I bought them from Conrad Eschenberg.

The convention room was surreal. I don't think I could have ever imagined that one day I'd have over 150,000 vintage comics in my collection (inventory, really) [Laughter]. I read comics for the fun of it. I collected comics for investment and just to have and share with my friends.

Did you ever drift away from comics?

VZ: I remember when I started getting interested in girls, I stopped collecting for awhile.

Girls, cars or rock and roll seem to be some of the main reasons guys who read comics gave them up at one point or another. What made you go back?

VZ: I was on a ski trip and this guy who worked at Forbidden Planet (a major comic store here in New York City) was hanging out at the lodge reading *Amazing Spider-Man* #300 and I lost my mind when I saw what

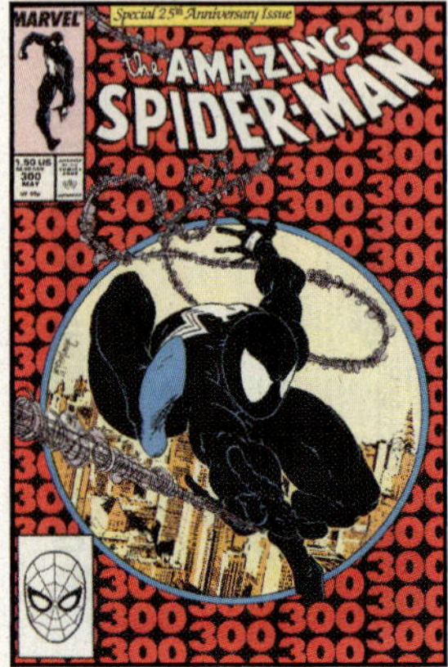

McFarlane was doing with Spidey. It was just amazing (pun intended). I started collecting again right after that.

You of course are known as one of the major comic dealers in the world today. How did you make the jump from collector to dealer?
VZ: When I was about 16 years old I started dealing with my friend who lived across the street from me. We didn't know what we were doing really but we knew what we liked and how to buy. We had an ad in the *Comics Buyer's Guide* for VM Comics (our initials) and we started buying. I also got a lot of leads and deals from kids in school and referrals. I was becoming the Comic Kid in Rockaway, where I grew up.

Were you an immediate success as you started your selling career?
VZ: When I started, I barely knew how to grade. I knew nothing about the Golden Age. I didn't even really know who Kirby was. But I loved comic books and I soaked up the information like a sponge. The thing I have always had going for me is that if I am passionate about something, I want to learn everything I can about that subject. I have been at this for a long time and I still learn something new all the time.

How did your partnership with Steve and Metropolis come about?
VZ: Steve and I started doing business together in the early '90s. After a few years of buying and selling with one another we ended up buying some big collections together, one of them being the Spokane Collection. To this day the Spokanes are some of the best books I have ever seen. In 1998 Steve invited me to the city for drinks at a Flat Iron District restaurant called America.

At that time he approached me about being his partner. Needless to say, I was very flattered. We had some challenges ahead of us. Steve and I had become best friends and strong business partners. We both wanted to make sure we did this

right. We worked for almost a year on a partnership agreement and on July 1, 1999 we merged our companies and I moved my business into Manhattan. It was a very exciting time.

Over the years we have built up Metropolis, we started a production company called Metropolis Entertainment and sold a TV show called *The Wrong Coast* to AMC and built ComicConnect.com, a second brand in the premier online marketplace for vintage comics, art and memorabilia. Partnerships are not easy. I am proud to say that [as we are doing this interview] we are coming up on the 13th anniversary of our merger. That is quite an accomplishment for any two partners but especially impressive considering how strong willed and opinionated both of us are. I believe Steve and I have remained close and successful because we are both very focused on the success of our companies, taking care of our customers and growing the comic market.

I wake up very excited to see what the day will bring, what new record we can make or break and checking out great, old comic books. And yes, there are times when I find myself stopping in the middle of the day to read a Golden Age comic I've never seen before, a classic Silver Age yarn or a book I remember reading from my youth from the '70s.

Do you see any changes in the market since your early days?
VZ: Since I began selling the market has changed a lot. The advent of the Internet, eBay, CGC, the rise of Image and Valiant, the comic market collapse, GPA, becoming partners with Steve at Metropolis, starting ComicConnect.com, the sale of the first million dollar comic (we sold an *Action Comics* #1 8.0 for $1 million) have all sculpted the market into what it is today. So many things have changed.

What are you most proud of in your career as a dealer?
VZ: That is a tough question. I have always tried to get comic books and collecting the respect it deserves. Comic

books are one of the only true American art forms. When I first started out full time after college I hated when people asked me what I did for a living. I'd tell them I sold comic books and the next question was "Can you make a living doing that?" Times have changed and I don't get that question any more. Every time I do a TV news interview or appear as a vintage comic expert on a TV show I always treat the subject matter with the respect it deserves. I also think my companies, Metropolis and ComicConnect.com have consistently taken the comic book business to the next level. We hold the record for the three most expensive comic books ever sold and have sold more *Action* #1s over the last four years than the rest of the industry combined over the last 10 years.

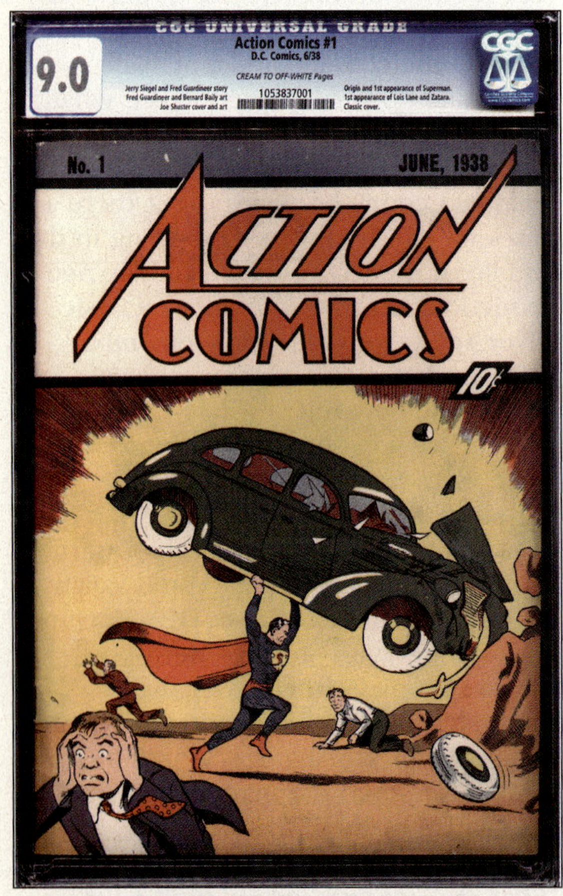

ACTION COMICS #1,
CGC CERTIFIED 9.0
which sold for $2,161,000
in November 2011.

You've also done an internet radio show, *Comic Zone Radio*, correct?
VZ: *Comic Zone Radio* started in 2005 when I was approached by an online radio station called World Talk Radio. They called asking me if I new someone who could host a radio show about comics. I quickly answered "Yes, me!" And guess what? I got the job. I must admit I was really nervous the first six months. I would get butterflies in my stomach and it took me awhile to get comfortable. I did the show for about five years. I made hardly any money off the show though at its height we had four sponsors and averaged 8,000 listeners per episode. [It] was my way of giving back to the comic community. I loved hosting the show and started developing a decent interview technique over time. One of the best pieces of advice I ever got on interviewing a guest was to listen. It was that simple. Although I did hours of research for each guest sometimes the best questions came out of their answers.

Who have been some of your guests on the show?
VZ: My guests included Stan Lee (twice), Frank Miller, Todd McFarlane, Art Spiegelman, Bernie Wrightson, Alex Ross, actors David Carradine and Thomas Jane, director Bryan Singer, comedy writer and art collector David Mandel and hundreds of other artists, writers, comic dealers, CGC graders, restoration experts, comic historians and more. Possibly one of my best interviews was with Jay Maybruck, the original founder of Sparkle City Comics. This was a four-part interview and Jay really delved into the dark side of his comic dealing days.

All of the shows are archived and free at www.comiczoneradio.com. Even though I haven't done a show since 2009, I still get requests to bring the show back. I was really touched that at least a half dozen comic fans at the Super Con in London came up to me to thank me for doing the *Comic Zone* and asked me to bring it back. I loved hosting *CZR* and I promise I will try. Finding the time

AMAZING FANTASY #15 CGC CERTIFIED 9.6 which sold for $1,100,000 in March 2011.

Amazing Fantasy #15 is still one of the best books you could possibly buy for investment. Competition is fierce. I am inspired by my competition every day. I want my companies to be the best they can be and I meet with my teams all the time to find ways to improve our company. Customer service has always been the core of my business and I make sure that comes across with people.

What about the new sellers coming into the market? There seems to be a lot of them. What do you say to them when they talk to you?
VZ: I think everybody today is a dealer. Customers are smart and if they see a book they can make a buck on they will try. I say learn the market. Watch for trends and learn how to spot restoration.

How do you think digital comics options will affect the hobby?
VZ: Comics will continue to be published on paper for a long time to come because people collect and buy and sell comics. Having said that if you can find a way to sell a digital comic book for more money than perhaps you can with paper, comics will disappear. Digital comics will help grow the market as the kids growing up today who wouldn't buy a paper comic book will buy them online. Plus digital comics are pretty cool. You can blow up panels and really see the detail. Very cool stuff!

is the hard part due to the breakaway success of ComicConnect.com and of course Metropolis' continued success. Thank you to all the listeners and supporters, and if you haven't listened to one of the shows please do.

So how do you see the state of the hobby today?
VZ: I notice that more people are coming into the market every day. Golden Age is on the rise. The Atlantic City collection we auctioned off in 2011 is a testament to the trend toward the Golden Age.

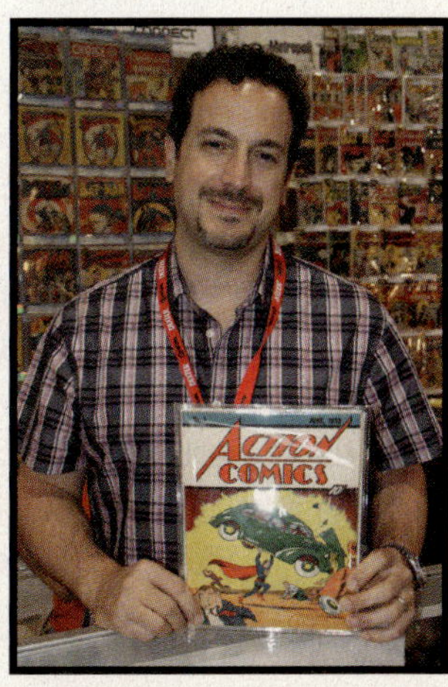

BY SCOTT BRADEN

BEAU SMITH

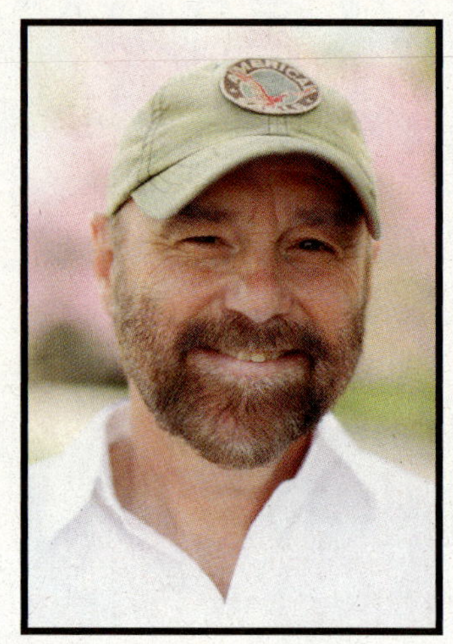

One of the many great things about the funny book business is that the fans have a voice in what transpires in their favorite books, as well as the chance – with the right guidance, the right story ideas, and the right contacts – to creatively participate in the four-color process of making comic books. Take veteran creator Beau Smith, for example. In his West Virginia-based Flying Fist Ranch and thereabouts, he first entered comics as a prolific letter column writer – which in turn helped him become a fan-favorite comic book scribe for DC Comics' Guy Gardner: Warrior and his creator-owned Wynonna Earp, among other projcets. Yeah, we know what you're thinking — if all he did was write to comic book publishers, then what was the secret of his success? Read on and find out.

As a fan, you were a prolific letter column writer. How did you decide which comic books to write to?

Beau Smith: Back in the late 1970s, before I began my professional writing career, before the internet, before fax machines and other sources of communication technology, I figured that the only way an aspiring writer was going to make any connection with Marvel and DC comics was to write letters to the editors. The letter columns in the back of the comic books were the focal point of fan/reader communication. That was where I was going to do my networking. I decided that I would write a letter of comment to each comic book that I bought each week, and that put me at about 10 letters a week. I only wrote to the comic books that I liked and read. I wasn't going to waste my time and money writing to comic books that I didn't enjoy. I knew then I had to market myself differently from the other folks writing letters, so I signed my full name, Stephen Scott Beau Smith. I also made sure that I did my best to make each letter entertaining as well as constructive. I must of done something right because from 1978 through 1986 I had over 300 letters printed in comics. It also helped when I attended conventions and introduced myself to editors. I'd usually get the "Hey! I know you! You're the guy with four names that writes me all the time!" Well, it worked. Pretty soon editors were sending me advance copies of upcoming series so that I would write letters for their letters pages. Relationships were built and soon the editors asked me to send in pitches and story ideas. I'm sneaky like that.

Did your letter column writing introduce you to other future comic book creators?

Beau Smith: Yup! There were other guys that were doing the same thing I was during that time period. We would sometimes exchange letters and shared opinions. Some of the other creators that were writing letters during that time period were, Mark Waid, Todd McFarlane, Chuck Dixon, Kurt Busiek, Kevin Dooley, just to name a few. In fact, if my faded memory serves me right, there was an issue of *Supergirl* that had letters from me, Todd McFarlane and Mark Waid in the same letters page. Before I started writing letters of comment to comics I remember growing up reading the printed letters of future comic book creators such as Dave Cockrum, Marv Wolfman, Len Wein, Tony Isabella, Gerry Conway, Frank Miller, Gary Groth, Dean Mullaney, and many others. I made some really great lifetime friends from the letter columns.

Did your letter column writing introduce you to editors?

Beau Smith: Yeah, it did. I met DC editors and creators Alan Gold (*Blue Devil*), Ernie Colon (*The Flash*), Murray Boltinoff, (*G.I. Combat*), Robert Kanigher (*Sgt. Rock)*, Joe Kubert (*Sgt. Rock*), and Marvel Editors and creators Jim Shooter, Walt Simonson, Louise Simonson, Tom DeFalco, and Roy Thomas. All of them were super helpful

Alter-ego "Beau La Duke" in action.

in getting me started in writing comic books in one way or another. Walt Simonson sent me plot proposals to learn from, Joe Kubert gave me advice on how best to write for an artist, and Robert Kanigher became a very good friend and taught me hours and hours of story telling lessons. I couldn't ask for a better foundation for my career.

Which editors did you first work with as a young comic book writer?

Beau Smith: My first editor was Cat Yronwode at Eclipse Comics where my writing career began. Cat was a tough, but fair editor. She put my grammar-poor butt through boot camp and I thank her for that. I needed it badly. She pretty much left me alone with my story ideas and characters, giving me the freedom to create and I appreciated that. At DC Comics, Kevin Dooley was my first editor there on my *Green Lantern Quarterly* story. Kevin was a huge help in the fact that he trained me on how to work with DC Comics and long established characters. He and his then assistant editor, Eddie Berganza, were wonderful sounding boards on creative ideas and character traits. Tight bonds were made. Tim Truman was my player/coach at Eclipse Comics when I started out. He knew the creative ropes and how much slack or how tight they needed to be. We was an immense help in forming the way I write and see a story. I also have to mention, even though he was not an edi-

tor of mine, early on, writer Mike Baron took me under his wing and taught me a lot about writing by sending me his layout scripts from *Nexus* and *The Badger*. I still have them today. My friend Chuck Dixon also taught me a lot with his scripts that help me crawl through the mine field of how to pitch an editor.

As a comics pro, which conventions did you first go to when you were starting out?

Beau Smith: Living in Huntington, West Virginia, I didn't really have much access early on to conventions. Before he went to work for Marvel Comics in promotions, Steve Safeel, a Huntington native, worked with Marshall University in putting on a sci-fi Convention here in Huntington. That was my first one back in 1983. Ron Frenz was the comic book guest there. We struck up a lifetime friendship there. The next year I was sent to my first really major convention, Chicago Con. I was sent there via Westfield Comics to give a reader's report to their subscribers in the *Westfield Newsletter*. To this day, that 1983 Chicago Con is my favorite. A ton of wonderful memories were made there and it still seems like a dream to me in my mind. It was there I met such creators as Sergio Aragonés, Mike Grell, Jim Shooter, Peter David, Robert Greenberger, John Romita, Sr. and so many more. My first convention as a professional in

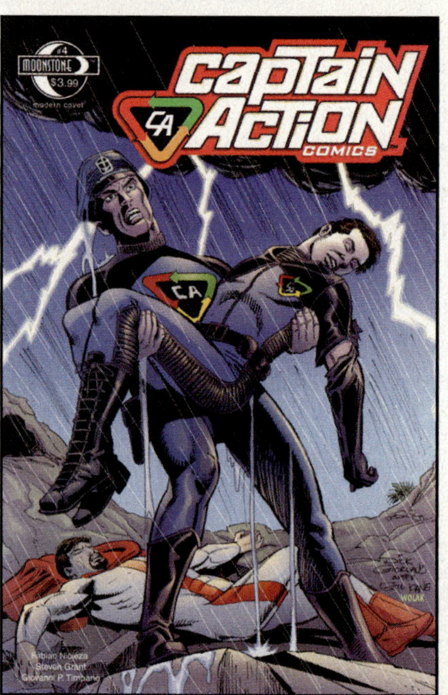

comics was the 1987 San Diego Comic Con. I was the Sales Manager for Eclipse Comics as well as writing "Beau La Duke's Tip For Real Men" in the back of Tim Truman's *Scout* comics. That con also doubled as a honeymoon for my wife, Beth and me. An amazing time was had. This was before San Diego had remodeled the downtown and Gas Lamp area. In fact, now that I think about it, this Summer celebrates my 25 years working in comics!

How did you enter the business and become a comics pro?

Beau Smith: It was during that 1984 Chicago Con that I met Tim Truman for the first time. Tim was doing *GrimJack* at First Comics. We hit it off through our mutual West Virginian accents. We talked a long time about our West Virginia roots and remained in contact from that con forward. In 1987 Tim contacted me and told me that Eclipse Comics was looking for a Sales Manager. I was working in sales and marketing at that time for a local audio/video chain here in Huntington. Tim suggested that I apply for the job with Eclipse publisher, Dean Mullaney. The ABA (American Bookseller's Association) was being held in Washington, D.C. that year, so Dean flew me in to meet and work the show with him, Tim and Chuck Dixon. That was also my first meeting with Diamond Comics Distributors, Eclipse's biggest distributor at the time. I had a good meeting with

Steve Geppi and Bill Schanes, once again, more lifetime friends in comics. Dean offered me the job, my only stipulation was that I wouldn't have to move. That was no problem since most of my work would be done by phone and traveling to the various conventions, distributor meetings and retail stores. I loved it and worked for Eclipse until 1994. Today, all these years later, I am once again working for Dean Mullaney at The Library Of American Comics through IDW Publishing.

You worked with many different companies as a comics pro. Which of those companies did you enjoy working for the most?
Beau Smith: As I mentioned, I think I enjoyed working for Eclipse Comics the most, as they say, your first is always retains the fondest memories. My time as VP of Marketing for Image Comics, Todd McFarlane Productions and McFarlane Toys was without a doubt the wildest. I got to be a part of something brand new from the start and work with it to make it one of the biggest creative changing forces in comics. It was the wild frontier in many ways, no rules, no boundaries and sometimes just flat out crazy. I enjoyed my years as VP at IDW Publishing a lot in the sense that I once again got to work for another friend and former Eclipse alumni, Ted Adams. IDW was without a doubt the smartest run company I have ever

worked for. Ted Adams is the best business mind in comics today bar none. Just look at where the company has gone in such a short time. Its foundation is rock solid and its future is amazing.

What projects have you been working on lately?
Beau Smith: Currently on the business end, I'm the director of marketing for The Library Of American Comics. On the writing end, I'm working on a creator-owned western project of mine for Dark Horse called *200 People to Kill*. Originally the artist was my friend Eduardo Barreto, but since Eduardo's passing last year, I am currently looking at new submissions for the project. Earlier this year, I had my *Wynonna Earp: The Yeti Wars* series come out from IDW as well as a couple of my *Classic Captain Action* stories at Moonstone. For the future, I'm working on new plots for my *Cobb* series and another *Wynonna Earp* series. As always, I am the columnist for my long running pop culture column, "Busted Knuckles" for Comics Bulletin (comicsbulletin.com) as well as my "Beauology 101 column for Westfield Comics (www.westfieldcomics.com). I am always seeking out new opportunities as a writer and on the marketing end of comics, so the phone rings and I take the calls. I hope the next 25 years turn out to be as much fun as the first.

BY JOHN CLARK

DON NEWTON

Having an older friend and mentor from whom a person may draw encouragement and inspiration while young in life is a condition that some are fortunate to experience. I am happy to have had that experience between the ages of 15 and 21 and for me, my friend was Don Newton.

Don was born November 12, 1934 in St. Charles, Virginia and was 34 when I first met him, through an ad for back-issue comic books which I had placed in G.B. Love's *The Rocket's Blast Comicollector*, the most widely circulated fanzine/adzine of the period. He was already an accomplished artist, trained in classical oil painting and was working as an art teacher for Washington Elementary School in Phoenix, Arizona, where we both lived. Don had discovered fandom a couple of years before and used the *Rocket's Blast* as his main vehicle to increase his collection of Golden Age comics, *Captain Marvel Adventures* in particular. He also became a regular contributor of covers to the fanzine, which

also published a comic strip he had tried to syndicate, *The Savage Earth*, in serialized form from 1968 to 1970.

Even though Don earned his living as an art teacher and even though he was a highly talented oil painter, his true love was comic books and his greatest aspiration was to become a full-time comic book illustrator. He regularly submitted samples to the major comic book publishers of the day and his determination finally paid off in 1974 when Nicola Cuti, an editor at Charlton (better known today as the co-creator of E-Man), saw his samples and was impressed by Newton's layout skills and his mastery of human anatomy.

Cuti gave Newton a trial story which passed muster and was published in *Ghost Manor* #18. Don then became a regular in the Charlton horror line, placing stories in a majority of issues through the next year until he took on the duties of regular feature artist for Charlton's *The Phantom*, beginning with #67 in 1975.

A dynamic panel and the cover from *The Phantom #67*, Don Newton's first on the title.

bullpen, first in 1979, pencilling an *Avengers Annual,* and again in 1981 to again work on *The Avengers.* Paul Levitz soon convinced Newton to return to DC, however, where he remained for the rest of his career, working as one of the regular artists on *Batman* and *Detective.* During his tenure at DC, Don worked with many of the legends of the industry, including Denny O'Neill, Gerry Conway, Elliot S! Maggin, Roy Thomas, Dan Adkins, Paul Rubinstein, Terry Austin, and many others. He also had a hand in the creation and design of three prominent DC supporting characters, Ch'p of the Green Lantern Corps, as well as Killer Croc and Jason Todd from the Batman series.

Don had a good relationship with Cuti, Joe Gill, George Wildman, and others at Charlton and he enjoyed his work, but their rates were low and he always aspired to work at Marvel or DC. While still working for Charlton he managed to pick up some incidental work on single issues of several Marvel titles, including *Ghost Rider* (inking Don Heck), several pages for *Giant-Size Defenders,* and a painted cover for *Unknown Worlds of Science Fiction Annual.*

His big break came when he was offered a gig drawing Aquaman for DC, through the influence of his friend Dan Adkins, who would be his regular inker for a three-year run on *Aquaman* and a concurrent run on *The New Gods.* Don's childhood ambition came to light in 1978 when he took over penciling chores on one of his two all-time favorite characters, Batman, beginning with *Batman #305.* That same year he fulfilled his long-time wish to pencil his other favorite super hero, Captain Marvel, in that character's final issue of *Shazam!* — #35.

Most of Don's career was at DC, with a couple of short forays into the Marvel

Don worked for DC steadily through 1984 when he succumbed to a heart attack due to complications arising from a throat infection, which he'd been fighting for several months. Even through his ailment, Don soldiered on, forcing himself to work and to produce the required allotment of penciled pages each day for the books he worked on. He died in a Mesa hospital on August 19, 1984 at the age of 49 and was survived by his mother, Hazel Milton (now deceased) and his son, Tony Newton. Don was to have taken over Roy Thomas' *Infinity Inc.* with #12. He had penciled a framing sequence for #11 and a "shelf story" to be used in case of emergency. Sadly, he was only able to pencil three pages of

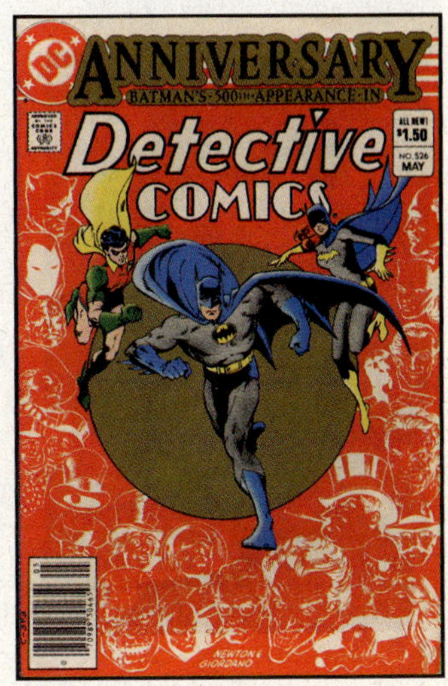

#12 before his death. The emergency story was subsequently inked by Joe Rubinstein and became Newton's last published work, *Infinity Inc.* #13, April 1985.

Despite the discrepancy of our ages, Don came to be my best friend and I deeply felt his loss, as did millions of comic book fans who were impressed and inspired by his dynamic art style. One of those "fans" was Robert Overstreet, whom Don met at a Houston comic convention in 1970, shortly after the publication of the first edition of *The Overstreet Comic Book Price Guide*. Don had several small paintings of various super heroes for sale at that convention and Overstreet was so impressed by them that he purchased all that Don had remaining. They became fast friends after that and when, in 1974, the *Guide* started featuring original covers, Overstreet commissioned Newton to paint the first one, a tribute to the Justice Society of America. Don was again commissioned in 1983 to paint an infinity cover of Batman, Superman, and Wonder Woman for the 13th edition of the *Guide*.

One version of the edition you now hold features a third painting for Overstreet done by Newton, which has not seen print until now.

John Clark, a veteran comic book creator, is the former Editor-in-Chief of Gladstone and of Gemstone Publishing's Disney line.

Don Newton's two covers for the *Overstreet Comic Book Price Guide*, #4 (1974) and #13 (1983).

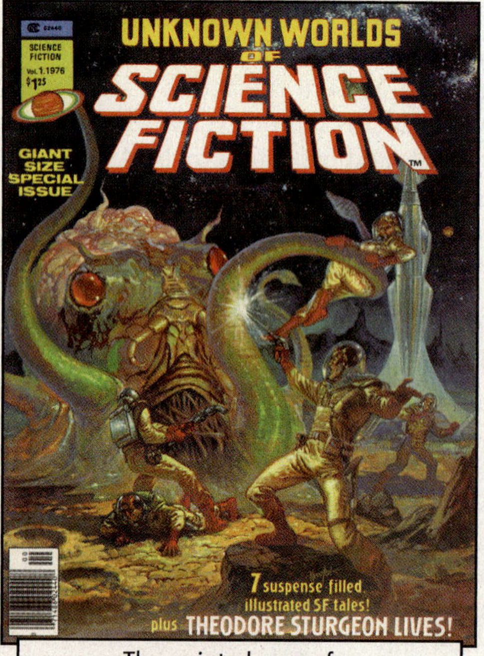

The painted cover for *Unknown Worlds of Science Fiction Special 1* (1976).

Newton fulfilled his long-time wish by pencilling his own adventures of Captain Marvel.

By Courtney Jenkins

Ross Richie

Ross Richie is the founder of BOOM! Studios, an independent, award-winning publisher of some of today's top titles in the comics industry. Founded in 2005 out of Ross' spare bedroom, BOOM! was named "Best Publisher (under 5% market share)" by Diamond Comics Distributors in both 2009 and 2010, and their comics have earned multiple Eisner and Harvey Awards.

In addition to turning out critically acclaimed comic books and graphic novels, Richie has also produced a number of successful independent film projects. His undeniable and absolute love for comics drives his continuous efforts to connect fans, bringing writers, artists, and audiences together.

In his words, comics provide "limitless possibilities; any story can be told. From superheroes to *Maus* and *Fun Home*. We're still exploring the boundaries of what can be done with the medium."

Richie's own journey began when, at six years old, he received a gift that he is not likely to forget. In an Easter basket from his mother, he found two comics. *Captain America* #207's dark storyline (think people being roasted in ovens) combined with aggressive artwork from Jack Kirby and Frank Giacoia to give young him nightmares. But, "The Fantastic Four was another story," he said. "The *Fantastic Four* was my first love. The art was enthralling (thank you George Pérez and Dave Hunt), the story totally engaging (thank you, Roy Thomas). *Fantastic Four* #178 sent me many an afternoon riding my bike down to the local drug store to buy comics and led to my career today."

No doubt that his natural talent and creativity were also factors in his career and ultimate success. As far back as elementary school, Richie exhibited talent as an artist. From junior high on, he studied painting and drawing and eventually entered college as a Fine Arts major. As his interests drifted, he ultimately graduated with a film degree, never imagining that his love for comics would lead to a career, rather envisioning a future as an artist or designer, perhaps going into advertising.

But sometimes things have a way of working out. When he found himself living in Los Angeles in 1993, surviving on credit cards, he capitalized on a connection made at a comics convention when he accepted a job offer from Tom Mason at Malibu Comics.

"For close to three years all of my fanboy dreams came true as I was at Malibu Comics when they published Gil Kane, Jim Starlin, Barry Windsor-Smith, Walter Simonson, Steve Gerber; the parade of stellar, top-of-the-line comic book talent that I grew up reading was just unstoppable," he remembered. "It was a masters' class on comic book publishing. I was given a lot of leeway in marketing. I built the San Diego booth for the company and saw what the costs were. I networked with retailers and learned the business from their perspective. I had a relationship with Diamond, so I understood how the system worked when I set up my account for BOOM!. I had instant credibility to set up a Diamond account. It was beyond critical for my success. It was the essential building block. I was able to see how a successful operation did it when Malibu was selling hundreds and hundreds of thousands of copies and was able to draft off those high-end relationships."

Over these years, he struck up a relationship with writer-artist Keith Giffen through a mutual friend, and ended up collaborating on a series for Image Comics called *Dominion*, which Richie wrote. Afterward, the inker of the second issue, Dave Elliott, reached out to him for help relaunching his comic book imprint Atomeka, a high-quality British publisher from the late 1980s that featured work from Alan Moore, Grant Morrison, Garth Ennis, Barry Windsor-Smith, Brian Bolland, and a score of other amazing talents.

"I had a lot of knowledge and relationships left over from my time at Malibu that could help out," Richie said.

Together, they successfully resurrected Atomeka, where Richie spent time working on some of his own projects, including *Hero Squared* with Giffen and J.M. DeMatteis. When Giffen came to Ross nearly a year later and suggested that he strike out on his own, "I thought he was crazy," he said. "But Keith is one of the few creators who has been working in the business for 35 years. It's like if Steven Tyler from Aerosmith tells you that you should have a career in music, you stop second-guessing yourself and take his compliment seriously, you know?"

With a little help and a lot of encouragement, Ross started BOOM!, beginning with just a phone, a computer, and himself in that spare bedroom. Reflecting on the company's success, he said, "You've got to be in publishing because it's your love. It's a thrill for me. There's a lot of heartbreak, there's a lot of excitement. It's great fun to see things surprise you with success. It's totally unique and the thing I love about it most is that you can do it with a tightly-knit team and create something remarkable and in a relatively

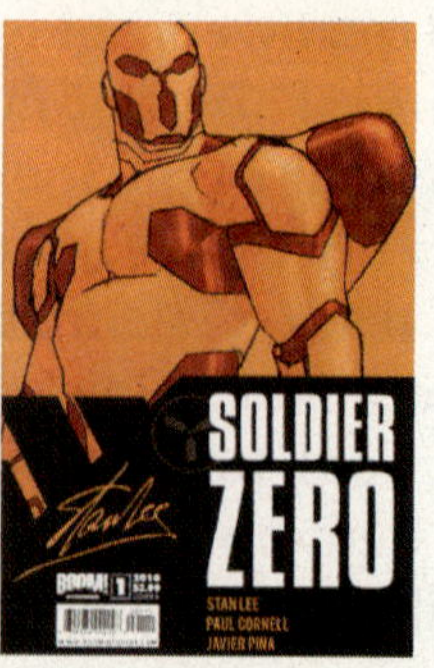

short amount of time connect with an audience."

"It's hard to single things out; even as I want to talk about publishing my favorite BOOM! series, I want to talk about collaborating with Denis Kitchen via our BOOM! Town imprint or indie music legend Daniel Johnston, or getting on the phone with Bruce Willis who had to give us the thumbs-up to do *Die Hard: Year One* or any number of dozens of moments that made me pinch myself."

One of BOOM!'s legacies will no doubt be their efforts to revitalize all-ages publishing in the direct market. As they move forward, the fanboy-turned-comics CEO has some thoughtful advice to share with the future Ross Richies of the world.

"The business is very hard to break into, but we often hire from our intern pool, so don't be afraid to do that. I know many publishers do that. Also make sure you network—go to signings (we conduct many during the year in L.A.). Shake hands, interact, and impress people. Don't be obnoxious. Don't be pushy. It's how I got my start 20 years ago—I went to a convention and talked to Malibu Comics," he said.

"If you are a creative person and want to write or draw, do it. And do it some more. Your first work is usually going to be rough, so get some critiques, get a thick skin, and don't quit. Neal Adams tells stories about how he used to tear Frank Miller apart when Miller was breaking in during the mid-1970s. Miller worked hard on his stuff and kept coming back again and again and again," he said. "Now with the web you can do your own work and put it on the web and send the URL to editors; it's a totally unique time. Go to conventions, meet writers and artists, get their advice, and listen to them. Put your heart and soul into it! Comic books are a medium of passion, and you can't succeed in this business without working very hard and caring a whole lot."

By Courtney Jenkins

John Jackson Miller

Leveraging his professional experience in journalism and publishing, John Jackson Miller turned an intense passion for comics into a job at *Comics Buyer's Guide*, becoming an editor and ultimately one of the most knowledgeable experts in the world about comic book circulation. In addition, he is now one of the top writers of *Star Wars* comics, having also written comics like *Iron Man* for Marvel, along with publishing two *Star Wars* prose novels. As if that weren't enough, he continues to maintain his own meticulous comics records and research on his Comics Chronicles website (www.comichron.com).

Miller started out reading Gold Key and Richie Rich titles, along with *Peanuts* mass-markets titles, and in his words, "I really got into them. I think as a kid, I felt that comics were the reading material specifically designed for us as kids. The funnies were the section of the paper that 'belonged' to us kids; we got comic books as giveaways at the shoe store and at the Big Boy restaurant. They felt accessible, and they inspired me to do my own comics."

As a precocious six-year-old, Miller began drawing pictures, putting them in sequence, and after adding some words— voila, he was publishing his own mini-comics. By the age of ten, he was casting Peanuts characters in his own stories, but realized that those characters truly belonged

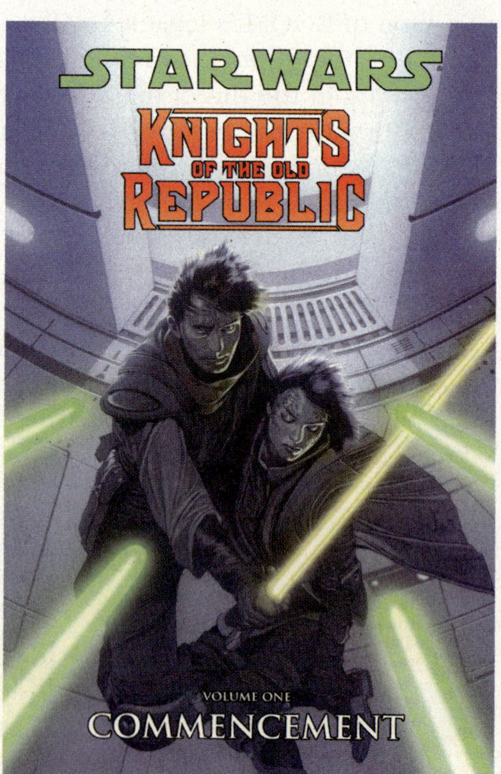

Star Wars Knights of the Republic: Commencement Volume One -2006

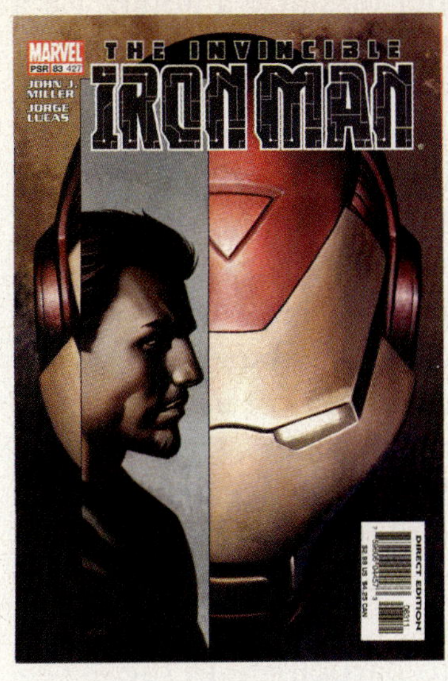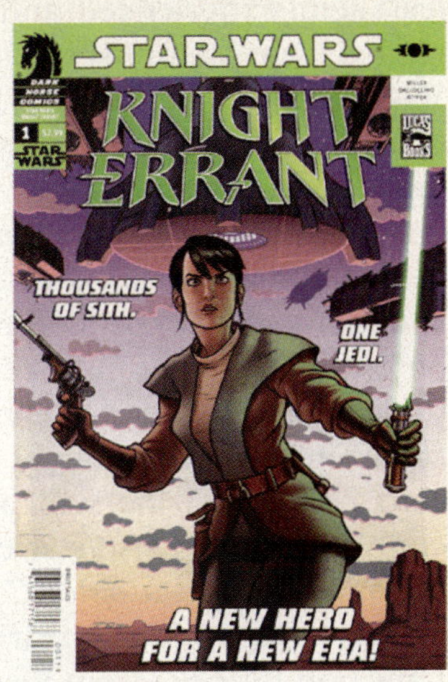

to Charles Schulz, and knew he needed to come up with his own stuff. In middle school, Miller's comics developed into series, each issue of the same length and containing a preview of the next edition. "It wasn't until eighth grade that we got a copy machine and I was able to sell subscriptions to my first mini-comics anthology. By high school, I was using the pages of fanzines like the Small Press Comics Explosion to advertise my stuff, and was still sending mini-comics around the country when I was in college. It would've been much easier if the Web was around then—I would have been doing webcomics instead!" Miller said.

While he was self-publishing his own comics, he was also becoming quite an educated and astute collector. Asked what he loves most about comics, Miller replied, "There's that participatory aspect I mentioned—also, I like that they exist both as an entertainment medium, and also as a collecting hobby. Where other people's mothers threw their comics away, my mother was a grade school librarian—she made me put my comics in order! So from a very early time I treated my old comics as more than just something I had read already—I considered them a library. Since that day, I have always taken care of my collection—all the comics are bagged and boarded and stored upright and spine-out in bookcases, not in comics boxes. This way, they really are more like a ready reference library."

In college, Miller briefly toyed with the idea of a career in spacecraft design, intending to take engineering courses and studying Russian so that he would be able to communicate with our would-be comrades in the space race. "Alas, somewhere between the Challenger disaster and my own inability to do calculus, I realized I'd better fall back on my self-publishing skills and get a journalism degree," he said. "I've been working in publishing ever since."

After college, Miller used his experience as the editor of the campus newspaper at the University of Tennessee to land his first full-time job: editing a line of lumber trade magazines. "It was pretty miserable for me—my interest in lumber wouldn't outweigh a toothpick. But it taught me to be able to write about anything. Fortunately, before that job ran me out of the business, I saw a *Comics Buyer's Guide* ad for an editor for their trade publication, *Comics Retailer*. The magazine had gone through several editors in its first two years, and with Don Thompson ailing, Maggie Thompson and her co-workers needed an experienced publishing hand in the office. I was at least semi-experienced, and happily moved from Memphis to faraway Wisconsin to take the job," he said.

"Don passed away a few months later, sad to say—but I worked with Maggie and her assistant Brent Frankenhoff to keep *Comics Buyer's Guide* (CBG) going, and that sort of expanded my portfolio onto the consumer magazine side of things. We also added games to the trade magazine, and later bought *Scrye*, the card game magazine, which I edited for a couple of years. I also started a book line, the *Standard Catalog of Comic Books*, for the company, and spearheaded the transition for *CBG* from weekly newspaper to monthly magazine. Later on, I managed editorial for the company's websites. So I got to reinvent the job a few times," Miller explained.

Soon, Miller found out that Marvel was looking to re-launch its Epic comics line and was seeking proposals from people in the comics publishing industry who had not yet actually written comics. Miller described his transition from writing about comics to writing the comics themselves: "After getting permission from my superiors, I drew on my Soviet Studies background to craft a Crimson Dynamo pitch, using the old Iron Man villain. That appeared in 2003 and led to a year on *Iron Man*—and then the *Star Wars* work after that. I finally left the day job in 2007 to write full time."

When asked which role he preferred, Miller explained, "Comics used to be my hobby—then they became my job. Now that I am writing comics for a living, writing about comics is again something of a hobby. My Comics Chronicles website [www.comichron.com] is really designed as a place for me to keep alive all the research I did in earlier years — and it provides me a way to participate in comics as a hobbyist historian. So it's a nice change of pace for me."

As a comics collector and hobbyist, one thing about Miller never changed: "I was a compulsive record-keeper. Having helped my mother organize a library for a school one summer, I learned about accession lists and inventory control— and so for several years I was keeping lots of records about when comics entered my collection, and how many I had. So comics collecting always had a data analysis aspect for me. I think the value of it all for me is perspective. When others are freaking out over a bad month in the new comics business, I'm able to put things into context—because I know first-hand how bad things got in the mid-1990s. And I have the data to back up what I'm saying."

The ability to participate in the comics industry in varying roles like these is one of the aspects of the business that Miller finds most worthwhile. For others interested in turning their passion for creating and collecting comics, Miller's advice is simple: "Write anything. Always write for an audience. I think there's no substitute for creating characters and situations that are all your own. Write to be seen, and people will find you."

Fan to Pro:

By Courtney Jenkins

John Haines

Longtime show dealer John Haines opened his specialty shop, Comics & Friends, smack in the middle of one of the worst recessions the U.S. has ever faced. In Mentor, Ohio, or anywhere else, it was a challenging environment. Against the odds, Haines has not only managed to make Comics & Friends a success, but is even looking forward to the next step. "We are now in our fourth year and considering opening a second location." A unique combination of personality and passion has enabled Haines to do what many could not.

His love affair with comics began at the barbershop, with a copy of *Incredible Hulk* #3. "It was an old ratty copy that had obviously been around for a while, but I was enthralled." He was hooked, but suffered his first major setback when his mother burned all of the comics lying around Haines' childhood bedroom. Illustrating his dedication and perseverance, Haines set right out, buying double copies and trading with other kids to rebuild his collection in no time.

His first trip to a convention cemented his love for the thrill of the hunt: "I hit that show with my entire net worth—$68. What did I get for it? Hold on to your seats, and remember that this was 1974: *Amazing Spider-Man* #1, *Avengers* #4, *Strange Tales* #114, *Captain America* #109, *Tales of Suspense* #63, *Fantasy Masterpieces* #3 through #7, *X-Men* #45 through #65 (fifteen cents each!), and best of all, Golden Age Timelys – *Captain America Comics* #42, *Marvel Mystery* #36, *Daring* #9, *Human Torch* #18, and *Sub-Mariner* #18 coverless. And I still had a few dollars left over."

All grown up, having worked as a computer programmer and part-time show dealer for years, Haines found himself ready for his next project and in spite of the less-than-ideal market conditions, opened his shop in September of 2009.

"Timing wasn't the issue to me. I had just ended a business relationship as an executive at a small private firm and had started a consulting firm that was doing pretty well. To me it was just another venture. I did want to open in a mall, which we did, and I did want my store to include pop culture items in addition to comics, which it does," he said.

Thanks to expert advice from store owners Haines had gotten to know at shows over the years, and a unique point-of-sale barcode system, Comics & Friends has been successful from the start.

"Sales have doubled, just like clockwork, every year since we opened," said Haines.

Continuously driven by his love for the archaeology, stories, and artwork that come with a career in comics, Haines advised fans interested in setting up shop, "Don't expect to make money right away – have a plan and stick to it. Be honest and forthright; your customers will thank you for it. Don't chase the short money, build a loyal base and treat them well."

As Haines looks toward the future for his store and himself, "Mostly now, it's the story. At this point, owning a particular comic is not the thrill that it was. Finding it is the thrill! Finding them is the most fun, and the most difficult part." And speaking of stories, Haines has one of the best about hunting down a collection—involving a decaying mansion, eight penny nails, and pork chops on Christmas Eve. But that's for another book…

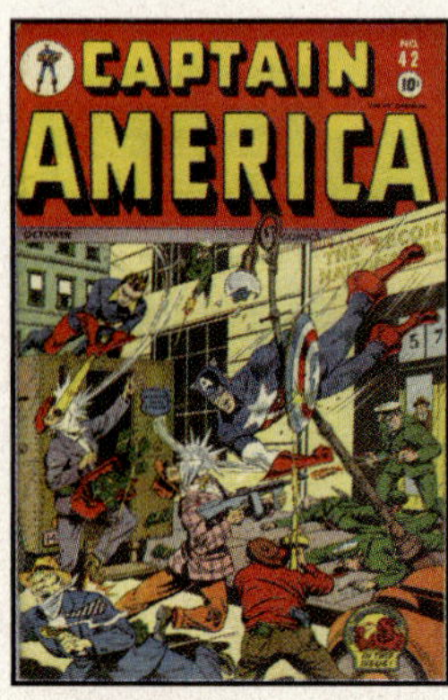 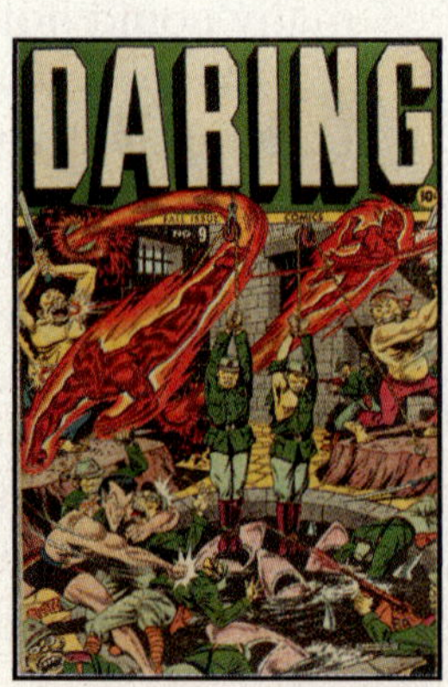 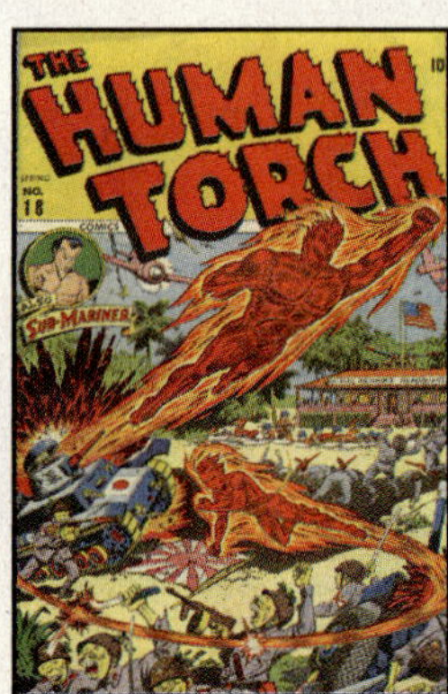

MIKE SAN GIACOMO

Mike San Giacomo is a nearly life-long comics fan who began working as a reporter at the Cleveland Plain Dealer *in 1989. There he has covered everything from statewide general assignment stories to breaking news, cops and courts. He also found a way to infuse his collecting passion into his job by writing the paper's column about comic books and becoming a go-to guy for pop culture-related material, including numerous articles about Superman. In addition, he's written his own comics as well.*

What was your first experience with comics?

I was about four or five when I discovered my brother's stash of Golden Age *All Star Comics*. I was fascinated by the incredible covers featuring the Justice Society. He read the comics to me and soon I was reading them on my own. I never stopped reading.

How long was it from that point until you considered yourself a collector?

I started buying my own comics from my meager allowance when I was in first grade, maybe seven years old. I shined shoes for quarters which went right to my comic book habit. I would keep the comics I bought in neat piles in my room. *Superboy*, *Superman* and *Batman* and later the *Justice League* were my favorites.

How did your collecting habits develop from there?

It just kept growing and growing. Back in the early sixties there were not that many new titles coming

out each month, not like today when there are 654 *Avengers* books every month. I also did a lot of trading comics with friends. And we had a used magazine shop that sold old comics six for a quarter. I practically lived there.

How did you become aware that you had an eye for why you liked some comics better than others?

While some friends were reading Harvey and Archie comics, I always went for the superhero books. I also became quite snobbish about some artists' work over others.

What was your first outlet for that?

For many years, I was just a reader and collector. While still in college studying journalism, I got a job as a part-time reporter at a newspaper in suburban Philadelphia. After a few months, I convinced them to allow me to write a series of features on comic books beginning in 1973. I started with the still amaz-

ing Denny O'Neil/Neal Adams in 1970 and did hero histories of major characters and storylines from DC and Marvel. I still regard the *Green Lantern/Green Arrow* series as one of the finest series in comics.

How did this part of your career develop further?
I have worked as a reporter since 1972 and would frequently sneak in news stories or features about comics into my newspapers. In 1993, after the "death" of Superman, I convinced my editor at the *Plain Dealer* in Cleveland (where I have worked since 1989) that the time was right to give comics their due in the mainstream. I was given a weekly column starting in 1993, long before the Internet rage, where I interviewed writers, artists and editors, previewed upcoming storylines and did tons of comic reviews. The comic column was also syndicated through the Newhouse Newspaper Chain to about 30 papers across the country. Several years ago, a new editor with little appreciation of comics cut my column back to once a month, though I still write numerous off-column stories about comics for the *Plain Dealer* in addition to the column. Writing about Cleveland native Superman is a sub-beat. I've written hundreds of articles about Superman and creators Jerry Siegel and Joe Shuster.

What was going on in the other areas of your career?
I love being a reporter covering hard news and features. I find it inspiring. In my years as a journalist I have covered everything imaginable from presidential visits to features on the homeless. I've won dozens of national and state awards for my work and traveled to foreign countries for stories. It's been great.

In addition to being a go-to guy for writing about comics and pop culture, you have also created comics such as *Tales of the Starlight Drive-In* and *Phantom Jack*. How different is that kind of writing from what you're usually doing? Do you enjoy it?

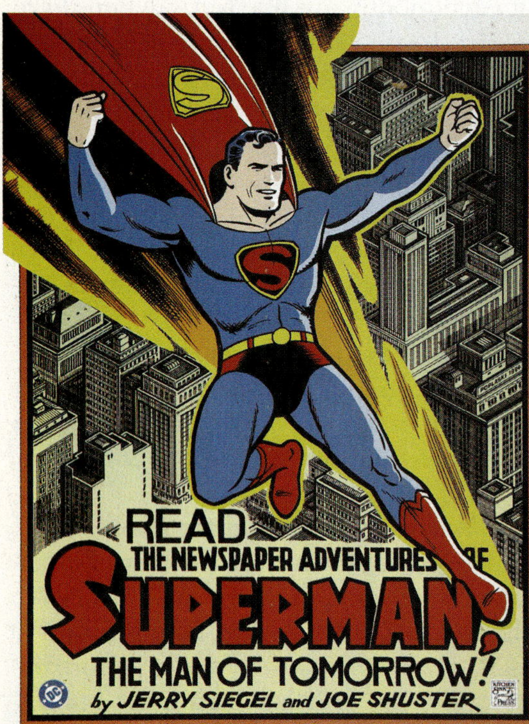

Writing about fellow Cleveland native Superman and creators Jerry Siegel and Joe Shuster seems fitting.

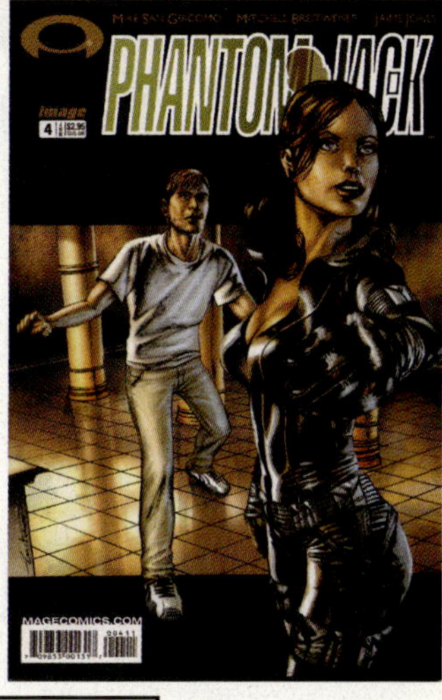

Phantom Jack, with art by Mitchell Breitweiser

I love it. I think a key moment came when I was writing *Phantom Jack* for Marvel's stillborn Epic Comics line (*Jack* was eventually published by Image and later by IDW). An editor wanted me to make some changes in dialogue and action and for a moment I fretted. Reacting like a reporter, I instinctively thought I would have to go out an re-interview people and gather more facts, which would take time. Then I remembered it was a comic book and I could make the characters say and do anything I wanted! What a concept.

What's the best part of writing about popular culture?

I love to introduce people to new things. I write a lot about music, films, books and the most gratifying moment for me comes when someone calls or emails me that they looked up a comic or a musician I wrote about and are now a huge fan. That makes it all worthwhile.

What would you say to someone who is considering going down a path similar to the one you've taken?

I say go for it. One thing I have learned about reviewing comics over the years, after having been on both the giving and the receiving end, is this: be fair. I'm not saying don't be tough in a review, I'm saying don't be a jerk. Be thorough, justify your criticisms and always remember that for every thing you might hate about a book, there is someone out there who will love it. Newspapers are in a tough time, with more resources going to the Internet, but people will always need someone trained to objectively report the news. It's just the platform that may change,

Has your career as a journalist ever influenced your comic writing?

Absolutely. Much of *Phantom Jack* is right from my own life, including *Jack's* origin and his adventures in Iraq. They were based on my actual experiences in the U.S. and Iraq. The text pieces in the *PJ* books are all based on true stories. My next project, *Chalk*, began with a newspaper assignment. I was covering a murder in Cleveland. It was midnight, the body and most of the police were gone. There was a full moon reflecting off the crude, chalk outline that was drawn around the now-

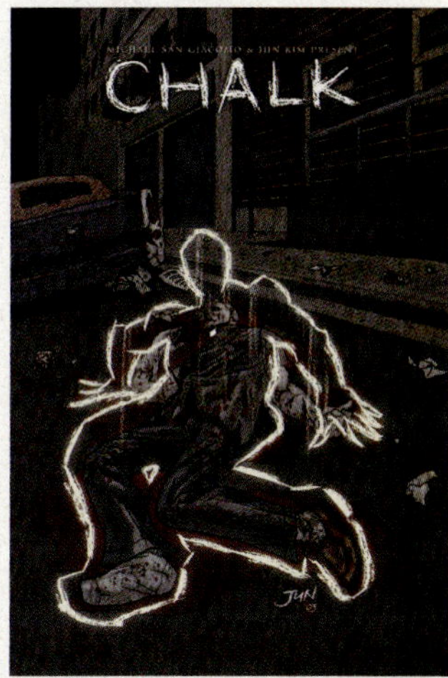

removed body. As I watched it, it seemed to shimmer and I wondered what it would be like if that outline came to life to avenge the victim? That is the high concept behind *Chalk*.

By Charlie Novinskie

Charlie Novinskie

No one starts out reading comic books and fantasizing about one day working professionally in comics. As a ten year old, all I wanted to know was who was stronger, the Hulk or the Thing, not how much it pays to be an editor in the comic industry. As we continue to read and collect comics there tends to be a tipping point that delineates that fine line between the fan and the professional. Let's face it, the majority of comic readers never aspire to work in comics, but it is nice to know that once the desire hits, there are viable options to make the transition into working professionally in comics.

My degree was in geology, and I spent 13 years working in the oilfields, certainly not the sort of training necessary to work in comics. But geology, while it sounds glamorous, is really a lot of sitting around in hotel rooms waiting for parts to show up for broken down drilling rigs. That free time meant plenty of time to not only read comics, but to also start writing letters to comics—letterhacking as it is referred to.

After all, I loved comics so much that I wanted to let the writers and artists know how I felt about their efforts. In fact, I wrote so many letters to Marvel Comics over a five-year period in the 1980s that I had hundreds of letters published. I had my counterparts, folks like Mark Lucas who wrote to DC, Malcolm Bourne who fancied Dark Horse and other indie comics, and others like Liz Holden, and the incomparable T.M. Maple! In 1991 the San Diego Con thought it would be a great idea to have a letterhack panel, and to our surprises, hundreds of people showed up!

Then one fine day a funny thing happened, I started receiving letters from these other letterhacks wanting to discuss comics. Eventually a letter from Joel Thingvall, Central Mailer for Capa-Alpha found its way to my mailbox. Capa-Alpha is the longest running APA about comics, and just so you know, APA stands for Amateur Press Association, i.e. a monthly way for comic fans to get together through the mail to discuss comics. Then, along with Robert Hough and others, we started our own APA—the Marvel Zombie Society APA, which ran for 150 issues. The world of fandom was opening up right before my very eyes. It was well organized many years earlier, but for me, it was a universe as broad and awe inspiring as any comic universe!

Then, the most interesting thing happened, I started receiving letters and phone calls from the editors at Marvel

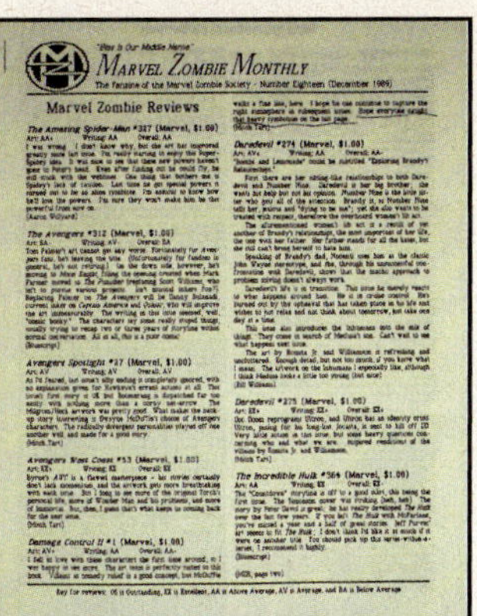

Comics, in particular, Jim Salicrup, editor of Spider-Man at the time, and Mark Gruenwald, editor and writer extraordinaire. Before I knew it Jim had me writing free-lance articles for *Marvel Age* magazine—my first professional paycheck—from Marvel no less!

All of it was just a progression of events that happened from getting my name out by writing letters and having them published. My intent was not to work in comics, but rather just share my enthusiasm with other fans. I'm sure many, many of today's top professionals can share similar stories of their transition from fandom to professional employment.

About that time, Jim Salicrup introduced me to David Anthony Kraft, publisher of the beloved and sorely missed publication, *Comics Interview*. I spent several years working as an associate editor, interviewing dozens of professionals for print.

Fans also have that wonderful opportunity to interact with professionals, today through e-mails, blogs, internet sites, and comic conventions. I remember my second San Diego Comic-Con, standing in line to meet writer Peter David. Peter was writing one of my favorite comics at the time, *Dreadstar* from First Comics. I had written dozens of letters, and had most of them printed in the letters pages of *Dreadstar*, so I was excited to meet Peter David. To my surprise, he was

as excited to meet me as I was to meet him! That's how the comic industry is—the interaction between fan and professional is so blurred that today's fan can easily be tomorrow's professional.

Fast forward out of the 1980s to the early 1990s when I receive a call from Jim Salicrup who just left Marvel for Topps Comics. He wanted me to move to New York, Brooklyn actually, to work as an assistant editor for Topps Comics. I've often stated that Jim was one of only a few people that could convince me to move from western Colorado to New York City—and he did it! From 1993-1998 I worked my way up from assistant editor to editor and finally sales and promotions manager of the entire line of Topps Comics— the Kirbyverse, *X-Files*, *Hercules*, *Xena*, *Jurassic Park*, *Mars Attacks* and many more great titles.

I made many life-long friends at Topps, folks like Jim, and Ira Friedman and Len Brown—way too many to list, and worked with many of my favorite writers and artists from my early days of comics: Don McGregor, Walter Simonson, and Roy Thomas to name just a few. The comics industry can be a great place to work and over time one learns that it truly is a small but tight knit group of hard working professionals. In my five years at Topps I often wondered why they paid me to do the things I did – travel to conventions, meet and work with creators, publish great comics – I'm glad they paid me, but in the long run I received much more than monetary value from that job.

I left Topps Comics on my own terms in 1998 after they decided to get out of the comic business. I moved back to Colorado and now live with my lovely wife Kristine in Lake Havasu City, Arizona. I consider myself more fan than pro these days, but I still have the wonderful privilege to continue to give back to the comic industry and those professionals that gave me so much enjoyment growing up.

As part of my job as sales and promotions manager at Topps Comics I did many great promotions with folks like Jim McLauchlin at *Wizard* magazine and J.C. Vaughn at *Overstreet's FAN*. Eventually, Jim McLauchlin went on to co-found and develop the Hero Initiative, the first non-profit organization designed to help comic creators in need get back on their feet. I've been on the Board of Directors of Hero Initiative for nearly 10 years and it gives me a great reason to stay in touch with some of the great statesmen of comics, including Roy Thomas, John Romita Sr., Walter Simonson, Denny O'Neil, Jim Valentino, George Perez, and Howard Chaykin.

Sure, I'm still collecting comics, but thanks to my involvement with Hero Initiative, I can keep one hand in the realm of professional status while enjoying the benefits of kicking back and being a fan. But best of all, I get to help a variety of creators in need, and for me, that gives me the satisfaction of giving back to many creators that provided me with many fond memories of growing up as a comic fan.

The opportunity exists, even today, for fans of comics to make it into the comics industry, in fact, if you ask just about any comics professional, they will tell you that they started out as comic fans. There are many different ways to break in, but I believe it is the only industry today that allows fans to become bona fide professionals.

If you're a fan reading comics with no aspirations of ever working in comics, you can have an entire life of enjoyment reading and collecting comics, or else you can develop your own path to working professionally in comics. But the best part of it all is that when it comes to being a fan or professional, you get to decide!

Charlie Novinskie continues to write about comics and trading cards from his home in Lake Havasu City, Arizona and serves as an Overstreet Comic Book Price Guide Advisor specializing in Silver Age comics and serves on the Board of the Hero Initiative. He can be reached at charlienovinskie@outlook.com

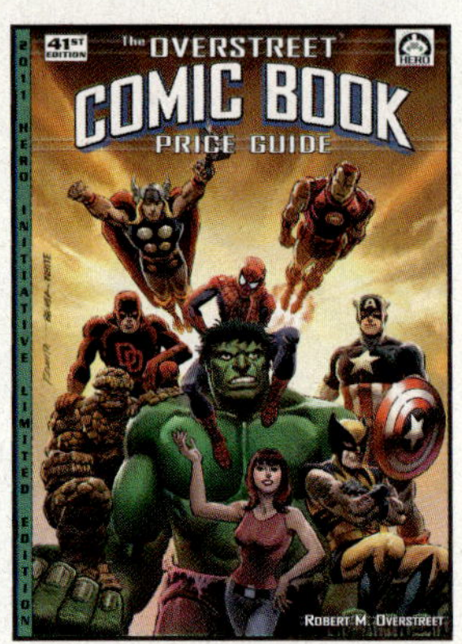

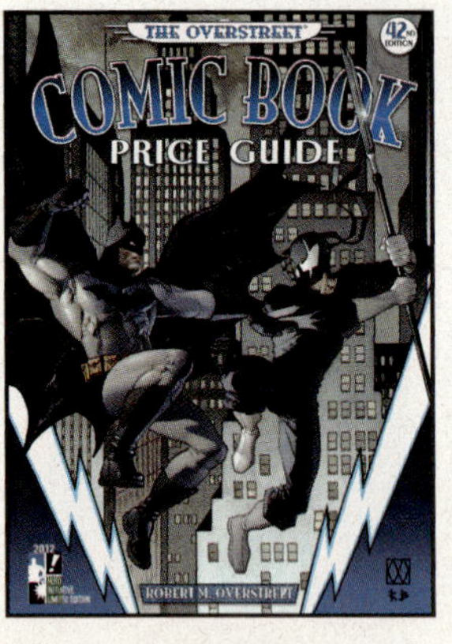

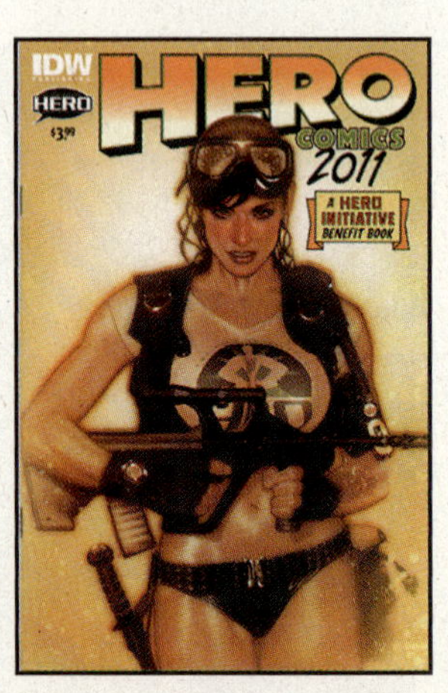

BY J.C. VAUGHN

JOSH NATHANSON

Josh Nathanson's ComicLink is a leading internet-based source for rare, vintage, high grade comic books and original comic art. Now best known as the company's founder, Nathanson started out as a fan, complete with a subscription to Marvel's X-Men.

You've told us previously your first comic book was a *Defenders Annual*. What were the circumstances when you saw it?

That's right. The first comic book that I bought was *Defenders Annual #1*. I was about 7. I found it at Silver Point Beach Club in the summer, where my parents took me as a child. People used to set up near the boardwalk to sell this and that and I remember walking back from camp one day and seeing the comic book sitting there in the middle of a pool of un-child-like things, like Tupperware and stuff. It was a beat up copy - these days, it would grade about a Good minus. I still have it for sentimental reasons.

How long from the time you first bought a comic book until you considered yourself a collector?

I was instantly a collector. Hooked immediately.

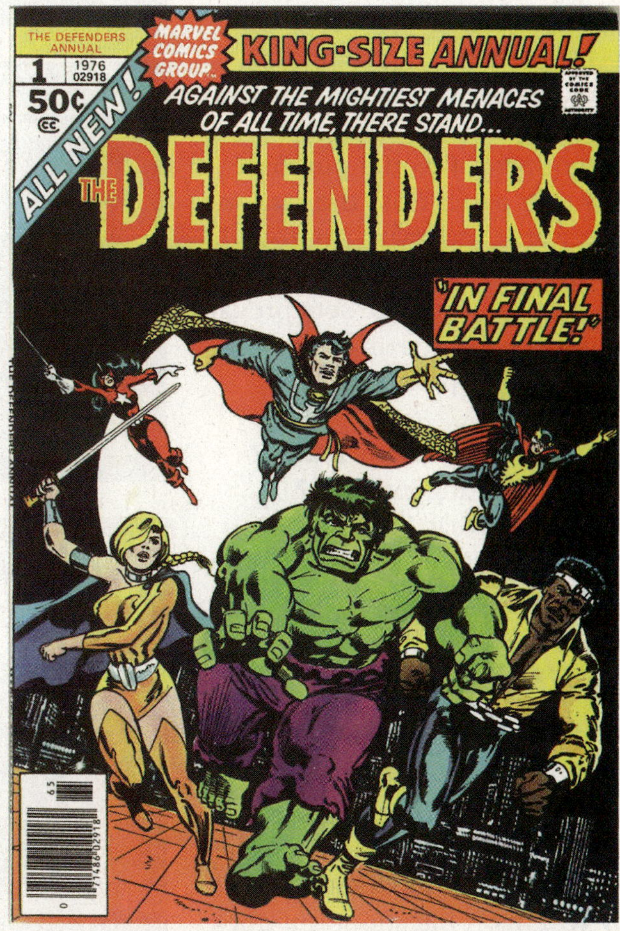

What were your early favorites? How did your collecting develop from that point?

Spider-Man and X-Men were my favorites early on. My good friend when I was young (elementary school) bought me a subscription to *X-Men* for my birthday. It was the first time that I got every single issue on a monthly basis and experienced that continuity of storytelling. It was something to look forward to, and then I started going to the comic book store religiously every month, and picked out multiple titles to collect. Then I was curious about the storylines that predated my collecting, and tried to get the earlier issues, starting with the most recent earlier issue that I didn't have.

You also collected baseball cards, too, right?

I did. I liked trying to find the rookies that would develop into stars based on their minor league stats. I would purchase cards in packs from the stationary stores and try to put together the complete sets, then tried to acquire complete sets predating this habit starting from the most recent prior set.

How did your family react to your collecting interests?

They liked that I had a hobby, and cared about this stuff. Before I was able to take the train myself to the comic store (where I also bought cards), I'd get a lift once a month from my parents, and they'd usually sit in the car and wait for me, under the train, on McDonald Avenue and Avenue P, in Brooklyn where I shopped at Pinocchio Discounts. A big shout out goes

to Bella, the proprietor, for putting up with the kid asking to see the stacks of comic books she had in the back because the conditions of the ones on her rack weren't up to my standards.

What made you think you could turn your interest into a business?

It was an evolution of my experiences and inspiration. At Cornell, in 1993, I think, one of the engineers introduced me to this novel thing called the Internet, and this was really before the browser really came into play, when the modem speed was 14.4 or maybe less. I used ftp to download sheet music because I was trying to teach myself guitar, and I found the newsgroup rec.comics.arts.marketplace. All of a sudden, there were back issues available to purchase easily over the Internet. It was fantastic, but hard to locate exactly what I wanted, in the grade I wanted it in. Very cool, but very time consuming.

After I graduated in 1995, I went to work for a Barclay's bank subsidiary at the time, on Wall Street, called BZW Securities. I wanted to become a trader. This doesn't happen overnight, I was placed as a temp in the operations department, the wrong department. Promises to shift me to the trading area weren't kept, and I lost my patience. I was not interested in what I was doing, and I was completing the job assigned every day by noon, and then I was doing the work of the lifers rather than being allowed to learn what interested me.

So, I got pretty fed up. It was never an option for me to work a job I wasn't interested in. My disillusionment turned to inspiration — I started thinking about how people come to this country with absolutely nothing and rise to become superstars by their sheer force of will. I decided that figuring out what I wanted to do was the hardest part. So, I looked at my interests outside of work and thought, "Wouldn't it be cool if I could spend my time at work, doing something I'd like to do anyway?" I'm not pro athlete caliber, I wasn't going to California to become a movie star, and so, I thought, there may be a way to turn my collecting interests into a business. It evolved from there. The challenge was to come up with a way to do that without a boatload of money.

What were the steps you took to do that?

I was determined to find a novel idea at a time when the Internet was just starting to become a place where people conducted business. eTrade was nothing more than a white screen with text when I started ComicLink. eBay started a year prior, in 1995, and I hadn't heard of it until I conceived of ComicLink. So, I just tried to think of what to do in a big way with comic books or sports cards, or both. I thought of rec.arts.comics.marketplace and how it would be great if there were an easier way to search for stuff.

I thought of the way the stock exchange is set up. Then, it hit me: I'd start a comic book exchange. Then I had to figure out how to make it work for both the buyer and seller. That's where the marketing plan came in. Then I started to go for my MBA just in case it didn't work out! So, I was setting up ComicLink with all my free time, working on Wall Street, and going for my MBA at night. I had no life and I think my friends thought I went off the deep end.

How did your business develop from there?

There is so much to say here, that there won't be enough room on your page. With a lot of hard work and countless decision points.

From the time you first started looking at comics, what do you think the biggest changes in the business have been?

The advent of the Internet as a means towards buying and selling comic books is with certainty the biggest change.

What sort of changes do you see in the marketplace over the next few years?

I think the marketplace has settled into a way of doing business that will continue. It is pretty evolved at this point.

TALES OF SUSPENSE #39
CGC CERTIFIED 9.6
Sold for $375,000
by ComicLink
in April 2012. © MAR

By **J.C. Vaughn**

Jason Kothari

For any fan who has thought "Wouldn't it be cool to own this?", Jason Kothari's journey as a fan would probably be one they'd be willing to take.

After Acclaim Entertainment filed for bankruptcy in 2005 – not even a decade after it had paid $65 million for VALIANT in 1994 – a group of investors led by Valiant fans Jason Kothari and Dinesh Shamdasani acquired the Valiant library of properties.

"Mr. Kothari and Mr. Shamdasani spent the next few years ensnared in legal battles tied to Valiant trademarks, but emerged unencumbered. They connected last summer with Mr. [Peter] Cuneo, who invested in the company and became its chairman. Gavin Cuneo, his son, became chief financial officer," *The New York Times* reported in July 2012, two months after their Valiant Entertainment launched its revived line with *X-O Manowar* #1 on May 2.

Following *X-O Manowar*, the new Valiant launched *Harbinger*, *Archer & Armstrong*, and *Bloodshot*. *Shadowman* is scheduled to launch as this book goes to press, with other titles slated to follow. New Valiant series rolling out invigorated discussions of the original series, and the days of *Eternal Warrior*, *Rai* and *Unity*.

"I grew up abroad in Hong Kong and there was only one comic book store there at the time. This was during the *Death of Superman*, *Batman: Knightfall*, and the creation of Valiant and Image, a very dynamic time for the industry. By reading magazines like *Wizard* and *Overstreet*, I saw there was more passion around Valiant than anything else, and I was curious to see what all this excitement was about," Jason Kothari said.

"Unfortunately, this one comic book store in the city did not initially carry many Valiant comics but this changed when they realized just how fast Valiant readership was growing and how engaged these readers were," he said.

"I started reading Valiant with *Bloodshot* #1 and then got a hold of some back issues; the more I read, the more fascinating I found the Valiant Universe. Getting into a new comic book universe at the ground floor and seeing it unfold was an amazing reading experience. I became a massive fan quickly, just like many of my peers, and then I couldn't get enough of it. It was like the *Star Wars* for my generation of comic book readers," he said.

"Valiant had unique heroes, compelling storytelling and paid excruciating attention to detail, making the reading experience so entertaining and immersive. The characters did unexpected but relatable things, the stories were interconnected with consequences felt throughout the Valiant Universe just like the real world, and there was a reason for almost everything so you paid close attention. Most of all, the characters were so interesting and memorable," he said.

Kothari said that like many other fans, when the original Valiant faded away, his enthusiasm for the characters and their universe did not.

"My interest in Valiant remained even when they stopped publishing new stories because of my fond memories and knowing the potential of what could have become. After all, Valiant was predicted by many people to become the next most popular library of characters. If they continued along their natural path and weren't acquired and mismanaged by video game company Acclaim Entertainment, who knows where they would be by now? Certainly, a number of the Valiant characters would have become household names today; that's where my role and the rebuilding of Valiant comes in, whether it is us or someone else, I truly believe it's their destiny. Selling 80 million comic books and eliciting the kind of passion it does, Valiant has simply too large and rabid a fanbase for this not to occur; it's just a matter of when. We're certainly doing everything we can to make this inevitable reality approach sooner rather than later," he said.

He hopes the things that made him a Valiant fan in the first place will win over others, both fans of the originals and those who have never read a Valiant comic before.

"The original Valiant titles that particularly resonated with me were *Harbinger*, *Shadowman*, *Rai*, and *Eternal Warrior*, and they conveyed important principles to me as a 12 year old: *Harbinger* taught me the mind has unlimited potential and what's right and wrong is a matter of perspective; *Shadowman* taught me not to avoid the dark or the things you fear in life but to face them head-on; *Rai* taught me that even the most powerful being in the world has the same challenges we all share, no less, and perhaps even more; *Eternal Warrior* taught me that with hard work, one man can make a real difference in this world. The characters and themes were so compelling and memorable," Kothari said.

"Today, I love all the new Valiant titles, but each for different reasons. You can't guess where *Harbinger's* story is going even from one page to the next; *Bloodshot* is such a dynamic action-packed book, it feels like a roller coaster and what a great epic action movie should be; every issue of *Archer & Armstrong* has made me laugh out loud at least once; *X-O Manowar* is a beautiful sci-fi epic unlike anything else; *Shadowman* is breath taking," he said.

"I'm so proud of the high-quality work our team and these exceptionally talented creators have done. We have rebuilt the business from the ground up like the original Valiant, with great storytelling as the primary goal above all else, from the team picked, to the budgets, to the production schedule, to the creators, and so on," he said.

As fans themselves, though, how do he and Shamdasani balance their responsibility to lead their company to success in this era with the desires of both older and newer Valiant fans?

"A healthy growing company in the long-run is best for everyone and this requires rebuilding the brand for old fans and continuously bringing in new fans. You'll notice all our books are great reads for both first time Valiant readers and existing Valiant fans because they're always created to be accessible yet familiar to those who are fans of the core concepts and themes from the original titles. Our creative goal is to have the Valiant Universe recognized and prized for consistently high-quality and accessible storytelling," he said.

What if he could tell his younger self that one day he'd own these characters and be responsible for bringing them back?

"I think my younger self would have found that to be a dream come true but also a tremendous responsibility. There are a lot of rabid Valiant fans out there, and every day we hope we are meeting their expectations. We love getting feedback from them to see how we can do things better. It's such an honor to be part of an industry with so many talented people, such a rich history and a bright shining future," he said.

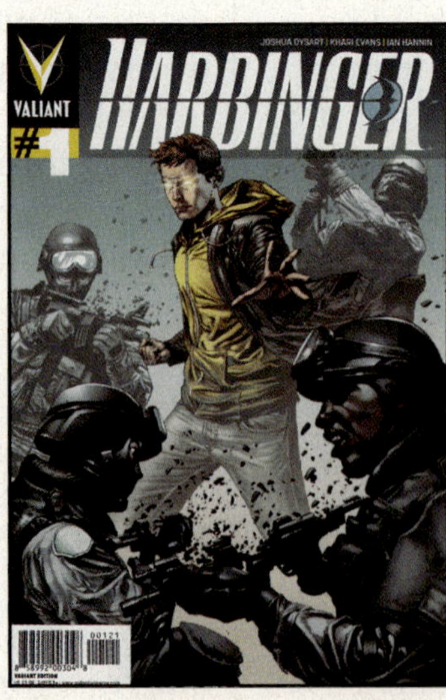

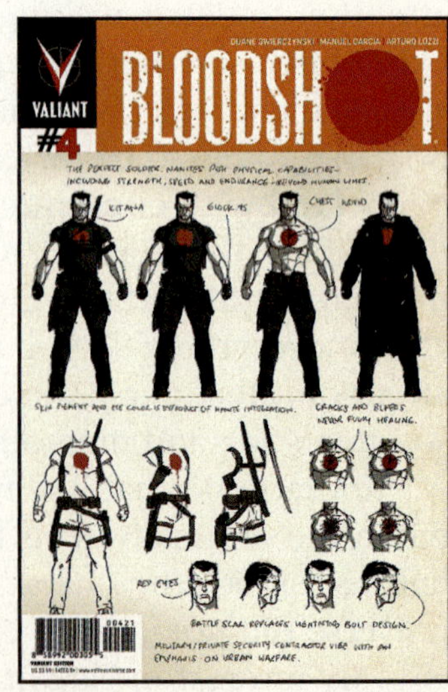

By **J.C. Vaughn**

Augie De Blieck, Jr.

For more than 15 years Augie De Blieck, Jr.'s "Pipeline" column, featured on the Comic Book Resources site, has been one of the most widely read review sources for comics.

What was your first experience with comics?

Augie De Blieck, Jr. (ADB): I remember a couple of Archie comics at a friend's house when I was a little kid, but it wasn't anything that stuck. I was more into the *G.I. Joe* and *Transformers* cartoons. That famous Marvel *G.I. Joe* TV ad didn't draw me into comics, either, as it did so many of my peers. I didn't start buying comics regularly until 1989, when I was 13. It was *Amazing Spider-Man* #318 that drew me in for good.

How long was it from that point until you considered yourself a collector?

ADB: What started as a time-killing hobby to replace my faded interest in baseball cards slowly grew into a collection. At first, I vowed not to be a "collector" again and just stacked the comics in old shoe boxes. A year or two later, I needed short boxes, bags, and boards to start seriously organizing them.

Today, I have a ridiculously large collection, but I'm still more a reader than a collector. I've long since given up trying to complete runs of comics for its own sake. Now, my problem is having too many books I want to read without the time to read them all.

How did your collecting habits develop from there?

ADB: It started with buying comics at the stationery store's spinner rack. The closest comics shop was too far away for me to ride my bike to, though it was an awesome experience when I walked into it for the first time a couple years later. *Walls* of comics? Wow. When one did open closer to me, I became a regular there on a weekly basis, though I don't think it was necessarily Wednesday afternoons. There followed bags and boards and occasional trips into the back issue bins. I didn't go to my first comics show until I was probably nearly ten years into the hobby.

The issue that started a fascination with comics, *Amazing Spider-Man* #318 (August 1989).

The short boxes of comics became long boxes. Organization became an on-going battle. As college gave way to "real life," I had a little extra disposable income and was able to pick up a lot of the back issues and collected editions of things I had only ever dreamed of reading. I filled in gaps and tried to better acquaint myself with the more recent history of comics.

If there's a focus to my collection today, it's in collecting more of the high-end collected editions. I love bookshelves filled with rows of hardcover books collecting my favorite series of the last 20 years.

How did you become aware that you had an eye for why you liked some comics better than others?
ADB: It started right away. Even when I didn't understand the production process of comics, I knew which Spider-Man title I favored. It was the one Todd McFarlane was drawing. I liked the character and read the other Spidey titles, but *Amazing* was the one I was happiest with.

I've always had an analytical mind, always trying to pick things apart to see how they work and how they come to be. Some people become car mechanics like that, while I became a comics critic.

What was your first outlet for writing about comics?
ADB: It started in the letters columns in the backs of the comics, themselves. I had nearly 400 letters published in the 1990s. There's no bigger thrill than flipping to the last page of a comic and finding your name in print.

How has your reviewing career progressed since you started?
ADB: Not all of the letters got published, of course. I realized I had more to say than anyone would ever read. Those words were going to waste. I started writing a regular review column on USENET. (For the kids, that's the internet's pre-cursor to message boards, which were the pre-cursor to Facebook and Twitter.) After one false start and a small break, I dedicated myself to a regular weekly schedule and have written Pipeline for the last 15 years, every week.

About two years in, I got an offer from the up-and-coming website, ComicBookResources.com, to join them. They had message boards and a twice-weekly news column, but no opinion column yet. I filled that gap and have never looked back.

Thanks to comics reviewing, I have a hobby that pays for itself. Who could ask for anything more?

What sort of standards do you set for yourself in reviewing comics?
ADB: First, be honest. Lying is far harder in the long term, anyway, and never helps your credibility. Even when I know my opinion is likely to be unpopular, I stick with it. I may have to explain it in better detail, but that's OK.

Second, judge the book you're given and not the book you wanted to read. Different types of books have different aims. While there are some universal truths to the medium of sequential storytelling, there are different ways to get there. A comedy comic is a far different beast from a superhero action book. Accept the differences and don't get snippy when one isn't the other.

Third, be as clear as possible. This is the hardest part. The internet is famous for parsing words, reading between lines, and imparting new meanings to fit an agenda. You can only do so much, but you have to try. That sounds a little defensive, I know, but it's not all together a bad thing. Trying to justify your every opinion certainly makes you consider things from more angles to be sure you know what you're talking about.

Are you able to really just enjoy a comic book, or is everything filtered through the perspective of thinking about reviewing it?
ADB: I try to read every comic for its own entertainment, but I mostly fail. On the other hand, it would be incredibly frustrating for me to read a really good book and not have an outlet to share that with. You take the good with the bad.

You have a major focus outside of comics, and that's photography. Do you think that being involved in something else is important for staying fresh in your perspective about comics, or does it not play that kind of role?

ADB: It's been a big help. I like to think I picked up on the artistic aspects of photography from studying comics for so long. But it's also true that the things I've learned from pursuing photography have lent themselves well towards discussing the art in comics. Things like focus, composition, and color are all major concerns in photography that also work in comic arts. I've written whole columns that were inspired by some overlap between photography and comics storytelling, so it definitely crosses over nicely.

I'm also a computer programmer (professionally and as a hobbyist), which has come in handy in recent years with the movement towards digital comics.

If someone was starting out blogging about comics or contributing to a site, what kind of advice would you offer?

ADB: Make a schedule and stick to it, first of all. The internet is a fickle place with lots of other choices. If you're not there when they expect you to be, they'll find someone else. It won't be easy to bring them back.

Also, have a voice. It might not be something your readers would pick up on at first glance, but you need to have a voice, or an angle, on your comics reviewing. Some people review comics from the perspective of a long-term superhero fan. Maybe you're a new reader. Maybe you have a feminist or political angle on the comics you read. Let that show. That will differentiate you from others and help to build your audience. The internet doesn't need Yet Another Boring Blogger. It needs more strong opinions and interesting voices.

You might not realize what that voice is at first. It's something that comes with time. If you don't start writing and don't continue writing regularly, you'll never figure that out.

One last Pro Tip: Everyone hates their earliest work. But everyone has to get through that first. Suffer through that, and you're well on your way.

BY COURTNEY JENKINS

ROB HUGHES

**Rob Hughes and Bob Kane
La Jolla, CA - August 1978**

Rob Hughes' foray into the world of comics began the same as many others': gifts of Mego "World's Greatest Superheroes" and G.I. Joe kits from Mom and Dad, the Justice League of America in *Superfriends* cartoons on Saturday mornings, and one campy 1966 *Batman* television show. It's doubtful, though, that many others can tell about the week that Bob Kane spent drawing and painting at their childhood home, as Hughes can.

Kane was in Hughes' hometown for the San Diego Comic Con, and there struck up a friendship with young Hughes and his family. "He spent a week with me and my family, drawing all sorts of

**The Outlaw Prince
Deluxe HC Edition**

pieces for us, including a magnificent 30" x 40" full color painting of Batman and Robin on patrol. Bob was very nice and patient with me since I was constantly asking him questions and he made me feel like I was his best friend. He nicknamed me "Batman, Jr." and told me to refer to him from then on as "Uncle Bob". Great memories and one of the high-lights of my childhood," recalled Hughes.

Remaining a dedicated Batman and comics fan, Hughes said, "I did not really think about making a career of it until I started dealing vintage comics part time in college. It provided an excellent opportunity for me to make some money on the side and eventu-

Bob Hughes and Bob Kane
with Batman painting
La Jolla, CA - August 1978

ally blossomed into a full time business."

That business quickly expanded as Hughes branched out into writing for *Comic Book Marketplace* and *The Overstreet Comic Book Price Guide*, running his Archangels site for fine vintage collectibles, and even writing his own graphic novels, *The Outlaw Prince* and *Luna Moon-Hunter*.

"Creating and producing comic books is much more difficult than I had ever imagined. Nonetheless, it has imparted a real admiration for the writers and artists that I grew up reading and given me a strong appreciation for the art of panel-to-panel storytelling," he said.

This deep appreciation for the art and the epic stories that the art tells is what continues to drive him. "I believe that when a person is blessed to have the rare opportunity to do something they love and have a great deal of passion for, that is

incentive enough to give it your all. If your heart is not in it, I think that is when purpose is defeated and fulfillment is absent."

"The competition is very fierce. But, if comics are your passion, and this is really what you feel you are called to do, then figure out what part of the business you like and are gifted in and try and break in to that particular area. Talk with as many professionals as you can, especially at shows and get those superb comic book magazines that are presently being published as *Alter Ego*, *Comic Book Marketplace*, *Back Issue* and such. Make sure to get the back issues of these periodicals as well since they really provide the reader with invaluable history and information by very passionate and knowledgeable writers and artists. If knowledge is truly power, then get reading and networking. It's the same for any business out there. The more effort you put in, the more you'll get out of it," he said.

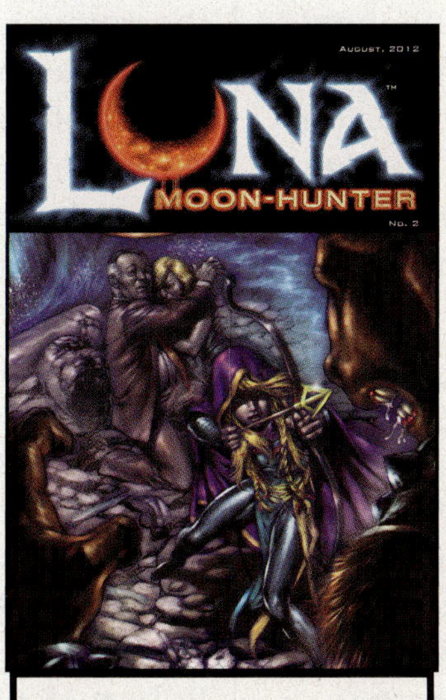

Luna Moon-Hunter #2

BY **J.C. VAUGHN**

STEVE GEPPI

It started, appropriately enough, with a love of comics. Disneys. ECs. Archies. You name them, he read them.

Born in the Little Italy section of Baltimore, Steve Geppi started working early to help support his mother. Even at age nine, though, comics were part of the mix. His first job was bundling comics and magazines for a local used magazine dealer and he opted to receive part of his compensation in comics.

As he grew up and began to raise a family, he took a job with the U.S. Postal Service. It was while working there that he happened upon his young nephew, George Kues, reading a comic book.

He has said on numerous occasions that a host of memories came flooding back. He quickly started purchasing back issues where he could, even asking customers on his mail route if they had any old comics they would be willing to sell. He began attending weekend comic shows and soon was setting up as a dealer. He was soon earning more money from buying and selling comics than he was from his day job.

"I opened Geppi's Comic World, a small store on Edmondson Avenue in Baltimore in 1974 in the basement of a TV repair shop," Geppi said. "Originally it was mainly a place to house my inventory between weekend conventions, but it quickly grew to be much more than that.

He had four stores operating in the Baltimore area when in 1982 he heard that his distributor was failing. The move from regional retailer to national distributor was a roll of the dice, but Diamond Comic Distributors was born. Today Diamond is the world's largest distributor of English-language comics serving as the exclusive distributor for many of the comic industry's leading publishers.

While today the archival publishing aspect of the comic book industry is flourishing, in 1994 it was much more of a niche undertaking. Geppi said that was his reason for forming Gemstone Publishing that year.

"I wanted to find a way to preserve and promote the history of this great medium, and so Gemstone was born," he said. The company acquired the assets of Overstreet Publications, which included *The Overstreet Comic Book Price Guide* and the services of its author, Robert M. Overstreet.

"It was one of those things that

some of my fellow collectors and dealers used to say: 'Wouldn't it be great to own the *Guide* someday?' And then it came true," he said.

Also along the way he acquired E. Gerber Products, a company that makes collecting supplies. He also purchased *Baltimore* magazine, the oldest city magazine in the country, which perhaps tipped his hand at what was to come later.

In January of 1995, he opened *Diamond International Galleries*, a gallery devoted to comics, comic collectibles and related art. The gallery drew visitors from all over the world, and became a popular place to host events and parties. In 2004, he added Hake's Americana & Collectibles, the oldest established pop culture auction house, to the Diamond International Galleries team.

"For many years, the Gallery was widely perceived as the singular showplace for comic character collectibles. I wanted it to highlight the level on which I thought comics, original comic art, and other rare, vintage, pop culture collectibles should be shown. Given the right venue, I always believed they would demand recognition from the culture as a whole," he said.

Less that 12 years later, he realized another dream when he took the concept to a much larger level with the September 2006 opening of Geppi's Entertainment Museum.

In mid-2005, he had announced GEM's formation in a 17,000 square foot facility in Camden Station, one of the historic buildings at the city's famous Camden Yards sports complex.

Immediately next door to Oriole Park and across the street from the Baltimore Convention Center, GEM not only showcases the comic book arts, but it spotlights the role of entertainment and popular culture in the mainstream culture since the nation's founding.

On Wednesday, September 6, 2006 GEM hosted a grand opening gala for the Baltimore and greater Maryland community including business, social and political leaders from around the region. Maryland's then-governor, Robert L. Ehrlich, State Superintendent of Schools Dr. Nancy Grasmick, and numerous other dignitaries represented the state, county and city officials. Many other Baltimore dignitaries were in attendance as well.

The following night centered more on the

comics industry and for it Geppi was joined by then-DC Comics President and Publisher Paul Levitz, Dark Horse Comics President Mike Richardson, cartoonist Jerry Robinson, fantasy artist Frank Frazetta, and activist Martin Luther King III, and many others.

Martin Luther King III was one of Steve Geppi's guests at the museum's opening.

"The point for both groups was to show them our commitment to comics and pop culture and our desire to share this vital American history with those who might have forgotten it and those who might never have known it previously," he said.

"None of us live forever, but I've been fortunate enough to be the steward of so many great collectibles that I can't help but want to share part of that experience," he said.

After two days of official grand opening events, the museum opened to the public on September 8. The reviews were, to say the least, spectacular.

"The 17,000-square-foot space takes up the second and third floors of the former Camden train station here, whose main floor is home to the Sports Legends at Camden Yards museum. Geppi's Entertainment Museum celebrates the colorful characters and collectibles that have emerged from comic strips and comic books since the late 1800s. Its packed displays - of

(Top) Former Marvel Comics Editor-in-Chief Jim Shooter, then-DC Comics President and Publisher Paul Levitz, and Steve Geppi survey the crowd during the collectibles industry grand opening of GEM. (Above) Famed fantasy illustrator Frank Frazetta, Comics Buyer's Guide editor Maggie Thompson and writer-artist Billy Tucci

movie posters, animation cels, action figures, board games, advertisements and more - chronicle the evolution of these characters, often reflecting the periods of American history from which they emerged," *The New York Times* said.

"As you wander through the lobby wondering all along how much more impressive the rest of the exhibit could be, you receive your answer immediately on crossing the threshold into the museum's main hallway. The walls are easily 20 feet tall and are covered from top to bottom (well, about 3-4 feet from the floor) with posters, original artwork, cartoon cels, cereal boxes and virtually anything else you could imagine that has some sort of pop culture icon emblazoned on it. Far from being overwhelmingly busy, with seemingly disparate images that you might assume would be at odds with each other fighting for your attention instead coming together to form a tapestry telling the story of American culture," ComicBook Resources.com said.

"To tour the new Geppi's Entertainment Museum in Camden Station is to reunite with those legions of imaginary characters who have instructed generations of Americans from infancy to old age," said the *Baltimore Sun*.

GEM 4-1-1

Geppi's Entertainment Museum is open to the public at 301 W. Camden Street, Baltimore, MD 21201, immediately next door to Oriole Park at Camden Yards, immediately across the street from the Baltimore Convention Center. GEM is situated on the second and third floors of Baltimore's historic Camden Station, right above another museum, Sports Legends at Camden Yards.

The hours of operation are 10 AM to 6 PM Tuesday-Sunday (closed on Mondays). GEM offers different membership levels for individuals, families, groups and corporations. Additional information is available by phone at (410) 625-7060 or on GEM's website, www.geppismuseum.com

INSIDE THE TOONSEUM

BY SCOTT BRADEN

What began as a small gallery within the Children's Museum of Pittsburgh, the ToonSeum – which opened in 2007 – became an outlet for many different types of cartooning. The museum, which is now located in Pittsburgh's Cultural District, shows its attendees excellent examples of the four-color art of comics — and beyond. Now, Mandi Bridgeman – the ToonSeum's director of marketing and programming – illuminates the secrets behind the multifaceted museum.

**If I was a newcomer to ToonSeum, what would I expect to see?
Mandi Bridgeman:** Newcomers would see something different all the time! The exhibits rotate every few months. We exhibit original art from comic books, animation, comic strips, editorial cartoons, books, greeting cards, gaming and much more. From superheroes to Saturday mornings, the ToonSeum is always evolving and changing its exhibitions.

**Where did the name "ToonSeum" come from?
Mandi Bridgeman:** This was actually a decision that was made because of the internet! There was the Cartoon Art Museum San Francisco, and the Comic and Cartoon Art Museum in New York. So anyone searching for a cartoon art museum would bring those up on the web. If we were to do a search for us we wouldn't really have unique hits. So it was decided to create a new word and concept. Taking the words cartoon and museum to create ToonSeum. It has allowed us to have a unique identity and experience branding.

**Who are some of the many artists that have their art shown at ToonSeum?
Mandi Bridgeman:** So many! Tom Richmond from *MAD Magazine*,

Joker creator Jerry Robinson, *Wonder Woman* artist Trina Robbins, *Pearls Before Swine*'s Stephan Pastis, editorial cartoonist Ted Rall. The list goes on and on and on, and we add new ones every year.

What are some of the events – past and present – held at ToonSeum?

Mandi Bridgeman: The ToonSeum has had some of the coolest events in Pittsburgh. Martini's and Toons featuring Playboy artist Doug Sneyd, The Return of Saturday Mornings with the performers behind Big Bird, Gary Gnu and Mr. McFeeley, Geek Nights, Dr. Sketchy — it's a long, long list. And, you never know who will show up: recently George Takei showed up at our Gotham Nights event!

Where do your attendees hail from? Are they mostly from Pittsburgh or elsewhere?

Mandi Bridgeman: About 60 percent of our guests are from out of town. They are tourists, convention goers, and most surprising, guests who have come just to see us! We have had guests from as far away as Italy who have flown in just for the opening of an exhibit here at ToonSeum.

Is the ToonSeum mostly for adults, or can the whole family come and enjoy it?

Mandi Bridgeman: Well, that's like asking "Who are cartoons for?" Cartoons are for everyone, but not all cartoons are for everyone! There is something here for the whole family. But they each find something different!

What does the ToonSeum offer adults? What does it offer kids?
Mandi Bridgeman: The ToonSeum offers programs and exhibits for all ages. Adults enjoy our wine and workshop nights, and kids enjoy our hands on how to draws. The exhibits can vary widely from kid-friendly to adults only, and of course there is something for everyone in our gift shop!

Scott Braden is a freelance journalist, comics historian, and nearly life long collector. He is a former staff editor at Gemstone Publishing

**Visit the ToonSeum
in Pittsburgh's Cultural District
945 Liberty Avenue, Pittsburgh, PA 15222
(412) 232-0199
www.toonseum.org**

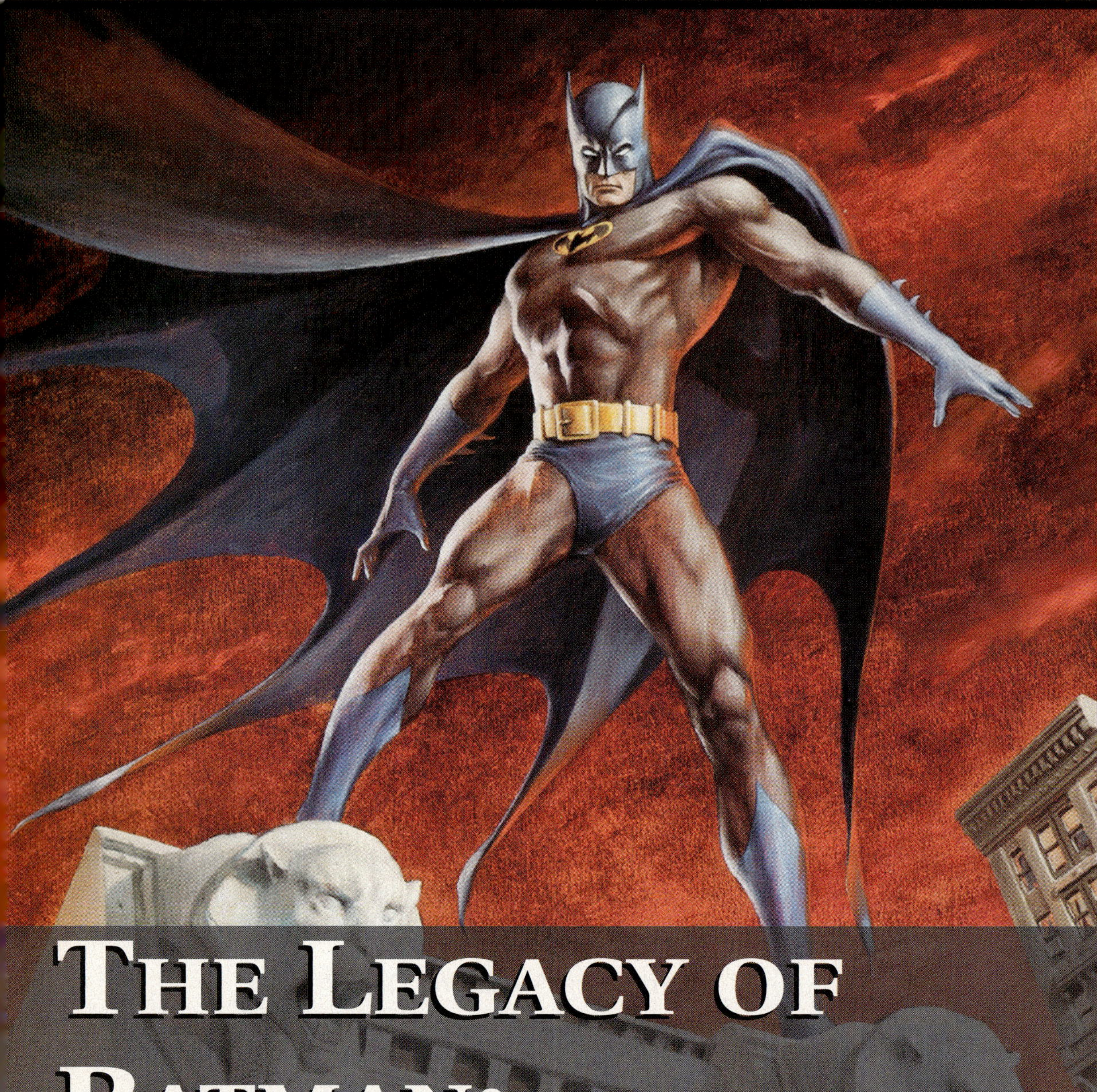

THE LEGACY OF BATMAN: SON OF THE DEMON

By Rob Hughes

Overstreet Advisor, dealer and comics writer Rob Hughes makes the case for why 1987's **Batman: Son of the Demon**, the first Batman graphic novel, is one of the most important Batman stories ever.

*The introduction of The Bat–Man in the very first panel of
Detective Comics #27, a brooding avenger of the twilight.*

Darkness descends over the sprawling cityscape and the full moon rises with the majestic magnificence of a medieval monarch to take her nocturnal throne, unrivaled in splendor and glory. Lunar light illuminates this manmade jungle of concrete and stone, brick and mortar, as the ghostly fingers of cool bay fog creeps down trash-filled alleyways. Hot sewer steam rises from manholes with a stygian stench that causes the denizens of the underworld to stir and scurry. A signal, sent from police headquarters, pierces the skyline to call forth the Gotham guardian from his lone patrol over these seedy streets.

With gleaming eyes and the silent grace of a panther, he prowls across rain-slicked rooftops as the shadows stand at attention at his passing. Sleek and powerful, his body is sculpted to physical perfection and his genius is trained to a razor's edge for the intense demands of his crusade against crime. His unparalleled senses are apex, fully attuned to every detail and nuance of the city's heartbeat.

This is the world he was born into; the theatre for which he was created. He pauses for a moment to survey the scene below, standing stalwart upon grim gargoyles as he cuts a towering and imposing figure against the deep crimson sky, black storm clouds swirling above—the harbinger of a coming tempest that would alter the life of the Batman like none other before or since.

From inception to conception, the darkly atmospheric, mysterious and moody presentation of the Dark Knight Detective is considered by most as the quintessential interpretation of the Batman character, beloved by readers and seasoned collectors alike. This was the way he was conceived more than seven decades ago by writer Bill Finger and artist Bob Kane for *Detective Comics #27* (May, 1939). The initial idea was Kane's, inspired by the unprecedented smashing success and overwhelming popularity of Jerry Siegel and Joe Shuster's Superman (*Action Comics #1*, June 1938), with the iconic defining details supplied by Finger to make the character a grim and brooding avenger of the twilight.

Finger and Kane's hero was a workingman's hero, much in the tradition of the famous pulp character, the Shadow; and in stark contrast to the bright and bold demi-god from Krypton. Bruce Wayne was not born the Batman, but had to exhaustively train himself, both physically and mentally, to become a superhero. For a little more than a year, his creators, along with writer Gardner Fox, presented a fascinatingly haunting stage for their laconic loner that was highly influenced by film noir with heavy use of shadows and dramatic lighting. Kane's artwork was quite stylistic, and yet completely mesmerizing as it perfectly fit the dark mood and enigmatic ambiance of the environment that this "strange and weird creature of the night" inhabited.

Those very early tales by Finger and Fox were written with such intricate storylines and a genuine sense of mystery and intrigue that they rank as perhaps, the very finest stories of the Golden Age period. The initial concept and storytelling style, so intriguing and engrossing, was soon abandoned for a lighter, more adolescent friendly approach soon after the introduction of Robin, the Boy Wonder in *Detective Comics #38* (April, 1940). Bouncing joyfully from panel to panel with a beaming smile and endless energy, Robin infused a strong sense of idyllic boyhood hope and bright Hollywood glamour that had been absent from the strip. This change, though lamentable to some, was quite significant, and most likely necessary for the long-term survival of the strip that would last for nearly 30 years.

The Age of Adams

Along came Neal Adams. In the late 1960s, Adams was a young artist of extraordinary talent and unmatched vision, a throwback to such legendary illustrators as Alex Raymond, Hal Foster, Frank Frazetta, and Al Williamson, who actually had the revolutionary idea of returning Batman to the night, just as Finger and Kane has originally created him. The super-hype of "Batmania", which had sprung forth from the campy *Batman* television series starring Adam West

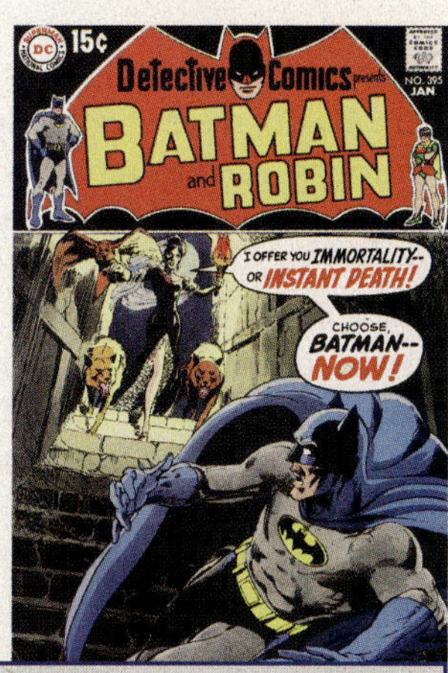

*Denny O'Neil and Neal Adams were
"taking Batman back to May of 1939",
starting in Detective Comics #395.*

as Batman and Burt Ward as Robin for three seasons on ABC from January 1966 to March 1968, had all but faded into oblivion and it was time once again for a change in direction—a much more serious direction.

Adams' goal was to restore Batman back to his roots, re-cloak him with the somber shadows and unleash this "dread creature of the night" upon an unsuspecting underworld and the public at large. He had approached DC editor Julie Schwartz for a Batman gig, but Schwartz turned him down flat. Not one to be denied, Adams then walked down the hall to Murray Boltinoff's office who was the editor of *The Brave and the Bold* comic that teamed Batman with other superheroes of DC's pantheon. In an extensive interview recorded by Mark DiFruscio for *Back Issue #50* (TwoMorrows Publishing, 2011), Adams explained, "So I asked Murray, 'I would like to do one of your Brave and Bold stories.' And he said, 'Sure, no problem.' And I said, 'But one thing, I would just like to take the stories from the daytime and place them at night.'" Boltinoff replied, "Go ahead. Whatever you want. Are you going to change the stories?" To which Adams responded, "'No, I'm not going to change a word. I just want to put them at night. And I'd like [Batman] rather than walk through a door, come in through a window.' Made more sense to me. Hide in the shadows. Little things like that."

Soon after, an irritated Schwartz gruffly ordered Adams into his office demanding, "Why are all these letters saying the only [good] Batman at DC Comics is in *Brave and Bold*?" Schwartz could be cantankerous and stubborn, but he certainly wasn't stupid and he perceived that his young star artist was definitely onto something here. In his wisdom, he awarded Adams Batman and teamed him with a seasoned writer named Denny O'Neil, who had worked as a reporter for a newspaper and had actual experience on the police and hospital beats. These two titan talents were absolutely ideal for where Batman needed to return—the grim glory of his inception and the gritty reality of the mean streets of Gotham City. This was, beyond any doubt, a momentous moment in the entire mythos of Batman. O'Neil and Adams literally made history here with unforgettable stories of such magnitude and influence that they are celebrated to this very day.

O'Neil was likewise interviewed for *Back Issue #50*, where he explained, "What I thought we were doing was taking Batman back to May of 1939 and doing what Kane and Finger had done. What we were really doing was kind of remembering what we thought [Batman] should have been. What we thought it was. And that was our interpretation [beginning with] 'Secret of the Waiting Graves'" in *Detective Comics #395* (January 1970). Adams added, "So what Denny was doing was right. And hopefully what I was doing was right. But we all kind of got it. It was no secret that we were doing Batman right. It was fun, it was dark, it was mysterious. And you know what? It still is. It's pretty much the same as it was then. Everybody gets it." Reflecting back upon Schwartz's fateful matching of writer and artist, Adams said, "He made the best and most sound judgment you could possibly make. And revolutionized comic books. Denny and I didn't revolutionize comic books. Julie Schwartz did. We did our job."

O'Neil summed it up beautifully, "What comics did, and what Neal and I did, was magic realism. But then, comics and pulps had been doing it since the '30s."

The Next Level

In 1971, these three legends raised the bar even higher when they collaborated to create an arch villain of monumental proportions—Ra's al Ghul—an anti-Christ type of would-be world dictator whose ultimate goal was to remake mankind and Planet Earth in his own image via global genocide. For *Back Issue #10* (TwoMorrows Publishing 2005), Peter Sanderson wrote an in-depth article titled, "The Lives and Times of Ra's al Ghul," in which the creation, origin, and career of al Ghul is explored in detail. In

*This iconic cover of **Batman** #232 introduced the "Head of the Demon" Ra's al Ghul to the Batman mythos.*

it, O'Neil hypothesized that, "He [Adams] and Schwartz saw a need for a new Batman villain, a mastermind who would be different from the Joker and the other costumed crooks associated with the character." O'Neil stated that, "We didn't want just another street thug with a costume and a fancy name. We were going for grandeur."

Schwartz came up with the foreboding name, which translated from Arabic as "Head of the Demon", and Adams brought forth the look of Ra's entirely from his own imagination. Adams explained that Ra's was meant to be "a character who is based in reality, which is sort of what our goal was at the time. In other words, come up with a villain, like Superman has Luthor, who is in some ways the equal of Batman, [and] not put him in a funny costume, but still make him striking." Not an easy task. Drawing from these concepts, Adams gave Ra's a high forehead; as he explained, "A high forehead is often regarded as a signifier of high intelligence. It shows confidence." He also gave him deep, expressive eyes and a prominent brow that reflected the stern, non-nonsense persona of an unforgettable and very powerful presence. Then he added one last defining detail. In his words, he thought, "Here's another thing I can do that might make the character even more significant, give him no eyebrows. I removed the eyebrows, and it really made the character striking. Y'know, what's interesting about that is if you don't explain it sometimes, it's even cooler. So removing the eyebrows was important to me in that it created an air of mystery."

Ra's al Ghul's debut came in the classic tale, "Daughter of the Demon" for *Batman #232* (June 1971, in which he shows up unannounced in the Batcave to seek out Batman's aid to rescue his beautiful daughter, Talia, from some unknown abductor who had likewise kidnapped Robin. The adventure eventually takes Batman, Ra's, and his giant bodyguard Ubu to Mount Nanda Devi, situated in the remote and dangerous Himalayas. Here, standing upon a ledge overlooking a deep crevice, Ra's makes a very profound and revealing confession: "It is a beauty to which my soul responds…so stark, so pure…as untainted as my desert home! I am cursed with a love for emptiness…desolation!" Soon after, Batman is reunited with Robin and exposes the whole journey for a ruse, a "staged and complicated quest…," but is quite baffled as to the reason why. A question to which Ra's responds, "Your admirable mind has reasoned all save the obvious…that my darling Talia loves you! My organization is vast…! I consider retiring from my activities—! I had to satisfy myself that you are a worthy successor to me!…

A worthy Son-in-Law!" The tale concludes with a panel of Talia kissing a rather startled Batman ever so gently on his cheek.

An unexpected ending to the harrowing adventure in Batman #232.

The lovely, yet quite complex Talia (created by O'Neil and artist Bob Brown) first appeared in *Detective Comics #411* (May 1971) in the story, "Into the Den of the Death-Dealers!" (cover by Adams, script by O'Neil, pencils by Brown and inks by Dick Giordano). In this tale, Batman tracks the villain Dr. Ebenezer Darrk, former president of the League of Assassins, to his lair in Asia where he meets and rescues Talia from his clutches. After a falling out with Ra's, Darrk had abducted Talia in retaliation and she ends up killing him in order to save Batman's life.

Talia is an exotic beauty, perhaps a cross between the Mediterranean and the Far East, possibly Mongolia, and Adam's version is considered the definitive one. In *Back Issue #10*, the artist said, "There is a certain sexiness you can enter into a character, and that was what I wanted to do with her. And so the idea was to take this woman, who is beautiful, and that is your first conception of her, and make her capable. And that to me was the most important thing, to be sexy and capable. Talia is the forerunner of the action heroines who are so common in pop culture today." Indeed, she proved herself most capable by aiding and saving Batman's life on several occasions over the years. O'Neil added, "I've always seen Talia as dignified. Kind of a stately, Grecian statue."

This story arc that introduced Ra's in *Batman #232* continued in *Batman #242* "Bruce Wayne – R.I.P." (Jun, 1972), *#243* "The Lazarus Pit" (August 1972) and concluded in *#244* "The Demon Lives Again" (September 1972). In this climatic chapter, the Detective tracks al Ghul to his desert lair and eavesdrops to hear him admit, "I have been called a criminal and genius…and I am neither! I am an artist! I have a vision…of an earth as clean and pure as a snow-swept mountain…or the desert outside!" To which Batman angrily responds, "It is the vision of a madman!" Ra's immediately challenges

Batman to a duel-to-the-death with scimitars. He readily agrees and the two engage one another under the sweltering sun. The intense combat is unexpectedly interrupted by the sharp sting of a scorpion upon Batman's ankle, and Ra's leaves his fallen foe to his fate. Talia tarries behind long enough to secretly administer some anti-venom that saves the Detective's life. And, like a desert wraith, he rises from the dunes in the cool of the evening to re-emerge with unabashed rage at al Ghul's tent and defeats the shocked villain who asks, "By the gods! You pursue me past your dying…! Are you man—or fiend from hell?" Batman and Talia embrace once more before he departs with Ra's slung over his shoulders into the desert night.

These stories are the way that these characters were created and introduced into the storyline; with Ra's al Ghul now firmly established as a major adversary, and his gorgeous daughter Talia, a genuine love interest for Batman. The stage was set for the complex and ever-revolving relationship of these three personalities to be explored and expanded upon even further.

Batman, Son of the Demon

Fifteen years later, the man of the hour was Mike W. Barr, a talented writer who had co-created *Batman and the Outsiders* with Jim Aparo after the cancellation of the long running title *The Brave and the Bold* with issue #200 (July 1983). Enjoying the success of his maxi-series *Camelot 3000* (DC, 1982-85), illustrated by English artist Brian Bolland (who would go on to draw *Batman: The Killing Joke* in 1988), Barr approached his editor at DC, Dick Giordano, about an idea of publishing graphic novels. Marvel had already been doing so since 1982, having released more than 20 by this time, and were doing quite well with them. Some of the more notable titles in the *Marvel Graphic Novel* series included (#1) *Death of Captain Marvel* by Jim Starlin (1982), (#4) *The New Mutants* by Chris Claremont and Bob McLeod (1982), (#5) *X-Men: God Loves Man Kills* by Claremont and Brent Eric Anderson (1983), and (#21) *Marada the She-Wolf* by Claremont and John Bolton (1985).

Barr felt that DC was missing a really big boat with titanic potential. In an informative side bar article in *Back Issue #10*, Barr said, "I had a contract with DC to do a Batman graphic novel, and I had come up with the idea to do a Ra's al Ghul story because I had always liked the character and Denny was over at Marvel at the time, so he had really no claim on it anymore. I came up

with the idea of Talia being pregnant with Batman's child. And then later on she would lose the child."

But Barr, a true maverick and trend-setting author, was not content with such a safe and secure, status-quo-restored ending. He believed that since this was to be the very first Batman graphic novel, published in larger, prestige format on high-quality paper stock carrying a cover price of $14.95 (20 times that of a regular comic book—$0.75 at the time)—the readers would want something more than your typical cliché ending. He wanted a really significant, even life-changing event for Batman to occur within the story. Barr explained, "So I said to Dick that at the end, if it turns out she really has not lost the baby, that the baby's out there, that's going to be a punch that they're not going to be able to forget. And I think I was right. I don't know if anybody's been able to forget it."

But, Giordano balked. The thought of Batman, one of DC's stalwart pillars of success since the 1930s, actually having a child out of wedlock seemed anathema. An ironic mindset since DC's flagship hero Superman had bedded Lois Lane without a wedding in the feature film *Superman II* (portrayed by Christopher Reeve and Margot Kidder in 1981). Were they actually married in the movie, or did DC simply look the other way here since it was the glamorous lights of Hollywood? Who knows? Nevertheless, Giordano was hesitant. Barr had anticipated this and showed him the comic *Batman Spectacular DC Special Series #15*, published in the summer of 1978, written by O'Neil, penciled by Michael Golden, and inked by Giordano

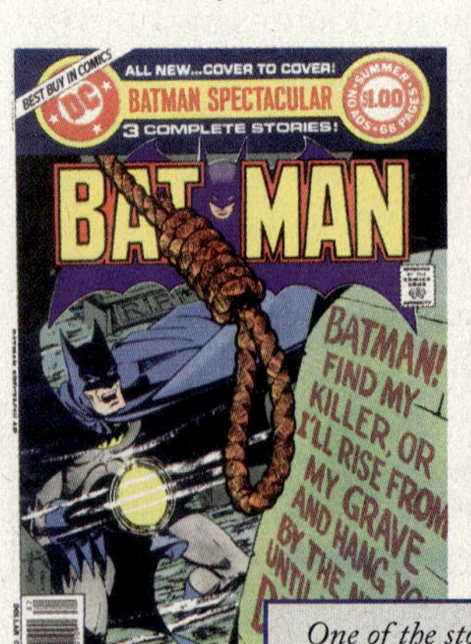

*One of the stories in **Batman Spectacular DC Special Series #15** featured a Wedding of Batman and Talia.*

himself. The special featured the story, "I Now Pronounce You Batman and Wife!", in which Ra's marries Batman to Talia aboard his large tanker somewhere in the Atlantic and outside the jurisdiction of the U.S. When Batman responds, "I don't remember saying 'I do'!" Ra's interjects, "Not necessary! In my nation, the consent of the female and her father are sufficient for marriage!" Satisfied, Giordano signed off on Barr's controversial plot; one which proved rather explosive in subsequent years.

The graphic novel was titled *Batman: Son of the Demon* (*SOD*), and Barr really pushed for something special. He wanted a truly epic and more mature saga that pushed the envelope by testing the limits of how far he could take Batman as a character. He wanted not only to expand the existing readership, but potentially reach an entirely new audience as well. Hence, the story had to be bigger and better than your typical comic book—more sophisticated, engaging, and impactful. In short, it had to be downright unforgettable. Barr explained, "The dilemma for me was how far could I push Batman past his present stories that were running in *Batman* and *Detective Comics*? In essence, how violent and how intense can I get and still remain true to the basic core of the character. I mean, Batman is not Dirty Harry who can kick down a door and start blasting away the bad guys."

Another important hurdle was finding an artist who would do the book justice. When asked about how Jerry Bingham came to be involved in the project, Barr answered, "I initially asked Brian Bolland, whom I had done *Camelot 3000* with, but he said that he was not interested in doing a graphic novel and no one else suitable seemed to be available at the time. I then wrote an article for the CBG (*Comics Buyers Guide*) that stated that I was working on the very first Batman graphic novel and was looking for an artist. Jerry [who was best known for his Kirby Award winning graphic novel *Beowolf* (First Comics, 1984)] read the article and called me up."

With Bingham signed on, Barr completed the *SOD* plot on December 15, 1985. Barr explained, "I wrote *Son of the Demon* 'Marvel style.' Sending Jerry a detailed [page by page] plot outline but no dialogue, nor panel breakdowns. In June of 1986, I began receiving copies of the penciled pages and began filling in the dialogue. By August of 1986, I had all the penciled pages with completed dialogue. The book was released one year later in August of 1987." Barr also noted, "In the original plot, there was an additional scene in which Batman follows a lead to the tough streets of Watts in South Central L.A. "This however, was left out of the final book.

On Bingham's part, the artwork for *SOD* took him a year and a half to complete. Each individual page required an average of three full days to complete the pencil and ink stages, and then another day or two to apply Dr. Martin's watercolors upon blue lines of the art. The black and white artwork was rendered on huge 15" x 20" sheets of heavy illustration paper supplied by the DC offices. Of special note is that Bingham choose to ink with an old fashioned quill pen—a painstaking process of dip and apply, dip and apply. The process not only demanded a great deal of skill, but also time and patience. The exceptional detail and outstanding rendering of his careful pen and ink work is vibrantly displayed in each and every panel—a testament to his tremendous talent and dedication to his profession.

In an exclusive interview with Bingham, when asked about the reason he chose to use an old fashioned quill pen in inking the interior pages, he replied, "At the time, the only options I knew were quill or brush. India ink had to be black because the printing process wasn't very forgiving and any translucency came across as muddy. A couple books tried to experiment with printing from pencils—Gene Colan drew all his

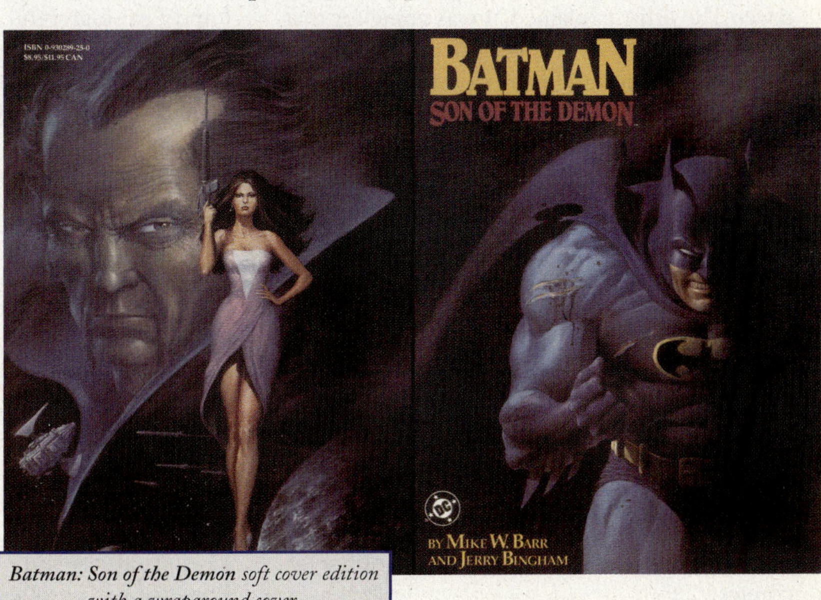

Batman: Son of the Demon soft cover edition with a wraparound cover.

comics in tone and his pencils were gorgeous but (I believe) difficult to translate for some inkers, so he was the perfect choice to try this with—but the printing process of the era didn't do it justice. Still, anything he did looked great."

SOD is considered Bingham's *magnum opus*, a true masterpiece in illustrative storytelling. His classic art style in this book is reminiscent of such legendary talents as Hal Foster and Neal Adams. When asked if the large size format of the graphic novel influenced his decision making in the panel breakdowns, Bingham answered, "No. When I started this project, all I knew was the standard for the industry at the time. The only GN adaptation that I enjoyed was the ability to bleed the art beyond the outside borders of the panels." At the time, standard comics, while occasionally bleeding a figure from one panel to the next, the outside borders were a fairly rigid construct—if not by mandate, at least in this young artist's mind.

Originally, *SOD* was supposed to only be printed in soft cover format, but when the editor and several of the DC executives saw the original artwork for the pages, they were so blown away at the epic beauty and genuine mastery of the work that they immediately decided to produce a deluxe hardcover edition in addition, one which would include an introduction from Luke Skywalker himself—Mark Hamill.

Bingham produced a spectacular, full oil painting for the title page of the hardcover edition—a piece that is considered to be one of the most iconic images ever created of Batman—-as well as an additional oil wrap around cover for the soft cover. The artist explained, "I was going for that Iconic Batman look. I'm sure I'm not the first to envision Batman standing on a rooftop with gargoyles of some sort, and there really isn't much of Batman and skyscrapers in the story, but it was the first Batman graphic novel and I went for the epic approach. I used a dry brush technique for the background clouds. Stylistically, my painting approach was still in its infancy, I was mostly self-taught, so what you see is what you got."

"The building [to the lower right of Batman's figure] was inspired by the work of the great New York cityscape artist, Richard Estes. I remember one year at the San Diego Comic Con, a fan came up to my table with a tattoo of the cover on his arm."

Of Bingham's art for *SOD*, Barr has said, "I feel it is the finest work Jerry has ever done in comics."

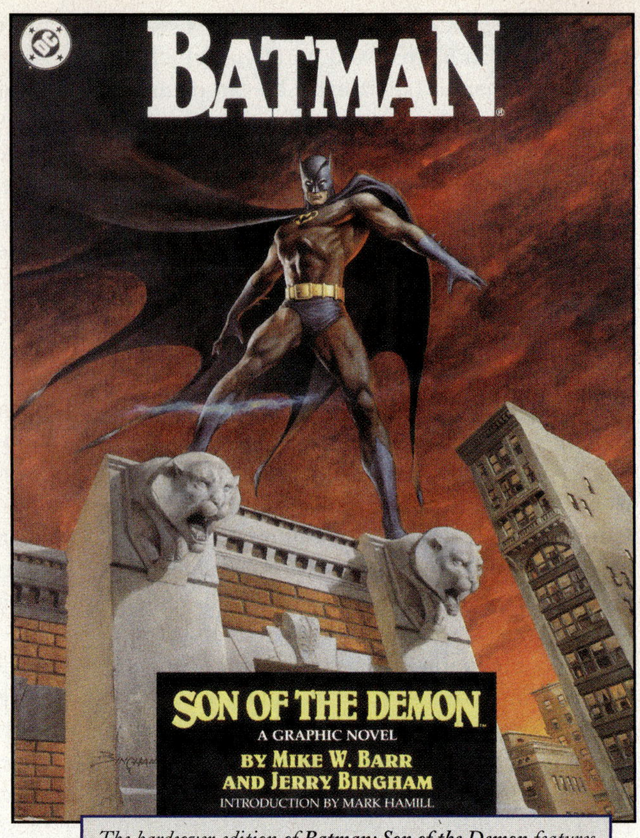

*The hardcover edition of **Batman: Son of the Demon** features Batman in an iconic pose on this oil painting cover.*

When asked about any classical influences as an artist, Bingham answered, "If there is a classical feel to my art, it's probably because I have over a hundred influences. I try to get something out of every artist I enjoy. But regarding comics, my two greatest influences growing up were Big John Buscema and Neal Adams. Jack Kirby was, by impetus. But Buscema, the style. I lived and breathed his books, thrilled at every new issue, and I'm so grateful he was as prolific as he was and left such a mountain of work behind."

With this graphic novel, Giordano opened the gate for these two thoroughbred talents who strove with such passion that they would lift Batman to a pinnacle in graphic literature that few others have been able to equal to this very day.

The Saga Begins

The *Son of the Demon* saga opened ominously with a four panel prologue in a remote desert-like region where Ra's al Ghul rises up from a deep crevice in the earth's surface, perhaps even out of hell itself. Barr wrote, "The earth screams, like a woman giving birth…"

When asked about this striking scene and whether or not he was implying some sort of supernatural subtext here, Barr replied, "To the best of my recollection, the original plot for

SOD played right off of my story 'The Messiah of the Crimson Sun' in *Batman Annual #8* (1982) with Ra's being revived from his 'death' in that story. I believe I was later told that Ra's had not been used since *Annual #8*, so I just cobbled together a moody, but non-specific resurrection scene. I was able to use prose and art to hook together the theme of storms and birth that weave in and out throughout the tale."

Bingham further explained: "I liked the layout of this page. I like geometrical compositions and was conscious of directional lines and the placement of important elements, the transitions between distant, extreme close-up, close-up, and receding…"

"Panel #1: abstract, directional lines formed by the clouds and a lightning-like crack in the earth…all pointing directly to the clutching hand in extreme close-up…"

"Panel #2: the negative space (sans caption) is necessary for that hand to pop…the hand pointing at the close-up of Ra's face…"

"Panel #3: Ra's hands are positioned in a way that one can draw a straight line from the panel-one clouds, through the "straight" pinky on the panel-two hand, down and across to the heavy shadows on panel four…and the all-important split in the earth."

"Panel #4: The receding Ra's is becoming insignificant and the panel is more about the now vertical lightning crack in the earth…."

"The best composition keeps the eye moving where the artist wants it to go. Much of what I describe is thought out in the initial thumbnails, with the minor accents and details contributing as the page develops."

Strangely, there is not one full splash page used in *SOD*. When asked about this omission, and whether or not his approach to the script was any different because of the larger format in which the book was going to be printed, Barr recalled that the prestige format would provide for much larger images and thus, convey a grandiose feel throughout. He said, "I recall thinking that with the larger format we could probably keep the same amount of panels and make them more panoramic, to 'open it up,' as they say in Hollywood, so the larger panels would be that much more spectacular. That may have been one of the reasons the book was done from a plot rather than a full script, to give Jerry the best possible advantage to use the expanded format."

On the same topic, Bingham interjected, "I would have loved large splash pages, but I personally hate more than six panels per page and as I recall, if I had any difficulty breaking down the visuals on this book, it was because the script was pretty complicated and I was trying to force multiple actions into a single panel just to get a little breathing room. For me, storytelling comes first. It is what comics are all about. Beyond artistic style, and making pretty pictures, the movie must play out without difficulty for the viewer. Everything else is personal, artistic taste."

After this brief prologue, the tale cuts to a half splash that depicts an establishing aerial shot of the Gotham Chemical Plant, which has been surround by police squad cars and a SWAT unit in a tense stand-off with a group of international terrorists. The insurgents hold a number of hostages, have access to deadly chemicals, and are not interested in any type of negotiations with Commissioner Gordon's police force. An unnamed sadistic terrorist grabs a very frightened woman in late pregnancy named Nancy by her hair and points his Uzi to her head, yelling defiantly out the window, "Listen up, cops! I gotta fat lady here! You try anything, she buys it! You follow? Well?"

Gordon simply replies, "Professional negotiators are on their way!"

Unimpressed, the terrorist screams back, "Screw your negotiators, man!"

"Have it your way, junior…"

Batman: Son of the Demon begins with Ra's Al Ghul rising up from a deep crevice, as if rising from Hell itself.

Gordon thinks, "...but I guarantee, you won't like the alternative...!" as he peers up in the night sky at the bright bat-signal boldly emblazoned upon a cloud.

This scene is a powerful ode to the Kane-Finger and O'Neil-Adams classic collaborations with a very strong emphasis on mood and atmosphere, while simultaneously building tremendous, tangible tension through the antics of the antagonists. The terrorist who has set his eyes upon Nancy is particularly vile as he threatens to ravish her right in front of her husband, but, before doing so, flips up his switchblade boasting, "...and what I want most...is to brand this bitch...put his mark on her..." In utter hopelessness, with tears steaming down her face, Nancy shuts her eyes tight and turns away as he begins to slowly carve the letter "Q" in her cheek. The vile act is beyond brutal, the savagery and humiliation infuriating in this extremely intense moment packed with such raw emotion that it prompts the reader to scream out for immediate retribution. This is storytelling at its very finest, and Barr and Bingham were really firing on all cylinders here—in, beyond any doubt, one of the best and most moving panels of the entire book.

With careful examination, readers may notice that each one of the terrorists have this strange "Q" etched somewhere on their bodies as a signifier (as we would learn later on in the tale) of the one man whom they serve under—Qayin. When asked if this "Mark of Qayin" branding was meant to have any connection to the infamous Mark of Cain in the Old Testament's Book of Genesis 4:15, in which God places a mark on Cain after he had murdered his younger brother Abel, Barr said, "That's exactly right. That was a thematic resonance I thought was too good to pass up. And if Qayin is Cain, then Batman, later in the story, becomes Abel, since they're both sons of Ra's al Ghul."

It is at this point in the story that the dreaded Batman makes his first appearance with a powerful punch to the back of the terrorist's cranium. In response, the antagonist fires wildly in a enraged daze, but our hero has secured himself once more in the shadows. Three more perpetrators open fire and Batman tosses a couple of gas pellets to produce a thick smokescreen that causes chaos and uncertainty among the crazed criminals. Pressing his advantage, the manhunter flows in and out of the darkness with the silent speed and grace of a deadly jungle cat, taking out the terrorists one by one until only a single perpetrator remains on the floor. One that grabs Nancy, threatening to murder her if his unseen opponent does not show himself in five seconds. After a quick countdown, the Batman boldly steps into full view and cryptically states, "Time's up." The terrorist spins and fires at a blitzing Batman who takes a couple of bullets in his side, while a few others slam into the barrels behind him, barrels full of highly pressurized toxic chemicals that violently spew out at full force into the shocked villain's face. In this horizontal action panel, Batman strikes perhaps his most famous pose by dramatically sweeping his azure cloak across his body for protection—the classic Golden Age stance created and immortalized by Kane himself. The black ooze instantly melts the flesh from the gunman's face as he looks up and curses Batman by saying, "God damn you...!" Batman leers down at his defeated foe with laconic indifference and ironically responds, "Looks like he got you first."

But, the caped crusader's task is not yet finished as he quickly climbs the stairs of a towering smoke stack, leaps onto the helicopter that

Jerry Bingham's skill in choreographing a thrilling fight scene is on display here.

was hovering to extract the terrorist team, and makes short work of the gunner and pair of pilots as the helicopter explodes like an erupting volcano.

During all of this, Commissioner Gordon has been looking on with grave concern, ordering the Harbor Patrol to begin searching the river for bodies. That is, until Batman surfaces with a deep gasp, asking his friend of the welfare of the hostages. The concerned crusader returns to check on the hostages and eyes a doctor giving medical attention to a wounded terrorist who had been accidently shot by one of his own men. Batman grabs the doctor and angrily demands, "That man can wait, doctor." The ruffled doctor responds, "He—hee has some rights, you know." Batman declares, "That woman has more."

With broad muscular shoulders that seem to carry the weight of the world, Batman moves over to speak with Nancy and her husband Mark, "Are the two of you all right, Ma'am?"

Mark answers, "Why..er…yes…thank you for all your…your help, Batman…"

"And your child?" he further questions.

Nancy responds, "I…I think he's fine…thank you…"

"Good," comments Batman, "…a child needs his parents…it's a terrible thing for a child to have to grow up alone."

Barr's dialogue here is significant on various levels, as it simultaneously reveals sophisticated subtext and introduces two profound themes of the story, while reflecting back on Batman's tragic and sorrow filled past. When asked about these all-important themes, expressly that of (#1) Batman as a Christ-like figure and (#2) that of the father/son relationship explored throughout *SOD*, Barr explained, "Superman is most often mentioned when discussing Christ figures in comics, but I think Batman also qualifies. He suffered immensely by the deaths of his parents, but, rather than turning inward and becoming bitter, he made the deliberate choice to try to prevent others from suffering as he has, risking his life every day to aid people he has never met.

"The father-son/parent-child relationship is expressed in many ways in *SOD*, from the pregnant woman Batman saves in the story's opening scene to the relationship between Harris Blaine Sr. to [Harris Blaine] Junior and Batman to Ra's al Ghul. Qayin's motivation comes from the deaths of his parents. Even Batman and Qayin become Ra's' sons during the story, making them, in an odd way, brothers. This kind of parallel structure and reemphasized theme is pure gold if a writer knows how to utilize it.

"That's why Robin isn't in the story. The inclusion of the Boy Wonder would seem a natural in a story dealing with father-son themes, but I felt that including Robin as Batman's symbolic son would dilute the intensity both of the relationship between Batman and Ra's al Ghul, and the relationship between Batman and Talia when Batman learns Talia is pregnant. When Batman learns that, their child has to become the primary focus of any father-son relationship he might be involved in."

Symbolism in the Son of Demon

This idea of Batman as a Christ-like character has many parallels and like comparisons in the world of superheroes; most notably that of Superman (as mentioned) and the Silver Surfer—beings from far-off, alien worlds, endowed with god-like powers and abilities, and graced with great compassion and concern for mankind and the betterment of the human race as a whole. Batman is a more down-to-earth and realistic example of this. A man of flesh and blood, just like us; with a keen intellect and possessing a relentless drive to battle evil and protect the good, God-fearing, and law-abiding citizens of his city. A man who has chosen a life of hard discipline and extreme self sacrifice for the dream of a much safer and secure world is one some might call a modern day King David.

Barr touched upon a very intriguing subtext in this scene—that of the rights of a victim versus the rights of the criminal. If an individual chooses to commit a crime—a deliberate and violent crime—one that violates the basic rights of another, how much claim should they have to their own rights? And to what extent should they be able to make claim to these rights, especially if they have blatantly disregarded the sanctity and welfare of their fellow human being? Should they be able to "hide" behind these rights, be protected by them in a court of law? It can be argued that Batman would ascribe to the words of Jesus Christ here, who said , "Woe unto the world because of offences! for it must needs be that offences come; but woe to that man by whom the offence cometh!" (Matthew 18: 7).

Origins

Following the powerful first scene, Batman swings off, chastising himself for diving in the very polluted Gotham River with an open wound, and soon alights down into a nearby alleyway for a brief rest. Due to the contamination of the river and the amount of blood loss, he collapses into unconsciousness as the statuesque silhouette of a beautiful woman approaches from behind.

And then Bruce Wayne dreams, as Barr wrote, "His eyes close…and every time his eyes close, he watches his parents die." Here, Barr and Bingham recapped Batman's famous origin; from the horrendous moment he witnessed the senseless murder of his parents at the hand of the murderous street thug, Joe Chill, to the night he stood before his parents grave and swore to wage war on all criminals, and finally to that fateful, life-altering evening in his study at Wayne Manor when he was, at last, inspired to become what fate had destined him to be. Everything was made crystal clear in one of the most spectacular and spooky panels of the entire story. Barr wrote, "…denied a normal life of family and friends …driven by a force greater than himself…" Bingham outdid himself here, illustrating a young Bruce getting to his feet, completely mesmerized as a huge man-bat climbs in through the window to confront him and grimly declaring, "I have chosen you, Bruce Wayne…you are mine, and you will become me…I am your true father…and you are my son." Once again, Barr touches upon the all-important father/son relationship theme in a much more surreal and symbolic manner.

The next panel harkens back to the early Golden Age, featuring a vintage Batman with full batwings and talons chasing down a fleeing thief—an homage to the classic first-year Bob Kane Batman when Kane rendered his character as a "dark creature of the night", with his black cape unfurling behind him to appear like enormous batwings. This brief origin sequence in the graphic novel is a brilliant depiction of the main object of Bruce's inspiration rendered as a giant man-bat. This idea was never seen before, as all the other origin retellings show a regular bat flying in the window. When asked about this unique vision of Batman's origin, Barr recalled, "I really do not remember if I wrote the script with a regular bat flying into Bruce's study, or if I wrote something like a 'huge bat-creature' climbs in through the window."

An Every Man

Following the dream sequence, Bruce awakes with sweat pouring down his face in the Batcave and calls for Alfred, but he is greeted by Talia, the second main player of *SOD*, who says, "I followed you from the factory, beloved…I knew you would need assistance, even though you would not admit it yourself." Here, Barr gave us a subtle look into the very psyche of Batman here. He is a loner at heart, and possessed with a fierce independence; a man who has trained himself to the apex of human skill and endurance, with great pride and confidence in his abilities, and possessing the knowledge to solve any mystery and handle any danger that could possibly present itself. However, he is also a man who is reluctant to ask for aid in his time of need, or to admit his own limitations, as seen in the next two panels as both Talia and Alfred object to Bruce not resting to heal his recent wounds. As he dons his bat-garb, Bruce stubbornly responds, "I don't recall asking for a vote." Talia sighs, "You can be most exasperating at times."

Barr explained, "I have had many a conversation about Batman with Denny (O'Neil) and Frank (Miller). I used to hang out with them quite often when we lived in New York. Many of these discussions have lasted for hours, but I've never seen Batman as a mentally incapacitated person nor insane. He is not a man who borders on being psychotic. He is just very determined and fully dedicated in his mission. Batman is like a larger-than-life, religious character. Christ-like! Here to help and aid mankind in his struggles against evil and tyranny. He has chosen the road of self-sacrifice and self-denial for the betterment of mankind and benefit of us all. In short, Batman is a role model in the truest sense."

In the next scene, Batman and Talia head off to police headquarters to meet with Commissioner Gordon, who provides intelligence on the terrorist group they captured at the Gotham Chemical Plant. Since each bears the letter "Q" carved into their flesh he hypothesizes that they work for the mysterious Qayin, an international terrorist who has never been captured. He has never even been photographed.

Batman interjects, "A terrorist and murderer…like his namesake, Cain." The Detective then explains how Qayin has connections to General Yossid of Golatia. In this story, Golatia is a fictional Middle Eastern country named after the Biblical Philistine giant Goliath and landlocked between Turkey and Iran with the massive U.S.S.R. looming ever so close to the north. Batman then asks about the chemicals that were in the barrels which Qayin's men were trying to heist and Gordon informs him that they were, "an experimental preparation, to be used in… pluviculture," the (real) science of rainmaking.

Armed with his newfound knowledge, they visit "Blaine – Pearson Research", the company owned and run by Dr. Harris Blaine. Batman bypasses the security system to find Dr. Blaine dead on his desk, poisoned only seconds before their arrival and clutching, "a star chart…of the constellation Perseus…focusing on the binary star…Algol?" After a quick interrogation of Blaine's partner, John Pearson, son Harris Blaine, Jr., and Professor Margaret Trask, who gives Batman Blaine's research papers on pluviculture, the Detective strides off and grimly declares, "Justice will be done. I promise."

Next, readers find the group soaring in Talia's Learjet, where she asks, "What do you study so intently, beloved?" Batman answers, "Algol is a star whose name literally means 'the Ghul', or 'the Demon.' Your father? Ra's al Ghul? 'The Demon's Head?'" This clue, plus the fact that Ra's had once tried to recruit Dr. Blaine to his cause back in *Batman #242* (June 1972), causes the Detective to strongly suspect that his old foe is responsible even though he is not entirely sure if Ra's is even alive. Talia objects, saying that her father, if alive, would never take the life of Harris Blaine and when he presses the issue, also asking about her interest in Qayin, Talia concludes, "I…I can say no more." To this, Batman reflects, "I understand… I hope someday I'll experience that kind of respect, that kind of loyalty…that kind of love… the love of a child for his father." This is a clever foreshadow from Barr.

They land at "Demon's Head", a secluded mountain citadel carved right into the face of the rock. Disembarking, Batman remarks, "That voice…I knew he was still alive…but I didn't let myself believe it…until now." The hero once again is confronted by his age-old arch nemesis, Ra's al Ghul—the third and final star player of *SOD*—who stands alongside Dr. Weltmann, supervising the construction of a new Lazarus Pit. Ra's turns, saying, "Who? Ah, the Detective…I might have known you would intrude, even as I prepare my greatest campaign." He then addresses his daughter, "Is it your intension to betray me again, as you did the last time we met?"

Talia bravely answers, "I would not hope to…but I do what I must, father, as do you." Ra's replies, "Spoken like flesh of my flesh! You will dine with me." This dialogue exchange between the trio is a reference back to Barr's story, "Messiah of the Crimson Sun" in *Batman Annual #8* (1982) where Batman witnesses the apparent death of Ra's.

Batman and Bond

At this stage, *SOD* has taken on a much grander scope, even epic in scale, much in the tradition of Ian Fleming's master spy James Bond 007 adventures. When asked about this inferred influence, Barr said, "Ra's was created to be a larg-er-than-life, James Bond style of villain. One who posed a global threat to mankind, not just a local one to Gotham City like the Joker, Penguin, and Two-Face.

"Ra's is a very powerful, very real adversary with a genius intellect that would challenge Batman to the 'nth' degree—one who would really test his meddle. With the added element of Talia as a love interest, Batman would also have to deal with his difficult and inner most emotions and feelings for his adversary's daughter that could very well be his undoing if not handled carefully and correctly.

"It's a multi-themed and multi-layered plot that has reflections from Fleming's 007 novel, *On Her Majesty's Secret Service* (April 1963), wherein one of the main characters, Marc-Ange Draco (head of the largest European crime syndicate), offers Bond his only daughter, the beautiful Contessa Teresa "Tracy" di Viccenzo, in marriage."

Tracy has many similarities to Talia; a beautiful, resourceful, and headstrong young woman that aids Bond in escaping from his main adversary, SPECTRE. Bond is smitten and marries Tracy, but the happy ending is not to be as she is viciously gunned down in Bond's car on their honeymoon.

Dining with the Enemy

In the next scene of *SOD*, at a grand dinner table that would make any monarch green with envy, Batman sits at one end and Ra's at the other, with Talia in between, yet conspicuously closer to Batman than her father. Could there be a subtle suggestion here by Bingham of where her loyalties rest? Bingham answered, "I deliberately designed the panel that way in order to visually show that Talia, at least at this time, was closer to Batman than her own father. And yet, she is obviously not sitting right next to Batman out of respect for her father." Talia is the "bridge" that will bind these two colossal personas together.

Batman questions Ra's about the murder of Dr. Harris Blaine, to which Ra's responds, "I assure you, Detective, I was in no way involved in Blaine's death. Indeed, the rendering useless of such an intellect is distasteful to me."

Batman rises to respond with one of the best lines of the entire book, "You'll understand if I need to be convinced." He pushes his interrogation further by asking, "…tell me, Ra's, have you ever had any dealings with a man named Qayin?"

Disgusted, Ra's rises and leans forward with a very threatening posture, demanding, "Qayin? You dare mention his name to me?"

Talia interjects, "Father, he doesn't know…"

Batman presses, "Then there is a connection?" And Ra's, deflated, slowly sinks back into his chair saying, "Most assuredly, Detective. Qayin is the murderer of my wife."

Batman is taken aback at this shocking revelation, as Talia remises, "My mother. I barely remember her…but she was so beautiful…" Ra's adds, "She remains so, in our hearts, daughter. Never forget that." Al Ghul then reflects back upon some very tragic and most painful history, revealing that he had once been the head of a covert military organization that battled the Axis powers during World War II. He was the godfather and guardian to a young boy named Quinlan, the son of one of his trusted lieutenants. Ra's reveals that he sent Quinlan's parents on a secret mission to the Japanese city of Hiroshima on August 6, 1945, saying, "A date of some historical significance, I think you will recall, Detective."

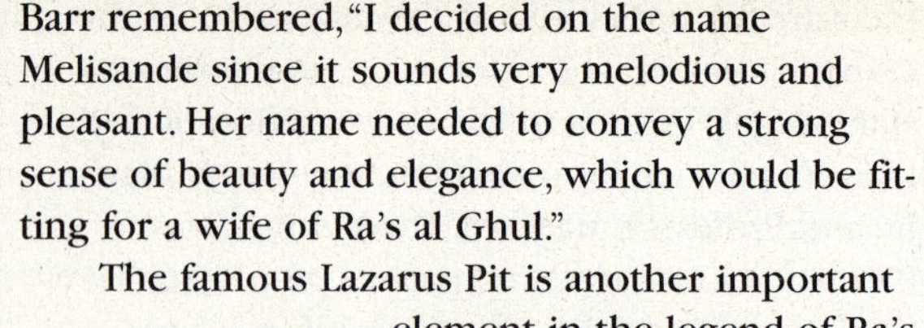

Qayin, the man who killed Talia's mother.

Quinlan was devastated at the death of his parents as Ra's continues, "…from that day forward, he became moody, fatalistic, obsessed with the subject of death. He demanded we call him Qayin, after the variation on the name of the first murderer." Tragedy really struck home when Ra's wife, Melisande, caught Qayin snooping around in the secret room where Ra's kept an early version of the Lazarus Pit. Since the room was forbidden to all save Ra's himself, Qayin flees in horror, and in doing so, pushes Melisande into the pit. Ra's grimly concludes, "Her death was instantaneous…"

Batman asks, "And Talia saw it?" To which she answers, 'Yes…"

Here, the artist presented an exquisite rendering of a close-up of Talia as a young girl in this sorrowful scene, in what was like the first of its kind.

This is a very intriguing and enlightening origin story, the first of its kind to reveal any sort of family history of Ra's al Ghul. Talia witnessing the death of her mother no doubt struck a deep chord with the compassionate Batman, who had likewise witnessed first-hand the murder of his own beloved mother, Martha. When asked about his initial ideas behind creating a wife for Ra's,

Barr remembered, "I decided on the name Melisande since it sounds very melodious and pleasant. Her name needed to convey a strong sense of beauty and elegance, which would be fitting for a wife of Ra's al Ghul."

The famous Lazarus Pit is another important element in the legend of Ra's al Ghul that has its origins in Biblical history; the resurrection of Lazarus by Jesus Christ being one of the most memorable and sensational miracles in the Holy Scriptures. The Pit is generally thought of to consist of an unknown, yet very potent concoction of terrestrial chemicals that bubble up at various key points in the Earth's crust, usually at the intersection of the mysterious ley lines. The raw, powerful energy that rises up to the surface infuses these chemicals with super strong rejuvenating healing powers. The Pit can heal the sick, diseased, and injured, restore youth, and even raise the dead. However, if a healthy person were to be put into the pit, they would perish, like Melisande.

Barr explained, "The whole idea behind the Lazarus Pit is that of resurrection and re-birth. Being born again."

The revealing origin story brings us to the core, the most significant moment of *SOD*, in which Ra's offers an alliance with Batman to track down and bring Qayin to justice—one that he accepts. Ra's then ups the ante by saying, "…and with this position comes the hand of my daughter. To accept the first is to accept the second, there is no middle ground. Do you still accept my offer, Detective?"

Batman responds with the classic, "I do" and readily admits that he has never been able to fully forget Talia nor keep her from his thoughts. Here, Bingham laid out a stunning and tasteful two-page spread love scene where Batman and Talia consummate their marriage. When Batman asks Talia about the need for a formal ceremony, she says, "Beloved, have you so quickly forgotten? There already has been…my father once married us, in an attempt to keep you from interfering with his plans. In his country, only the consent of the bride is required for a marriage…" A reference to the O'Neil-Golden story in *Batman Spectacular DC Special Series #15* (Summer 1978).

From their marriage bed, we then change

venues to the small Middle Eastern country of Golatia and her military dictator, General Yossid. The general strides down a gloomy prison wing of an ancient stone fortress amidst lamentable cries for help and mercy, all the while cursing the enveloping darkness. He pauses before the imposing Qayin, a burly behemoth with a disturbing taste for torture and brutality. A brief conversation follows, by which it becomes obvious that both parties are jockeying for position and using one another in their lust for greater power. Their conversation concludes with false promises and Qayin strides away when his personal physician asks to see him. An x-ray of Qayin's rib cage reveals a large black spot of decay, and Qayin asks, "I'm dying, am I not?"

"Yes," replies the doctor. Qayin asks, "How long?"

"A matter of weeks. Eight, perhaps…more likely six," says the doctor. Qayin cryptically murmurs, "That will be enough time…enough time to either save myself, or take the world with me."

Commenting on this scene, Barr said, "Qayin's disease was left vague on purpose. I wanted to convey with a strong implication that he was dying from his own internal rottenness; his own personal evil that is a canker consuming him from the inside out."

Asked about the visual design of Qayin, Bingham explained, "I really don't recall any design notes on Qayin—blame my age—perhaps the writer said he was a big strong guy, which was obvious by his ability to crush a man's ribcage with his bare hands, maybe he mentioned the scar, but the design was mine, as simple as it was."

From the prison in Golatia, Barr returned readers to al Ghul's mountain fortress and Bingham rendered a wonderful establishing shot of Batman and Ra's sitting at a chess match to further establish that subtext. In this shot, the pair sit upon a jutting rocky crag that provides for an awe-inspiring panoramic view of the surrounding majestic mountains with three massive windows towering behind them. It is a stunning panel, which provides for that truly epic feel. They discuss their newfound, yet fragile friendship, and Ra's reflects with his classic mantra—one that is nearly verbatim from his statement in *Batman #232*—saying, "Detective, as you know, I am cursed with a love for emptiness…desolation. It is a beauty to which my soul responds…as pure, as untainted as the deserts of my birth.

"I deem it my mission to purify this planet, to restore it to its former beauty…a mission I will brook no interference in…" Yikes!

His statement of mindset re-conjures up the very thought-provoking idea that of Ra's al Ghul representing a type of anti-Christ, the would-be world conqueror and dictator whose ultimate goal is to remake the planet and mankind in his own image, ruled by his absolute and uncontested will. Readers are reminded here that Ra's is a very powerful and charismatic overlord of great resources, possessed with unparalleled ambition and bodacious bravado, a political and military leader who speaks with great swelling words infused with sinister supernatural power and influence. Under his power, one would imagine that any rival to his plans for a global utopia or "New World Order" would not be tolerated. Barr said that he sees Ra's as, "A total fascist! In his mind, he is the only one who has the solution to mankind's problems and he believes that there is no other way of looking at things."

Ra's' radical sentiments are not merely comic book fiction, as history has shown, but representative of the extremist belief that mankind needs to "purify the planet" through global genocide.

What follows next is an exciting and action-packed seven-page scene in which Batman, Talia, and a small group of al Ghul's men break into Cape Canaveral by night in order to sabotage the launch of a weather satellite that the Detective is convinced Qayin will use against mankind. They fail, with Batman engaging in a quick, yet brutal melee with Qayin, the two combatants only being separated by the powerful blast of the rocket ship being sent into orbit.

Returning to "Demon's Head" base, Ra's is pleased that they have established a direct connection between Qayin and the nation of Golatia, but Batman is somber, disappointed at their failure to thwart the launch and concerned about losing one of Ra's soldiers named Donal. Talia interrupts their conversation to drop a bomb on her husband's world, one that would become another landmark moment in the legend of the Batman.

She beckons Batman, "Beloved, a word?"

He counters, "Can't it wait, Talia?"

She insists, "It cannot."

He concedes, "Now, Talia, what's so impor—"

"Beloved, I am with child. I am pregnant", she announces, with Batman being dumbfounded at the monumental news. He then embraces her saying, "That's wonderful!" After a heartfelt congratulations from Ra's, Batman ponders, "A child. We'll name it Thomas…or Martha, if it's a girl. It'll be the happiest baby in the world."

The pace then quickens considerably by whipping up a rousing rodeo of high-paced action and intense confrontations supplied with tense and tight dialogue. Back at the Golatia

A new twist to the Batman mythos.

desert fortress, Qayin savagely tortures Donal until he screams out for a mercy killing saying, "Please! …You said you would kill me with no pain if I told you where al Ghul is."

Qayin coldly answers, "So I did." The broken soldier pleads, "I have told you…"

Qayin peers down at Donal with cruel eyes to remark, "So you have…and so I will." The burly giant then puts his huge hands on either side of Donal's head as the terrified soldier asks, "What are you…No!"

Qayin coolly remarks, "I am keeping my promise." and with an frightening display of strength, crushes Donal's skull with his bare hands as hot blood spews out all over the wall. He wipes his hands coldly, concluding, "Well, I kept half my promise."

Cutting back to Demon's Head, Batman and Talia are sharing a quiet and tender moment alone. In the meantime, outside, a squadron of military helicopters approach the mountain locale. Batman gives Talia a beautiful ornate jeweled necklace and Talia promises, "Whenever I wear it, I shall think of you…and I shall wear it always."

Asked if there any special significance to the jeweled necklace, Barr offered his insight, "To my recollection, the necklace had not appeared before. Knowing the way my mind works, I probably searched back issues for some prop to use for this purpose, but found none, and so created one. It was a visual way of connecting the baby to Talia, letting the reader know this is the child of Bats and Talia."

Bingham continued, "This is obviously after

Talia has told Batman that she is pregnant and they are really beginning to connect emotionally here, as symbolized by the necklace."

In the next scene, the security door suddenly begins to crack and then explodes, "…like the sudden violence of a summer storm" as Barr described, and Qayin's commando force storm into the landing bay. A quick engagement ensues with Batman and Talia suddenly caught in a furious firefight. Batman appears far too preoccupied with the safety of his wife and unborn child, and he and Talia are nearly slain in a flurry of bullets before he can secure her behind the protection of the bay dock doors.

Talia calls for help while thinking, "Killed. He was almost killed…He may yet be…all because he is trying to protect me." Batman escapes the oncoming force to rendezvous with Ra's. He informs al Ghul that he is through with the mission and that Talia's safety is all that matters to him now and they will be departing as soon as possible.

Another security door is blown to smithereens and Qayin now stands before the Lazarus Pit, his only hope of being cured of his deadly disease. The giant boasts, "..and at last…the Lazarus Pit is mine."

Ra's appears seemingly out of nowhere on a large monitor to intercept his old enemy saying, "I think not, Qayin."

Qayin fires back, "al Ghul. I commend your courage in daring to face me…in my moment of triumph." Ra's coolly responds, "You always spoke too quickly, Qayin. You may recall the story of Moses…who was permitted to see the Promised Land…but never to enter it." With this, Ra's detonates the complete destruction of the Pit in a wonderful metaphor by Barr! Qayin's commando

The jeweled necklace - more than just a symbol of emotional connection.

force is soon overrun and they begin to flee the base, while Qayin himself, bloodied and bruised, pushes himself up from under the rubble and swears swift vengeance upon al Ghul and the world.

Back in Golatia, Qayin has usurped control of the American weather satellite and orders his scientist to have it create a full-blown hurricane and send it over the border to the Soviet Union in the hopes of inciting World War III. Horrified at this prospect, General Yossid interjects saying, "Stop this immediately…"

Qayin pulls the general away from the satellite controls stating, "Your will no longer matters, General…I have grown weary of you." In an absolutely chilling four panel progression drawn by Bingham, the evil Qayin once again displays his extraordinary strength and disdainful taste for cruelty as he crushes Yossid's ribcage in his burly hands.

Bingham has said that he sees this as Qayin's "Darth Vader" moment, where he is bombastically showcasing his physical superiority in the most terrifying manner. The artist continued, "The four panel sequence really works well because of the close-up reaction shot of Qayin." His sinister and sadistic smirk betrays not only his immense capacity for evil works, but the awful fact that he takes great pleasure in doing them.

Continuing the saga, *SOD* depicts Mikhail Gorbachev, head of the Soviet Union, placing an emergency phone call to the President of the United States, Ronald Reagan to inform him that the hurricane caused by the U.S. satellite has entered Russia and is devastating several villages. Gorbachev further adds that if the storm comes within 100 miles of Moscow, it will be considered an act of war, strongly implying that Russia will retaliate with a full out nuclear strike.

Back at Demon's Head, Batman and Ra's are discussing their next move when Talia faints in the arms of her father. In the medical ward, Barr and Bingham provided readers with a somber scene, in which a weeping Talia informs her husband, "I am well, beloved,…" She turns away from him to add, "I…I have lost the baby." The use of body language in this scene by Bingham provides a most superb hint of subtle subtext. The next panel is a masterstroke of Bingham's quill pen as he drew our hero in total isolation, with no borders and no background whatsoever; Batman, devastated by this news, is hunched over with clenched fists in extreme emotional anguish, feeling very much alone as he hears Talia explain, "…all the strife of the raid…all the exertion…Beloved, I am very sorry." This is a very

heartfelt piece, so skillfully done by Bingham to really hammer home the psychological pain that our hero is experiencing—the realization of profound loss.

Bingham explained ,"Notice how small the figure Batman is here. His whole world has just crashed down upon him. He is isolated and all alone. He feels impotent and insignificant."

Believing that his child is no more, Batman can resume his mission with little concern for his own safety and thus, joins Ra's and his own men to confront Qayin. Because of Qayin's fixation on Biblical history, Batman informs Ra's that the terrorist leader's base will be on Mt. Ararat, the landing place of Noah's Ark after the Great Deluge. Ra's team parachute in and take Qayin's men by surprise. When one of the patrol guards has al Ghul dead in his sights, Batman drops down upon him from above to save Ra's life. Securing the perimeter, Batman and Ra's enter the compound and confront Qayin in his control center.

The beastly giant turns to greet the intruders, "Welcome. I knew you would find me."

Batman boldly declares, "Then you have to know it's over."

To which Qayin boasts, "I know no such thing…I remain to be convinced."

Batman and Ra's jump down to the platform floor with the Detective ordering, "Ra's, deactivate the radar screen controls…Qayin is mine."

A fierce fight ensues with Batman engaging Qayin while Ra's stands at the control board of the weather satellite in this most critical moment of mental crises as he ponders the possibilities of having such a powerful device in his personal arsenal. He pulls out the live wires from the circuit board to bypass the access code but hesitates, thinking to himself, "…but such a waste. Such a device would do much for my cause to see the planet purified…made new…"

Barr deliberately placed the very fate of the world in the hands of this arch nemesis of Batman in order to build the highest level of climatic anticipation possible. Now, at the very brink of achieving his lifelong goal of seeing Earth born anew out of destruction, what would this sworn and self-styled world ruler do? At this fateful moment, Ra's al Ghul decides, "No matter. My campaign may be set back…but it must be done." He touches the wires together and the weather satellite appears back on radar as U.S. missile command fires a flurry of rockets to destroy it.

Ra's leans over a defeated Qayin, advising him to turn over his knowledge of terrorist groups to the authorities. The fallen giant

Talia sends Bruce Wayne away.
Sadly, they are not destined to be together.

responds, "I am a dead man anyway, al Ghul…and so are you." Qayin quickly grabs Ra's with one hand and the live wires in the other, holding them to Ra's face saying, "I may not see the world die before me, but at least I shall take with me the murderer of my parents!"

Just before he can slay his lifelong and most-hated enemy, Batman suddenly leaps to the rescue with a powerful and fateful kick to Qayin's jaw. The burly beast becomes entangled within the live sparkling wires, and is electrocuted in the process. Bingham explained, "Notice, that in this panel I did not draw the floor. I wanted to show that Qayin is grounded, literally being fused to the floor itself."

Looking down upon his fallen foe, Ra's remarks, "Perhaps now he is at peace."

Batman responds by dipping his finger in Qayin's blood and drawing a "Q" on his cheek, grimly concluding, "Perhaps…I hope not."

Bingham offered an interesting insight on this scene, "Batman is placing Qayin's own mark upon his cheek, in direct payback for his terrorist cutting his mark on Nancy's cheek back in the opening scene at the Gotham Chemical Plant."

Barr returned readers to the medical ward at Ra's base to witness a tender scene between Batman and Talia, who is still recovering in bed. Talia tells him, "I would be alone."

Batman removes his cowl, saying, "All right, I'll come back later…" She interrupts, "No, beloved…I wish you to leave."

Emotionally spent, Bruce surrenders, "All right Talia…I wish things had…our lives don't seem…maybe someday…I'm sorry." He leaves her to solitary mourning.

As Batman walks away, a sorrowful Ra's says, "I, too, am sorry…my son."

Bruce Wayne in sorrowful reflection, as
a man, not the Batman

In consideration of this sorrowful, yet significant scene, both writer and artist offered their thoughts. At the end of Barr's story 'Messiah of the Crimson Sun' in *Batman Annual #8*, Talia says, 'My father wished us to be married, beloved…and once, I, too, desired that…but now, I wish only that you leave.' Here, at the end of *SOD*, Talia asks Batman to leave once again after lying about losing their baby. If Talia loves him so much, always calling Batman her "beloved", why does she keep asking him to leave her?

Barr answered, "Like many star-crossed couples, they live together happily for a while, but something always comes along to spoil it. It may be that they're destined not to be together for any amount of time. But when they are together, it's pretty good for each of them."

Bingham continued, "Talia sends Bruce Wayne away because she knows that he would never be the Batman she loves and admires so much if he were to stay with her. He's way too protective and preoccupied with her safety, especially if children were involved. She feels that it is probably best for them not to be together and is willing to sacrifice their marriage for his well being."

Towards the end of the epic, the locale shifts back to Gotham City, where Batman clears up the remaining plot threads with Commissioner Gordon. Batman departs out the window into the face of a rainstorm as Gordon says, "You'd better get inside, it looks like the storm is about to break."

Batman grimly answers, "Commissioner…it already has."

In one of the final scenes, Bingham provided one last profound look of our unmasked hero, standing stoically silent upon a high rooftop in sorrowful reflection as the rain descends in relentless sheets, like heavy tears from the heavenly host. Bingham said, "This panel I drew with his cowl down to convey that Bruce is not the Batman, the iconic legend of lore, here. No. Here, he is just a man, like you and me. A man of flesh and blood who is experiencing great pain and regret like any ordinary human being."

The *Son of the Demon* saga closes at Brooksdale Orphanage with a nurse proudly presenting a newborn baby boy to an unnamed but delighted couple—a baby who has a beautifully wrought necklace of ornate jewels laid across his body. His adopted mother promises, "…he'll be the happiest baby in the world."

With all of the dramatic action, readers may have been left wondering, "Who exactly is the Son of the Demon?" Barr's answer: Batman is the Son of the Demon. Ra's recruits him to marry his daughter, Talia, who is the Daughter of the

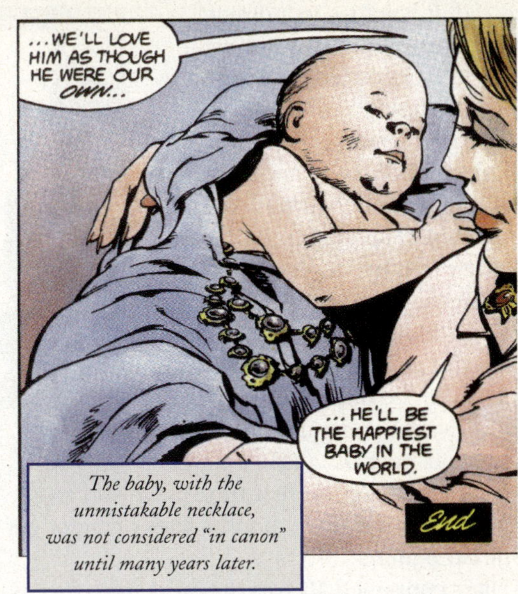

The baby, with the unmistakable necklace, was not considered "in canon" until many years later.

Demon, and thus becomes al Ghul's literal son-in-law. With this, Ra's then considers Batman his son, calling him such in the book, and eventual heir to his vast empire."

As previously mentioned, *Batman: Son of the Demon,* published in August 1987, was the very first Batman graphic novel ever produced, and a very important historical event in the ever-growing mythos of one of the most famous and beloved characters in the rich history of comic books. One may think this would call for a good deal of promotion via an aggressive ad campaign from the publisher. Interestingly enough, according to aside bar article featured in *Back Issue #10*, Barr explained, "There was no advertising for [*SOD*] whatsoever, which surprised me, because you'd think it'd be a fairly high-profile project with the popularity of Batman, and this being the first Batman graphic novel and all that…So DC did no advertising on it whatsoever, and despite this, the book did sell out anyway. In fact, in terms of sales, the revenue from *SOD* pushed DC ahead of Marvel in the direct market for the first time since 1971. Or rather, it was the first time since 1971 that DC beat Marvel in revenues," a most remarkable feat that even *Batman: The Dark Knight Returns* mini-series (1986) and *Batman: The Killing Joke* one-shot (1988), failed to accomplish.

Fans may think that the DC brass would have been ecstatic and chomping at the bit for a sequel as soon as possible. And so did Barr, but what he suddenly encountered was a solid stonewall. Barr explained, "So, as soon as I heard that [*SOD*] had done so well, I immediately contacted DC and said, 'Let's do a sequel.' [But], they would not entertain any notion of it. They wanted to do another Batman graphic novel with me, but they didn't want to do a direct sequel to *SOD*." DC was not even willing to acknowledge the validity of *SOD* being part of the official Batman storylines such as were appearing in *Batman* and *Detective Comics*. Remember, that at this time, the Elseworlds book line had not been released by DC yet.

Bingham reflected with a sense of irony, "So here I was, the artist of one of the most successful Batman books ever, the biggest selling graphic novel in the company's history, actually pushing DC above Marvel no less in sales for the first time in over a 15 years, and six months later I cannot get work. Go figure?"

Barr continued, "It was dropped from the canon the instant that it hit print." DC had a huge hit on their hands, the type of book all publishers dream of—a simultaneous commercial and critical success. The graphic novel was a total cash cow, for which they were more than willing to collect the revenues from, but were ashamed to claim the responsibility of due to the controversial nature of the story.

So, what was the real problem? Why was a book that was so financially successful and so well received by the readers left to languish in limbo for nearly two decades? The answer is hard to pinpoint definitively. Was it envy of the book's success? Jealousy of Barr and Bingham's talents and fast-growing popularity? Perhaps it was some petty power play by competing executives, possibly a personal grudge, or maybe someone simply thought that Barr had pushed the envelope a bit too far this time, going beyond his allotted jurisdiction with Batman? Barr was told by one DC executive that *SOD* seemed, "inappropriate for the characters and storyline as [DC was] then interpreting them."

The same *Back Issue #10* article went on to mention that it may not have been DC's decision to make anyway. Barr mentioned that he had a phone conversation with the head honcho at DC, publisher Jenette Kahn, "I was told by Jenette Kahn herself…that she had been told by the higher-ups at Warners that if there's another graphic novel with the son of Batman and Talia in it, she would be fired." Barr continued, "I think that may have been an excuse not to do anything with the book or the character."

When asked about why the soft cover trade paperback of *SOD* is still in print, Barr answered, "Because it makes money for [DC]."

Even though it seems DC choose to look

Ibn al Xu'ffasch (seated right), in league with Lex Luthor in 1996's Kingdom Come.

upon *SOD* as a "black sheep," the influence and time-tested lasting impact of the book is undeniable. Batman and Talia's child would soon show up in various books under various names, depending upon the interpretation of the particular writer and artist. Examples include:

Brotherhood of the Bat (1995)
In the Elseworlds story, the character is named Tallant Wayne, who crusades against his grandfather, Ra's al Ghul.

Kingdom Come (DC, 1996)
In Alex Ross and Mark Waid's Elseworlds miniseries, the character's name is Ibn al Xu'ffasch – Arabic for "Son of the Bat" – who shows up as part of Lex Luthor's Mankind Liberation Front. Ross wrote, "Xu'ffasch is the heir to Ra's al Ghul's secret empire for one simple reason: he is Ra's grandson. The child sired by Ra's daughter Talia and his greatest enemy, The Batman, made his first appearance in the *Son of the Demon* graphic novel by Mike W. Barr and Jerry Bingham."

Batman #655-658 (2006)
In Grant Morrison and Andy Kubert's story arc "Batman and Son," expands upon the original *SOD* storyline, the boy is named Damian Wayne. Raised by Talia under the tutorship of the League of Assassins, Damian is a problematic protégé—narcissistic, spoiled and violent—which poses quite a challenge for Batman in his efforts to properly train and direct the boy. It is this character that has merged into the main Batman storylines.

Batman Bride of the Demon (1990)
The sequel that Barr did follow *SOD* with artwork by Tom and Eva Grindberg.

Young Damian Wayne is a prominent figure in current Batman lore, taking up the mantle of Robin.

Nonetheless, the very profound question still lingers, had DC given Barr carte blanche for a *SOD* sequel, what would he have done with the characters and story?

According to Barr, "Well, at the end of *SOD*, Batman and Ra's are both unaware of the existence of the child. In the sequel, both would have become aware of the boy and begin to move heaven and earth to get to him first. Both Batman and Ra's see the boy as their legitimate heir and want custody in order to raise and train the boy the way they each see fit. And Talia would be right smack in the middle of this titanic clash."

What about the jeweled necklace? Would Barr have included this in the follow up sequel to *SOD*? He answered, "Almost certainly. I'm very big on visual motifs and their reuse to establish story theme."

Barr expounded a bit further on his thoughts regarding the all-important relationship between the two protagonists—when asked, "Would Batman and Talia still be married in your opinion since they consummated their marriage in *SOD*?", he replied, "I believe so, though they would certainly be in the midst of a long-term separation. The original version of the sequel would have taken care of that, as well as resolving the matter of the child."

Special thanks to Mike W. Barr and Jerry Bingham for their time and generosity.

COLLECTING ORIGINAL COMIC ART

Todd McFarlane's original cover art for 1990's *Amazing Spider-Man* #328 sold for $657,250, the highest price ever realized for a piece of original comic art, at Heritage Auctions July 26-28, 2012 event in Beverly Hills, California.

That same sale saw McFarlane's cover for *Amazing Spider-Man* #317 sell for $143,400, his *Marvel Tales* #235 cover go for $56,762.50, and two of his interior pages from *Amazing Spider-Man* #319, Page 1 and Page 19, realize $28,680 each.

Frank Miller and Klaus Janson's original art for *Batman: The Dark Knight Returns* #3 Page 10 became the previous single most valuable piece of American comic art to ever sell when it brought $448,125 as part of Heritage's May 5, 2011 auction.

Prior to that, Miller's original cover for *Daredevil* #188 sold for $101,575 at Heritage on Friday, May 21, 2010.

In recent years, there have been record prices paid for the works of many different creators spanning a multitude of genres.

The record-setter for original comic art: the cover of *Amazing Spider-Man* #328 at $657,250.

Peanuts Sunday pages and dailies by Charles Schulz and many other comic strip originals attract plenty of attention and high prices as well.

It might be surprising then, to hear Steve Borock, Senior Consignment Director of Heritage, say that prospective comic art collectors should concentrate on collecting what they love, not what they think is going to sell for a record price… but that's precisely what he does.

"Is it even a question? Collect what you love," Borock said.

He said that doesn't mean what you love can't be worth big money, but that if you're going to have to live with it and look at it and risk losing money on it, it better be something you can enjoy.

There are very few other rules for collecting, he said.

Know your budget. Only buy what you can afford. That may seem pretty basic, but emotions are powerful forces and can compel us to reach beyond our means. Specifically, don't purchase a piece of comic art for which the expense will only force you to turn around and sell it in short order.

Know whether the piece you are considering has a personal appeal to you or is one that has appeal to everyone. This can have a major effect if you are unexpectedly forced to sell the art. Obviously the broader the appeal, the more demand for the piece it would be reasonable to expect.

"Ask yourself 'Will I at least be able to get some of the money back when I go to sell it?'" Borock said.

He also pointed out that there are at least as many niches in collecting original comic art as there are in comic books. You can collect favorite heroes, favorite villains, first appearances, last appearances, genre themes, publishers and in many other ways.

You can also, of course, collect by creator.

And in addition to McFarlane and Miller

From Frank Miller and Klaus Janson, this $448,125 interior page from *Batman: The Dark Knight Returns #3*.

there are many to choose from. Try Neal Adams, Murphy Anderson, Jim Aparo, Sergio Aragonés, Matt Baker, Carl Barks, John Buscema, Dave Cockrum, Palmer Cox, Jack Davis, Dan DeCarlo, Steve Ditko, Will Eisner, Bill Everett, Frank Frazetta, Jean Giraud (Moebius), Larry Hama, Carmine Infantino, Jack Kirby, Joe Kubert, Harvey Kurtzman, Jim Lee, Russ Manning, Winsor McCay, Mike Mignola, Mart Nodell, George Pérez, Mac Raboy, Jerry Robinson, Marshall Rogers, John Romita, Sr., John Romita, Jr., Don Rosa, Kurt Schaffenberger, John Severin, Marie Severin, Joe Shuster, Bill Sienkiewicz, Joe Simon, Walter Simonson, Jim Steranko, Dave Stevens, Curt Swan, Alex Toth, Michael Turner, Mike Wieringo, Al Williamson or Wally Wood, for instance (Of course they are all Overstreet Hall of Fame artists and there are only a few known examples of work by some of them).

But don't limit your choices by who's in our hall of fame or *any* hall of fame. It keeps coming back to what *you* like personally and what you can afford. After that, there are many different approaches.

Noted comic art collector Nick Katradis shared his.

"When purchasing original comic art, before we take into consideration our own nostalgic connection which attracts us to the page, or whether it's the artist and/or inker who we prefer, there are several structural qualities to look for," Katradis said.

"One wants to look for a page where the main character appears in as many panels as we can find. One should look for pages where the villain is present also, if possible. Other qualities are, if a page has a double panel or features a larger than normal panel; that is also quite desirable," he said.

"More qualities to look for are when an important thing happens on the page, which affects the continuity of the story and/or is of long term importance to the character (first appearance, death, change in costume, etc.)," he said.

"Lastly, the condition of the page is also important. One has to make sure there are not too many defects (too much white-out, cut-outs, glue residue, ink stains/smudges, browning of the paper, etc). All these things can affect eye appeal and affect the overall desirability of the page, and its value in the future if one chooses to sell it," he said.

For Katradis personally, he said, the most important quality is nostalgia.

"I believe that without the emotional attachment that a piece of comic art creates, all other qualities are secondary. That is why I collect mostly Bronze Age, from 1971 to 1979, because it's the time period I grew up reading comics in the early 1970s," he said.

He said that when he started collecting comic art in 2002, he concentrated on buying mostly covers and splash pages. As time passed, however, he found that panel pages are just as important, and in some ways more satisfying than owning the cover or the splash to the comic.

"As the collecting mentality kicked in, once I owned one page in a story that I liked, when another page came to market I would always try to buy it to attempt to complete the story. In most cases, this is

This Charles Schulz Sunday *Peanuts* page for April 10, 1955 fetched $113,525 at auction.

futile and in a lot of cases it is not economically feasible. But it sure is fun trying!" he said.

After nostalgia, Katradis echoes Borock's call to look for an artist whose comic work you love.

"For example, I love Sal Buscema's work on *Captain America* from the 1970s. So I collect any example I can find. I also love Jim Aparo's *Brave & The Bold*, *Spectre*, *Aquaman*, and *Phantom Stranger*, also from the 1970s," he said.

"Other collectors in the hobby typically try to find a piece of art from a comic that the artist is known for. For example, a Ditko or John Romita *Amazing Spider-Man* page, a Jack Kirby *Fantastic Four* or *Captain America* page, a John Buscema *Conan* or *Avengers* page, etc.," he said. "Although I also try to get a representative sample of each great artist's work, it is not the main focus of my collecting comic art."

An important factor both Borock and Katradis focused on was that collectors should actually enjoy what they collect.

"If you're not enjoying it, why are you doing it?" Borock asked.

"Collecting comic art from the 1970s is pure nostalgia for me," Katradis said. He believes the nostalgic impulse is key, while Borock didn't narrow it down as much by that factor as whatever art really grabs the purchaser. Either way, the reason is that a hobby, no matter how lucrative, should be something that brings pleasure to the participant.

"Most of my day's work involves real estate, mortgages, and stocks. So when I get home and after my wife and I put our kids to bed, it's nice to go to my home office and play with my comics and my comic art collection. This great hobby literally lets me recapture the innocence of my youth every day. It is the only time I can feel like I did back in 1972 as an 11 year old, when the most important thing in my life was Superman, Captain America, The Sub-Mariner, and the Hulk," Katradis said.

He said the first place to start looking is eBay.

"Even though these days the pickings are slim, if you are diligent and opportunistic, you can find a panel page from your youth that you can treasure, and at a fair price too, most of the time," he said.

"I would also go to comicartfans.com. Bill Cox has created an incredible site with over 350,000 pieces of comic art. Here is where you can look for days, weeks, and months, for all the comic art you ever wanted to see. If there is a page you like, you can politely inquire if it's for sale. A lot of times, you strike up a deal," he said.

"I would also look through the dealers' websites. You can find most of the main sites on comicartfans.com, on the border of each page. You can click on the site, and you are there. If you are looking for a high end piece of art, chances are that you will find it on a dealer's site. However, this is also where you will pay dearly for it. Dealers know the value of each piece, and they know how hard it would be to replace each piece once they sold it, so the prices are not cheap, but the selection is vast and quite impressive," he said.

It's also wise to familiarize yourself with the various auction sites as well. Some pieces there go for surprisingly reasonable rates, while others set records. Either way, in our information-is-king world, it's best to be informed, no matter what your specialty.

This watercolor original art used on the Calvin & Hobbes 1989-90 calendar sold for $107,550.

Collecting Character Toys

By Ted Hake

One of the many different niches of collecting is character toys or, more broadly, character collectibles. We asked noted expert Ted Hake, founder of Hake's Americana, to outline same basic thoughts about what goes into character collecting.

COLLECTING MAKES SENSE

Much research and speculation on why people collect is in print. Here are a few thoughts on a related but different subject – why collecting in general and collecting toys and related pop culture objects in particular makes sense.

As we proceed through our lives, we all acquire a multitude of objects. Indeed, the acquisition of objects is one of the most basic human traits. Our cave men ancestors who put forth the effort to acquire that extra measure of food, fur, firewood, weapons and tools were the ones likely to survive the longest.

In today's society, most of us rather quickly and easily acquire the necessities for day-to-day living.

Many of us have the time, energy, money and intellectual curiosity to acquire objects beyond the necessities. We are able to acquire objects that bring us a sense of satisfaction and enjoyment. Our lifetime accumulations make us all collectors in a general sense, but when we seek out, acquire and appreciate a particular type of object we have a focus, the hallmark of a true collector.

So why does collecting make sense? Many interests and pursuits share with collecting a wide range of psychological and emotional benefits. These may include simply providing a means of relaxation to offering opportunities for communication and interaction with people who share a common interest. The pursuits which bring these benefits often require financial expenditures. The bonus astute collectors realize is that rather than dissipating financial resources, they are actually increasing their wealth over time.

Since the mid-1960s, the buying and selling of new and old collectibles has grown to a multi-billion dollar industry. This is rather amazing considering that Webster's New World Dictionary defines "collectible" as: "any of a class of old things, but not antiques, that people collect as a hobby, specifically a thing of no great intrinsic value."

Collectors spending billions on things "of no great intrinsic value" must have clear goals in mind and be rewarded with benefits or this economic activity would never have grown to its present level. If one's goals are solely financial, that person is more properly termed an investor rather than a collector. For collectors, financial benefits are often an important consideration and a positive bonus, but there are more important considerations.

Collectors feel passionate about the objects they seek and search for them with enthusiasm. The collector identifies with those objects emotionally. There is recognition intellectually of an item's historical importance or appreciation of its physical qualities. Sometimes, as with toy collecting, the emotional connection with objects is intensely personal.

Toys are most closely associated with childhood. Our memories of childhood, both the trials and triumphs, stay with us until our demise. Some say, in a negative way, that toy collectors are out to recapture their youth. The reality is that toy collectors never lost their youth. Toys are collected as a way to keep us in touch with our youth. Toy collections bring our past experiences to life in a physical form to be sensed visually and tactically and thus enhancing precious memories.

Developing all the nuances of astute collecting and the evolution of a collector's focus takes time. The journey is rewarding in many ways. In contrast to our daily obligations and concerns, collecting is an adventure to be savored, a way to express and enjoy our passions. It makes sense.

FINDING IT

Even if a collector is precisely focused on what objects will be collected, he needs a framework of knowledge against which potential acquisitions may be evaluated. Honing these skills is an evolving process which should be an enjoyable journey of appreciation. The goal is to absorb the knowledge and develop the techniques that allow the collector to evaluate objects and recognize quality when it presents itself.

The resources to acquire this knowledge framework are plentiful, and with the Internet, more accessible than ever. For toy collectors there are numerous museums, reference books such as this one covering a multitude of specialties to those on precisely defined subjects and clubs devoted to specific collectibles or favorite characters and personalities.

Many collector clubs publish member rosters and hold conventions. Find and meet collectors in the local area who share similar interests and travel to conventions, shows and in-person auctions. Observing and participating are the building blocks of an educated collector. An excellent source to learn about happenings in the world of vintage toys, along with new issues for collectors, is *Scoop*, a free weekly e-newsletter sponsored by the publisher of this book, Gemstone Publishing (on the web at http://scoop.diamondgalleries.com).

When it comes to finding items, newer collectors who don't thoroughly know their items of interest are advised to know their dealer. Unlike Internet auction sites where both the authenticity and condition of items may be misrepresented, innocently or with malice, there are many nationally known sources for guaranteed authentic material such as Hake's Americana & Collectibles and other established entities.

As a collector's knowledge and confidence in his focus area grows, he may safely expand his searches for items with less concern about overpaying or purchasing reproductions. Although the odds of a significant find vary greatly, potential sources include garage sales, newspaper want ads, local auctions, single owner or multi-dealer retail stores, general or specialized show venues, Internet auction sites, and in person or catalogue/phone/Internet bidding specialized auctions with a field of nationwide or even worldwide bidders.

If the venue is an auction, some beforehand preparation is recommended. Is authenticity guaranteed or are items sold "buyer beware?" Know the terms of sale including bidding increments, applicable buyer's premium and returns policy. If at all possible, personally inspect items of interest. If that isn't possible, ask condition questions in advance or deal with auctioneers whose condition statements are known to be accurate and trustworthy. Decide in advance what each item of interest is worth to you. One approach is to pick an amount you would be happy to pay and a second amount as the maximum you are willing to pay. Remember to calculate and add in any buyer's premium the auction may require. Do not exceed your maximum without careful consideration. There are, however, those special items. Will the extra bid and money paid now to acquire a special piece have much future significance or will that be overshadowed by regret for a missed opportunity? The answer is part of the process of knowing ourselves and becoming astute collectors.

BUYING IT

When a purchase is made, the collector is putting his knowledge and instincts to the test. He is operating in a marketplace created by people with a shared interest in owning a particular object.

For vintage collectibles, as opposed to new creations designed for collector appeal, the rules of supply and demand are important, but actually secondary to the critical third factor of condition.

Supply, or rarity, is an assessment of availability. Vintage collectibles, for a variety of reasons, were produced in finite quantities and have various survival rates. Often, rarity is further increased as surviving examples enter collections to be held long-term. For example, many collections assembled in the 1960s and 1970s era of greater availability were brought to market in the 1990s and purchased by new owners who may hold them for a quarter century or longer.

Demand is an assessment of popular appeal. Levels of interest may vary over time and in some narrow specialties even be influenced by the actions of just a few individual collectors. The important issue for a person selecting a collecting focus is to find a subject with a demand level that results in a value structure comfortably in tune with available finances. Collecting goals must realistically match collecting resources. In establishing values, condition is the third and frequently most influential critical con-

sideration. Rarity and demand being equal, an item with a significant condition problem results in the elimination of a large percentage of the potential buyers. An item in exceptionally choice Near Mint or Mint condition may add to the universe of potential buyers.

There are numerous additional factors that influence an item's perceived value. Among these are considerations of historical importance, provenance, physical size, aesthetic qualities and subject qualities that may attract interest from several distinct groups of collectors. On top of this, in auctions the unknown emotional motivations of competing bidders provide the wild card factor.

When the buying decision is imminent, reflect on whether the item conforms to your collecting focus. Does it grab your attention, pique your interest, spark your enthusiasm? Apply brutal, rigorous standards. You are taking one of many steps that together are going to play a big role in determining the future potential value of your collection. Try to buy the best example that fits your budget or that will likely ever present itself for purchase. Step up for important pieces. A few dollars "too much" now may quickly become irrelevant in terms of satisfaction and potential growth in value.

Restored items require the collector to balance many factors. How desirable do you find this item? Will an unrestored example likely be encountered soon? Is the restoration done professionally and not obvious? Is the piece sufficiently discounted in relation to an undamaged example? If the answers fit your goals and standards, make the purchase.

Restoration takes many forms depending on the material substance of the object. From mending a box corner split, to filling in a rim flake, to the near total restoration of a lithographed tin image – nearly all things are possible for the professional restorer. The processes require skill, practice, and the correct materials. Many items are made worse, rather than better, by over-confident amateurs. Responsible sellers must volunteer the degree of restoration to potential buyers.

REPRODUCTIONS AND FANTASIES

Not all reproductions are created equally. Licensed or properly authorized reproductions, indelibly marked as such, allow people to own wonderful objects at reasonable prices. Unfortunately, other reproductions are created by people who deceive for profit. The collector's best defense is acquiring knowledge about a chosen specialty and patronizing dealers and auction houses who unconditionally guarantee their merchandise as authentic. Surprisingly, many big names in the auction world do not guarantee authenticity. Read the fine print prior to participating as a bidder.

TAKING CARE OF IT

When a collectible is acquired, the collector becomes its custodian, responsible for its well being. This is not much of a burden and in fact should be enjoyed, but there are some basic maintenance principles to apply.

First, remove any adhesive price tags as quickly as possible. The longer these are in place the more firmly they adhere. Also, an inked price may bleed through the tag and stain the item. In most cases, a few drops of adhesive solvent will do the item no harm. Let the solvent do its work for a few seconds and usually the tag will then easily lift off without taking along surface paper or paint.

If the seller marked the item with a price in pencil, it may be left alone or erased. Above all, don't write the purchase price on the item. Record keeping should be done in a notebook or on the item's holder, not on the item itself.

Mylar bags are recommended for paper items with acidic paper such as comic books or pulp magazines. Pinbacks may go into glass covered "butterfly" mounts. However, these mounts in a stack create pressure and the glass may adhere to the paint on lithographed tin buttons. If this type of case is used, litho pinbacks should be stored separately in individual holders. Three dimensional objects are best stored on shelves in closed cases to protect them from accumulating dust and particularly tobacco smoke residue.

Collectibles in the home face their greatest threats when stored in attics and basements or any

location that receives direct sunlight. Also dangerous to many printed items are fluorescent lights, which may fade colors very quickly. Any extreme — heat, light, moisture, smoke — presents dangers to be avoided. Glue, tape, pen and pencil should never be applied directly on the item. Do nothing to degrade it. Its future value depends in part on the custodial care it receives.

SELLING IT

Once acquired, some collectors abhor the thought of parting with a single object. The collection becomes a fortress with a one-way door. This approach is one extreme, but if it brings satisfaction, it's the correct approach for that collector.

Another approach is to test and fine-tune judgments by periodically entering the marketplace. This concept is particularly worthwhile for the more seasoned collector whose tastes and sense of appreciation has evolved over time. Being open to "trading up" and culling earlier mistakes will likely be a valuable learning experience and a financial benefit, at least in the long-term.

A collector may stay in touch with the retail marketplace without becoming a seller. This takes time and study, but is easily accomplished by attending shows or reviewing auction results. Entering the marketplace will likely provide different useful insights. Selling venues might include a hobby publication advertisement, taking a table at a show, consigning to an auction, listing items on public Internet auctions, and selling directly to a dealer or another collector.

The potential benefits of the selling experience may include: raising the collection's quality; establishing valuable relationships with dealers, auction houses and other collectors; receiving feedback on just how astute were the original purchases of the items now for sale; and a host of other insights to help continually refine collecting goals and skills.

COLLECTING MOVIE POSTERS

By Bruce Hershenson

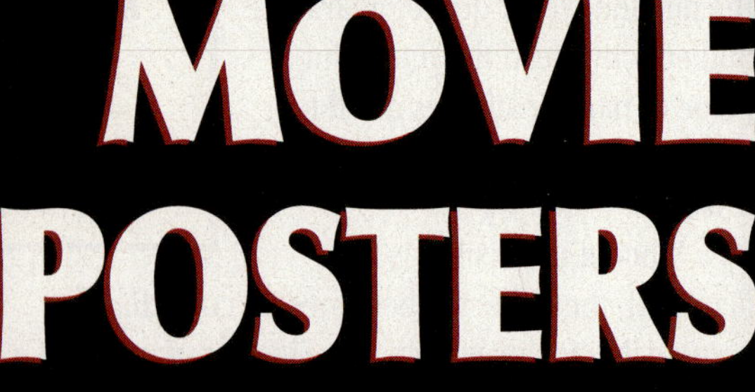

This 1921 one-sheet was auctioned at Christie's East in 1990 for $39,600.

Almost everyone has heard of collecting coins, stamps, baseball cards and of course, comic books, but only a surprisingly small number of people have even heard of collecting original vintage movie posters! Why is that? Because the other types of collectibles were *all* originally sold directly to the general public, and in very large quantities, so large numbers survive, and there is always the chance of someone discovering a large collection lurking in anyone's attic.

But movie posters (the ones displayed at the movie theaters) were never sold to the general public (at least not until the 1970s), and even if you begged a theater owner to give you one, they could not, because that poster was needed to be used for display at the next theater showing that movie. The *only* people to have movie posters were the owners of "poster exchanges", the companies that distributed posters to theaters. On rare occasions, movie posters are found in closed down theaters or in the homes of former theater owners, or in torn down buildings where they were used for insulation between walls and under floors!

So the rarity of older movie posters is many times that of *any* other collectible! In the movie poster hobby, when there are 50 examples of a poster from the 1930s, that is considered a "common title," and there are lots of titles from the 1930s and earlier where not even *one* example of the movie poster is known to exist, and many others where only a few are known.

This rarity surprisingly works against the hobby growing. Quite often I am contacted by people who want a specific poster, and would be happy to pay above what it has sold for the past few times, and I have to tell them that it is likely that all the known examples are in collections where the owners would likely not sell at any price.

It is also hard to get new collectors when there is next to no one who started collecting as a child. Millions of people started out collecting coins, stamps, baseball cards and of course, comic books when they were young, and when they get older and start having disposable income, they often return to the hobby of their youth, which is almost never collecting movie posters!

But recent years have seen a major new branch of the movie poster collecting hobby emerge. Starting after the great success of *Star Wars* in 1977, and the insatiable demand for posters that the movie produced, the creators of movie posters started selling them directly to dealers, who then re-sold them directly to collectors. While there are a few very rare titles and styles of posters, most post-1980 posters are available in *far* larger numbers than the older posters.

Even into the 1990s, the number of full-time poster dealers, collectible shows and auctions was very low. In 1990, I organized the first ever all movie poster auction by a major auction house, and it took in just under $1,000,000 (with one poster from *The Cabinet of Dr. Caligari* auctioning for $39,600!), but such auctions were few and far between.

In 1999, the Internet (primarily through eBay) finally brought a way for new collectors to easily enter the hobby and I moved my million dollar business entirely onto eBay that year, and over the next few years my list of customers grew from 2,500 to over 25,000, and my sales doubled to over $2,000,000 a year!

In 2008, I moved my entire business off

We auctioned this *King Kong* at Christie's East in 1994 for $97,100.

eBay onto my own site, eMoviePoster.com, and over the four years since have nearly doubled my sales to just under $4,000,000 a year, and we auction an unbelievable 110,000 posters per year! In addition there are now several other competing auction sites, and hundreds of dealers with often elaborate selling sites, many with thousands or tens of thousands of posters online.

Best of all, an awful lot of posters can be purchased for well under the cost of a reproduction of the very same poster. Around half of the 110,000 posters we auction each year sells for $14 or under, with many thousands selling for a few dollars or under. A new collector with a modest budget can still put together a fun collection of posters that can easily be displayed and enjoyed on their walls.

We recently auctioned an excellent example of this first James Bond one-sheet for $1,450.

We recently auctioned this rare original Italian 39" x 55" for *The Good, The Bad, and the Ugly* for $1,850.

What is the best way to enter the hobby? The first stop should be our Auction History database at http://www.emovieposter.com/agallery/archive.html where you will find just under three quarters of a million accurate sales results, and almost all of them have enlargable images of the posters sold! Using this, you can quickly identify posters you might like to collect, and ones that fit the budget you have.

I often hear dealers tell new collectors that years later they will look back and regret many great deals they turned down, but I feel it is usually just the opposite. I advise new movie poster collectors to take their time and enter the hobby slowly, because their tastes are liable to evolve over time, and they don't want to find that they no longer want many of their earliest purchases.

I have been in this hobby so long (I have collected for over 40 years, and have auctioned full time for over 23) and I have reached the point where a lot of the collectors who bought from me many years ago are now turning to me to auction off their collections, and a large number of them have made a large profit from the money they spent on their collection over the years.

It is *this* that makes movie poster collecting such a great hobby. You can spend your time on a hobby you love, and have your walls filled with wonderful art throughout that time, and when the time comes that you want to sell your collection you will likely get far more back than you put into it. It doesn't get better than that!

What are some specifics about how to start? Here are some pointers:

1) **Buy a few inexpensive posters and see how you like them.** You can buy inexpensive frames to display them with from many sources. You may find over time that you lose interest in some of your purchases, but fortunately the frames are reusable

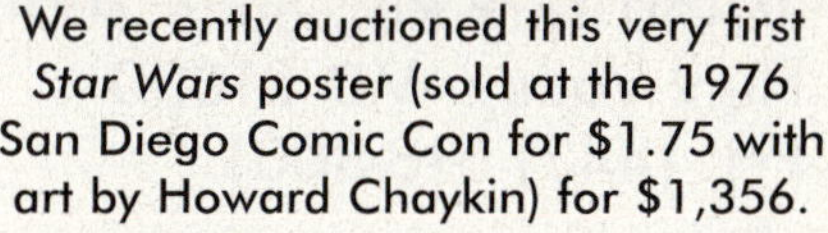

We recently auctioned this very first *Star Wars* poster (sold at the 1976 San Diego Comic Con for $1.75 with art by Howard Chaykin) for $1,356.

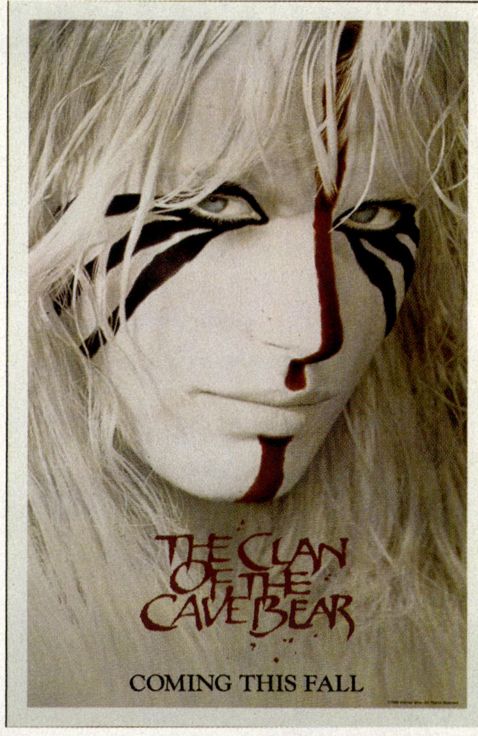

We recently auctioned this rare "teaser" one-sheet (incredible graphics for a lesser movie!) for $356.

because almost all posters are standard sizes.

2) **Consider collecting on a specific actor or theme.** You might try to get one poster here from all the Steven Spielberg movies, or you might collect posters from movies about car racing. The possibilities are limitless, because there have been movies about every subject under the sun for well over 100 years. Naturally you will find collecting in the most popular areas, like James Bond or *Star Wars*, is far more expensive than choosing some less popular area!

3) **Be prepared for your areas of interest to evolve or drastically change!** Lots of collectors find that as they get deeper into the hobby their choice of what to collect changes dramatically. Many collectors buy many inexpensive posters at first and later start buying fewer, more expensive posters.

4) **Don't forget that the main idea of collecting is to have fun!** If you also make money the day you sell your collection, great, but if it turns into something you don't enjoy, then you might as well get a part-time job. Buy what you personally love, but try not to overpay (except on very rarely offered items) because part of the fun is getting a poster you want at a price you wanted to pay!

I have done nothing but auction movie posters for the past 23 years, and been in collectibles for the past 45 years, and I am certain that there has *never* been a better time to collect vintage movie posters! Thanks to the Internet, you can see large full-color images of what you buy before you buy it, and there are tens of thousands of auctions every month, and millions of posters offered at fixed prices. If you take your time, you will likely be able to slowly put together an excellent collection of exactly what you want to collect, and at prices you want to pay!

Alternate Worlds
Yorktowne Plaza
72 Cranbrook Road
Cockeysville, MD 21030
PH: (410) 666-3290
AltWorldStore@comcast.net
www.Alternateworlds.biz

Dr. David J. Anderson, D.D.S.
5192 Dawes Avenue
Seminary Professional Village
Alexandria, VA 22311
PH: (703) 671-7422
FAX: (703) 578-1222
DJA2@cox.net

ArchAngels
4629 Cass Street #9
Pacific Beach, CA 92109
PH: (310) 480-8105
rhughes@archangels.com
www.archangels.com

Batman & Wonder Woman Collectors
P.O. Box 604925
Flushing, NY 11360-4925
batt90@aol.com
wwali@aol.com

Bill Cole Enterprises Inc.
P.O. Box 60
Randolph, MA 02368-0060
PH: (781) 986-2653
FAX: (781) 986-2656
sales@bcemylar.com
www.bcemylar.com

Certified Guaranty Company (CGC)
P.O. Box 4738
Sarasota, FL 34230
PH: (877) NM-COMIC
FAX: (941) 360-2558
www.CGCcomics.com

ComicConnect.com
873 Broadway
Suite 201
New York, NY 10003
PH: (888) 779-7377
PH: (212) 895-3999
FAX: (212) 260-4304
support@comicconnect.com
www.comicconnect.com

ComicLink Auctions & Exchange
PH: (617) 517-0062
buysell@ComicLink.com
www.ComicLink.com

Diamond Comic Distributors
10150 York Rd., Suite 300
Hunt Valley, MD 21030
PH: (443) 318-8001

Diamond International Galleries
1940 Greenspring Drive
Suite A-B
Timonium, MD 21093
PH: (888) 355-9800
PH: (443) 318-8438
GalleryQuestions@
    DiamondGalleries.com
www.DiamondGalleries.com

eMoviePoster.com
Bruce Hershenson
P.O. Box 874
West Plains, MO 65775
PH: (417) 256-9616
FAX: (417) 257-6948

Stephen A. Geppi
10150 York Rd.
Suite 300
Hunt Valley, MD 21030
PH: (443) 318-8203
gsteve@diamondcomics.com

Geppi's Entertainment Museum
301 West Camden Street
Baltimore, MD 21201
PH: (410) 625-7089
FAX: (410) 625-7090
www.geppismuseum.com

E. Gerber Products
1720 Belmont Ave.; Suite C
Baltimore, MD 21244
PH: (888) 79-MYLAR

GetCashForComics.com
PH: (866) 461-0640
buying@GetCashForComics.com

Hake's Americana
P.O. Box 12001
York, PA 17402
PH: (866) 404-9800
www.hakes.com

Heritage Auction Galleries
3500 Maple Avenue
17th Floor
Dallas, TX 75219-3941
PH: (800) 872-6467
www.HA.com

Heroes Aren't Hard to Find
1957 East 7th St.
Charlotte, NC 28204
PH: (704) 375-7462
HeroesOnline.com

Metropolis Collectibles
873 Broadway
Suite 201
New York, NY 10003
PH: (800) 229-6387
FAX: (212) 260-4304
buying@
    metropoliscomics.com
www.metropoliscomics.com

Midtown Comics
64 Fulton Street
New York, NY 10038
PH: (800) 411-3341
PH: (212) 302-8192
FAX: (646) 421-2033
info@midtowncomics.com
www.midtowncomics.com

Midtown Comics
459 Lexington Ave.
(Corner of 45th Street)
New York, NY 10017
PH: (800) 411-3341
PH: (212) 302-8192
FAX: (646) 421-2033
info@midtowncomics.com
www.midtowncomics.com

Midtown Comics
200 West 40th Street
New York, NY 10018
PH: (800) 411-3341
FAX: (646) 421-2033
info@midtowncomics.com
www.midtowncomics.com

Pedigree Comics, Inc.
12541 Equine Lane
Wellington, FL 33414
PH/FAX: (561) 422-1120
CELL: (561) 596-9111
DougSchmell@
    pedigreecomics.com
www.pedigreecomics.com

Superworld Comics, Inc.
456 Main St., Suite F
Holden, MA 01520
PH: (508) 829-2259
Ted@Superworldcomics.com
www.Superworldcomics.com

ADVERTISER INDEX

COMIC AND ANIMATION ART COLLECTING REVEALED!

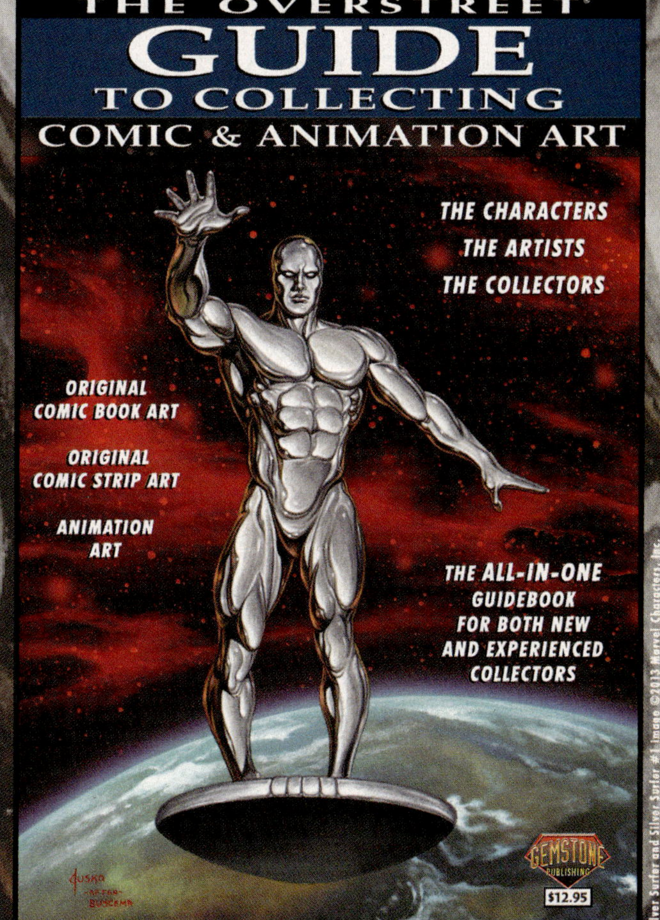

"Fantastic for a novice comic art or animation collector, but even better, even the most sea-soned hobbyist will find some new information in many of the incredible articles. Overstreet has done it again! Another great book for our wonderful hobby!"

-- Steve Borock
Senior Consignment Director
Heritage Auctions

"The perfect handbook to help understand the original comic book art market."

-- Dan Gallo
Comic Art Con

"There's no better one-volume introduction to collecting comics and animation art!"

-- Dean Mullaney
The Library of American Comics

"*The Overstreet Guide to Collecting Comic & Animation Art* is informative and incredibly exciting to read. It's full of pictures of incredible comic art, and a must-read for any comic art collector. The price is more than reasonable and the stories and art have a broad range of topics."

-- Nick Katradis
Collector

"Original narrative art is appreciated around the world. The basis of a cultural phenomenon, institutions routinely seek out and exhibit collections. It is amazing that a comprehensive guide that describes the factors and attributes that garner such attention has never been published until now."

-- Joe Mannarino
All Star Auctions

Insights for Beginners and Experienced Collectors Alike!

160 PAGES • FULL COLOR • SOFT COVER • $12.95

AT BETTER COMIC SHOPS NOW!

GEMSTONE PUBLISHING

WWW.GEMSTONEPUB.COM

COLLECTOR
BUYING PRE-1965
COMIC BOOKS
AND RELATED COLLECTIBLES

COMIC BOOKS
CLUB KITS · PREMIUMS
OTHER CHARACTER COLLECTIBLES

I am the
most serious collector
you'll ever find...
I LOVE THIS STUFF!

SEND YOUR SALE LIST!

Stephen A. Geppi
10150 York Road, Suite 300
Hunt Valley, MD 21030
443-318-8203
gsteve@diamondcomics.com